Drill and Review
Study Guide

for use with

Economics

Third Edition

David C. Colander
Middlebury College

Prepared by
David C. Colander
Middlebury College

Jenifer C. Gamber
Eastern Economic Journal

Irwin
McGraw-Hill

Boston, Massachusetts   Burr Ridge, Illinois   Dubuque, Iowa
Madison, Wisconsin   New York, New York   San Francisco, California   St. Louis, Missouri

Irwin/McGraw-Hill

A Division of The McGraw·Hill Companies

Drill and Review Study Guide for use with
ECONOMICS

Copyright ©1998 by MaxiPress. All rights reserved.
Previous edition 1995 by MaxiPress.
Printed in the United States of America.
The contents of, or parts thereof, may be reproduced for use with
ECONOMICS
David C. Colander
provided such reproductions bear copyright notice and may not be reproduced in
any form for any other purpose without permission of the publisher.

1 2 3 4 5 6 7 8 9 0 MP/MP 9 0 9 8 7

ISBN 0-256-17280-3

http://www.mhhe.com

Contents

Microeconomic Concepts: The Basics

Competition, Monopoly, and Market Structure

Thinking Like an Economist: Microeconomic Policy Debates

Distribution and Factor Markets

International Dimensions of Microeconomics

Preface to Students

We wrote this study guide to help you do well in your economics courses. Even using a great book like the Colander textbook, we know that studying is not all fun. The reality is: most studying is hard work and a study guide won't change that. Your text and lectures will give you the foundation for doing well. So the first advice we will give you is:

1. Read the textbook.
2. Attend class.

We cannot emphasize that enough. Working through the study guide will not replace the text or lectures; this study guide is designed to help you retain the knowledge from the text and classroom by practicing the tools of economics. It is not an alternative to the book and class; it is **in addition to them**.

Having said that, we should point out that buying this guide isn't enough. You have to *use* it. Really, if it sits on your desk, or even under your pillow, it won't do you any good. Osmosis only works with plants. This study guide should be well worn by the end of the semester — dog-eared pages, scribble beneath questions, some pages even torn out. It should look used.

WHAT CAN YOU EXPECT FROM THIS BOOK?

This is a *drill and review* study guide, which means that it concentrates on the terminology and models in your text. It does not expand upon the material in the textbook; it reinforces it. It primarily serves to give you a good foundation to understanding principles of economics. Your professor has chosen this study guide for you, suggesting that your economics exams are going to focus on this kind of foundational understanding. You should be sure of this: if your professor is going to give you mainly essay exams, or complex questions about applying the foundations (like the more difficult end-of-chapter questions in your textbook) this study guide will not be enough to ace that exam.

This study guide is designed to prepare you for straightforward multiple choice, short-answer, and short-problem exams. The structure of this study guide reflects that focus. The main parts are short-answer, matching definitions to their terms, problems, and multiple choice questions.

Still, your exam questions may differ from the questions in this book — especially the multiple choice questions. We made these questions up, and compared to those of many professors; they tend to be on the hard side. They focus far less on facts and recall and more on analysis and understanding of the economic models in the text. To get an idea of what your exams will be like, ask your professor to take a look at these questions and tell the class whether they are representative of the type of questions that will be on the exam. And if they will differ, how.

HOW SHOULD YOU USE THIS STUDY GUIDE?

This book works best if you have attended class and read the book. Ideally, you were awake during class and took notes, you have read the textbook chapters more than once, and have worked through some of the questions at the end of the chapter. (So, we're optimists.)

Just in case the material in the book isn't fresh in your mind, before turning to this study guide it is a good idea to refresh your memory about the material in the text. To do so:

1. Read through the margin comments in the text; they highlight the main concepts in each chapter.

2. Turn to the last few pages of the chapter and reread the chapter summary.

3. Look through the key terms, making sure they are familiar. (O.K., we're not only optimists, we're wild optimists.)

Even if you do not do the above, working though the questions in the study guide will help to tell you whether you really do know the material in the textbook chapters.

STRUCTURE OF THE STUDY GUIDE

This study guide has two main components: (1) a chapter-by-chapter drill and review and (2) three pre-tests based upon groups of chapters.

Chapter-by-chapter drill and review

Each chapter has seven elements:

1. A chapter at a glance: A brief exposition and discussion of the learning objectives for the chapter.
2. Short-answer questions keyed to the learning objectives.
3. A word scramble.
4. A test of matching the terms to their definitions.
5. Problems and exercises.
6. Multiple choice questions.
7. Answers to all questions.

Each chapter presents the sections in the order that we believe they can be most beneficial to you. Here is how we suggest you use them:

Learning Objectives: These should jog your memory about the text and lecture. If you don't remember ever seeing the material before, you should go back and re-read the textbook chapter. The numbers in parentheses following each learning objective refer to the page in the text that covers that objective. Remember, reading a chapter when you are thinking about a fantasy date is almost the same as not having read the chapter at all.

Short-Answer Questions: The short-answer questions will tell you if you are familiar with the learning objectives. Try to answer each within the space below each question. Don't just read the questions and assume you can write an answer. Actually writing an answer will reveal your weaknesses. If you can answer them all perfectly, great. But, quite honestly, we don't expect you to be able to answer them all perfectly. We only expect you to be able to sketch out an answer.

Let's give you an example of what we mean. The first short-answer question for Chapter 1 is, "What are the five important dimensions economic learning?" The answer is "economic reasoning, economic terminology, economic insights, economic institutions, and economic policy options." There are many ways of dividing up what you learn, so if you don't get this list perfect, it is not a big problem in our view. If your exam is a multiple choice exam, the possible answers will jog your memory.

Of course, some other questions are important to know. For example, if there is a question about the economic decision rule and you don't remember that it excludes past costs and benefits, you need more studying. So the rule is: Know the central ideas of the chapter; be less concerned about the specific presentation of those central ideas.

After you have sketched out all your answers, check them with those at the end of the chapter and review those that you didn't get right. Each question is based upon a specific learning objective in the text. For those you didn't get right, you may want to return to the textbook to review the material covering that learning objective.

Word Scrambles: This is meant as a diversion for you. We have chosen what we believe are three key terms from each chapter and mixed up the letters. If you like word scrambles, do it; if you don't, just look up the terms in the answers to see if your three key terms in that chapter matched our three key terms.

Match the Terms and Concepts to Their Definitions: Since the definitions are listed, you should get most of these right. The best way to match these is to read the definition first, and then find the term on the left that it defines. If you are not sure of the matching term, circle that definition and move on to the next one. At the end return to the remaining definitions and look at the remaining terms to complete the matches. After completing this part, check your answers with those in the back of the chapter and figure our what percent you got right. If that percent is below the grade you want to get on your exam, try to see why you missed the ones you did and review those terms and concepts in the textbook.

Problems and Exercises: Now it's time to take on any problems in the chapter. These problems are more difficult than the short-answer questions. These problems focus on numerical and graphical aspects of the chapter.

Working through problems is perhaps one of the best ways to practice your understanding of economic principles. Even if you are expecting a multiple choice exam, working through these problems will give you a good handle on using the concepts in each chapter.

If you expect a multiple choice exam with no problems, you can work through these fairly quickly, making sure you understand the concepts being tested. If you will have a test with problems and exercises, make sure you can answer each of these questions accurately.

Work out the answers to all the problems in the space provided before checking them against the answers in the back of the chapter. Where our answers differ from yours, check to find out why. The answers refer to specific pages in the textbook so you can review the text again too.

Most of the problems are objective and have only one answer. A few are interpretative and have many answers. We recognize that some questions can be answered in different ways than we did. If you cannot reconcile your answer with ours, check with your professor. Once you are at this stage — worrying about different interpretations — you're ahead of most students and, most likely, prepared for the exam.

Multiple Choice Questions: The last exercise in each chapter is the multiple choice test. We leave it for last because it serves to test the breadth of your knowledge of the text material. Multiple choice questions are not the final arbiters of your understanding. They are, instead, a way of determining whether you have read the book and generally understood the material.

Take this test after having worked through the other questions. Give the answer that most closely corresponds to the answer presented in your text. If you can answer these questions you should be ready for the multiple choice part of your exam.

Work through all the questions in the test before grading yourself. Looking up the answer before you try to answer the questions is a poor way to study. For a multiple choice exam, the percent you answer correctly will be a good predictor of how well you will do on the test.

You can foul up on multiple choice questions in two ways—you can know too little and you can know too much. The answer to knowing too little is obvious: Study more—that is, read the chapters more carefully (and maybe more often). The answer to knowing too much is more complicated. Our suggestions for students who know too much is not to ask themselves "What is the answer?" but instead to ask "What is the answer the person writing the question wants?" Since, with these multiple choice questions, the writer of the question is the textbook author, ask yourself: "What answer would the textbook author want me to give?" Answering the questions in this way will stop you from going too deeply into them and trying to see nuances that aren't supposed to be there.

For the most part questions in this study guide are meant to be straightforward. There may be deeper levels at which other answers could be relevant, but searching for those deeper answers will generally get you in trouble and not be worth the cost.

If you are having difficulty answering a multiple choice question, make your best guess. Once you are familiar with the material, even if you don't know the answer to a question you can generally make a reasonable guess. What point do you think the writer of the question wanted to make with the question? Figuring out that point and then thinking of incorrect answers may be a way for you to eliminate wrong answers and then choose among the remaining options.

Notice that the answers at the end of the chapter are not just the lettered answers. We have provided an explanation for each answer — why the right one is right and why some of the other choices are wrong. If you miss a question, read that rationale carefully. If you are not convinced, or do not follow the reasoning, go to the page in the text referred to in the answer and reread the material. If you are still not convinced, see the caveat on the next page.

Questions on Appendices: In the chapters we have included a number of questions on the text appendices. To separate these qustions from the others, the letter A precedes the question number. They are for students who have been assigned the appendices. If you have not been assigned them (and you have not read them on your own out of your great interest in economics) you can skip these.

Answers to All Questions: The answers to all questions, including rationales for those answers, appear at the end of each chapter. They begin on a new page so that you can tear out the answers and more easily check your answers against ours. We cannot emphasize enough that the best way to study is to answer the questions yourself first, and then check out our answers. Just looking at the questions and our answers may tell you what the answers are but will not give you the chance to see where your knowledge of the material is weak.

Pretests

Most class exams cover more than one chapter. To prepare you for such an exam, we provide multiple choice pretests for groups of chapters.

In these pretests each chapter will not be represented equally. Some chapters cover more important concepts and will be tested more heavily. This is most likely the approach your professor will take when designing your classroom test.

We suggest taking these under test conditions. Specifically,

Use a set time period to complete the exam.
Sit at a hard chair at a desk with good lighting.

For these exams, answer each question fully, and complete the entire exam before grading yourself. These pretests consist of 25-50 multiple choice questions from the selected group of chapters. These questions are identical to earlier questions so if you have done the work, you should do well on these.

Each answer will tell you the chapter on which the question is based, so if you did not cover one of the chapters in the text for your class, don't worry if you get that question wrong. If you get a number of questions wrong from the chapters your class has covered, worry.

There is another way to use these pretests which we hesitate to mention, but we're realists so we will. That way is to forget doing the chapter-by-chapter work and simply take the pretests. Go back and review the material you get wrong.

However you use the pretests, if it turns out that you consistently miss questions from the same chapter, return to your notes from the lecture and reread your textbook chapters.

A FINAL WORD OF ADVICE

That's about it. If you use it, this study guide can help you do better on the exam by giving you the opportunity to use the terms and models of economics. However, we reiterate one last time: The best way to do well in a class is to attend every class and read every chapter in the text as well as work through the chapters in this study guide. Start early and work consistently. Do not do all your studying the night before the exam.

A CAVEAT

There is always a chance that there's a correct answer other than the one the book tells you is the correct answer, or even that the answer the book gives is wrong.

We've tried hard to avoid those instances, but we're all human, and make mistakes. If you find a mistake, check the rationale at the end of the chapter justifying the chosen answer, and see if that convinces you. If the rationale does not match the answer given in this book, assume the error is typographical. If that is not the case, and you still think another answer is the correct one, write up an alternative rationale and e-mail Professor Colander the question and the alternative rationale. Professor Colander's e-mail is:

colander@middlebury.edu.

When he gets it he will either send you a note thanking you immensely for finding an example of incorrect reasoning, or explain why we disagree with you. If you're the first one to have pointed out an error he will also send you a copy of a case book in economics—just what you always wanted, right?

David Colander
Jenifer Gamber

Acknowledgements

We want to thank a number of students who worked through the study guide. Umar Serajuddin was helpful in choosing and revising second edition questions and suggesting new ones. We hope that the year he spent on the textbook and this study guide before going on to graduate school at the University of Maryland proved helpful. Senake Gajameragedara provided invaluable help making sure all the answers are correct. Helen Reiff provided her sharp eye in proofreading. Tom Thompson helped with encouragement and general guidance. We would also like to thank our families for giving us the support we needed to get this study guide done.

Dedicated to

Emily and William

Zach and Kasey

Chapter 1: Economics and Economic Reasoning

Chapter at a glance

1. Three central coordination problems any economic system must solve are: (6)

    1) What to produce.
    2) How to produce it.
    3) For whom to produce it.

    Most economic coordination problems involve perceived scarcity.

2. Five important dimensions of economics are: (7)

    1) Economic reasoning   *Is really benefit/cost analysis. If the benefits of something outweigh its costs, then do it. If not, don't.*

    2) Economic terminology   *Need to know what the terms and concepts mean. Learn them as you go!*

    3) Economic insights *General statements about what causes what—how an economy works (sometimes called economic theories, laws, models, or principles).*

    4) Economic institutions *Need to learn the structure or make-up of businesses, government and society and how they interact.*

    5) Economic policy options *There is more than one way to achieve an end or goal. Need to be aware of the different options and try to choose the "best."*

3. If the relevant benefits of doing something exceed the relevant costs, do it. If the relevant costs of doing something exceed the relevant benefits, don't do it. (9)

    Really need to think in terms of the marginal, or "extra" benefits (MB) and marginal, or "extra" costs (MC) of a course of action.

    Rational decision-making:
    If MB>MC =>Do more of it because "it's worth it."
    If MB<MC =>Do less of it because "it's not worth it."

    NOTE: The symbol "=>" means "implies" or "logically follows."

4. Opportunity cost is the basis of cost/benefit economic reasoning; it is the benefit foregone, or the cost of the next-best alternative to the activity you've chosen. In economic reasoning, that cost is less than the benefit of what you've chosen. (11)

    Opportunity cost => "What must be given up in order to get something else." Opportunity costs are often "hidden." Need to take into consideration all costs.

5. Economic reality is controlled by three invisible forces: (12)

    What happens in a society can be seen as the reaction and interaction of these 3 forces.

    1) The invisible hand (economic forces);
    The market forces of demand, supply, and prices, etc.

    2) The invisible handshake (social and historical forces);
    The impact of generally accepted social morals and customs.

    3) The invisible foot (political and legal forces).
    Political and legal forces affect decisions too.

6. Microeconomics considers economic reasoning from the viewpoint of individuals and builds up; macroeconomics considers economic reasoning from the aggregate and builds down. (17)
    Microeconomics (micro) => concerned with some particular segment of the economy.
    Macroeconomics (macro) => concerned with the entire economy.

7a. _Positive economics_ is the study of what is, and how the economy works. (19)
    Deals with "what is" (objective analysis).

7b. _Normative economics_ is the study of what the goals of the economy should be. (19)
    Deals with "what ought to be" (subjective analysis).

7c. The _art of economics_ is the application of the knowledge learned in positive economics to the achievement of the goals determined in normative economics. (19)

The art of economics is sometimes referred to as "policy economics."

"Good" policy tries to be objective. Tries to weigh all the benefits and costs associated with all policy options and chooses that option in which the benefits outweigh the costs to the greatest degree.

See also, Appendix A: "Economics in Perspective"
See also, Appendix B: "Graphish: The Language of Graphs"

In Appendix B, remember:
2 types of relationships:

1) _Direct (Positive) Relationship_: expressed as an upward sloping curve.

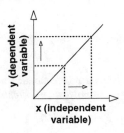

Note: as x increases, y increases; as x decreases, y decreases.

2) _Inverse (Negative) Relationship_: expressed as a downward sloping curve.

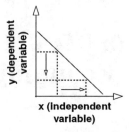

Note: as x increases, y decreases; as x decreases, y increases.

Short-answer questions

1. What are the five dimensions of economic learning? (LO2)

2. What are the three central problems that every economy must solve? (LO1)

3. What is scarcity? Why is defining economics in terms of scarcity problematic? (LO1)

4. State the economic decision rule. (LO3)

5. Define opportunity cost. (LO4)

6. Explain the importance of opportunity cost to economic reasoning. (LO4)

7. Define the three invisible forces that operate in the real world. (LO5)

8. How does microeconomics differ from macroeconomics? Give an example of a macroeconomic issue and a microeconomic issue. (LO6)

9. Define positive economics, normative economics, and the art of economics. How do they relate to one another? (LO7)

Word Scramble

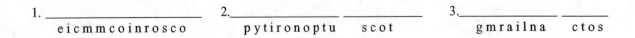

1. _____   2._____ _____   3._____ _____
    e i c m m c o i n r o s c o   p y t i r o n o p t u   s c o t   g m r a i l n a   c t o s

Match the Terms and Concepts to Their Definitions

___ 1. art of economics

___ 2. economic decision rule

___ 3. economic forces

___ 4. economic reasoning

___ 5. economic theory

___ 6. economics

___ 7. economy

___ 8. invisible foot

___ 9. invisible hand theory

___ 10. invisible handshake

___ 11. macroeconomics

___ 12. marginal benefit

___ 13. microeconomics

___ 14. opportunity cost

___ 15. positive economics

___ 16. scarcity

a. Additional benefit above what you've already derived.
b. Generalizations about the working of an abstract economy.
c. If benefits exceed costs, do it. If costs exceed benefits, don't.
d. Making decisions on the basis of costs and benefits.
e. The study of individual choice, and how that choice is influenced by economic forces.
f. The forces of scarcity.
g. The benefit forgone, or the cost, of the best alternative to the activity you've chosen.
h. The study of what is, and how the economy works.
i. The insight that a market economy will allocate resources efficiently.
j. Social and historical forces that play a role in deciding whether to let market forces operate.
k. The institutional structure through which individuals in a society coordinate their diverse wants or desires.
l. The study of inflation, unemployment, business cycles, and growth primarily from the whole to the parts, focusing on aggregate relationships and supplementing the analysis with microeconomic insights.
m. The study of how human beings coordinate their wants.
n. Goods available are too few to satisfy individuals' wants.
o. Political and legal forces that play a role in deciding whether to let market forces operate.
p. The application of the knowledge learned in positive economics to the achievement of the goals determined in normative economics.

Problems and Exercises

1. State what happens to scarcity for each good in the following situations:

   a. New storage technology allows college dining services to keep peaches from rotting for a longer time. (Good: peaches).

   b. More students desire to live in single-sex dormitories. No new single-sex dormitories are established. (Good: single-sex dormitory rooms).

2. State as best you can:

   a. The opportunity cost of going out on a date tonight with the date you made last Wednesday.

   b. The opportunity cost of breaking the date for tonight you made last Wednesday.

c.   The opportunity cost of working through this study guide.

d.   The opportunity cost of buying this study guide.

3.   Assume you have purchased a $15,000 car. The salesperson has offered you a maintenance contract covering all major repairs for the next 3 years, with some exclusions, for $750.

a.   What is the opportunity cost of purchasing that maintenance contract?

b.   What information would you need to make a decision based on the economic decision rule?

c.   Based upon that information how would you make your decision?

4.   State for each of the following whether it is an example of an invisible foot, invisible hand, or invisible handshake at work:

a.   Warm weather arrives and more people take Sunday afternoon drives. As a result, the price of gasoline rises.

b.   In some states, liquor cannot be sold before noon on Sunday.

c.   Minors cannot purchase cigarettes.

d.   Many parents will send money to their children in college without the expectation of being repaid.

Multiple Choice Questions

1. Economic reasoning
    a. provides a framework with which to approach questions.
    b. provides correct answers to just about every question.
    c. is only used by economists.
    d. should only be applied to economic business matters.

2. Scarcity could be reduced if
    a. individuals work less and want fewer consumption goods.
    b. individuals work more and want fewer consumption goods.
    c. world population grows and world production remains the same.
    d. innovation comes to a halt.

3. In the textbook, the author focuses on coordination rather than scarcity as the central point of the definition of economics because
    a. economics is not really about scarcity.
    b. scarcity involves coercion, and the author doesn't like coercion.
    c. the author wants to emphasize that the quantity of goods and services depends upon human action and the ability to coordinate that human action.
    d. the concept "scarcity" does not fit within the institutional structure of the economy.

4. In the U.S. economy, who is in charge of organizing and coordinating overall economic activities?
    a. Government.
    b. Corporations.
    c. No one.
    d. Consumers.

5. In the United States more fish is consumed on Friday than on any other day. This is due to the fact that
    a. fishing boats tend to come in on Thursday.
    b. the price of fish is lower on Thursday evenings.
    c. fish would spoil over the weekend.
    d. the Catholic religious tradition limited eating meat on Fridays until recently.

6. You bought stock A for $10 and stock B for $50. The price of each is currently $20. Assuming no tax issues, which should you sell if you need money?
    a. Stock A.
    b. Stock B.
    c. It doesn't matter which.
    d. You should sell an equal amount of both.

7. In deciding whether to go to lectures in the middle of the semester, you should
    a. include tuition as part of the cost of that decision.
    b. not include tuition as part of the cost of that decision.
    c. include a portion of tuition as part of the cost of that decision.
    d. only include tuition if you paid it rather than your parents.

8. In making economic decisions you should consider
    a. marginal costs and marginal benefits.
    b. marginal costs and average benefits.
    c. average costs and average benefits.
    d. total costs and total benefits, including past costs and benefits.

9. In arriving at a decision, a good economist would say that
    a. one should consider only total costs and total benefits.
    b. one should consider only marginal costs and marginal benefits.
    c. after one has considered marginal costs and benefits, one should integrate the social and moral implications and reconsider those costs and benefits.
    d. after considering the marginal costs and benefits, one should make the decision on social and moral grounds.

10. In making decisions economists use only
    a. monetary costs.
    b. opportunity costs.
    c. benefit costs.
    d. dollar costs.

11. The opportunity cost of reading Chapter 1 of the text
    a. is about 1/20 of the price you paid for the book because the chapter is about one twentieth of the price of the book.
    b. zero since you have already paid for the book
    c. has nothing to do with the price you paid for the book.
    d. is 1/20 the price of the book plus 1/20 the price of the tuition.

12. Rationing devices that our society uses include
    a. the invisible hand only.
    b. the invisible hand and invisible handshake only.
    c. the invisible hand and invisible foot only.
    d. the invisible hand, the invisible foot, and the invisible handshake.

13. If at Female College there are significantly more females than males (and there are not a significant number of gays)
    a. economic forces will be pushing for females to pay on dates.
    b. economic forces will be pushing for males to pay on dates.
    c. economic forces will be pushing for neither to pay.
    d. economic forces are irrelevant to this issue. Everyone knows that the males always should pay.

14. Individuals are prohibited from practicing medicine without a license. This is an example of
    a. the invisible hand.
    b. the invisible handshake.
    c. the invisible foot.
    d. the invisible brain.

15. A recent development is that birth mothers are being given more control over specifying the socioeconomic background and other characteristics of the family she is giving her baby to. This is an example of _____ in action.
    a. the invisible hand.
    b. the invisible handshake.
    c. the invisible foot.
    d. the invisible brain.

16. In studying economics,
    a. one should develop a micro foundation first.
    b. one should develop a macro foundation first.
    c. one should study the totality and develop simultaneously a micro and macro foundation.
    d. one should develop a metro foundation for micro and macro.

17. Which of the following is an example of a macroeconomic topic?
    a. The effect of a frost on the Florida orange crop.
    b. Wages of cross-country truckers.
    c. How the unemployment and inflation rates are related.
    d. How income is distributed in the United States.

18. The statement, "The distribution of income should be left to the market," is
    a. a positive statement.
    b. a normative statement.
    c. an art-of-economics statement
    d. an objective statement.

19. "Given certain conditions, the market achieves efficient results" is an example of a
    a. positive statement.
    b. normative statement.
    c. art-of-economics statement.
    d. subjective statement.

A1. Economics that focuses on formal interrelationships is called
    a. Walrasian economics.
    b. Marshallian economics.
    c. Smithian economics.
    d. good economics.

A2. Marshallian economics differs from Walrasian economics in that
    a. it is more concerned with income distribution.
    b. it has more heart.
    c. it takes institutions and political and social dimensions more
       into account.
    d. it focuses more on supply and demand.

B1. In the graph on the right the point A represents
    a. a price of 1 and a quantity of 2.
    b. a price of 2 and a quantity of 2.
    c. a price of 2 and a quantity of 1.
    d. a price of 1 and a quantity of 1.

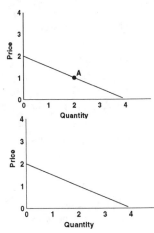

B2. The slope of the line in the graph to the right is
    a. 1/2.
    b. 2.
    c. minus 1/2.
    d. minus 2.

B3. At the maximum and minimum points of the nonlinear curve, the value of the slope is equal to
    a. 1.
    b. zero.
    c. minus 1.
    d. indeterminate.

B4. Which of the four lines in the accompanying graph at the right has the larger slope?
    a. A.
    b. B.
    c. C.
    d. A and C.

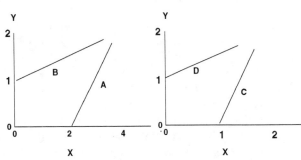

Answers

Short-answer questions

1. Five important dimensions of economic learning are: economic reasoning, economic terminology, economic insights, economic institutions, and economic policy options. (7)

2. The three central problems that every economy must solve are (1) what to produce, (2) how to produce it, and (3) for whom to produce it. (6)

3. Scarcity occurs when there are not enough goods available to satisfy individuals' desires. Defining economics in terms of scarcity is problematic for two reasons. First, scarcity is a perceived concept. If individuals could be encouraged to work more and want less, scarcity could be reduced or even eliminated. Second, the quantity of usable resources depends upon technology and human action. Defining economics in terms of scarcity suggests that eliminating scarcity would eliminate economics. Even if scarcity did not exist, society would still face a coordination problem. The coordination definition of economics includes scarcity but is a much more inclusive definition. (6)

4. If the relevant benefits of doing something exceed the relevant costs, do it. If the relevant costs of doing something exceed the relevant benefits, don't do it. (9)

5. Opportunity cost is the benefit forgone, or the cost, of the best alternative to the activity you have chosen. (11)

6. Opportunity cost is the basis of cost/benefit economic reasoning. In economic reasoning, opportunity cost is less than the benefit of what you have chosen. (11)

7. The three invisible forces are the invisible hand, the invisible handshake, and the invisible foot. The invisible hand is the price mechanism, the rise and fall of prices that guides our actions in a market. The invisible handshake is social and historical forces that play a role in deciding whether to let market forces operate. The invisible foot is political and legal forces that play a role in deciding whether to let market forces operate. (12)

8. Microeconomic theory considers economic reasoning from the viewpoint of individuals and builds up while macroeconomics considers economic reasoning from the aggregate and builds down. Microeconomics studies things like household buying decisions. Macroeconomics studies things like the unemployment rate. (16-17)

9. Positive economics is the study of what is and how the economy works. Normative economics is the study of what the goals of the economy should be. The art of economics is the application of the knowledge learned in positive economics to the achievement of the goals one has determined in normative economics. (19)

Word Scramble   1. microeconomics   2. opportunity cost   3. marginal cost.

Match the Terms and Concepts to Their Definitions
1-p; 2-c; 3-f; 4-d; 5-b; 6-m; 7-k; 8-o; 9-i; 10-j; 11-l; 12-a; 13-e; 14-g; 15-h; 16-n.

Problems and Exercises

1. a. Scarcity will fall because fewer peaches will rot. (12)
    b. Scarcity of single-sex dorm rooms will rise since the number of students desiring single-sex dorm rooms has risen, but the number available has not. (12)

2. a. The opportunity cost of going out on a date tonight that I made last Wednesday is the benefit forgone of the best alternative. If my best alternative was to study for an economics exam, it would be the increase in my exam grade that I would have gotten had I studied. Many answers are possible. (11-12)
    b. The opportunity cost of breaking the date for tonight that I made last Wednesday is the benefit forgone of going out on that date. It would be all the fun I would have had on that date. Other answers are possible. (11-12)

c. The opportunity cost of working through this study guide is the benefit forgone of the next-best alternative to studying. It could be the increase in the grade I would have received by studying for another exam, or the money I could have earned if I were working at the library. Many answers are possible. (11-12)

d. The opportunity cost of buying this study guide is the benefit forgone of spending that money on the next-best alternative. Perhaps it is the enjoyment forgone of eating two pizzas. Other answers are possible. (11-12)

3. a. The opportunity cost of purchasing the maintenance contract is the benefit I could receive by spending that $750 on something else like a moon roof. (11-12)

b. I would need to know the benefit of the maintenance contract to assess whether the cost of $750 is worthwhile. (11-12)

c. For me the benefit of the maintenance contract is the expected cost of future repairs that would be covered and the peace of mind of knowing that future repairs are covered by the contract. The cost is the opportunity cost of using the $750 in another way. If the benefit exceeds the cost, do it. If the cost exceeds the benefit, do not do it. (11-12)

4. a. This is an example of the invisible hand. (12)

b. This is an example of the invisible foot. Some states have laws, called blue laws, against selling liquor on Sundays altogether or selling it before noon. (12)

c. This is an example of the invisible foot. This is a federal law. (12-14)

d. This is an example of a social force, the invisible handshake. (12-14)

Multiple Choice Questions

1. a. As discussed on page 8, the textbook author clearly believes that economic reasoning applies to just about everything. This eliminates c and d. He also carefully points out that it is not the only reasoning that can be used; hence b does not fit. So the correct answer must be a.

2. b. On page 6 of the textbook, the author states that the problem of scarcity could be reduced if individuals worked more and wanted less. Scarcity results when more people want more of something than is currently available.

3. c. On page 8 of the book the author emphasizes the human action reason for focusing on coordination. He explicitly points out that scarcity is important, but that the concept, coordination, is broader.

4. c. As discussed on page 8, the invisible hand of the market coordinates the activities and is a composite of many individuals rather than just any one individual. If you were tempted to say b, corporations, your instincts are right, but the "overall" eliminated that as even a possible answer.

5. d. This is an example of cultural norms affecting demand, as is discussed on page 8. The other answers might have some validity but they are far less significant than d.

6. c. As is discussed on pages 9 and 10 of the book, in making economic decisions you consider that only costs from this point on are relevant; historical costs have no relevance. Since the prices of the stocks are currently the same, it doesn't matter which you sell.

7. b. As discussed on page 9, in economic decisions, you only look at costs from this point on; sunk costs are sunk costs, so tuition can be forgotten. In economic decisions, forward looking marginal costs and marginal benefits are focused on.

8. a. The economic decision rule is "If benefits exceed costs, do it." As is discussed on pages 9 and 10 of the text, however, the relevant benefits and relevant costs to be considered are marginal (additional) costs and marginal benefits. The answer d is definitely ruled out by the qualifying phrase referring to past benefits and costs. Thus, only a is correct.

9. c. As the textbook points out on pages 9 and 10, economists use a framework of costs and benefits initially, but then later they add the social and moral implications to their conclusions. Adding these can change the estimates of costs and benefits, and in doing so can change the result of economic analysis, so there is an integration between the two. (This was a hard question which required careful reading of the text to answer correctly.)

10. b. As discussed on pages 10 and 11 of the text opportunity costs include measures of nonmonetary costs. The other answers either do not include all the costs that an economist would consider, or are simply two words put together. The opportunity costs include the benefit forgone by undertaking an activity.

11. c. As discussed on pages 10-12 the correct answer is that it has nothing to do with the price you paid since that is already paid, so a and d are wrong. The opportunity cost is not zero, however, since there are costs of reading the book. The primary opportunity cost of reading the book is the value of the time you're spending on it which is determined by what you could be doing with that time otherwise.

12. d. As discussed on pages 12 and 13 of the text, all of these are rationing devices. The invisible hand works through the market and thus is focused on in economics. However the others also play a role in determining what people want, either through legal means or through social control.

13. a. As discussed on pages 12 and 13 of the text, if there are significantly more of one gender than another, dates with that group must be rationed out among the other group. Economic forces will be pushing for the group in excess supply (in this case women) to pay. Economic forces may be pushing in that direction even though historical forces may push us in the opposite direction. Thus, even if males pay because of social forces, economic forces will be pushing for females to pay.

14. c. As discussed on page12-14 of the text, legal forces are called the invisible foot.

15. a. As discussed on page 13 of the text, even though the invisible hand is not allowed to operate directly in the adoption market, it operates indirectly. It gives more power to the supplier of something that's in short supply, so when there is excess supply we are likely to see rules changed to reflect more the desires of that supplier. That's what's happening here.

16. c. As discussed on page 17, neither micro nor macro is prior; one needs both a micro foundation for macro and a macro foundation for micro. Thus, the best answer is c. The d answer, metro foundation, is meaningless. What is a metro foundation? We don't know. (Actually, if it had said "metafoundation" it might have been justifiable as an answer, but it did not.) Be careful when you see something totally unfamiliar such as the d answer here. It's often thrown in there to make sure you really know what you are talking about. Alternatively, it might be that the individual making out these questions had to think of four alternatives and sometimes there are only three likely ones.

17. c. As discussed on pages 16 and 17, Macroeconomics is concerned with inflation, unemployment, business cycles and growth. Microeconomics is the study of individuals. The distribution of income is a micro topic because it is concerned with the distribution of income among individuals.

18. b. As discussed on page 19, this could be either a normative or an art-of-economics statement, depending on whether there is an implicit "given the way the real-world economy operates to best achieve the growth rate you desire." Since these qualifiers are not there, "normative" is the preferable answer.

19. a. As discussed on page 19 this is a positive statement. It is a statement about *what is*, not about what should be.

A1. a. As discussed in Appendix A, page 23, Walrasian economics focuses on formal relationships.

A2. c. This is a hard question because each of the four answers is in some sense true. However, the focus of the discussion in Appendix A, page 23, is on Marshallian economics considering the social and political dimensions more so than Walrasian economics. Thus, c is the best answer.

B1. a. As discussed in Appendix B, page 23 and 24, a point represents the corresponding numbers on the horizontal and vertical number lines.

B2. c. As discussed on page 26 of Appendix B, the slope of a line is defined as rise over run. Since the rise is -2 and the run is 4, the slope of the above line is minus 1/2.

B3. b. As discussed on page 27 of Appendix B, at the maximum and minimum points of the curve the slope is zero.

B4. c. As discussed in Appendix B, page 26, the slope is defined as rise over run. Line C has the largest rise for a given run so c is the answer. Even though, visually, line A seems to have the same slope as line C it has a different coordinate system. Line A has a slope of 1 whereas line B has a slope of 2. Always be careful about checking coordinate systems when visually interpreting a graph. (See pages 28-29).

Chapter 2:
The Economic Organization of Society

Chapter at a glance

la. <u>Capitalism</u> is an economic system based on private property and the market. It gives private property rights to individuals, and relies on market forces to coordinate economic activity. (32)
Capitalism ("market-oriented economy") is characterized by:
(I)   mainly private ownership of resources
(II) market system solves the What? How? and For whom? problems.

1b. <u>Socialism</u> is, in theory, an economic system that tries to organize society in the same way as most families are organized—all people should contribute what they can, and get what they need. (33-34)
Socialism ("government-controlled economy") is characterized by:
(I)   government control over resources
(II) government solves the What? How? and For whom? problems.

✔ *All real-world economies have elements of both capitalism and socialism.*

2. Exhibit 1 in the textbook shows capitalism's and Soviet-style socialism's solutions to the three central planning problems. (35)

Capitalism's solutions to the central economic problems:
1.   What to produce: what businesses believe people want, and is profitable.
2.   How to produce: businesses decide how to produce efficiently, guided by their desire to make a profit.
3.   For whom to produce: distribution according to individuals' ability and/or inherited wealth.

Soviet-style socialism's solutions to the three problems:
1.   What to produce: what central planners believe is socially beneficial.
2.   How to produce: central planners decide, based on what they think is good for the country.
3.   For whom to produce: central planners distribute goods based on what they determine are individuals' needs.

3. Markets coordinate economic activity by using the price mechansim to direct individuals' self-interest into society's interest. (37)
Unbridled, pure or laissez-faire capitalism led to many abuses. This created support for at least some socialism.

✔ *We now have "Welfare Capitalism"—a mix of capitalism and socialism.*

4. Remember this graph:

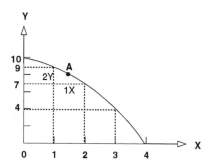

<u>*Production Possibilities Curve*</u>
Shows the trade-off (or opportunity cost) between two things.
The slope tells you the opportunity cost of good X in terms of good Y. In this particular graph you have to give up 2 Y to get 1 X when you're around point A. (40)

5. The principal of increasing marginal opportunity cost states that opportunity costs increase the more you concentrate on the activity. In order to get more of something, one must give up ever-increasing quantities of something else. (41)

Production Possibility Curve

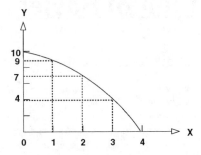

Production Possibility Table

		Opportunity cost of X
X	Y	_(amount of Y which must be foregone)_
0	10	
		>1
1	9	
		>2 Note: As you get more of X
2	7	
		>3 you have to give up larger
3	4	
		>4 amounts of Y.
4	0	

6. When individuals trade, using their comparative advantages, their combined production possibility curve shifts out. (43)

Specialization and trade along the lines of comparative advantage is mutually beneficial to all involved.

Markets and trading make people better off.

7. Because decisions are contextual, what the prodution possibility curve for a particular decision looks like depends upon the existing insitutions, and the analysis can be applied only in that institutional and historical context. (46)

The production possibility curve is an engine of analysis to make contextual choices, not a definitive tool to decide what one should do in all cases.

See also, Appendix A: "The History of Economic Systems."

Short-answer questions

1. What is capitalism? (LO1)

2. What is socialism? (LO1)

3. How does a capitalist economy solve the three central economic problems? (LO2)

4. How does a Soviet-style socialist economy solve the three central economic problems? (LO2)

5. How can markets coordinate economic decisions without the active involvement of government? (LO3)

6. Design a grade production possibility curve and show how it demonstrates the concept of opportunity cost. (LO4)

7. State the principle of increasing marginal opportunity cost. (LO5)

8. What would the production possibility curve look like if opportunity cost were constant? (LO5)

9. Explain what happens to the production possibility curve with trade and why trade makes individuals better off. (LO6)

10. Why is the production possibility curve more useful in discussing small changes than it is when discussing changes in entire economic systems? (LO7)

A1. Why did feudalism evolve into mercantilism?

A2. Why did mercantilism evolve into capitalism?

A3. Explain what is meant by the statement that capitalism has evolved into welfare capitalism.

Word Scramble

1. _____   2._____   3._____

     a c i i l m o s s   a a c i i l p s s t t   n f c c e y f i i e

Match the Terms and Concepts to Their Definitions

____ 1. comparative advantage

____ 2. economic system

____ 3. feudalism

____ 4. NIMBY

____ 5. Industrial Revolution

____ 6. principle of increasing marginal opportunity cost

____ 7. productive efficiency

____ 8. production possibility curve

____ 9. private property rights

____ 10. socialism

____ 11. Soviet-style socialism

____ 12. welfare capitalism

a. Control of an asset or a right given to an individual or a firm.

b. Period when technology and machines rapidly modernized industrial production and mass produced goods replaced handmade goods.

c. Economic system in which the market operates but government regulates markets significantly.

d. Economic system that tries to organize society in the same way that families do — people contribute what they can and get what they need.

e. Economic system that uses central planning and government ownership of the means of production to answer the questions what to produce, how to produce it, and for whom to produce it.

f. Represents Not In My Back Yard; a phrase used by people who may approve of a project, but don't want it to be near them.

g. Political system divided into small communities in which a few powerful people protect those who are loyal to them.

h. The set of economic institutions that determine a country's important economic decisions.

i. The advantage that attaches to a resource when that resource is better suited to the production of one good than to the production of another good.

j. In order to get more of something, one must give up ever-increasing quantities of something else.

k. A curve measuring the maximum combination of outputs that can be obtained from a given number of inputs.

l. Getting as much output for as few inputs as possible.

Problems and Exercises

1. Suppose a restaurant has the following production possibility table:

Labor devoted to pizza in % of total	Output of pizza in pies per week	Labor devoted to spaghetti in % of total	Output of spaghetti in bowls per week
100	50	0	0
80	40	20	10
60	30	40	17
40	20	60	22
20	10	80	25
0	0	100	27

a. Plot the restaurant's production possibility curve.

b. What happens to the marginal opportunity cost as the output of bowls of spaghetti increases?

c. What would happen to the production possibility curve if the restaurant found a way to toss and cook pizzas faster?

d.   What would happen to the production possibility curve if the restaurant bought new stoves and ovens that cooked both pizzas and spaghetti faster?

2.   Suppose Ecoland has the following production possibilities table:

% resources devoted to production of guns	Number of guns	% resources devoted to production of butter	Pounds of butter
100	50	0	0
80	40	20	5
60	30	40	10
40	20	60	15
20	10	80	20
0	0	100	25

a.   Plot the production possibility curve for the production of guns and butter. Put guns on the horizontal axis.

b.   What is the per unit opportunity cost of increasing the production of guns from 20 to 30? From 40 to 50?

c.   What happens to the opportunity cost of producing guns as the production of guns increases?

d.   What is the per unit opportunity cost of increasing the production of butter from 10 to 15? From 20 to 25?

e.   What happens to the opportunity cost of producing butter as the production of butter increases?

f.   Given this production possibility curve, is producing 26 guns and 13 pounds of butter possible?

g.   Is producing 34 guns and 7 pounds of butter possible? Is it efficient?

3.   Show, given the following production possibility tables and using production possibility curves, that the United States and Japan would be better off specializing in the production of either food or machinery and then trading rather than producing both food and machinery themselves and not trading.

| United States Production per year | | Japan Production per year | |
Tons of food	Thousands of units of machinery	Tons of food	Thousands of units of machinery
10	0	12.2	0
8	5	10	1
6	10	7.5	2
4	15	5	3
2	20	2.5	4
0	25	0	5

4.   Assume that France can produce wine at 25 francs per bottle and can produce butter at 5 francs per pound. Assume that Italy can produce wine at 16,000 lire per bottle and butter at 10,000 lire per pound.

   a.   In terms of pounds of butter, what is the opportunity cost of producing wine in each country?

   b.   Who has the comparative advantage in producing butter?

   c.   Which country should most likely specialize in wine and which should specialized in butter?

Multiple Choice Questions

1. An economic system works via
    a. the invisible hand.
    b. the invisible hand and the invisible foot.
    c. the invisible hand and the invisible handshake.
    d. the invisible hand and the invisible foot and the invisible handshake.

2. For a market to exist, you have to have
    a. public property rights.
    b. private property rights.
    c. a combination of public and private property rights.
    d. coordination rights.

3. In a pure capitalist society, the concept of fairness embodied is
    a. to each according to their needs; from each according to their ability.
    b. to each according to their ability; from each according to their needs.
    c. them that works, gets; them that don't, starve.
    d. everyone gets enough, but those who work harder get more.

4. In theory
    a. socialism is an economic system that tries to organize society in the same ways as most families organize, striving to see that individuals get what they need.
    b. socialism is an economic system based on central planning and government ownership of the means of production.
    c. socialism is an economic system based on private property rights.
    d. socialism is an economic system based on markets.

5. Soviet-style socialism is
    a. an economic system that tries to organize society in the same ways as most families organize, striving to see that individuals get what they need.
    b. an economic system based on central planning and government ownership of the means of production.
    c. an economic system based on private property rights.
    d. an economic system based on markets.

6. In capitalism, the "what to produce" decision is made by
    a. what people want.
    b. what firms believe people want and will make a profit for the firms.
    c. what government believes people want and will make a profit for the government.
    d. what central planners believe is socially beneficial.

7. In Soviet-style socialism, the "what to produce" decision is made by
    a. what people want.
    b. what firms believe people want and will make a profit for firms.
    c. what government believes people want and will make a profit for government.
    d. what central planners want or what they believe is socially beneficial.

8. The U.S. economy today can best be described as
    a. socialist.
    b. pure capitalist.
    c. welfare capitalist.
    d. state socialist.

9. If the opportunity cost of good X in terms of good Y is 2Y, so you'll have to give up 2Y to get one X, the production possibility curve would look like
   a. a.
   b. b.
   c. c.
   d. d.

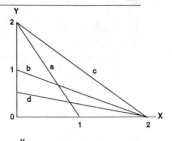

10. If the opportunity cost of good X in terms of good Y is 2Y, so you'll have to give up 2Y to get one X, the production possibility curve would look like
    a. a.
    b. b.
    c. c.
    d. d.

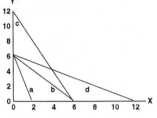

11. If the opportunity cost of good X in terms of good Y is 2Y, so you'll have to give up 2Y to get one X, the production possibility curve would look like
    a. a.
    b. b.
    c. c.
    d. a, b, and c

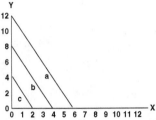

12. If the opportunity cost is constant for all combinations, the production possibility frontier will look like
    a. a.
    b. b.
    c. c.
    d. d.

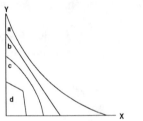

13. If the principle of increasing marginal opportunity cost applies at all points, the production possibility curve looks like
    a. a.
    b. b.
    c. c.
    d. d.

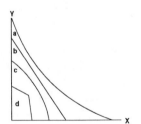

14. Given the accompanying production possibility curve, when you're moving from point C to B the opportunity cost of butter in terms of guns is
    a. 1/3.
    b. 1.
    c. 2.
    d. 3/2.

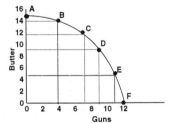

15. In the graph to the right, in the range of points between A and B there is
    a. a high opportunity cost of guns in terms of butter.
    b. a low opportunity cost of guns in terms of butter.
    c. no opportunity cost of guns in terms of butter.
    d. a high monetary cost of guns in terms of butter.

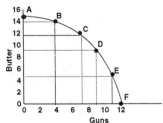

16. In the accompanying production possibility diagram, point A would be
    a. an efficient point.
    b. a super-efficient point.
    c. an inefficient point.
    d. a non-attainable point.

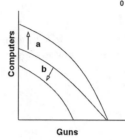

17. A law about the growth of efficiency of computers states that computer chip technology doubles the efficiency of computers each year. If that holds true, which of the four arrows would demonstrate the appropriate shifting of the production possibility curve?
    a. a.
    b. b.
    c. c.
    d. d.

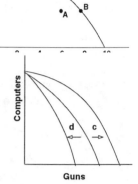

18. Say that methods of production are tied to particular income distributions, so that choosing one method will help some people but hurt others. Say also that method A produces significantly more total output than method B. In this case
    a. method A is more efficient than method B.
    b. method B is more efficient than method A.
    c. if method A produces more and gives more to the poor people, method A is more efficient.
    d. one can't say whether A or B is more efficient.

19. If the United States and Japan have production possibility curves as shown in the diagram on the right, at what point would they most be after trade?
    a. A
    b. B
    c. C
    d. D

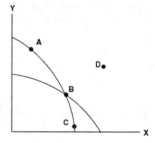

A1. In feudalism the most important invisible force was
    a. the invisible hand.
    b. the invisible handshake.
    c. the invisible foot.
    d. the invisible brain.

A2. When there is not a lot of significant technological change
    a. feudalism is highly inefficient.
    b. feudalism is reasonably efficient.
    c. technological change has no relation to whether feudalism would be efficient or not.
    d. feudalism is inefficient, no matter what.

A3. In mercantilism, the guiding invisible force is
    a. the invisible hand.
    b. the invisible foot.
    c. the invisible handshake.
    d. the invisible brain.

A4. Mercantilism evolved into capitalism because
    a. government investments did not pan out.
    b. the Industrial Revolution undermined the craft guilds' mercantilist method of production.
    c. the guilds wanted more freedom.
    d. serfs wanted more freedom.

A5. Marx saw significant tension between
   a. rich capitalists and poor capitalists.
   b. capitalists and government.
   c. capitalists and the proletariat.
   d. government and the proletariat.

A6. Asian economies tend to be
   a. more feudalistic than the U.S. economy.
   b. more capitalistic than the U.S. economy.
   c. more socialistic than the U.S. economy.
   d. more mercantilist than the U.S. economy.

A7. State socialism is an economic system in which
   a. business sees to it that people work for their own good until they can be relied upon to do that on their own.
   b. business sees to it that people work for the common good until they can be relied upon to do that on their own.
   c. government sees to it that people work for their own good until they can be relied upon to do so on their own.
   d. government sees to it that people work for the common good until they can be relied upon to do so on their own.

Answers

Short-answer questions

1. Capitalism is an economic system based on private property and the market. It gives private property rights to individuals, and relies on market forces to coordinate economic activity. (32)

2. Socialism is an economic system that tries to organize society in the same way as do most families — all people should contribute what they can, and get what they need. (33)

3. A capitalist economy solves the problem what to produce: what businesses believe people want and think they can make a profit supplying. It solves the problem how to produce: businesses decide how to produce efficiently, guided by their desire to make a profit. It solves the problem for whom to produce: distribution according to individuals' ability and/or inherited wealth. (35)

4. A Soviet-style socialist economy solves the problem what to produce: what central planners believe is socially beneficial. It solves the problem how to produce: central planners decide, based, one hopes, on what they think is good for the country. It solves the problem for whom to produce: central planners distribute goods based on what they determine are individuals' needs. (35)

5. The invisible hand — the price mechanism — guides the actions of suppliers and consumers to the general good. That is, competition directs individuals pursuing profit to do what society needs to have done. Markets coordinate economic decisions by turning self-interest into social good. (37)

6. The production possibility curve shows the highest combination of grades you can get with 20 hours of studying economics and English. The grade received in economics in on the vertical axis and the grade received in English is on the horizontal axis. The graph tells us the opportunity cost of spending any combination of hours on economics and English. For example, the opportunity cost of increasing your grade in economics by 6 points is decreasing your English grade by 4 points. (38-39)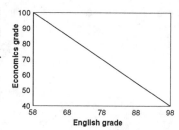

7. The principle of increasing marginal opportunity cost states that in order to get more of something, one must give up ever-increasing quantities of something else. (41)

8. Such a production possibility curve would be a straight line connecting the maximum number of units that could be produced of each product if all inputs were devoted to one or the other good. (40)

9. By comparing individual production possibility curves, one can determine those activities in which each has a comparative advantage. By concentrating on those activities for which one has a comparative advantage and trading those goods for goods for which others have a comparative advantage, individuals can end up with a combination of goods not attainable without trade. The production possibility curve shifts out with trade. (41-43)

10. The production possibility curve is best used given an existing economic system because an economic system determines relationships that affect costs in everyday decisions and in production. The example in the text of how changing from socialism to capitalism would affect the production possibility curve is a good example of how the production possibility curve can mask the probability that beneficial result of major structural changes may take many years. (45-46)

A1. Feudalism evolved into mercantilism as the development of money allowed trade to grow, undermining the traditional base of feudalism. Politics rather than social forces came to control the central economic decisions. (53-54)

A2. Mercantilism evolved into capitalism because the Industrial Revolution shifted the economic power base away from craftsmen toward industrialists and toward an understanding that markets could coordinate the economy without the active involvement of the government. (54-55)

A3. Capitalism has evolved into welfare capitalism. That is, the human abuses marked by early capitalist developments led to a criticism of the market economic system. Political forces have changed government's role in the market, making government a key player in determining distribution and in making the what, how, and for whom decisions. This characterizes the U.S. economy today. (55-57)

Word Scramble   1. socialism   2. capitalists   3. efficiency

Match the Terms and Concepts with Their Definitions

1-i; 2-h; 3-g; 4-f; 5-b; 6-j; 7-l; 8-k; 9-a; 10-d; 11-e; 12-c.

Problems and Exercises

1. a. The restaurant's production possibility curve is shown to the right. (39)
    b. The number of pizza pies that must be given up to make an additional bowl of spaghetti increases as the number of bowls of spaghetti produced increases. (40)

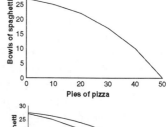

    c. If the restaurant found a way to toss and cook pizzas faster, the production possibility curve would rotate out along the pizza axis as shown on the right. (43)

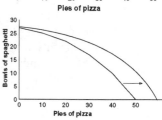

    d. The production possibility curve would shift out to the right as shown in the figure on the right. (43)

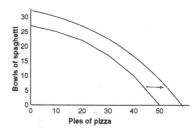

2. a. The production possibility curve is a straight line as shown on the right. (39-40)
    b. The opportunity cost of increasing the production of guns from 20 to 30 is 0.5 pounds of butter per gun. The opportunity cost of increasing the production of guns from 40 to 50 is also 0.5 pounds of butter per gun. (40-41)

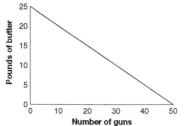

    c. The opportunity cost of producing guns stays the same as the production of guns increases. (41-42)
    d. The opportunity cost of increasing the production of butter from 10 to 15 is 2 guns per pound of butter. The opportunity cost of increasing the production of butter from 20 to 25 is 2 guns per pound of butter. (41-42)
    e. The opportunity cost of producing butter stays the same as the production of butter increases. (41-42)
    f. Producing 26 guns and 13 pounds of butter is not attainable given this production possibility curve. We can produce 20 guns and 15 pounds of butter. To produce six more guns, Ecoland must give up 3 pounds of butter. Ecoland can produce only 26 guns and 12 pounds of butter. (41-42)
    g. Ecoland can produce 34 guns and 7 pounds of butter. To see this, begin at 30 guns and 10 pounds of butter. To produce 4 more guns, 2 pounds of butter must be given up. Ecoland can produce 34 guns and 8 pounds of butter, which is more than 34 guns and 7 pounds of butter. This is an inefficient point of production. (41-42)

3. The production possibility of producing food and machinery for both Japan and the United States is shown in the graph on the right. The combined production possibility curve with trade is also shown. Clearly, trade shifts the production possibility curve out, showing that the two countries are better off with trade. The United States has a comparative advantage in the production of machinery. It must give up only 0.2 tons of food for each additional thousand units of machinery produced. Japan must give up 2.5 tons of food for each additional thousand units of machinery produced. A specific example is if Japan produced 12.5 tons of food and no machines while the United States produced 0 tons of food and 15 thousand units of machinery, Japan could offer the United States 2 tons of food for 3 thousand units of machinery. The United States would be at point A and Japan would be at point B. Each would be able to attain a level of production not attainable before. (41-42)

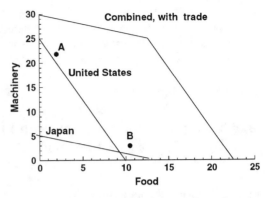

4. a. In France, the opportunity cost of producing wine is 5 pounds of butter. In Italy, the opportunity cost of producing wine is 1.6 pounds of butter. Calculate this by finding how much butter must be forgone for each bottle of wine in each country. (41-42)

  b. France has the comparative advantage in producing butter because it can produce butter for a lower opportunity cost. (41-42)

  c. Italy should specialize in producing wine and France should specialize in producing butter assuming one can produce only wine and the other must produce only butter. This is concluded from the principle of comparative advantage. (41-42)

Multiple Choice

1. d   As discussed on page 31, an economic system works via the interaction of all three invisible forces.

2. b   As discussed on page 32, markets require private property rights because these give people the framework within which they can trade from one to another and markets rely on trading. Markets also require government, but government and public property rights are not the same thing, which rules out a and c. And d is a throwaway answer.

3. c   As discussed on page 33, c represents the concept of fairness in a pure capitalist economy. In a welfare capitalist economy d would be a possible answer. We should also point out that c leaves out issues of inheritance and luck, which complicate the ethics of capitalism, but c is nevertheless by far the best answer.

4. a   As discussed on page 33, a is the correct answer. If the question had said "Soviet-style socialism," b would have been an acceptable answer, but Soviet-style socialism was a response to real-world implementation problems, not part of the theory of socialism.

5. b   As discussed on page 34, b is the correct answer. If the question had said simply "socialism." a would have been an acceptable answer, but given that it said Soviet-style socialism, b is the preferable answer.

6. b   As discussed in Exhibit 1, page 35, the correct answer is b.

7. d   As discussed Exhibit 1, page 35, the correct answer is d. We should point out that this is *ideally*; in practice, central planners may not be concerned with society. Thus c is a possible answer, but the term "profit" makes it unacceptable. Planners would not get profit—they might get rich, but it wouldn't be through profits.

8. c   See pages 37 and 38 of the text.

9. a   As discussed on page 39, the production possibility curve tells how much of one good you must give up to get more of the other good; here you must give up 2Y to get one X, making a the correct answer.

10. c   As discussed on page 39, the production possibility curve tells how much of one good you must give up to get more of another good. Opportunity costs is a ratio; it determines the slope, not the position, of the ppc curve. Thus, the correct answer is c because the 12 to 6 trade-off reduces to a 2 to 1 trade-off.

11. d   As discussed on page 39, the production possibility curve tells how much of one good you must give up to get more of the other good. Opportunity costs is a ratio; it determines the slope, not the position, of the ppc curve. Since all have the same correct slope, all three are correct, so d is the right answer.

12. b   As discussed on pages 39 and 40 of the book, if the opportunity costs are constant, the ppc is a straight line, so b must be the answer.

13. c   As discussed on pages 40 and 41 of the book, with increasing marginal opportunity costs, as you produce more and more of a good, you will have to give up more and more of the other good to do so. This means that the slope of the ppc must be bowed outward, so c is the correct answer. (See Exhibit 3, page 40 for an in-depth discussion.)

14. d   As discussed on page 40, the slope of the ppc measures the trade-off of one good for the other. Since moving from point c to b means giving up 3 guns for 2 pounds of butter, the correct answer is 3/2 or d.

15. b   As discussed on page 41, the flatter the slope, the higher the opportunity cost of the good measured on the vertical axis; alternatively, the flatter the slope the lower the opportunity cost of that good measured on the horizontal axis. In the AB range the slope is flat so guns have a low opportunity cost in terms of butter; one need give up only one pound of butter to get four guns.

16. c   As discussed on page 44 (See Exhibit 5), point A is an inefficient point.

17. a   As discussed on page 44 (See Exhibit 5), technological change that improves the efficiency of producing a good shifts the ppc out in that good, but not in the other good. So a is the correct answer.

18. d   The answer is "You can't say," as discussed on page 43. The term "efficiency" involves *achieving a goal as cheaply as possible.* Without specifying one's goal one cannot say what method is more efficient. The concept efficiency generally presumes that the goal includes preferring more to less, so if any method is more productive, it will be method A. But because there are distributional effects that involve making additional judgments, the correct answer is d. Some students may have been tempted to choose c because their goals involve more equity, but that is their particular judgment, and not all people may agree. Thus c would be incorrect, leaving d as the correct answer.

19. d   As discussed in Exhibit 4 on page 42, with trade, both countries can attain a point outside each production possibility curve. The only point not already attainable is D.

A1. b   As discussed on page 53, in feudalism tradition reigned.

A2. b   As discussed on page 53, as long as society doesn't change too much, tradition operates reasonably well. Hence b is the best answer.

A3. b   As discussed on page 53, in mercantilism government directed the economy.

A4. b   See page 54.

A5. c   See page 55. To the degree that government was controlled by capitalists, d would be a correct answer, but it is not as good an answer as c, which represents the primary conflict. Remember, you are choosing the answer that best reflects the discussion in the text.

A6. d   See page 57, where it is stated that Asian economies have many similarities to mercantilism.

A7. d   See pages 56 and 57.

Chapter 3: Supply and Demand

Chapter at a glance

1. The <u>law of demand</u> states that the quantity of a good demanded is <u>inversely related</u> to the good's price. When price goes up, quantity demanded goes down. When price goes down, quantity demanded goes up. (60)

✔ *Law of Demand (Inverse Relationship):*
   arrows move in $\uparrow P \Rightarrow \downarrow Q_d$
   opposite directions $\downarrow P \Rightarrow \uparrow Q_d$

   Law of Demand expressed as a <u>downward-sloping curve</u>:

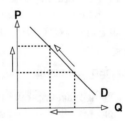

2a. The law of demand is based upon opportunity cost and individuals' ability to substitute. If the relative price of a good rises, the opportunity cost of purchasing that good will also rise and demanders will substitute for it a good with a lower opportunity cost. (61)
   As the P of beef $\uparrow$ s, we buy more chicken.

2b. The law of supply, like the law of demand, is based on opportunity cost and the individual firm's ability to substitute. Suppliers will substitute toward goods for which they receive higher relative prices. (68)
   If the P of wheat $\uparrow$ s, farmers grow more wheat and less corn.

3. Changes in quantity demanded are shown by movements along a demand curve. Shifts in demand are shown by a shift of the entire demand curve. (62-63) *(Note: "Δ" means "change.")*
   Don't get this confused on the exam!
   ΔQ_d is caused <u>only</u> by a Δ in the P of the good itself.

✔ $\Delta P \Rightarrow \Delta Q_d \Rightarrow$ *movement along a given D curve*

   $\uparrow P \Rightarrow \downarrow Q_d$: *movement along a curve (e.g. from point A to point B).*

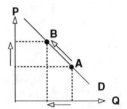

   ΔD is caused only by Δs in the shift factors of D(<u>not</u> a Δ in the P of the good itself!)
✔ <u>Δ in shift factors of D $\Rightarrow$ $\Delta D \Rightarrow$ shift of a D curve</u>

✔ *Know what can cause an increase and decrease in demand:*
   $\uparrow D \Rightarrow$ <u>*Rightward Shift*</u> $\downarrow D \Rightarrow$ <u>*Leftward Shift*</u>

4. To derive a demand curve from a demand table you plot each point on the demand table on a graph and connect the points. (64)

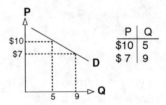

P	Q
$10	5
$ 7	9

5. The <u>law of supply</u> states that the quantity supplied of a good is <u>directly related</u> to the goods' price. When price goes up, quantity supplied goes up. When price goes down, quantity supplied goes down. (68)

✔ *Law of Supply (Direct Relationship):*
arrows move in $\uparrow P \Rightarrow \uparrow Q_s$
same direction $\downarrow P \Rightarrow \downarrow Q_s$

Law of Supply expressed as an <u>*upward-sloping curve*</u>*:*

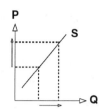

6. Just as with demand, it is important to distinguish between a shift in supply (a shift of the entire supply curve) and a movement along a supply curve (a change in the quantity supplied due to a change in price). (69-70)
   Don't get this confused on the exam!
   ΔQ_s *is caused* <u>*only*</u> *by a* Δ *in the P of the good itself.*

✔ $\Delta P \Rightarrow \Delta Q_s \Rightarrow$ *movement along a given S curve.*

   $\uparrow P \Rightarrow \uparrow Q_s$*: movement along a curve (e.g. from point A to point B).*

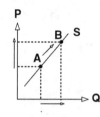

   ΔS *is caused only by* Δs *in the shift factors of S (*<u>*not*</u> *a* Δ *in the P of the good itself!)*
✔ <u>Δ *in shift factors of S* $\Rightarrow \Delta S \Rightarrow$ *shift of a S curve*</u>

✔*Know what can cause an increase and decrease in supply:*
  $\uparrow S \Rightarrow$ <u>*Rightward Shift*</u> $\downarrow S \Rightarrow$ <u>*Leftward Shift*</u>

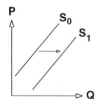 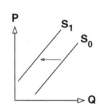

7. To derive a supply curve from a supply table, you plot each point on the supply table on a graph and connect the points. (70-72)

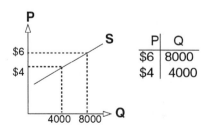

P	Q
$6	8000
$4	4000

8. The three dynamic laws of supply and demand are:
   1. If quantity demanded is greater than quantity supplied, prices tend to rise; when quantity supplied is greater than quantity demanded, prices tend to fall. (72-73)
   2. The larger the difference between quantity demanded and quantity supplied, the greater the pressure for prices to rise (if there is excess demand) or fall (if there is excess supply). (73)
   3. When quantity demanded equals quantity supplied, prices have no tendency to change. (73-74)

✔ <u>*Know this!*</u>
   1. If $Q_d > Q_s \Rightarrow$ Shortage $\Rightarrow P$ will $\uparrow$.
   2. If $Q_s > Q_d \Rightarrow$ Surplus $\Rightarrow P$ will $\downarrow$.
   3. If $Q_s = Q_d \Rightarrow$ Equilibrium $\Rightarrow$ no tendency for P to change (because there is neither a surplus nor a shortage).

Shortage	Surplus	Equilibrium
$(Q_d > Q_s)$	$(Q_s > Q_d)$	$(Q_s = Q_d)$
P is below equilibrium	P is above equilibrium	

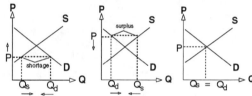

ALSO NOTE:

$\uparrow D \Rightarrow \uparrow P; \uparrow Q$ $\downarrow D \Rightarrow \downarrow P; \downarrow Q$

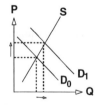 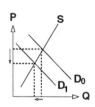

$\uparrow S \Rightarrow \downarrow P; \uparrow Q$ $\downarrow S \Rightarrow \uparrow P; \downarrow Q$

 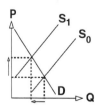

See also, "Appendix A: Algebraic Representation of Demand, Supply, and Equilibrium."

Short-answer questions

1. What is the law of demand? (LO1)

2. What does the law of supply say would most individuals do if their wage increased? Relate your answer to opportunity cost and substitution. (LO2)

3. Suppose the price of Red Hot Chili Pepper CDs rose 2% and the average price of all other goods rose 10%. What does the law of demand say would happen to the quantity of Red Hot Chili Pepper CDs demanded? (LO2)

4. Demonstrate graphically a shift in demand. (LO3)

5. Demonstrate graphically a movement along a demand curve. (LO3)

6. Draw a demand curve from the following demand table. (LO4)

    Demand Table

Q	P
50	1
40	2
30	3
20	4

7. State the law of supply. (LO5)

8. Demonstrate graphically the effect on the supply of Red Hot Chili Pepper CDs of a new technology that reduces the cost of producing Red Hot Chili Pepper CDs. (LO6)

9. Demonstrate graphically the effect of a rise in the price of Red Hot Chili Pepper CDs on supply. (LO6)

10. Draw a supply curve from the following supply table. (LO7)

Supply Table

Q	P
20	1
30	2
40	3
50	4

11. State the first dynamic law of supply and demand and demonstrate it graphically. (LO8)

12. State the second dynamic law of supply and demand and demonstrate it graphically. (LO8)

13. Given the graph on the right, at what price is there no pressure on price to change? Why? (LO8)

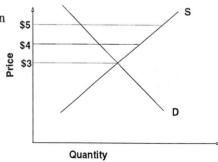

Word Scramble

1. _____   2._____   3._____
   b e i i i l m q r u u   l p p s u y   a e e i l r t v   c e i p r

Match the Terms and Concepts to Their Definitions

___ 1. demand curve

___ 2. equilibrium price

___ 3. excess supply

___ 4. factors of production

___ 5. first dynamic law of supply and demand

___ 6. law of demand

___ 7. law of supply

___ 8. market demand curve

___ 9. movement along a supply curve

___ 10. quantity demanded

___ 11. relative price

___ 12. second dynamic law of supply and demand

___ 13. shift factor of demand

___ 14. shift in supply

___ 15. third dynamic law of supply and demand

a. A specific amount that will be demanded per unit of time at a specific price. Refers to a point on a demand curve.

b. Curve that tells how much of a good will be bought at various prices.

c. If how much of a good is supplied is affected by a shift factor, there is said to be a shift in supply. Graphically, a shift in supply will cause the entire supply curve to shift.

d. In a market, the larger the difference between quantity supplied and quantity demanded, the greater the pressure on prices to rise (if there is excess demand) or fall (if there is excess supply).

e. Method of representing a change in the quantity supplied. Graphically, a change in quantity supplied will cause a movement along the supply curve.

f. More of a good will be demanded the lower its price, other things constant. Also can be stated as: Less of a good will be demanded the higher its price, other things constant.

g. More of a good will be supplied the higher its price, other things constant. Also can be stated as: Less of a good will be supplied the lower its price, other things constant.

h. Price of a good compared to the price of some other good.

i. Quantity supplied is greater than quantity demanded.

j. Resources, or inputs, necessary to produce goods.

k. Something, other than the good's price, that affects how much of the good is demanded.

l. The price toward which the invisible hand (economic forces) drives the market.

m. The horizontal sum of all individual demand curves.

n. When quantity demanded is greater than quantity supplied, prices tend to rise; when quantity supplied is greater than quantity demanded, prices tend to fall.

o. When quantity supplied equals quantity demanded, prices have no tendency to change.

Problems and Exercises

1. Draw two linear curves on the same graph from the following table, one relating P with Q_1 and the other relating P with Q_2.

P	Q_1	Q_2
25	50	110
30	60	100
35	70	90
40	80	80
45	90	70

a. Label the curve that is most likely a demand curve. Explain your choice.

b. Label the curve that is most likely a supply curve. Explain your choice.

c. What is equilibrium price and quantity? Choose points above and below that price and explain why each is not the equilibrium price.

2. You are given the following individual demand tables for compact discs.

Price	Juan	Philippe	Ramone
$7	3	20	50
$10	2	10	40
$13	1	7	32
$16	0	5	26
$19	0	3	20
$22	0	0	14

a. Determine the market demand table.

b. Graph the individual and market demand curves.

c. If the current market price is $13, what is the total market demand? What happens to total market demand if price rises to $19 a disc?

d. Say that a new popular Vanilla Ice compact disc hits the market which increases demand for compact discs by 25%. Show with a demand table what happens to the individual and market demand curves. Demonstrate graphically what happens to market demand.

3.   Draw a hypothetical demand and supply curve for cyber cafes — coffee houses with computers hooked up to the Internet with access to daily newspapers (among other things) at each table. Show how the equilibrium price and quantity is affected by the following:

   a.   A technological breakthrough lowers the cost of computers.

   b.   Consumers' income rises.

   c.   A per-hour fee is charged to coffee houses to use the Internet.

   d.   The price of newspapers in print rises.

   e.   Possible suppliers expect Cyber cafes to become more popular.

4.   The invention of a self-milking cow machine allows cows to milk themselves. Not only does this reduce the need for higher-cost human assistance in milking, but it also allows the cow to milk herself three times a day instead of two, leading to both a healthier cow and increased milk production.

   a.   Show the effect of this innovation on the equilibrium quantity and price of milk.

   b.   Show the likely effect on equilibrium price and quantity of apple juice (a substitute for milk).

A1. The supply and demand equation for strawberries is given by

$Q_s = -10 + 5P$
$Q_d = 20 - 5P$

where P is price in dollars per quart, Q_s is millions of quarts of strawberries supplied, and Q_d is millions of quarts of strawberries demanded.

   a.   What is the equilibrium market price and quantity for strawberries in the market?

   b.   Suppose a new preservative is introduced that prevents more strawberries from rotting on their way from the farm to the store. As a result supply of strawberries increases by 20 million quarts. What effect does this have on market price and quantity sold?

   c.   Suppose it has been found that the spray used on cherry trees has ill effects on those who eat the cherries. As a result, the demand for strawberries increases by 10 million quarts. What effect does this have on market price for strawberries and quantity of strawberries sold?

A2. In Bangladesh, it is common for ear cleaners (individuals who clean other people's ears) to offer their services to passers-by along the road. The supply and demand equations for ear cleaners can be expressed as

$Q_s = -20 + 8P$
$Q_d = 40 - 12P,$

where P is price in takas (currency in Bangladesh) and quantity is interpreted as thousands of ear cleaners.

   a.   What is the equilibrium market price and quantity of ear cleaners?

   b.   Suppose the incomes of consumers in Bangladesh rise and the demand for ear cleaners to clean ears increases by 20 thousand. What is the resulting equilibrium price and quantity of ear cleaners?

   c.   Suppose the Health Department of Bangladesh relaxes a previous regulation that only high quality cotton can be used for ear cleaning. Many ear cleaners switch to less-expensive lower-quality cotton and the supply of ear clearners increases by 10 thousand at each price. What is the new equilibrium price and quantity of ear cleaners?

Multiple Choice Questions

1. The law of demand states
   a. more of a good will be demanded the lower its price, other things constant.
   b. more of a good will be demanded the higher its price, other things constant.
   c. people always want more.
   d. you can't always get what you want at the price you want.

2. If the weather gets very hot, what will likely happen?
   a. The supply of air conditioners will increase.
   b. Quantity demanded of air conditioners will increase.
   c. Demand for air conditioners will increase.
   d. The quality demanded of air conditioners will increase.

3. If the price of air conditioners falls, there will be
   a. an increase in demand for air conditioners.
   b. an increase in the quantity demanded of air conditioners.
   c. an increase in the quality demanded of air conditioners.
   d. a shift in the demand for air conditioners.

4. In partial equilibrium analysis one assumes
   a. other things constant and forgets them.
   b. other things are not constant.
   c. other things are constant but one brings them back into the analysis later when one applies it.
   d. other things are not constant, and one partially fits them into the analysis.

5. The demand curve has just shifted in. Which of the following would not be an explanation?
   a. The price of some other good has risen.
   b. The price of some other good has fallen.
   c. The price of this good has fallen.
   d. Society's income has fallen.

6. In Brazil in the 1980s the price of pencils doubled in a year, but simultaneously so did the price of almost every good. In applying the law of demand, one would expect
   a. the quantity demanded of pencils to increase.
   b. the quantity demanded of pencils to decrease.
   c. the quantity demanded of pencils to remain constant.
   d. the demand for pencils to increase.

7. Using the standard axes, the demand curve associated with the following demand table is

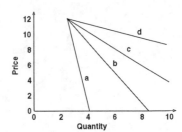

Demand Table		
	p	q
a. a		
b. b	7	5
c. c	9	4
d. d	11	3

8. There are many more substitutes for good A than for good B.
   a. The demand curve for good A will likely be flatter.
   b. The demand curve for good B will likely be flatter.
   c. You can't say anything about the likely relative flatness of the demand curves.
   d. The demand curve for good B will likely shift out further.

9. To derive a market demand curve from two individual demand curves
    a. one adds the two demand curves horizontally.
    b. one adds the two demand curves vertically.
    c. one subtracts one demand curve from the other demand curve.
    d. one adds the demand curves both horizontally and vertically.

10. The market demand curve will always
    a. be flatter than the individual demand curves that make it up.
    b. be steeper than the individual demand curves that make it up.
    c. have the same slope as the individual demand curves that make it up.
    d. be unrelated to the individual demand curves and slope.

11. The movement in the graph at the right from point A to point B represents
    a. an increase in demand.
    b. an increase in the quantity demanded.
    c. an increase in the quantity supplied.
    d. an increase in supply.

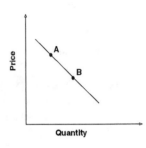

12. The law of supply states that
    a. more of a good will be supplied the higher its price, other things constant.
    b. less of a good will be supplied the higher its price, other things constant.
    c. more of a good will be supplied the higher its price, other things changing proportionately.
    d. less of a good will be supplied the higher its price, other things changing proportionately.

13. In the graph on the right, the arrow refers to
    a. a shift in demand.
    b. a shift in supply.
    c. a change in the quantity demanded.
    d. a change in the quantity supplied.

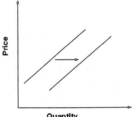

14. The market supply curve for the following two individual supply curves
    S_1 and S_2 would be
    a. S_3.
    b. S_4.
    c. S_5.
    d. S_6.

15. If there is an improvement in technology one would expect
    a. a movement along the supply curve.
    b. a shift upward of the supply curve.
    c. a shift downward of the supply curve.
    d. a movement down along the supply curve.

16. You're the supplier of a good and suddenly a number of your long-lost friends call you. Your good is most likely
    a. in excess supply.
    b. in excess demand.
    c. in equilibrium.
    d. in both excess supply and demand.

17. At which point will you expect the stronger downward pressure on prices?
    a. a.
    b. b.
    c. c.
    d. d.

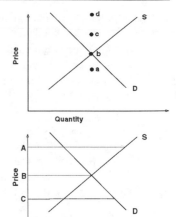

18. If the invisible handshake and invisible foot are strong in the following
    diagram
    a. you expect the equilibrium price to be at A.
    b. you expect the equilibrium price to be at B.
    c. you expect the equilibrium price to be at C.
    d. it is difficult to know where to expect the equilibrium price to be
       unless one knows more about these other invisible forces.

19. If the demand for a good increases you will expect
    a. price to fall and quantity to rise.
    b. price to rise and quantity to rise.
    c. price to fall and quantity to fall.
    d. price to rise and quantity to fall.

20. If there is a flood, what will likely happen to the price of bottled water?
    a. It will rise.
    b. It will fall.
    c. It will remain the same.
    d. It will fall to zero.

A1. The supply and demand equations for Nantucket Nectar's Kiwi-berry juice are given by
    $Q_s = -4 + 5P$ and $Q_d = 18 - 6P$ respectively, where price is dollars per quart and quantity is thousands of
    quarts. The equilibrium market price and quantity is
    a. P = $2, Q = 6 thousand quarts.
    b. P = $3, Q = 6 thousand quarts.
    c. P = $14, Q = 66 thousand quarts.
    d. P = $22, Q = 106 thousand quarts.

A2. The supply and demand equations for sidewalk snow removal in a small town in Montana are given by $Q_s =$
    $-50 + 5P$ and $Q_d = 100 - 5P$ respectively, where price is in dollars per removal and quantity is numbers of
    removals per week. It snows so much that demand for sidewalk snow removals increases by 30 per week.
    The equilibrium market price and quantity is
    a. P = $15, Q = 6 sidewalk snow removals.
    b. P = $15, Q = 6 sidewalk snow removals.
    c. P = $18, Q = 66 sidewalk snow removals.
    d. P = $18, Q = 40 sidewalk snow removals.

A3. The supply and demand equations for sidewalk snow removal in a small town in Montana are given by $Q_s =$
    $-50 + 5P$ and $Q_d = 100 - 5P$ respectively, where price is in dollars per removal and quantity is numbers
    of removals per week. (Same equations as for A2.) Suppose snowfall is so light demand for sidewalk snow
    removals decreases by 10 per week. The equilibrium market price and quantity is
    a. P = $18, Q = 40 sidewalk snow removals.
    b. P = $16, Q = 30 sidewalk snow removals.
    c. P = $14, Q = 20 sidewalk snow removals.
    d. P = $8, Q = 10 sidewalk snow removals.

A4. The supply and demand equations for beef in England are given by $Q_s = -18 + 7P$ and $Q_d = 72 - 8P$ respectively, where price is in £ per pound and quantity is millions of pounds of beef per year. Mad cow disease reduces the supply of beef by 15 million pounds per year. What is the new equilibrium price and quantity of beef?

  a. P = £5/lb, Q = 32 million pounds of beef per year.
  b. P = £6/lb, Q = 24 million pounds of beef per year.
  c. P = £7/lb, Q = 16 million pounds of beef per year.
  d. P = £7/lb, Q = 31 million pounds of beef per year.

A5. The supply and demand equations for beef in England are given by $Q_s = -18 + 7P$ and $Q_d = 72 - 8P$ respectively, where price is in £ per pound and quantity is millions of pounds of beef per year. (Same equations as in A4.) Mad cow disease reduces the supply of beef by 15 million pounds per year and subsequent fear by consumers reduces demand by 30 million pounds per year. What is the new equilibrium price and quantity of beef?

  a. P = £3/lb, Q = 18 million pounds of beef per year.
  b. P = £5/lb, Q = 2 million pounds of beef per year.
  c. P = £7/lb, Q = 46 million pounds of beef per year.
  d. P = £9/lb, Q = 30 million pounds of beef per year.

Answers

Short-Answer Questions

1. The law of demand states that the quantity of a good demanded is inversely related to the good's price. When price goes up, quantity demanded goes down. (60)

2. The law of supply states that as the price of supplying a good rises, the quantity supplied will rise. According to this law, most individuals would choose to supply more labor if their wage increased. By working more hours, individuals forgo the benefit of leisure, so as wages increase, the opportunity cost of not working increases and individuals will substitute work for leisure. (68)

3. Since the money price of all goods has risen 10% and the money price of Red Hot Chili Pepper CDs has risen 2%, the relative price of Red Hot Chili Pepper CDs has fallen 8%. The law of demand states that as the relative price of a good falls, the quantity demanded rises. Remember, it is the good's relative price, not its money price, that the law of demand refers to. The opportunity cost of buying a CD has fallen (because its relative price has fallen) and individuals will substitute away from all other goods toward Red Hot Chili Pepper CDs. (60-61)

4. A shift in demand is shown by a shift of the entire demand curve resulting from a change in a shift factor of demand as shown in the graph on the right. (63)

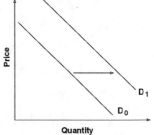

5. A movement along a demand curve is a change in quantity demanded resulting from a change in price as is shown in the graph on the right as a movement from Q_0 to Q_1. (63)

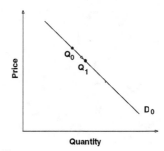

6. To derive a demand curve from a demand table, you plot each point on the demand table on a graph and connect the points. This is shown on the graph on the right. (64)

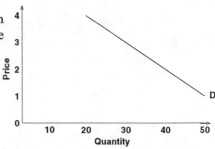

7. The law of supply states that the quantity of a good supplied is directly related to the good's price. When price goes up, quantity supplied goes up. (68)

8. A new technology that reduces the cost of producing Red Hot Chili Pepper CDs will shift the entire supply curve to the right from S_0 to S_1, as shown in the graph on the right. (69-70)

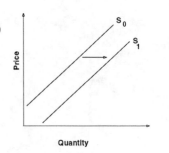

9. A rise in the price of Red Hot Chili Pepper CDs from P_0 to P_1 results in a movement along a supply curve to the right; quantity of Red Hot Chili Pepper CDs supplied will rise from Q_0 to Q_1 as shown in the graph on the right. (69)

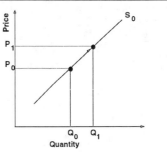

10. To derive a supply curve from a supply table, you plot each point on the supply table on a graph and connect the points. This is shown on the graph on the right. (70)

11. The first dynamic law of supply and demand states that (a) when quantity demanded is greater than quantity supplied, prices tend to rise and (b) when quantity supplied is greater than quantity demanded, prices tend to fall. Each case is demonstrated in the graph on the right. Price tends away from P_1 and P_2 and toward P_0. (72-73)

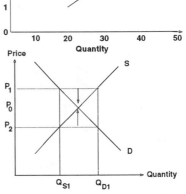

12. The second dynamic law of supply and demand states that in a market, the larger the difference between quantity supplied and quantity demanded, the greater the pressure on prices to rise (if there is excess demand) or fall (if there is excess supply). This demonstrated in the graph on the right. At P_2, the pressure for prices to fall toward P^* is greater than the pressure at P_1 because excess supply is greater at P_2 compared to excess supply at P_1. (73)

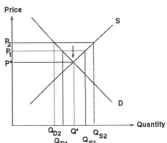

13. Assuming only market forces are operating, at price $3 there is no pressure for prices to change because quantity demanded equals quantity supplied. At $4 and $5, quantity supplied exceeds quantity demanded and there is excess supply; prices will tend to fall. The third dynamic law of supply and demand states that when quantity supplied equals quantity demanded, prices have no tendency to change. (73)

Word Scramble 1. equilibrium   2. supply   3. relative price

Match the Terms and Concepts to Their Definitions
1-b; 2-l; 3-i; 4-j; 5-n; 6-f; 7-g; 8-m; 9-e; 10-a; 11-h; 12-d; 13-k; 14-c; 15-o.

Problems and Exercises

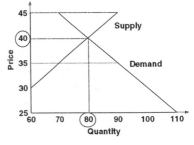

1. The linear curves are shown on the right. (60-69)
   a. As shown in the graph, the downward sloping curve is a demand curve. We deduce this from the law of demand: more of a good will be demanded the lower its price. (60-69)
   b. As shown in the graph, the upward sloping curve is a supply curve. We deduce this from the law of supply: more of a good will be supplied the higher its price. (60-69)
   c. The equilibrium price and quantity are where the demand and supply curves intersect. This is at $P = \$40$, $Q = 80$. At a price above $40, such as $45, quantity supplied exceeds quantity demanded and there is pressure for price to fall. At a price below $40, such as $35, quantity demanded exceeds quantity supplied and there is pressure for price to rise. (60-69)

2. a.   The market demand table is the summation of individual quantities demanded at each price as follows (64-65):

Price	Market quantity demanded
$7	73
10	52
13	40
16	31
19	23
22	14

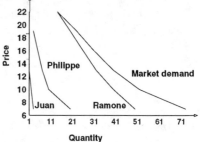

b.   The individual and market demand curves are shown to the right of the demand table. (64-65)

c.   At $13 a disc, total market demand is 40 discs. Total market demand falls to 23 when the price of discs rises to $19 per disc. (64-65)

d.   Quantity demanded at each price rises by 25% for each individual and for the market as a whole. The new demand table is shown below. Graphically, both the individual and market demand curves shift to the right. The graph on the right shows the rightward shift in market demand. (64-65)

Price	Juan	Philippe	Ramone	Market
$7	3.75	25	62.50	91.25
$10	2.50	12.5	50	65
$13	1.25	8.75	40	50
$16	0	6.25	32.5	38.75
$19	0	3.75	25	28.75
$21	0	0	17.5	17.5

3. A hypothetical market for cyber cafes is drawn on the right. (76-77)

a.   A technological breakthrough that lowers the cost of computers will shift the supply of cyber cafes to the right as shown. Equilibrium price will fall. Equilibrium quantity will rise. (76-77)

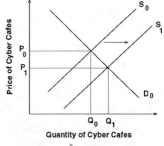

b.   A rise in consumers' income will shift the demand for cyber cafes to the right as shown in the graph to the right. Equilibrium price will rise. Equilibrium quantity will rise. (76-77)

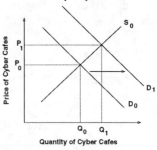

c.   If a fee is charged to coffee houses to use the Internet, the supply of cyber cafes will shift to the left as shown. Equilibrium price will rise. Equilibrium quantity will fall. (76-77)

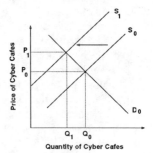

d. If the price of newspapers in print rises, the demand for cyber cafes will shift to the right as shown. Equilibrium price will rise. Equilibrium quantity will rise. (76-77)

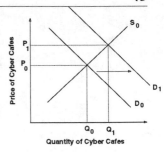

e. If possible suppliers expect cyber cafes to become more popular, the supply of cyber cafes will shift to the right as shown. Equilibrium price will fall. Equilibrium quantity will rise. (76-77)

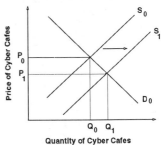

4. a. This innovation will shift the supply curve to the right. Equilibrium price will fall. Equilibrium quantity will rise. (76-77)

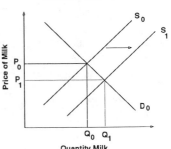

b. The market demand and supply for apple juice is shown on the right. As a result of the fall in milk prices, the demand for apple juice shifts to the left. Equilibrium price will fall. Equilibrium quantity will fall. (76-77)

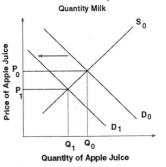

A1. a. Equating Q_s to Q_d and then solving for equilibrium price gives us $3 per quart. Substituting $3 into either the demand or supply equation, we find that equilibrium quantity is 5 million quarts. (81-83)

b. Since supply increases by 20 million quarts, the new supply equation is $Q_s = 10 + 5P$. Equating this with the demand equation, we find the new equilibrium price to be $1 per quart. Substituting into either the new supply equation or the demand equation we find that equilibrium quantity is 15 million quarts. (81-83)

c. With demand increasing, the new demand equation is $Q_d = 30 - 5P$. Setting Q_s equal to Q_d and solving for price we find equilibrium price to be $4 per quart. Substituting this into either the new demand or supply equation we find equilibrium quantity to be 10 million quarts. (81-83)

A2. a. Setting the demand and supply equations equal to one another, we find equilibrium price of 3 takas per ear cleaner. Substituting 3 takas into either the demand or supply equation we find equilibrium quantity to be 4 thousand ear cleaners. (81-83)

b. With increased demand for ear cleaners, the new demand equation becomes $Q_d = 60 - 12P$. Setting supply equal to demand, we find that the new equilibrium price is 4 takas per ear cleaner. Substituting 4 takas into either the demand or supply equation, we find equilibrium quantity to be 12 thousand ear cleaners. (81-83)

c. As supply rises by 10 thousand ear cleaners, the new supply equation becomes $Q_s = -10 + 8P$. Setting this new supply equation equal to the demand equation, we find equilibrium price to be 2.5 takas. Substituting 2.5 takas into either the demand or supply equation, we find equilibrium quantity to be 10 thousand ear cleaners. (81-83)

Multiple Choice

1. a   As discussed on page 60, the correct answer is a. A possible answer is d, which is a restatement of the law of demand, but since the actual law was among the choices, and is more precise, a is the correct answer.

2. c   As discussed on pages 62 and 63, it is important to distinguish between a change in the quantity demanded and a change in demand. Weather is a shift factor of demand, so demand, not quantity demanded, will increase. Supply will not increase; the quantity supplied will, however. Who knows what will happen to the quality demanded?—We don't.

3. b   As discussed on pages 62 and 63, when the price falls there is a movement along the demand curve which is expressed by saying the quantity demanded increased.

4. c   As discussed on page 62, in partial equilibrium analysis one assumes other things constant but keeps these other things in the back of one's mind and adds them back later.

5. c   The price of this good is the only one of the four that would cause a movement along a demand curve. The others are all shift factors. Some of you may have thought that 'a' was a possible answer since, generally, a rise in the price of another good shifts the demand curve for a good out, not in. That's true generally, but there are cases where goods are complements and the rise in the price of another good will shift the demand for this good in. Since c is clearly a correct answer, you didn't have to know this information to answer the question. We suggest the following rule: if one answer fits choose it; worry about fine distinctions later and only if you have time. If you can't figure out whether one answer might be right, choose the one you are sure is right. See page 63.

6. c   As is discussed on page 60, it is important to remember that partial equilibrium supply/demand analysis refers to relative price. This question focuses on one dimension of that relative price issue. Since all prices went up in the same proportion, the relative price of pencils has not changed. Therefore, the law of demand would predict no change in the quantity demanded of pencils.

7. b   This demand curve is the only demand curve that goes through all the points in the table. See page 64.

8. a   This is a hard question at this point in the course because it is not explicitly discussed in the text. However, the basic ideas are found from pages 60 to 63 of the text, and if you understand the idea behind the law of demand, you will be able to deduce that the more substitutes, the flatter the demand curve, assuming roughly the same quantities are demanded and they are drawn on the same axes. The reason is that an equal rise in price will cause individuals to switch to other goods more, the more substitutes there are.

9. a   As discussed in the text on pages 64 and 65 (Exhibit 4), market demand curves are determined by adding individuals' demand curves horizontally.

10. a   Since the market demand curve is arrived at by adding the individual demand curves horizontally, it will always be flatter. See page 65.

11. b   The curve slopes downward, so we can surmise that it is a demand curve; and the two points are on the demand curve, so the movement represents an increase in the quantity demanded, not an increase in demand. A shift in demand would be a shift of the entire curve. (See Exhibit 2, page 63 of the text.)

12. a   As discussed on page 68, the law of supply is stated in a. The others either have the movement in the wrong direction or are not holding all other things constant.

13. b   It is a shift in supply because the curve is upward sloping; and it's a shift of the entire curve, so it is not a movement along. See page 69.

14. c   The market supply curve is determined by the horizontal addition of individual supply curves. See pages 70-72.

15. c   As discussed on page 70, technology is a shift factor of supply so it must be a shift of the supply curve. Since it is an improvement, it must be a shift downward—at each quantity the price will be lower.

16. b   When there is excess demand, demanders start searching for new suppliers, as discussed on page 73.

17. d   This is an example of the second dynamic law of supply and demand: the greater the difference between quantity supplied and quantity demanded, the greater the pressure for the prices to rise or fall. See pages 73-74.

18. d   There is no way of choosing among a, b, and c without knowing the relative strengths and direction of these other forces. The other forces are likely to move the equilibrium price away from B, but they might be working against each other, leaving equilibrium price unchanged. So the best answer is d. See pages 71-74.

19. b   Since this statement says demand increases, it is the demand curve shifting. Assuming an upward sloping supply curve, that means that quantity will rise and price will rise. See page 77.

20. a   A flood will likely bring about a significant increase in the demand for bottled water since a flood makes most other water undrinkable. Assuming an upward sloping supply curve, this will cause the price of bottled water to rise. See pages 76-77.

A1. a.   Setting the supply and demand equations equal to one another we find equilibrium price and quantity to be option a. (81)

A2. d.   The new demand equation is $Q_d = 130 - 5P$. Setting this equal to the supply equation and solving for equilibrium P and Q gives you option d. (81-83)

A3. c.   The new demand equation is $Q_d = 90 - 5P$. Setting this equal to the supply equation and solving for equilibrium P and Q gives you option c. (81-83)

A4. c.   The new supply equation is $Q_s = -33 + 7P$. Setting this equal to the supply equation and solving for equilibrium P and Q gives you option c. (81-83)

A5. b.   The new demand and supply equation are $Q_d = 42 - 8P$ and $Q_s = -33 + 7P$ respectively. Setting this equal to the supply equation and solving for equilibrium P and Q gives you option b. (81-83)

Chapter 4:
Using Supply and Demand

Chapter at a glance

1. Price ceilings cause shortages; price floors cause surpluses. (86, 91)

   A price ceiling is a legal price set by government below equilibrium. A price floor is a legal price set by government above equilibrium.

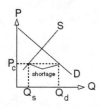

   Price Ceiling   **Price Floor**

2. Supply and demand can shed light on a variety of real-world events. (86-89)

   Supply and demand analysis is not just an academic exercise! Businesspeople, policy makers, and others find it extremely useful. You can too. See "Problems and Applications" and "Brain Teasers" for this and the last chapter.

3. As long as one remembers what prices and quantities go on each axis, exchange rate determination can be described by supply and demand graphs. (90-91)

   Most countries' currencies are traded in foreign exchange markets. The interaction of demand and supply determines the currency's value (price)–just as if does for any other good.

4. Taxes and tariffs raise price and reduce quantity. Quotas are a numerical limit on the number imported. (95-97)

   A tariff is an excise tax on an imported good. Any excise tax imposed on suppliers shifts the supply curve up by the amount of the tax. Rarely is the tax entirely passed on to consumers in the form of a

higher price. Although a quota can have the same effect as a tariff, suppliers prefer quotas becuase the suppliers get the revenues.

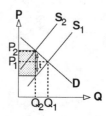

With tax t, price rises to P_2 and the government collects revenue shown by the shaded region. A quota Q_2 has the same effect on price and quantity. The difference is in who gets the revenue.

5. When analyzing the aggregate, small effects that can be put aside in micro can add up, and hence cannot be forgotten. (97-98)

   The fallacy of composition is the false assumption that what is true for a part will also be true for the whole. This means that what is true in microeconomics, may not be true in macroeconomics.

6. When there is an interdependence between supply and demand, a movement along one curve can cause a shift of the other curve. Thus, supply and demand analysis used alone is not enough to determine where the equilibrium will be. (99-100)

   When the "other things are constant" assumption is not realistic, then feedback effects can become relevant. The degree of interdependence differs among various sets of issues. That is why there is a separate micro and macro analysis–microeconomics and macroeconomics.

   See also, Appendix A: "Algebraic Representation of Interferences with Demand and Supply."

Short-answer questions

1. What is a price ceiling? Demonstrate graphically the effect of a price ceiling on a market. (LO1)

2. What is a price floor? Demonstrate graphically the effect of a price floor on a market. (LO1)

3. Demonstrate graphically what happens to the equilibrium price and quantity of m&ms if they suddenly become more popular. (LO2)

4. Demonstrate graphically what happens to the equilibrium price and quantity of oranges if a frost destroys 50 percent of the orange crop. (LO2)

5. Demonstrate graphically what happens in the following situation: Income in the U.S. rose in the 1990s and more and more people began to buy luxury items such as caviar. However, about that same time, the dissolution of the Soviet Union threw suppliers of caviar from the Caspian Sea into a mire of bureaucracy, reducing their ability to export caviar. Market: Caviar sold in the United States. (LO2)

6. Draw the supply and demand for U.S. dollars, remembering to label the axes. Explain what creates the demand and supply for U.S. dollars. (LO3)

7. Demonstrate graphically how the government maintains a fixed exchange rate when demand for its currency rises. (LO3)

8. Why are rent controls likely to worsen an existing shortage of housing? (LO1)

9. Demonstrate graphically what happens to equilibrium price and quantity when a tariff is imposed on imports. (LO4)

10. What is the difference between partial equilibrium and general equilibrium analysis? (LO5)

11. How is the fallacy of composition related to why economists separate micro from macro economics? (LO5)

12. What happens to equilibrium price and quantity when supply and demand are interdependent? (LO6)

Word Scramble

1._____ _____ 2._____ 3._____ __ _____

   c r e i p   g c i e l n i   p r i e t o n d i e c a   y a l f c l a f o n p s c i m t i o o o

Match the Terms and Concepts to Their Definitions

____ 1. price ceiling

____ 2. price floor

____ 3. depreciation

____ 4. nonconvertible currency

____ 5. fixed exchange rate

____ 6. rent control

____ 7. excise tax

____ 8. tariff

____ 9. quota

____ 10. partial equilibrium analysis

____ 11. fallacy of composition

a. A fall in the exchange rate.

b. Analysis that is partial or incomplete and holds other things equal.

c. Tax that is levied on a specific good.

d. The false assumption that what is true for a part will also be true for the whole.

e. A government-imposed limit on how high a price can be charged.

f. A quantitative restriction on the amount that one country can export to another.

g. Price ceiling on rents set by government.

h. A government-imposed limit on how low a price can be charged.

i. The rate at which a currency can be exchanged is set by the government.

j. A currency that cannot be freely exchanged except at the government set rate.

k. Excise tax on an imported good.

Problems and Exercises

1. The following table depicts the market supply and demand for milk in the United States.

Price in dollars per gallon	Quantity of gallons supplied in 1,000 of gallons	Quantity of gallons demanded in 1,000 of gallons
$1.50	600	800
$1.75	620	720
$2.00	640	640
$2.25	660	560
$2.50	680	480

a. Graph the market supply and demand for milk.

b. What is the equilibrium market price and quantity in the market?

c. Show the effect of a government imposed price floor of $2.25 on the market price, quantity supplied, and quantity demanded.

d. Show the effect of a government imposed price ceiling of $2.25 on the market price, quantity supplied, and quantity demanded.

e. Show the effect of a government imposed price ceiling of $1.75 on the market price, quantity supplied, and quantity demanded.

f. Show the effect of a government subsidy of $0.50 per gallon on the market demand and market supply table. What happens to the equilibrium price and quantity for milk? (You do not need to give specific values).

2. What would happen to equilibrium price and quantity in the previous problem if the government imposes a $1 per gallon tax on the sellers and as a result supply decreases by 100 thousand gallons? What price would the sellers receive?

3. Graphically show market demand and supply curves with government-set prices that best described the market for the majority of consumer goods in Soviet-style socialist economies.

4. Suppose 1994 Phoenix Suns games with 200,000 tickets sell out in preseason at a price of $30. Some people did not get tickets. Also assume that tickets are scalped during the season. ("Scalping" is the name given to the buying of tickets at a low price and reselling them at a high price.)

    a. Demonstrate this situation at preseason with supply and demand curves.

    b. Demonstrate the effect of an unbeaten Suns record on the supply and demand for scalped tickets mid-season. What happens to equilibrium price?

5. The invention of a self-milking cow machine allows cows to milk themselves. Not only does this reduce the need for higher-cost human assistance in milking, but it also allows the cow to milk herself three times a day instead of two, leading to both a healthier cow and increased milk production.

    a. Show the effect of this innovation on the equilibrium quantity and price of milk.

    b. Suppose farmers have decried the effects of this new technology on price and have lobbied the government to set the price floor for milk at the price before the invention. Show the result for equilibrium price, quantity supplied, and quantity demanded in the market.

6. Describe what likely happens to market price and quantity for the particular goods in each of the following cases:

    a. A technological breakthrough lowers the costs of producing tractors in India while there is an increase in incomes of all citizens in India. Market: tractors.

    b. The United States imposes a ban on the sales of oil companies that do business with Libya and Iran. At the same time, very surprisingly, a large reserve of drillable oil is discovered in Barrington, Rhode Island. Market: Oil.

c.   In the summer of 1996, many people watched the Atlanta Summer Olympics on NBC instead of going to the movies. At the same time, thinking that summer time is the peak season for movies, Hollywood released a record number of movies. Market: movie tickets.

d.   After a promotional visit by Michael Jordan to France, a craze for Nike Air shoes develops, while a worker strike in Nike's manufacturing plants in Honduras decreases the production of these shoes. Market: Nike shoes.

e.   Due to restored political and economic stability, demand for tourism and foreign investment in South Africa increases. At the same time, an increased number of South Africans want to hold their own currency. Market: SA rand. (The rand is the South African currency.)

7.   The supply and demand for Ireland's currency, the punt, is given by the following diagram. It currently trades at price of P_1.

a.   If left to the market, would the punt appreciate or depreciate? Would goods imported into Ireland become more or less expensive?

b.   What does its government need to do to maintain the exchange rate fixed at P_1?

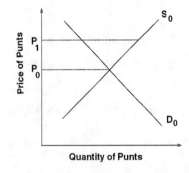

8.   Buchananland wants to restrict its number of auto imports from Zachstan. It is trying to decide whether it should impose a tariff or set quotas on Zachstani cars. With the help of a diagram, explain why auto makers in Zachstan have hired a lobbyist to persuade the government of Buchananland to set quotas instead of imposing tariffs.

A1. The supply and demand equations for roses are given by $Q_s = -10 + 3P$ and $Q_d = 20 - 2P$ respectively, where P is dollars per dozen roses and Q is dozens of roses in hundred thousands.

    a.   What is the equilibrium market price and quantity of roses sold?

    b.   Suppose the government decides to make it more affordable for individuals to be able to give roses to their significant others, and sets a price ceiling for roses at $4 a dozen. What is the likely result?

    c.   It is highly likely that because of the resulting distortion in the market due to the price ceiling at $4, a number of highly dedicated, and perhaps desperate, individuals will resort to buying roses for their significant others in the black market. What will the black market price for roses likely be?

    d.   Suppose the government decides to tax the suppliers of roses $1 per dozen roses sold. What is the equilibrium price and quantity in the market? How much do buyers pay for each rose they buy for their significant others? How much do suppliers receive for each rose they sell?

    e.   Suppose the government decides instead to impose a $1 tax on buyers for each dozen roses purchased. (Government has determined buying roses for love to be a demerit good.) What is the equilibrium price and quantity in the market? How much do the buyers pay, and the sellers receive?

Multiple Choice Questions

1. If there is an effective price ceiling
   a. the quantity demanded exceeds the quantity supplied.
   b. the quantity supplied exceeds the quantity demanded.
   c. the demand exceeds supply.
   d. the supply exceeds demand.

2. If a price ceiling is instituted that is above the equilibrium price, then
   a. the quantity demanded exceeds the quantity supplied.
   b. the quantity supplied exceeds the quantity demanded.
   c. the quantity supplied equals the quantity demanded.
   d. the demand exceeds the supply.

3. If the government institutes a price floor at P_0 in the accompanying diagram, which of the following represents the likely quantity supplied?
   a. Q_0.
   b. Q_1.
   c. Q_2.
   d. Q_3.

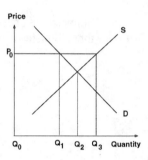

4. If the government institutes a price floor at P_0 in the accompanying diagram, which of the following points represents the likely quantity supplied?
   a. Q_0.
   b. Q_1.
   c. Q_2.
   d. Q_3.

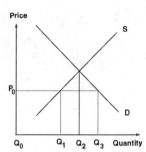

5. The equilibrium price in a market is given in the graph on the right. Is this
   economy most likely
   a. a socialist economy?
   b. a capitalist economy?
   c. a Soviet-style socialist economy?
   d. a welfare capitalist economy?

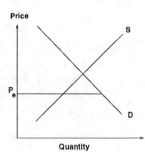

6. If the government set rent controls at P_c the black market rental price of
   housing will be
   a. P_c.
   b. P_e.
   c. P_m.
   d. at or between P_c and P_m.

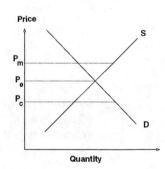

7. What will likely happen to the price and quantity of Gillette's Advanced Performance shaving cream as demand for it increases?
   a. The price will rise, and as a result, quantity will fall.
   b. Both price and quantity will rise.
   c. The price will fall, and quantity will rise.
   d. The price will fall, what happens to quantity is not clear.

8. Assume that the cost of shipping automobiles from the U.S. to Japan decreases. What will likely happen to the equilibrium price and quantity of cars made in the U.S. and sold in Japan?
   a. The price will rise, and quantity will fall.
   b. Both price and quantity will rise.
   c. The price will fall, and quantity will rise.
   d. The price will fall, what happens to quantity is not clear.

9. What will likely happen to equilibrium price and quantity of paper if school enrollment increases while a tornado destroys the largest paper mill in Tanzania?
   a. The price will increase, and so will quantity.
   b. The price will increase, and quantity will decrease.
   c. The price will decrease, but what happens to quantity is not clear.
   d. The price will increase, but what happens to quantity is not clear.

10. What will likely happen to the price and quantity of light bulbs as the costs of manufacturing them increases, while cheap alternative solar bulbs invented by University of Colorado student Paolo Raden are introduced into the market?
   a. The price will decrease, but what happens to quantity is not clear.
   b. What happens to price isn't clear, but quantity will increase
   c. What happens to price isn't clear, but quantity will decrease.
   d. It is not clear what happens to either price or quantity.

11. What will likely happen to price and quantity of roses in Babylon if the major purchasers of roses, women, decide that men (for whom women buy the roses) are too unreasonable to deal with, while the men, in frustration, destroy many commercial rose gardens?
   a. The price will decrease, but what happens to quantity is not clear.
   b. What happens to price isn't clear, but quantity will increase
   c. What happens to price isn't clear, but quantity will decrease.
   d. It is not clear what happens to either price or quantity.

12. What will likely happen to the price and quantity of cricket bats in Trinidad as interest in cricket dwindles following the dismal performance of the national cricket team, while at the same time taxes are repealed on producing cricket bats?
   a. The price will decrease, but what happens to quantity is not clear.
   b. The price will decrease, and quantity will increase.
   c. The price will increase, but what happens to quantity is not clear.
   d. It is not clear what happens to either price or quantity.

13. What will likely happen to the price of Venezuelan currency (Bolivars) in terms of dollars if demand for its exports falls while its nationals want to get their money out of Venezuela due to economic instability?
   a. It will fall.
   b. It will basically remain the same.
   c. It will rise.
   d. It is difficult to say.

14. In the foreign exchange market for Mexican pesos and U.S. dollars, the demand for the peso reflects
    a. The demand by Mexican citizens for U.S. goods.
    b. The demand by U.S. citizens for Mexican goods.
    c. The supply by Mexican citizens of Mexican goods.
    d. The demand by Mexican citizens for Mexican goods.

15. If a currency has appreciated in value, you know that
    a. It will take more of the currency that has appreciated to buy other currencies.
    b. It will take less of the currency that has appreciated to buy other currencies.
    c. Foreign goods will cost more to import.
    d. Domestic goods will cost less to foreigners.

16. What will likely happen to the value of the Malaysian ringgit in terms of dollars as more foreigners want to invest in Malaysia, and at the same time Mahathir Perot, a wealthy Malaysian businessman, decides to sell his huge holdings of Malaysian ringgit?
    a. It will fall.
    b. It will remain the same.
    c. It will rise.
    d. It is difficult to say.

17. A fixed exchange rate involves a currency
    a. that cannot be freely exchanged except at the government set rate.
    b. that can be exchanged freely.
    c. where the rate at which a currency can be exchanged is set by government.
    d. where the rate which is maintained by the invisible handshake.

18. Under a fixed exchange rate, if there is excess demand for its currency, the government
    a. must reduce the supply of its currency.
    b. must increase the supply of its currency.
    c. must increase the demand for its currency.
    d. must let the invisible hand operate.

19. Given the supply and demand curves on the right, to impose the equivalent of a quota of 5,000 computers, the amount of tariff that has to be imposed on each computer is
    a. below $2,000.
    b. $2,000.
    c. $2,500.
    d. above $2,500.

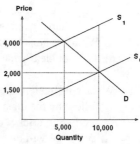

20. For governments
    a. tariffs are profitable compared to quotas because tariffs can help them collect revenues.
    b. quotas are profitable compared to tariffs because quotas can help them collect revenues.
    c. neither quotas nor tariffs can help collect revenues.
    d. both quotas and tariffs are sources of revenues.

21. The fallacy of composition is
    a. the false assumption that what is false for a part will also be false for the whole.
    b. the false assumption that what is true for a part will also be true for the whole.
    c. the false assumption that what is false for a whole will also be false for the part.
    d. the false assumption that what is true for a whole will also be true for the part.

22. Partial equilibrium analysis is most likely applicable without modification for interdependencies to
   a. the egg market.
   b. the aggregate labor market.
   c. the aggregate goods market.
   d. the savings/investment market.

A1. The supply and demand equations for umbrellas in Holland are $Q_s = -30 + 10P$ and $Q_d = 95 - 15P$ respectively, where P is the guilder price of umbrellas and Q is thousands of umbrellas per week. The Dutch government sets a price ceiling for umbrellas at 4 guilder per umbrella. What will likely happen in the market for umbrellas?
   a. Quantity supplied will exceed quantity demanded by 10 umbrellas per week.
   b. Quantity supplied will exceed quantity demanded by 25 umbrellas per week.
   c. Quantity demanded will exceed quantity supplied by 15 umbrellas per week.
   d. Quantity demanded will exceed quantity supplied by 25 umbrellas per week.

A2. The supply and demand equations for umbrellas in Holland are $Q_s = -30 + 10P$ and $Q_d = 95 - 15P$ respectively, where P is the guilder price of umbrellas and Q is thousands of umbrellas per week. (The same as in A1.) What will likely happen if the floor is set at 4 guilder?
   a. Quantity supplied will exceed quantity demanded by 10 umbrellas per week.
   b. Quantity supplied will exceed quantity demanded by 25 umbrellas per week.
   c. Quantity demanded will exceed quantity supplied by 15 umbrellas per week.
   d. Quantity demanded will equal quantity supplied.

A3. The supply and demand equations for Arizona Ice Tea in Arizona is given by $Q_s = -10 + 6P$ and $Q_d = 40 - 8P$; P is price of each bottle in dollars; and quantity is in hundreds of thousands of bottles per month. Suppose the state government imposes a $1 per bottle tax on the suppliers. The market price the suppliers receive and the equilibrium quantity in the market are
   a. $3 per bottle and 8 hundred thousand bottles per month.
   b. $3 per bottle and 16 hundred thousand bottles per month.
   c. $4 per bottle and 8 hundred thousand bottles per month.
   d. $4 per bottle and 16 hundred thousand bottles per month.

A4. The supply and demand equations for Arizona Ice Tea in Arizona is given by $Q_s = -10 + 6P$ and $Q_d = 40 - 8P$; P is price of each bottle in dollars, quantity in hundreds of thousands of bottles per month. (The same as in A4.) Suppose the state government imposes a $1 per bottle tax on the demanders. The likely price the suppliers receive and the equilibrium quantity after the tax is imposed are
   a. $3 per bottle and 8 hundred thousand.
   b. $44/14 per bottle and 208/14 hundred thousand.
   c. $4 per bottle and 8 hundred thousand.
   d. $58/14 per bottle and 208/14 hundred thousand.

Answers

Short-Answer Questions

1. A price ceiling is a government imposed limit on how high a price can be charged. An effective price ceiling below market equilibrium price will cause $Q_D > Q_S$ as shown in the graph on the right. (86)

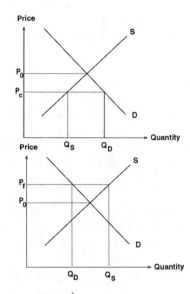

2. A price floor is a government imposed limit on how low a price can be charged. An effective price floor above market equilibrium price will cause $Q_S > Q_D$ as shown in the graph on the right. (91)

3. Increasing popularity of m&ms means that at every price, more m&ms are demanded. The demand curve shifts out to D_1, and both equilibrium price and quantity rise to P_1 and Q_1 respectively. (86-90)

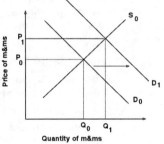

4. A frost damaging oranges means that at every price, suppliers are willing to supply fewer oranges. The supply curve shifts to the left to S_1, and equilibrium price rises to P_1, and quantity falls to Q_1. (86-90)

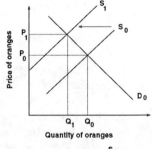

5. The demand curve for Russian caviar shifts out; the supply shifts in; the price rises substantially. What happens to quantity depends upon the relative sizes of the shifts. (86-90)

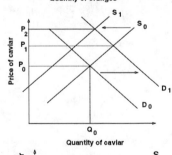

6. The demand and supply for U.S. dollars is shown in the graph on the right. The y-axis is labelled "price of U.S. dollars in foreign currency per U.S. dollar" and the x-axis is labelled "quantity of U.S. dollars." The demand for U.S. dollars is created by the demand by foreigners for U.S. goods and assets. The supply of U.S. dollars is created by the demand by U.S. citizens for foreign goods and assets. (86-91)

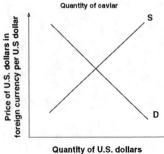

7. With a fixed exchange rate, the government adjusts its demand or supply for its currency to offset any change in private or international demand or supply for the currency so that it can maintain the exchange rate fixed. Supposing the demand for currency shifts out to D_1, to keep the exchange rate constant, the government must increase the supply of currency to S_1. (90-91)

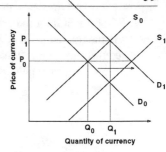

8. Rent controls are price ceilings and result in shortages in rental housing. As time passes and as the population rises, and the demand for rental housing also rises, other ventures become more lucrative relative to renting out housing. Owners have less incentive to repair existing buildings, let alone build new ones, further reducing the supply of rental housing. The housing shortage increases. (92-94)

9. As a tariff of t is imposed, the supply curve shifts leftward to S_1 by the amount of the tariff. The equilibrium price goes up and quantity goes down. (95)

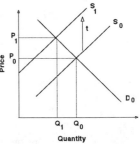

10. Partial equilibrium is the analysis that is partial or incomplete because it holds other things equal, whereas general equilibrium is the analysis that considers all changes. (97)

11. Fallacy of composition is the false assumption that what is true for a part will also be true for the whole. In micro, economists isolate an individual person's or firm's behavior and consider its effects, while the many side effects are kept in the background. In macro, those side effects become too large and can no longer be held constant. These side effects are what account for the interdependence of supply and demand. Macro, thus, is not simply a summation of all micro results; it would be a fallacy of composition to take the sum of each individual's (micro) actions and say that it is the aggregate (macro) result. (97-98)

12. When supply and demand are interdependent, a movement along one curve can cause a shift in the other curve. Equilibrium price and quantity change as there is movement toward equilibrium. (98-100)

Word Scramble   1. price ceiling   2. depreciation   3. fallacy of composition

Match the Terms and Concepts with Their Definitions
1-e; 2-h; 3-a; 4-j; 5-i; 6-g; 7-c; 8-k; 9-f; 10-b; 11-d.

Problems and Exercises

1. a. The market supply and demand for milk is graphed on the right.
   b. The equilibrium market price is $2 and equilibrium quantity in the market is 640 thousand gallons of milk. This is point A on the graph on the right. (84-86)

   c. A government imposed price floor of $2.25 is shown in the figure on the right. Since it is a price above market price, quantity supplied (660) exceeds quantity demanded (560) by 100 thousand gallons. (91)

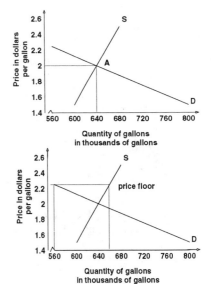

d. A government imposed price ceiling of $2.25 will have no effect on the market price of $2 per gallon since it is a ceiling above equilibrium price. Equilibrium quantity in the market remains at 640 thousand gallons. This is shown on the right. (84-86)

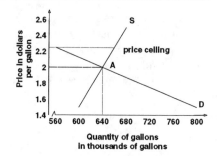

e. A government imposed price ceiling of $1.75 is below market price. Quantity supplied (620 thousand gallons) will be less than quantity demanded (720 thousand gallons) by 100 thousand gallons as shown on the right. (85-86)

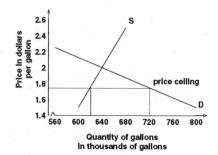

f. A government subsidy of $0.50 per gallon will change the market supply and demand table as follows:

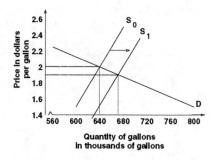

Price in dollars per gallon	Quantity of gallons supplied in 1,000 of gallons	Quantity of gallons demanded in 1,000 of gallons
$1.50	640	800
$1.75	660	720
$2.00	680	640
$2.25	700	560
$2.50	720	480

The supply curve shifts to the right as shown in the figure on the right side of the demand table. Equilibrium price will be lower than $2 and equilibrium quantity will be higher than 640 thousand gallons, though from the table it is not clear where precisely they will be. (95-96)

2. Because of the tax, the quantity supplied for every price level will decline. The supply and demand table will change as follows:

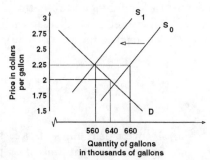

Price in dollars per gallon	Quantity of gallons supplied in 1,000 of gallons	Quantity of gallons demanded in 1,000 of gallons
$1.50	500	800
$1.75	520	720
$2.00	540	640
$2.25	560	560
$2.50	580	480

The market equilibrium price would be $2.25 and quantity would be 560 thousand gallons. Since the sellers will have to pay $1 tax on every gallon they sell, they will receive $1.25 per gallon milk. (95-96)

3. In Soviet-style socialist countries, prices of most consumer goods tended to be set below market equilibrium prices. The result was a shortage of goods. As shown on the graph to the right, at the price ceiling P_c, quantity demanded exceeds quantity supplied. (85-86)

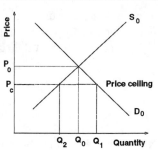

4. a. This situation is shown on the right. Supply is perfectly elastic at $30 until the maximum number of tickets, at which point it becomes perfectly inelastic. After 200,000 tickets are sold, no tickets are available at any price from the ticket booth. The demand curve can be any number of places on this graph, but it must intersect the supply curve at or to the right of 200,000 tickets. (88-89)

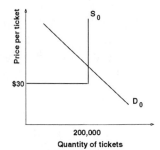

b. After preseason tickets are sold, the supply curve for tickets is now upward sloping (until the 200,000 level) because some current ticket holders are willing to sell their tickets (scalping). An unbeaten Suns record shifts the demand for Suns tickets to the right, increasing the scalping price of tickets. This is shown on the right. (88-89)

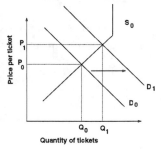

5. a. This innovation will shift the supply curve to the right. Equilibrium price will fall. Equilibrium quantity will rise. (88-89)

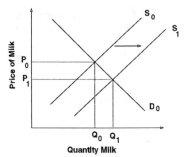

b. A price floor for milk at the price before the invention is shown on the right as $P_f = P_0$. Quantity supplied, Q_1, exceeds quantity demanded, Q_0. (91-92)

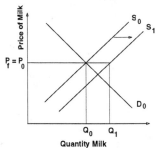

6. a. The supply curve will shift out from S_0 to S_1 as the new technology makes it cheaper to produce tractors. Increased incomes will shift the demand for tractors out from D_0 to D_1. Equilibrium price may go up, remain the same, or go down, depending on the relative shifts in the two curves. Equilibrium quantity, however, will definitely increase. (88-89)

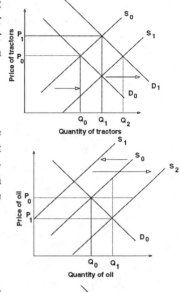

b. The ban on the companies doing business with Libya and Iran will shift the supply curve in from S_0 to S_1. The discovery of oil will, however, shift it back out to S_2. Depending on the relative shifts, equilibrium price and quantity will change. In the case shown in the diagram, the shift resulting from the discovery of the new oil source dominates the shift resulting from the ban, and the equilibrium price falls and quantity goes up. (88-89)

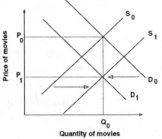

c. With more people watching the Olympics, the demand for movies shifts in from D_0 to D_1. At the same time the increased supply of movies will shift the supply curve out from S_0 to S_1. Equilibrium price will fall, and the change in equilibrium quantity will depend on the relative shifts in the curves. (88-89)

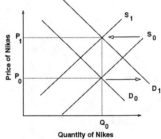

d. With more people demanding Nike Air shoes, the demand curve will shift out from D_0 to D_1. The worker strike will, however, reduce supply and shift it in from S_0 to S_1. The resulting equilibrium price will be higher, and the change in quantity depends on the relative shifts in the curves. (88-89)

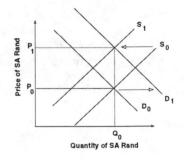

e. With increased demand for tourism and foreign investment in South Africa, the demand for its currency will increase, shifting the demand curve out from D_0 to D_1. At the same time, because more South Africans want to hold their own currency, the supply curve will shift in. The exchange rate will appreciate. The quantity traded will go up or down depending on the relative shifts in the supply and demand curves. (88-89)

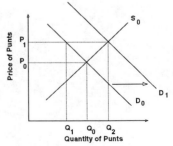

7. a. If left to the market, the punt would depreciate. That is, it would take fewer amounts of a foreign currency to purchase the same number of punts. Since the punts would purchase fewer amounts of a foreign currency, imports would cost more. (90)

b. To maintain the exchange rate at P_1 dollars, which is above the equilibrium price, and therefore at a level where quantity supplied exceeds quantity demanded, the government of Ireland will have to buy Q_1-Q_2 of its own currency. As it will do so, the demand for its currency will shift out from D_0 to D_1. (91-93)

8. The supply and demand equilibrium are at price P_e and quality Q_e. If quotas for Zachstani cars are set at Q_2, the price received for each car sold is P_2, which is well above P_t, the price they would normally sell for at that quantity. A tariff of t would have to be imposed to reduce imports to Q_2 reflected by the supply curve shifting in to S_1. In both cases, consumers pay Zachstan producers P_2 for each car. In the case of the quota, Zachstan producers keep P_2 for each car. In the case of the tariff, Zachstan producers must give up t for each car sold. Profits are higher with the quota. For this reason they have the lobbyist lobbying for quotas. (95-97)

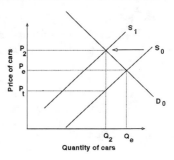

A1.a. Equating Q_s and Q_d, then solving gives equilibrium price \$6 and quantity 8 hundred thousand dozen. (103)

 b. If price ceiling is set at \$4, $Q_s = 2$, and $Q_d = 12$; resulting shortage is 10 hundred thousand dozen. (103)

 c. This is a bit tricky. Since price ceiling is at \$4, only 2 hundred thousand dozen roses will be supplied in the market. To find the black market price you have to see what the demand price of roses will be if quantity is 2 hundred thousand dozen. Solving for $Q = 2$ in the demand equation gives demand price at \$9. The black market price will be somewhere between \$4 and \$9. (103)

 d. If a \$1 tax is imposed on suppliers, the new supply equation will be $Q_s = -10 + 3(P-1) = -13 + 3P$. Equating this with Q_d gives equilibrium price \$6.40 and quantity 6-4/5 hundred thousand. Buyers pay \$6-3/5 for each rose they buy, and the sellers receive \$1 less than that, or \$5-3/5, for each rose they sell. (103)

 e. As a result of the tax, the new demand equation will be $Q_d = 20 - 2(P+1) = 18 - 2P$. Equating this with Q_s gives equilibrium price \$5.40 and quantity 6-4/5 hundred thousand. Buyers pay \$6.40 ($P + 1$) for each rose they buy, and the sellers receive \$5.40 for each rose they sell. (103)

Multiple Choice

1. a   As discussed on page 86, the correct answer here is the quantity demanded exceeds the quantity supplied. You don't use the terms demand and supply because that usage refers to the entire schedule.

2. c   Here the answer is the quantity supplied equals the quantity demanded because the price ceiling is put above the equilibrium price and hence is not effective. It would become effective only if the equilibrium price exceeded that price ceiling. See page 86.

3. d   You determine the quantity supplied in an effective price floor by determining where the price floor intersects the supply curve. Effective price floors create excess supply. See page 91.

4. c   In this case the price floor is not effective, so the market moves to the equilibrium price and quantity Q_2. See page 91.

5. c   In reality, Soviet-style socialist economies had shortages. In the others there is less of a reason to believe that the actual price would deviate from market equilibrium price. See page 34 of Chapter 2 and 92 of this chapter.

6. d   See discussion on Exhibit 5 in page 92.

7. b   As the demand curve shifts out, equilibrium market price and quantity will rise. See pages 88-89 of textbook for related discussion.

8. c   As the supply curve will shift out market price will fall while the quantity will rise. See pages 88-89 of text.

9. d   As school enrollment increases, the demand curve for paper will shift out. At the same time the supply curve will shift in because of the tornado. Price will definitely rise while quantity will change depending on the relative shifts in the curves. See pages 88-89 of textbook for related discussion.

10. c   The supply curve for light bulbs will shift in due to increased manufacturing costs, while the demand curve will shift in because of the cheap alternatives available. Price will change depending on the relative shifts of the curves while equilibrium quantity will decrease. See pages 88-89 of the textbook for related discussion.

11. c   As both the demand and the supply curve shift in, equilibrium quantity will fall and price will change depending in the relative shifts of the supply and demand curves. See pages 88-89.

12. a   Demand for cricket bats will fall, shifting the demand curve in, while the tax repeal will shift the supply curve out. Price will fall, and quantity will change depending on the relative shifts of the supply and demand curves. Related issues are discussed in pages 88-89 of the textbook.

13. a   With a fall in demand for Venezuela's exports, the demand curve for its currency will shift in, while the supply curve will shift out with its nationals wanting to get their money out of their country. The net result will be that the exchange rate will fall. See discussion pages 90 and 91 of textbook.

14. b   See page 91.

15. b   See page 91.

16. d   Since both demand and supply are increasing, the answer could be a, b, or c. Which it is depends on the relative shifts in the supply and the demand curves. So, d is the correct answer. See discussion on pages 91 and 92 of the textbook.

17. c   See page 92 of book.

18. b   See page 92 of textbook.

19. c   Per computer a tariff of $2,500 is needed to limit supply to 5,000. See page 95 of textbook.

20. a   See discussion on pages 95-97 of the textbook.

21. b   See page 97 of the textbook.

22. a   The smaller the market the more likely partial equilibrium analysis is applicable without modification. (97)

A1. d   Plugging in P = 4 in the supply and demand equations gives $Q_s = 10$, and $Q_d = 35$. So, quantity demanded exceeds quantity supplied by 25, and d is the correct answer. See page 103 of the textbook.

A2. d   Since the price floor is set below the equilibrium market price it has no effect on the market, and quantity supplied will equal quantity demanded. See page 103 of the textbook.

A3. a   A $1 per bottle tax on suppliers makes the supply equation $Q_s = -10 + 6(P - 1) = -16 + 6P$. Equating this with the demand equation gives equilibrium P = $4 and Q = 8 hundred thousand. The supplier receives $3 ($4 − $1). See page 103 of the textbook.

A4. a   A $1 per bottle tax on demanders makes the demand equation $Q_d = 40 - 8(P+1) = 32 - 8P$. Equating this with the supply equation gives equilibrium P = $3 and Q = 8 hundred thousand. The supplier receives $3. See page 103 of the textbook.

Chapter 5:
U.S. Economic Institutions

Chapter at a glance

1. Ultimately the U.S. economy's strength is its people and its other resources. (105)

   For a bird's-eye view of the U.S. economy see Exhibit 1 (sometimes called the "circular flow of income model"). Be able to draw and explain it.

   Note, there are 3 basic economic institutions:
   1) Businesses:
   *   a. Supply goods in goods market*
   *   b. Demand factors in factor market*
   *   c. Pay taxes and receive benefits from government*
   2) Households:
   *   a. Supply factors*
   *   b. Demand goods*
   *   c. Pay taxes and receive benefits from government*
   3) Government:
   *   a. Demands goods*
   *   b. Demands factors*
   *   c. Collects taxes and provide services*

2. Although businesses decide what to produce, they are guided by consumer sovereignty. (107)

   Businesses produce what consumers want.

3. The advantages and disadvantages of the three forms of business are shown in Exhibit 4 on page 110. (110)

   ✔ *Know the advantages and disadvantages of the three forms of business:*
   *   1) Sole Proprietorship*
   *   2) Partnership*
   *   3) Corporation*

4. Although, in principle, ultimate power resides with the people and households (consumer sovereignty), in practice the representatives of the people–firms and government–are sometimes removed from the people and, in the short run, are only indirectly monitored by the people. (112)

   Note:
   1) Do we control business and government or do they control us?
   2) The distribution of income (rich vs. poor) determines the "for whom" question. If you're rich you get more.
   3) The invisible handshake affects what business and government do or don't do.

5a. Two general roles of government are: (114)
   1. *As an actor:* Collects taxes and spends money.
   2. *As referee:* Sets the rules governing relations between households and businesses.

5b. Seven specific roles of government are: (116)

   1. Providing a stable structure within which markets can operate.

   What the government rules "ought to be" is debatable.

   2. Promoting workable, effective competition.

   Know the different consequences associated with competition vs. monopoly power.

   3. Correcting for external effects of individuals' decisions.

   ✔ *Know the distinction between positive and negative externalities and how government tries to correct for them.*

   4. Providing public goods that the market doesn't adequately supply.

   Government provides these by collecting taxes from everyone to try to eliminate the free-rider problem

5. Ensuring economic stability and growth.

Government tries to ensure:
  1. Full employment
  2. Low inflation
  3. Economic growth (which increases the
      standard of living)

6. Providing acceptably fair distribution of society's production among its individuals.

In order to redistribute money and therefore goods the government uses taxes (and other methods).

✔ *Know the difference between progressive, regressive, and proportional taxes.*

VII. Encouraging merit and discouraging demerit goods or activities.

Should government decide what is "good" or "bad" for us?

Government may:
  1) subsidize merit (socially desirable) goods
  2) tax demerit (socially undesirable) goods

✔ *The first 5 specific roles of government are economic roles which are generally less controversial while the last two are political roles.*

✔ *Government intervenes in the economy in an attempt to correct for "market failures." But just as the market can sometimes provide undesirable results, there is also government failure–government intervention which makes things worse.*

See also, Appendix A: "A Deeper Look at Business."
See also, Appendix B: "Households, Culture, and Ideology."

Short-answer questions

1. What are the three groups that comprise the U.S. economy? (LO1)

2. What is the role of each group in the economy? (LO1)

3. Draw a diagrammatic representation of the U.S. economy using these three groups. Label the market in which businesses and households interact. (LO1)

4. Although businesses decide what to produce, who ultimately makes the decision what to produce? (LO2)

5. What are the three major forms of businesses? (LO3)

6. Your friend wants to buy a coin-operated laundramat. Her brother has offered to be a partner in the operation and put up half the money to buy the business. They have come to you for advice about what form of business to create. Of course you oblige, letting them know the advantages and disadvantages of each. (LO3)

7. Why is much of the economic decision making done by business and government even though households have the ultimate power? (LO4)

8. What are two general roles of government? (LO5)

9. What are seven specific roles of government? (LO5)

10. What potential role does the government have when externalities exist? (LO5)

Word Scramble

1. _____ 2. _____ 3. _____
   c e i i m n o o p t t   r e n t a l i t e x y   f i o p r t

Match the Terms and Concepts to Their Definitions

___ 1. consumer sovereignty

___ 2. corporation

___ 3. entrepreneurship

___ 4. externality

___ 5. free rider

___ 6. macroeconomic externality

___ 7. merit goods or activities

___ 8. monopoly power

___ 9. partnership

___ 10. progressive tax

___ 11. public goods

___ 12. stock

___ 13. market failure

a. Ability to prevent others from entering a business field, which enables a firm to raise its price.
b. Situation in which the market does not lead to a desired result.
c. Business that is treated like a person, legally owned by its stockholders. Its stockholders are not personally liable for the actions of the corporate "person."
d. Business with two or more owners.
e. Certificate of ownership in a company.
f. Effect of a trade or agreement on third parties that people did not take into account when they entered the trade or agreement.
g. Externality that affects the levels of unemployment, inflation, or growth in the economy as a whole.
h. Goods whose consumption by one individual does not prevent their consumption by other individuals.
i. Person who participates in something for free because others have paid for it.
j. Principle that the consumer's wishes rule what's produced.
k. Tax whose rates increase as a person's income increases.
l. The ability to organize and get something done.
m. Things government believes are good for you, although you may not think so.

Problems and Exercises

1. List the three types of businesses from largest in number to smallest in number.

2. List the three types of businesses from largest in annual receipts to smallest in annual receipts.

3. For each of the following, state for which form or forms of business it is an advantage: Sole proprietorships, partnerships, or corporations:

    a. Minimum bureaucratic hassle.

    b. Ability to share work and risks

    c. Direct control by owner.

    d. Relatively easy to form.

    e. No personal liability.

    f.   Increasing ability to get funds.

4.   For each of the following, state for which form or forms of business it is a disadvantage: Sole proprietorships, partnerships, corporations:

    a.   Unlimited personal liability.

    b.   Possible double taxation of income.

    c.   Limited ability to get funds.

    d.   Legal hassle to organize.

5.   Order the following federal government income from largest to smallest: Social insurance taxes and contributions, excise taxes, individual income taxes, corporate income taxes.

6.   Order the following federal expenditures from largest to smallest: Interest, income security, national defense, health and education.

7.   For each of the following state what economic role government is playing or did play: Providing a stable institutional framework, promoting effective and workable competition, correcting for externalities, providing for public goods, ensuring economic stability and growth.

    a.   The judicial system recognizes the value of contracts of exchange between consumers and businesses.

    b.   A municipality prohibits smoking in malls.

    c.   The antitrust division of the government's Justice Department successfully pursued antitrust violations by AT&T in the 1980s.

    d.   The Federal Reserve (a semiautonomous branch of government) tries to keep the economy from overheating and from going into recession.

    e.   The federal government maintains an army.

8. State for each of the following tax tables whether the tax is progressive, regressive, or proportional.

a.

Tax rate	Income Level
10%	0-$10,000
10	$10,001-$30,000
10	$30,001-$60,000
10	$60,001 and above

b.

Tax rate	Income Level
35%	0-$10,000
30	$10,001-$30,000
25	$30,001-$60,000
20	$60,001 and above

c.

Tax rate	Income Level
8%	0-$10,000
10	$10,001-$30,000
16	$30,001-$60,000
24	$60,001 and above

Multiple Choice Questions

1. The labor force of the United States is approximately
    a. 100,000 people.
    b. 50 million people.
    c. 130 million people.
    d. 760 million people.

2. The population in the United States is approximately
    a. 10 million.
    b. 50 million.
    c. 270 million.
    d. 2 billion.

3. The ability to organize and get something done generally goes under the term
    a. the corporate approach.
    b. entrepreneurship.
    c. economicship.
    d. consumer sovereignty.

4. By number, the largest percentage of businesses are
    a. partnerships.
    b. corporations.
    c. sole proprietorships.
    d. nonprofit companies.

5. By receipts, the largest percentage of business is undertaken by
    a. partnerships.
    b. corporations.
    c. sole proprietorships.
    d. nonprofit companies.

6. Over-the-counter stock
    a. is traded on the New York Stock Exchange counter.
    b. is traded on all exchanges.
    c. is traded in odd lots.
    d. is not traded over a counter.

7. An odd lot refers to
    a. a set of shares in a strange company.
    b. shares not traded on the New York Stock Exchange.
    c. a purchase of fewer than 100 shares of a corporation.
    d. any non-even number of shares traded.

8. When a corporation's stock price goes up
    a. the corporation gets more revenue.
    b. the corporation gets less revenue.
    c. the corporation's revenue does not change.
    d. the yield on that company increases.

9. In reality, businesses are usually controlled by
    a. stockholders.
    b. managers.
    c. government.
    d. consumers.

10. The poverty level for a family of four in the United States is approximately
    a. $6,000 per year.
    b. $16,000 per year.
    c. $30,000 per year.
    d. $50,000 per year.

11. The largest percentage of state and local expenditures is on
    a. education.
    b. health and medical care.
    c. highways.
    d. income security.

12. The largest percentage of federal government expenditures is on
    a. income security.
    b. national defense.
    c. education.
    d. interest.

13. If an effect of a trade or agreement between two people affects some other party, that effect is called
    a. a monopoly.
    b. anti-competition.
    c. an externality.
    d. free ridership.

14. An example of a negative externality is
    a. education.
    b. pollution.
    c. government intervention.
    d. monopoly.

15. If the consumption of a good by one individual does not prevent its consumption by another individual, that good is called
   a. a public good.
   b. a private good.
   c. a macroeconomic good.
   d. a demerit good.

16. If the rates of a tax increase as a person's income increases, the tax is
   a. a progressive tax.
   b. a regressive tax.
   c. a proportional tax.
   d. a merit tax.

17. Economic theory says government should
   a. follow a policy of laissez-faire.
   b. get intricately involved in the economy.
   c. not get involved in the economy.
   d. base government intervention upon the costs and benefits.

A1. In the United States the fastest growing sector has been
   a. the manufacturing sector.
   b. the service sector.
   c. the agricultural sector.
   d. the government sector.

Answers

Short-Answer Questions

1. The three groups that comprise the U.S. economy are households, businesses, and government. (106)

2. Households supply factors of production to businesses; business produces goods and services and sells them to households and government. Government taxes businesses and households, buys goods and services from businesses and labor services from households, and provides goods and services to businesses and households. (106)

3. A diagrammatic representation of the U.S. economy is shown to the right. Households provide factors of production to firms in return to payment in the factor market. Households buy goods and services from businesses in the goods market. The government taxes businesses and households and provides goods and services to each of them. (106)

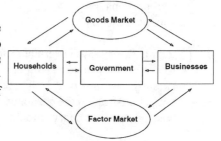

4. Although businesses decide what to produce, they are guided by consumer sovereignty. Businesses want to make a profit, so they will produce what they believe consumers will buy. That is not to say that businesses don't affect the desires of the consumer through advertising. (107)

5. The three major forms of businesses are sole proprietorship, partnership, and corporation. (109)

6. I would advise each of them to think hard about their situation. Each form of business has its disadvantages and advantages. If your friend wants to minimize bureaucratic hassle and be her own boss, the best form of business would be a sole proprietorship. However, she would be personally liable for all losses and might have difficulty obtaining additional funds should that be necessary. If her brother has some skills to offer the new business and is willing to share in the cost of purchasing the company, she might want to form a partnership with him. Beware, though: Both partners are liable for any losses regardless of whose fault it is. I would ask her if she trusts her brother's decision-making abilities.

   As a partnership they still might have problems getting additional funds. What about becoming a corporation? Her liability would be limited to her initial investment, her ability to get funds is greater, and she can shed personal income and gain added expenses to limit taxation. However, a corporation is a legal hassle to organize, may involve possible double taxation of income, and if she plans to hire many employees it involves monitoring problems once she becomes less involved. I would tell her she needs to weigh the costs and benefits of each option and choose the one that is best for her. (110)

7. Much of the economic decision making is done by business and government even though households have the ultimate power because in practice the representatives of the people — firms and government — are sometimes removed from the people. In the short run, government and business are only indirectly monitored by the people. (112)

8. Two general roles of government are referee and actor. (114)

9. Seven specific roles of government are (1) providing a stable structure within which markets can operate; (2) promoting workable, effective competition; (3) correcting for external effects of individuals' decisions; (4) providing public goods that the market does not adequately supply; (5) ensuring economic stability and growth; (6) providing acceptably fair distribution of society's production among its individuals; and (7) encouraging merit goods or activities and discouraging demerit goods or activities. (116)

10. The potential role for government when externalities exist is for government to institute policies that require market participants to take into account the effect of their actions on third parties. Government, however, cannot always institute policies that succeed in doing so without other negative effects. (117)

Word Scramble   1. competition   2. externality   3. profit

Match the Terms and Concepts to Their Definitions

1-j; 2-c; 3-l; 4-f; 5-i; 6-g; 7-m; 8-a; 9-d; 10-k; 11-h; 12-e; 13-b.

Problems and Exercises

1. Sole proprietorships, corporations, partnerships. (109)

2. Corporations, sole proprietorships, and partnerships. (Sole proprietorships and partnerships have equal percentages of annual receipts.) (109)

3. a. Sole proprietorship. No special forms are required to begin one. (110)
   b. Partnership. The owners have one another to work with and the financial risk is shared. (110)
   c. Sole proprietorship. This is a firm of one person who controls the business. (110)
   d. Partnership. This is easy to form relative to the easiest (sole proprietorship) and the hardest (corporation). (110)
   e. Corporation. The individual liability is only to the extent of the individual investment. (110)
   f. Corporation. Corporations are more developed firms and have more access to capital. (110)

4. a. Sole proprietorship and partnership. (110)
   b. Corporation. (110)
   c. Sole proprietorship and partnership. (110)
   d. Corporation. (110)

5. Individual income taxes, social insurance taxes and contributions, corporate income taxes, excise taxes. (110)

6. Income security, national defense, interest, health and education. (115)

7. a. Providing a stable institutional framework. (116)
   b. Correcting for externalities. (117)
   c. Promoting effective and workable competition. (117)
   d. Ensuring economic stability and growth. (118)
   e. Providing for public goods. (117-118)

8. a. Proportional because the rate remains the same regardless of income. (118)
   b. Regressive because the rate declines as income rises. (118)
   c. Progressive because the rate increases as income rises. (118)

Multiple Choice

1. c   See page 113.
2. c   See page 112.
3. b   See page 107, where entrepreneurship is defined.
4. c   See Exhibit 3, page 109.
5. b   See Exhibit 3, page 109.
6. d   See page 111.
7. c   See page 111.
8. c   Corporations get money only from new issues of stock. Their revenue does not change. The yield is the earnings divided by stock price, so that will fall, not increase, with a rise in the stock price. See page 111.
9. b   As discussed on page 112, although in theory stockholders control businesses, in reality generally managers do.
10. b   See page 113.
11. a   See Exhibit 7, page 115.
12. a   See Exhibit 8, page 115.
13. c   See page 117 for a definition of externality.
14. b   See page 117.
15. a   See pages 117-118.
16. a   See page 118.
17. d   As discussed on page 120, economic theory does not prescribe any particular role for government.
A1. b   As discussed on pages 123-124, the answer is the service sector.

Chapter 6:
An Introduction to the World Economy

Chapter at a glance

1. The industrial countries of the world have a large industrial base and a per capita income of about $20,000 a year; the developing countries of the world include low- and median-income economies that have a per capita income of between $300 and $2,000 a year. (131)

   There are also:
   1. high income oil exporting countries
   2. transitional economies
   3. Soviet-style socialist economies

   ✔ *Know the names of where all these countries are.*

2. Some major producing areas for some important raw materials are: (132)
   Aluminum–Guinea, Australia
   Cobalt–Zaire, Zambia, Russia
   Copper–Chile, U.S., Poland
   Iron–Russia, Brazil, Australia
   Zinc–Canada, Australia, Russia

   ✔ *Helps explain strategic roles some countries play in the world economy.*

   ✔ *Geography also helps explain why countries have the comparative advantages they do.*

3. Two ways in which *inter*national trade differs from *intra*national (domestic) trade are: (135)

   1. International trade involves potential barriers to trade; and

   Free and open international trade along the lines of comparative advantage is mutually beneficial to all economies involved.

   2. International trade involves multiple currencies.

   Foreign exchange markets exist to swap currencies.

4. By looking at an exchange rate table, you can determine how much various goods will likely cost in different countries. (135)

   An exchange rate table shows the relative value of other currencies in terms of the dollar and vice versa.

   In addition, note that a change in the exchange rate value of a currency will effect the country's balance of payments accounts. When the balance of payments account is in equilibrium, the quantity of a currency supplied equals the quantity of currency demanded.

5. Two important causes of a trade deficit are: (140)

   1. A country's competitiveness; and

   Reduced competitiveness ↑ s a trade deficit due to:
   a) relatively lower productivity
   b) and ↑ in the value of the country's currency.

   2. The relative state of a country's economy.

   A stronger economy means higher incomes, therefore more imports and a greater trade deficit.

6. Five important international economic institutions are: (141)
   1. The UN
   2. The WTO
   3. The World Bank
   4. The IMF; and
   5. The EU

   They are designed to enhance negotiations (to avoid trade wars).

   ✔ *Also know about global corporations.*

   ✔ *Think internationally because we live in a global economy.*

   See also, Appendix A: "Our International Competitors."

Short-answer questions

1. What is the per capita income of *the industrial countries of the world* and *the developing countries of the world*? (LO1)

2. Classifying countries by output levels misses some aspects of importance in the world economy. Name one of these. (LO1)

3. Where would you find information about the flows of resources among nations? Why is this information important? (LO2)

4. State two ways international trade differs from domestic trade. (LO3)

5. Based on Exhibit 3 on page 136, calculate the following: (LO4)

    a. How many British pounds would you receive for $100?

b.   What is the exchange rate for U. S. dollars in German marks?

c.   If 7.7 Hong Kong dollars equals one U.S. dollar, how many U. S. dollars equal one Hong Kong dollar?

6.   What are two important causes of a trade deficit? How does each affect the trade deficit? (LO5)

7.   What are the World Trade Organization (WTO) and the General Agreement on Trade and Tariffs (GATT)? How do they differ? (LO6)

8.   What are five important international economic institutions? (LO6)

Word Scramble

1. _____ _____ 2._____ 3._____ _____
      a a c e i m o p r t v   a a a d e g n t v   a f f i r s t   a d e r t   c d e f i i t

Match the Terms and Concepts to Their Definitions

___ 1. competitiveness

___ 2. foreign exchange market

___ 3. General Agreement on Tariffs and Trade (GATT)

___ 4. global corporations

___ 5. Group of Seven

___ 6. International Monetary Fund (IMF)

___ 7. NAFTA

___ 8. nontariff barriers

___ 9. trade deficit

___ 10. World Bank

___ 11. World Trade Organization

a. A multinational, international financial institution concerned primarily with monetary issues.

b. A country's ability to produce goods and services more cheaply than can other countries.

c. A multinational, international financial institution that works with developing countries to secure low-interest loans.

d. Corporations with substantial operations on both the production and sales sides in more than one country.

e. Group that meets to promote negotiations and coordinate economic relations among countries. The Seven are Japan, Germany, Britain, France, Canada, Italy, and the United States.

f. Indirect regulatory restrictions on exports and imports.

g. A past agreement among subscribing countries on certain limited conditions of international trade.

h. Market in which one country's currency can be exchanged for another country's.

i. The result of a country's imports exceeding its exports.

j. Free trade zone including the United States, Canada and Mexico.

k. An international organization committed to getting countries to agree not to impose new tariffs or other trade restrictions except under certain limited condition.

Problems and Exercises

1. State whether the trade restriction is a quota, tariff, or nontariff barrier.

   a. The U.S. charges Toyota Corporation 10% of the value of each Toyota imported into the United States.

   b. The EU allowed only beef that was not treated with growth-inducing hormones to be traded in EU markets.

   c. To encourage domestic production of automobile parts, Japan limits the importation of automobile parts according to a rigid schedule of numbers.

   d. The United States requires sheet metal used in the production of automobiles to be of a certain compound that is different than the compound used by foreign producers of sheet metal.

2. Assume that Germany can raise pork at a cost of 4 marks per pound and can raise beef at a cost of 8 marks per pound. In the United States, pork can be produced at $2 per pound and beef at $3 per pound.

    a. In terms of pounds of pork, what is the opportunity cost of producing beef in each country?

    b. Who has the comparative advantage in producing pork?

    c. Assume Americans eat 22,500 pounds of beef per year and 16,250 pounds of pork each year. Germans eat 10,000 pounds of beef and 20,000 pounds of pork each year. Which country should specialize in beef and which should specialize in pork?

3. Refer to the following table to answer the questions

Currency	U.S. $ equivalent	Currency per U.S. $
British pounds	_____	0.67
Italian lira	_____	1660.00
Chilean peso	_____	420.00
Swiss franc	0.67	_____
Japanese yen	0.009	_____

    a. Complete the blanks in the table above.

    b. How many Italian lire buys one dollar?

    c. How many Chilean pesos buy one Japanese yen?

    d.   How many U.S. dollars are needed to buy a British Rolls Royce at a cost of 75,000 pounds?

4.   Consider the following Balance of Payments account for the United States in 1960:

		Dollars in millions
	Current Account	
	Exports (goods and services)	19,658
	Imports (goods and services)	-14,758
	Net investment income	3,390
1.	Balance on the current account	_____
	Capital Account	
	Capital inflows	2,294
	Capital outflows	-4,099
2.	Balance on the capital account	_____
3.	Current and capital account balance	_____
4.	Official transactions account	_____
5.	Total	_____

    a.   Fill in the missing values on the balance of payments account.

    b.   Is the current account in deficit or surplus? Are Americans buying fewer foreign assets or are foreigners buying more U.S. assets?

    c.   What is the quantity of U.S. dollars demanded? What is the dollar value of foreign currencies demanded?

    d.   What is the U.S. doing on the foreign exchange market? How do you know?

5. As Exhibit 4 in Chapter 6 shows, the United States had a merchandise trade balance surplus for most years after World War II until the mid-1970s. Since then the merchandise trade balance has been in deficit. For each of the following events, explain how the event would affect the trade deficit.

   a. Technological innovations in the United States make U.S. firms more competitive.

   b. The exchange value of the dollar falls.

   c. The level of U.S. income rises.

Multiple Choice Questions

1. If you hear the term, "the industrial countries of the world," you will likely think of
   a. the United States, Australia, and the Sudan.
   b. Germany, Russia, and Japan
   c. Germany, Australia, and France.
   d. Saudi Arabia, the United States, and Germany

2. If a country can produce a good at a lower opportunity cost than another country can produce it, we say it has
   a. a comparative advantage in the production of that good.
   b. an export advantage in the production of that good.
   c. an import advantage in the production of that good.
   d. a production advantage in the production of that good.

3. Say the United States can produce widgets at $4 apiece and wadgets at $4 apiece while South Korea can produce widgets at 500 won apiece and wadgets at 200 won apiece.
   a. The United States has a comparative advantage in widgets.
   b. The United States has a comparative advantage in wadgets.
   c. The U.S. cost of widgets is lower.
   d. The U.S. cost of wadgets is lower.

4. If a country imposes numerical limitations on how much of a good can be shipped into that country, the country has imposed
   a. a quota.
   b. a tariff.
   c. a nontariff barrier.
   d. a customs fee.

5. In a foreign exchange market
    a. imports are exchanged for exports.
    b. exports are exchanged for imports.
    c. labor services, exports, imports, and currencies are exchanged.
    d. one currency is exchanged for another.

6. In the mid-1990s the United States
    a. has run rather large trade surpluses.
    b. has run rather large trade deficits.
    c. has run an approximate trade balance.
    d. has fluctuated between trade deficits and trade surpluses.

7. Debtor nations will
    a. run trade deficits.
    b. run trade surpluses.
    c. not necessarily run a trade surplus or a trade deficit.
    d. run foreign exchange sales.

8. Which of the following is NOT an account in the balance of payments accounts?
    a. exchange rate account
    b. current account
    c. capital account
    d. official transactions account

9. If a country is maintaining an exchange rate above its market equilibrium determined by private supply and demand for its currency, then that country's
    a. official transaction account would be in surplus.
    b. official transaction account would be in deficit.
    c. current account would be in surplus.
    d. current account would be in deficit.

10. If the U.S. economy expands relative to other countries' economies, other things constant, the U.S. trade balance will likely
    a. be unaffected.
    b. move toward both deficit and surplus.
    c. move toward surplus.
    d. move toward deficit.

11. When the U.S. dollar fell substantially relative to the yen in the mid-1990s, that fall had a tendency to
    a. both increase and decrease U.S. competitiveness.
    b. increase U.S. competitiveness.
    c. decrease U.S. competitiveness.
    d. have no effect on U.S. competitiveness.

12. Important international institutions include all the following except
    a. NAFTA.
    b. IMF.
    c. WTO.
    d. DU.

13. The Group of Five consists of
    a. Japan, Germany, Britain, France, and the United States.
    b. Japan, Germany, Britain, France, and Italy.
    c. Italy, Japan, Germany, Britain, and the United States.
    d. Canada, Japan, Germany, the United States, and France.

14. If a country is found guilty in the World Court
    a. its leaders will be put in jail.
    b. it will be forced by the UN to pay a fine.
    c. it may or may not comply with the remedy decreed by the Court, depending on whether it chooses to comply or not.
    d. its dues to finance the World Court will be doubled.

15. The general plan of NAFTA is
    a. to raise tariffs on most goods so the tariffs are equal among countries.
    b. to replace tariffs with quotas.
    c. to move towards political integration among Canada, Mexico, and the United States.
    d. to remove tariffs on most goods within 15 years of signing.

16. NAFTA
    a. is scheduled for elimination in the year 2010
    b. involves countries in all hemispheres.
    c. involves countries in the western hemisphere.
    d. is to be combined with the EU within 5 years.

A1. The EU is an economic free trade area
    a. but not a political organization.
    b. and a loose political organization.
    c. and a federation of individual countries.
    d. and a nation-state.

A2. The EU is moving towards the establishment of a single currency, which is to be called
    a. the European dollar.
    b. the Euro.
    c. the European mark.
    d. the European pound.

A3. Members of the European Union include
    a. Germany, France, and Switzerland.
    b. Great Britain, Spain, and Norway.
    c. Greece, Italy, and Switzerland.
    d. Greece, Denmark, and Portugal.

A4. The Japanese economy is sometimes called
    a. a neo-feudalist economy.
    b. a neo-capitalist economy.
    c. a neo-mercantilist economy.
    d. a neo-socialist economy.

A5. MITI refers to
    a. entrepreneurial dreamings, such as those of Walter Mitty.
    b. a Japanese government agency.
    c. a U.S. government agency.
    d. a UN agency.

A6. Some of the reasons for Japan's economic success include all the following except
    a. its population's commitment to hard work.
    b. its high level of saving.
    c. its population's individualism.
    d. its institutional commitment to exports.

Answers

Short-Answer Questions

1. The per capita income of *the industrial countries of the world* is about $20,000 per year. The per capita income of *the developing countries of the world* is between $300 per year and $2,000 per year. (131)

2. Classifying countries by output is one way to group countries. Countries with low output share similar problems with countries that have high per capita income. This classification, however, misses the strategic importance of some countries in the world. For instance, Saudi Arabia has a relatively small output, but its importance lies in its control of a significant portion of the world's oil supply, an important input to production worldwide. Other dimensions missed include cultural and social dimensions. (132-133)

3. You would find information about the flows of resources among nations in the library (for example, in *The Times Atlas of Natural Resources*). This information is important because a country's resources contribute to its strategic importance to the world economy. (133)

4. Two ways international trade differs from domestic trade are (1) international trade involves potential barriers to trade; and (2) international trade involves multiple currencies. (135)

5. a. £59: Look at Exhibit 4 and find British pounds. I find that on Tuesday the equivalent of one U.S. dollar was 0.59 pounds (column 3). Multiply this by 100 to find out how many pounds equal $100. (136)
    b. One would receive 1.56 German marks for one U.S. dollar. This is read right off the table, column 3. (136)
    c. 0.13 U.S. dollars. The reciprocal of the exchange rate from Hong Kong dollars to U.S. dollars is the exchange from U.S. dollars to Hong Kong dollars (1/7.7). (136)

6. Two important causes of a trade deficit are a country's competitiveness and the relative state of a country's economy. A country's competitiveness affects how cheaply a country can sell its goods. The more a country is competitive, the cheaper it can sell its goods and the lower its trade deficit will be. The relative state of a country's economy affects the trade deficit through imports. When U.S. income rises, so do imports, and the trade deficit worsens. The trade deficit also affects U.S. income. An increase in imports means U.S. production falls and U.S. income falls. (140)

7. The WTO is an organization committed to getting countries to agree not to impose new tariffs or other trade restrictions except under certain limited conditions. The GATT was an agreement among many subscribing countries on certain conditions of international trade. An important difference between the two is that the WTO has some enforcement mechanisms while GATT did not. (141)

8. Five important international economic institutions: the UN, GATT, the World Bank, the IMF, and the EU. (141-142)

Word Scramble　　　1. comparative advantage　　　2. tariffs　　　3. trade deficit

Match the Terms and Concepts to Their Definitions
1-b; 2-h; 3-g; 4-d; 5-e; 6-a; 7-j; 8-f; 9-i; 10-c; 11-k.

Problems and Exercises

1. a. Tariff because it is a tax on imports. (135)
    b. Nontariff barrier because this was not a tax or a numerical restriction on imports, but a regulation that had the effect of reducing imports. (135)
    c. Quota because it is a numerical restriction on imports. (135)

    d. Nontariff barrier because this is not a tax or a numerical restriction on imports, but it is a regulation that will have the effect of reducing imports. (135)

2. a. In the United States, the opportunity cost of producing one pound of beef is 1.5 pounds of pork. In Germany, the opportunity cost of producing one pound of beef is 2 pounds of pork. Calculate this by determining how much pork can be produced with $1 (or 1 DM in Germany) and how much beef can be produced with $1 (or 1 DM in Germany) and comparing the two. For the United States this is 1/2 pound of pork and 1/3 pound of beef. So, 1/2 pound of pork can be exchanged for 1/3 pound of beef. Or likewise, 1.5 pounds of pork can be exchanged for 1 pound of beef. (133-134)

    b. Germany has the comparative advantage in producing pork because the opportunity cost of producing pork in terms of forgone beef production is lower than it is in the United States. (133-134)

    c. The United States should specialized in beef because it has the comparative advantage in producing beef. Germany should specialize in pork because it has the comparative advantage in producing pork. This is concluded from the principle of comparative advantage. (133-134)

3. a. These blanks are filled in the table below. (135)

	Currency	U.S. $ equivalent	Currency per U.S. $
A	British pounds	1.49	0.67
B	Italian lire	0.0006	1660.00
C	Chilean peso	0.0024	420.00
D	Swiss franc	0.67	1.49
E	Japanese yen	0.009	111.10

    b. 1660 Italian lire buys one dollar. Look at column three, row B, for the exchange of lire per U.S. dollar. (135)

    c. One Japanese yen buys 3.78 Chilean pesos. Calculate this by first finding the yen per dollar (111.1) and Chilean pesos per dollar (420). To find Chilean pesos per Japanese yen, divide the Chilean peso per dollar by yen per dollar. (135)

    d. $111,940.30 are needed to buy a British Rolls Royce at a cost of 75,000 pounds. To calculate this, find the British pound per U.S. dollar (0.67) and divide this into the cost of the Rolls Royce in pounds. (112)

4. a. The missing blanks are filled in below:

      Current Account

	Exports	$19,650
	Imports	-14,758
	Net investment income	3,390
1.	Balance on the current account	<u>8,290</u>
	Capital Account	
	Capital inflows	2,294
	Capital outflows	-4,099
2.	Balance on the capital account	<u>-1,805</u>
3.	Current and capital account balance	6,485
4.	Official transactions account	<u>-6485</u>
5.	Total	0

    b. The current account is in surplus. Since capital inflows are less than capital outflows, the value of foreign assets bought by Americans exceed the value of U.S. assets bought by foreigners.

    c. The quantity of U.S. dollars demanded in 1960 equals imports plus capital outflows, or $18,857 million. The dollar value of foreign currencies demanded is exports plus capital inflows, or $21,944 million.

    d. Since the current and capital account balance is in surplus, the U.S. government must be selling $6,485 million U.S. dollars. We know this because the balance of payments must be zero, implying an official transactions account of $6,485 million, enough to offset the current and capital account surplus. (137-139)

5. a. Technological innovations in the United States making U.S. firms more competitive will tend to reduce the trade deficit. This is because U.S. goods will tend to be cheaper. Americans will substitute domestic goods for imports and foreigners will substitute U.S. exports for other goods. (140-141)

b. A fall in the exchange value of the dollar will tend to reduce the U.S. trade deficit. This is because U.S. goods will be cheaper. (140-141)

c. A rise in the level of U.S. income will tend to increase the U.S. trade deficit. This is because as domestic income increases, the demand for imports rises. (140-141)

Multiple Choice Questions

1. c   All other answers include at least one country that is not an industrial country of the world. See Exhibit 1, pages 130-131.

2. a   See page 133, where comparative advantage is defined. The other choices are simply words thrown together.

3. a   In the United States, producing one more widget costs one wadget; in South Korea producing one more widget costs 2.5 wadgets. So the opportunity cost of widgets is lower in the United States and therefore it has a comparative advantage in widgets. See page 133.

4. a   While it could be argued that quotas are a type of nontariff barrier, that is not the way they are defined in this text, and "quota" is the better answer. See page 135 of the text.

5. d   See page 135.

6. b   See Exhibit 4, page 138.

7. c   One must always distinguish between debt and deficit. A debtor nation may be running a trade surplus. See page 136.

8. a   The balance of payments account is comprised of the current account, the capital account, and the official transactions account. See page 139.

9. a   The government must be buying up the excess supply of its currency that is an inflow of its currency, which shows up as a positive official transactions balance. The country's current account could be in surplus or deficit depending upon what's happening with the capital account. (138-139)

10. d   As the U.S. economy expands, its imports increase, moving the trade balance towards deficit. See page 140.

11. b   As discussed on page 140, a fall in the value of a country's currency increases its competitiveness.

12. d   DU are two letters chosen at random. See pages 133, 141, and 142 for definitions of the others.

13. a   See page 142.

14. c   The World Court has no supra-national enforcement mechanism. See page 142.

15. d   See pages 133-134.

16. c   See pages 133-134.

A1. b   See page 147.

A2. b   See page 147.

A3. d   See Exhibit A1, page 148.

A4. c   See page 149.

A5. b   See page 150.

A6. c   See page 149. Japanese culture emphasizes cooperation far more than individualism.

Pretest I
Chapters 1 - 6

Take this test in test conditions, giving yourself a limited amount of time to complete the questions. Ideally, check with your professor to see how much time he or she allows for an average multiple choice question and multiply this by 25. This is the time limit you should set for yourself for this pretest. If you do not know how much time your teacher would allow, we suggest 1 minute per question, or 25 minutes.

1. Economic reasoning
   a. provides a framework with which to approach questions.
   b. provides correct answers to just about every question.
   c. is only used by economists.
   d. should only be applied to economic business matters.

2. In making economic decisions you should consider
   a. marginal costs and marginal benefits.
   b. marginal costs and average benefits.
   c. average costs and average benefits.
   d. total costs and total benefits, including past costs and benefits.

3. The opportunity cost of reading Chapter 1 of the text
   a. is about 1/20 of the price you paid for the book because the chapter is about one twentieth of the price of the book.
   b. zero since you have already paid for the book
   c. has nothing to do with the price you paid for the book.
   d. is 1/20 the price of the book plus 1/20 the price of the tuition.

4. "Given certain conditions, the market achieves efficient results" is an example of a
   a. positive statement.
   b. normative statement.
   c. art-of-economics statement.
   d. subjective statement.

5. In theory
   a. socialism is an economic system that tries to organize society in the same ways as most families organize, striving to see that individuals get what they need.
   b. socialism is an economic system based on central planning and government ownership of the means of production.
   c. socialism is an economic system based on private property rights.
   d. socialism is an economic system based on markets.

6. If the opportunity cost of good X in terms of good Y is 2Y, so you'll have to give up 2Y to get one X, the production possibility curve would look like
   a. a.
   b. b.
   c. c.
   d. d.

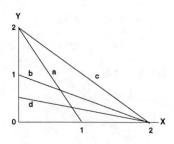

7. In the graph to the right, in the range of points between A and B there is
   a. a high opportunity cost of guns in terms of butter.
   b. a low opportunity cost of guns in terms of butter.
   c. no opportunity cost of guns in terms of butter.
   d. a high monetary cost of guns in terms of butter.

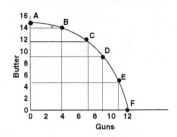

8. A law about the growth of efficiency of computers states
   that computer chip technology doubles the efficiency
   of computers each year. If that holds true, which of the
   four arrows would demonstrate the appropriate shifting of the production possibility curve?
   a. a.
   b. b.
   c. c.
   d. d.

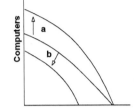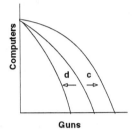

9. In partial equilibrium analysis one assumes
   a. other things constant and forgets them.
   b. other things are not constant.
   c. other things are constant but one brings them back into the analysis later when one applies it.
   d. other things are not constant, and one partially fits them into the analysis.

10. There are many more substitutes for good A than for good B.
    a. The demand curve for good A will likely be flatter.
    b. The demand curve for good B will likely be flatter.
    c. You can't say anything about the likely relative flatness of the demand curves.
    d. The demand curve for good B will likely shift out further.

11. The movement in the graph at the right from point A to point B represents
    a. an increase in demand.
    b. an increase in the quantity demanded.
    c. an increase in the quantity supplied.
    d. an increase in supply.

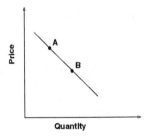

12. If there is an improvement in technology one would expect
    a. a movement along the supply curve.
    b. a shift upward of the supply curve.
    c. a shift downward of the supply curve.
    d. a movement down along the supply curve.

13. At which point will you expect the stronger downward pressure on prices?
    a. a.
    b. b.
    c. c.
    d. d.

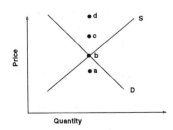

14. If there is an effective price ceiling
    a. the quantity demanded exceeds the quantity supplied.
    b. the quantity supplied exceeds the quantity demanded.
    c. the demand exceeds supply.
    d. the supply exceeds demand.

15. If the government institutes a price floor at P_0 in the accompanying diagram, which of the following points represents the likely quantity supplied?
    a. Q_0.
    b. Q_1.
    c. Q_2.
    d. Q_3.

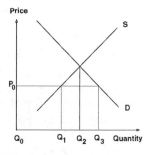

16. What will likely happen to the price and quantity of Gillette's Advanced Performance shaving cream as demand for it increases?
    a. The price will rise, and as a result, quantity will fall.
    b. Both price and quantity will rise.
    c. The price will fall, and quantity will rise.
    d. The price will fall, what happens to quantity is not clear.

17. What will likely happen to the price and quantity of cricket bats in Trinidad as interest in cricket dwindles following the dismal performance of the national cricket team, while at the same time taxes are repealed on producing cricket bats?
    a. The price will decrease, but what happens to quantity is not clear.
    b. The price will decrease, and quantity will increase.
    c. The price will increase, but what happens to quantity is not clear.
    d. It is not clear what happens to either price or quantity.

18. What will likely happen to the value of the Malaysian ringgit in terms of dollars as more foreigners want to invest in Malaysia, and at the same time Mahathir Perot, a wealthy Malaysian businessman, decides to sell his huge holdings of Malaysian ringgit?
    a. It will fall.
    b. It will remain the same.
    c. It will rise.
    d. It is difficult to say.

19. The fallacy of composition is
    a. the false assumption that what is false for a part will also be false for the whole.
    b. the false assumption that what is true for a part will also be true for the whole.
    c. the false assumption that what is false for a whole will also be false for the part.
    d. the false assumption that what is true for a whole will also be true for the part.

20. The ability to organize and get something done generally goes under the term
    a. the corporate approach.
    b. entrepreneurship.
    c. economicship.
    d. consumer sovereignty.

21. In reality, businesses are usually controlled by
    a. stockholders.
    b. managers.
    c. government.
    d. consumers

22. An example of a negative externality is
    a. education.
    b. pollution.
    c. government intervention.
    d. monopoly.

23. If a country can produce a good at a lower opportunity cost than another country can produce it, we say it has
    a. comparative advantage in the production of that good.
    b. an export advantage in the production of that good.
    c. an import advantage in the production of that good.
    d. a production advantage in the production of that good.

24. If a country is maintaining an exchange rate above its market equilibrium determined by private supply and demand for its currency, then that country's
    a. official transaction account would be in surplus.
    b. official transaction account would be in deficit.
    c. current account would be in surplus.
    d. current account would be in deficit.

25. The general plan of NAFTA is
    a. to raise tariffs on most goods so the tariffs are equal among countries.
    b. to replace tariffs with quotas.
    c. to move towards political integration among Canada, Mexico, and the United States.
    d. to remove tariffs on most goods within 15 years of signing.

Answers

1. a (1:1)	11. b (3:11)	21. b (5:9)
2. a (1:8)	12. c (3:15)	22. b (5:14)
3. c (1:11)	13. d (3:17)	23. a (6:2)
4. a (1:19)	14. a (4:1)	24. a (6:9)
5. a (2:4)	15. c (4:4)	25. d (6:15)
6. a (2:9)	16. b (4:7)	
7. b (2:15)	17. a (4:12)	
8. a (2:17)	18. d (4:16)	
9. c (3:4)	19. b (4:21)	
10. a (3:8)	20. b (5:3)	

Key: The figures in parentheses refer to multiple choice question and chapter numbers. For example (1:4) is multiple choice question 1 from chapter 4.

Chapter 7:
Economic Growth, Business Cycles, Unemployment, and Inflation

Chapter at a glance

1a. U.S. economic output has grown at an annual 2.5 to 3.5 percent rate. (158)

1b. Since 1945 the average expansion has lasted about 51 months. (163)

1c. In the 1980s and 1990s the target rate of unemployment has been between 5 percent and 6 percent. (166)

The target rate of unemployment has been called the "natural" rate of unemployment.

1d. Since World War II, the U.S. inflation rate has remained positive and relatively stable. (173)

2. Five important ingredients of growth are: (159)
1. Institutions with incentives compatible with growth;

Government policy can help or hinder growth–do you know how?

2. Technological development;

Technology not only causes growth, it changes the entire social and political dimensions of society.

3. Available resources;

Technological advances can help overcome any lack of resources.

4. Capital accumulation–investment in productive capacity; and

Can be: (1) Privately owned by business, (2) publicly owned and provided by government–our infrastructure, (3) human capital–investment in people, (4) social capital–institutions and conventions.

5. Entrepreneurship

This is the ability to get things done. It involves creativity, vision, and an ability to translate that vision into reality.

✔ *Growth is a goal because it increases the nation's absolute standard of living.*

✔ *Growth is measured as increases in real GDP from one year to the next.*

3. The four phases of the business cycle are: the peak, the downturn, the trough, and the upturn. (164)

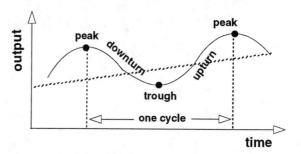

✔ *Note!*
   1) *There is an overall upward secular growth trend of 2.5-3.5% shown by the dotted line.*
   2) *We want to smooth out fluctuations because of the problems associated with them.*
   3) *2 problems with a downturn (recession) are (a) cyclical unemployment and (b) low growth rate.*
   4) *1 problem with upturn (expansion) is (a) demand-pull inflation.*

4a. The unemployment rate is measured by dividing the number of unemployed individuals by the number of people in the civilian labor force and multiplying by 100. (169)

Unemployment measures are imperfect but are still a good gauge of the economy's performance.

4b. Some microeconomic categories of unemployment are: reason for unemployment, demographic unemployment, duration of unemployment, and unemployment by industry. (172)

✔ *Know the different types of unemployment.*
✔ *Target rate of unemployment (5-6%) is the lowest rate of unemployment that policymakers believe is achievable under existing conditions (where inflation is not accelerating).*

5. Potential income is defined as the output that will be achieved at the target rate of unemployment and the target level of capacity utilization. It is difficult to know precisely where potential output is.(171)

Recession: Actual output (income) < Potential output.
Expansion: Actual output (income) > Potential output.

6a. Inflation is a continual rise in the price level. (173)

Price indexes are used to measure inflation; The most often used are the Producer Price Index (PPI), GDP deflator, and the Consumer Price Index (CPI).

6b. The "real" amount is the nominal amount divided by the price index. It is the nominal amount adjusted for inflation. (176)

Real means "inflation-adjusted."

7a. Cost-push inflation involves a rise in the price level resulting from restrictions on supply in a large number of markets When excess demand causes prices to rise it is referred to as demand-pull inflation. (177)

Typical Market in Demand-Pull Inflation   *Typical Market in Cost Push Inflation*

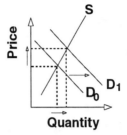 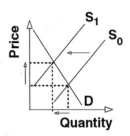

Both result in a higher price level. But, note the different directions in quantity (output).

7b. Expected inflation is the amount of inflation that people expect. Unexpected inflation is a surprise to them. (178)

We adjust to expected inflation by raising our prices or wages. However, this can create still more inflation. Demand-pull and cost-push inflation can feed on each other.

8. While inflation may not make the nation poorer, it does cause income to be redistributed and it can reduce the amount of information that prices are supposed to convey. (179)

Inflation hurts some, but benefits others.

Short-answer questions

1. What is the average rate of real growth in output in the United States since 1890 to the present? (LO1)

2. How long has the average expansion since mid-1945 lasted? (LO1)

3. In the 1980s and 1990s, what has been the target rate of unemployment? (LO1)

4. How did the inflation rate in the U.S. change in this century from pre-World War II to the post-World War II period (1950 to the present)? (LO1)

5. You've been called in by a political think tank to develop a strategy to improve growth in the U.S. What five things would you recommend that they concentrate on that would contribute positively to economic growth? (LO2)

6. Label the four phases of the business cycle in the graph to the right. (LO3)

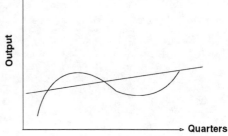

7. How is the unemployment rate calculated? (LO4)

8. Who in the United States does not work and is nevertheless not counted as unemployed? (LO4)

9. State two categories of unemployment for which microeconomic policies are appropriate. Why are such categories important to follow? (LO4)

10. How is the target rate of unemployment related to potential income? (LO5)

11. Define inflation. If there were no inflation what would happen to the distinction between a real concept and a nominal concept? (LO6)

12. Suppose the price of a Maserati in 1975 was $75,000 and the price of a Maserati in 1995 was $200,000. Your parents exclaim that the prices of Maserati's have risen by 166%! Wow! You tell them that the price of a Maserati really hasn't risen that much. They are confusing real and nominal concepts. Explain what you mean. (LO6)

13. What is the difference between cost-push and demand-pull inflation? (LO7)

14. Which of the two curves below better demonstrates a single market making a contribution to cost-pull inflation? To demand-pull inflation? (LO7)

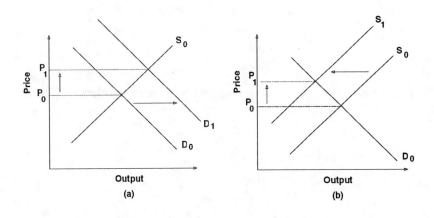

15. What is the difference between expected and unexpected inflation? (LO7)

16. What are two important costs of inflation? (LO8)

Word Scramble

1. _____ _____   2._____   3._____ _____
    b e i n s s s u   c c e l y   a f i i l n n o t   e e l m m n n o p t u y   a e r t

Match the Terms and Concepts to Their Definitions

___ 1.	business cycle
___ 2.	capacity utilization rate
___ 3.	Consumer Price Index
___ 4.	cyclical unemployment
___ 5.	demand-pull inflation
___ 6.	discouraged workers
___ 7.	frictional unemployment
___ 8.	full employment
___ 9.	GDP deflator
___ 10.	human capital
___ 11.	hyperinflation
___ 12.	inflation
___ 13.	leading indicators
___ 14.	Okun's rule of thumb
___ 15.	potential output
___ 16.	real output
___ 17.	recession
___ 18.	structural readjustments
___ 19.	structural unemployment
___ 20.	unemployment rate

a. A downturn that persists for more than two consecutive quarters.
b. A continual rise in the price level.
c. A one-percent change in the unemployment rate will cause income to change in the opposite direction by 2.5 percent.
d. An economic climate in which almost everyone who wants a job has one.
e. Index of inflation measuring prices of a fixed "basket" of consumer goods, weighted according to each component's share of an average consumer's expenditures.
f. Index of the price level of aggregate output of the average price of the components in GDP relative to a base year.
g. Indicators that tell us what's likely to happen in 12 -15 months.
h. Inflation resulting from the pressure exerted when the majority of markets in the economy experience increases in demand.
i. Inflation that hits triple digits (100 percent) or more per year.
j. Modifications in the types of goods produced and the methods of production.
k. Output that would materialize at the target rate of unemployment and the target rate of capacity utilization.
l. People who do not look for a job because they feel they don't have a chance of finding one.
m. People's knowledge.
n. Rate at which factories and machines are operating compared to the maximum rate at which they could be used.
o. The total amount of goods and services produced, adjusted for price level changes.
p. The upward or downward movement of economic activity that occurs around the growth trend.
q. The percentage of people in the labor force who can't find a job.
r. Unemployment caused by new entrants to the job market and people who have left their jobs to look for and find other jobs.
s. Unemployment resulting from changes in the economy itself.
t. Unemployment resulting from fluctuations in economic activity.

Problems and Exercises

1. For each of the following increases in the unemployment rate, state what will likely happen to income in the United States:

    a. Unemployment rate falls 2 percentage points.

    b. Unemployment rate falls 1 percentage point.

    c. Unemployment rate increases 3 percentage points.

2.   For each, state whether the unemployment is structural or cyclical.

   a.   Unemployment rises as output in the economy falls.

   b.   The demand for workers to make typewriters falls as more consumers switch to computers.

   c.   As the United States becomes a more high-tech producer, labor-intensive factories relocate to low-wage countries. Factory workers lose their jobs and the unemployment rate rises.

   d.   As it becomes more acceptable for mothers to work, more women enter the labor market looking for work. The unemployment rate rises.

   e.   Foreign economies slow and demand fewer U.S. exports. Unemployment rate rises.

3.   Calculate the following given the information about the economy in the table:

Total population	260 million
Noninstitutional population	200 million
Incapable of working	60 million
Not in the labor force	66 million
Employed	134 million
Unemployed	10 million

   a.   Labor force.

   b.   Unemployment rate.

4.   Create a price index for Green Bay Packer fans using the following basket of goods with 1997 prices as the base year.

Quantities in 1997	Prices 1997	1998
90 lbs of cheese	$2.50/lb	$2.00/lb
12 flannel shirts	$15/shirt	$20/shirt
16 football tickets	$25/ticket	$30/ticket

a.   What is the price of the basket of goods in each year? Show how the price index is 100 in the base year 1997.

b.   Using 1997 as the base year, what is the price index in 1998? By how much have prices risen?

c.   What are some potential flaws of this price index?

5.   Calculate the following given the following information about the economy in 1975, 1985, and 1995:

	1975	1985	1995
Nominal GDP (in billions of dollars)	1,630.6	4,180.7	_____
GDP deflator (index, 1992=100)	42.2	78.6	108
Real GDP (in billions of 1992 dollars)	_____	_____	6,756.48

a.   Nominal GDP in 1995.

b.   Real GDP in 1992 dollars in 1975 and 1985.

c.   Rise in prices from 1975 to 1985.

d.   Growth in nominal output from 1975 to 1985.

6.   Answer each of the following questions about nominal output, real output, and inflation:

a.   Nominal output increased from $6.5 trillion to $6.9 trillion from 1993 to 1994. The GDP deflator rose over that same year by 2.3%. By how much did real output increase?

b.   Real output increased from $4.9 trillion to $5.1 trillion from 1992 to 1993. The GDP deflator rose over that same year by 3%. By how much did nominal output increase?

c.   Real output decreased from $4.8 billion in 1990 to $4.7 billion in 1991. Nominal output rose by 2%. By how much did the price level rise from 1990 to 1991?

7.   For each of the following scenarios, state whether it is describing demand-pull or cost-push inflation.

a.   The money supply has been expanding rapidly. Consumers can't seem to find all the goods they want.

b.   The economy is operating above full employment. Workers are beginning to demand higher wages and firms are raising their prices (knowing that they will have no trouble selling their goods).

c.   Even though there are no shortages of goods, firms are finding that the prices of inputs to production are rising rapidly. Firms are forced not only to cut back production but to raise their prices to cover costs.

d.   In expectation of higher prices in the future, consumers stock up on goods now. Firms raise their prices just to keep pace with general inflation. They also see their inventories dwindle and increase production levels.

Multiple Choice Questions

1.   The secular trend growth rate in the United States is approximately
     a. 1 to 1.5 percent per year.
     b. 2.5 to 3.5 percent per year.
     c. 5 to 5.5 percent per year.
     d. 7 to 7.5 percent per year.

2.   Some people have argued that the two goals of (1) environmental protection and (2) economic growth that involves increased material consumption by individuals do not necessarily contradict each other because spending on the environment can create growth and jobs. This argument
     a. offers great hope for the future.
     b. is incorrect because environmental issues are not as important as material consumption.
     c. is correct because material consumption is not as important as the environment.
     d. is incorrect because the environmental projects will use the resources generated from growth, leaving little or nothing for increased personal consumption.

3.   Important ingredients of growth include all the following except
     a. technological development.
     b. significant resources.
     c. institutions and incentives compatible with growth.
     d. strong government.

4. Technological change increases output by
   a. increasing the amount of capital.
   b. decreasing the amount of capital.
   c. changing the nature of capital.
   d. increasing the amount of resources we have.

5. The business cycle characterized by the Great Depression occurred in the early
   a. 1900s.
   b. 1930s.
   c. 1950s.
   d. 1960s.

6. Leading indicators include
   a. manufacturing and trade sales volume.
   b. number of employees on non-agricultural payrolls.
   c. industrial production.
   d. new orders for goods and materials.

7. Under pure capitalism, the main deterrent of unemployment was
   a. pure government intervention.
   b. pure market intervention.
   c. the fear of hunger.
   d. immigration.

8. In the 1980s and 1990s the target rate of unemployment generally has been
   a. between 2 and 3 percent.
   b. between 3 and 5 percent.
   c. between 4 and 6 percent.
   d. between 7 and 8 percent.

9. Keynesians
   a. generally favor activist government policies.
   b. generally favor laissez-faire policies.
   c. believe that frictional unemployment does not exist.
   d. believe that all unemployment is cyclical unemployment.

10. Classicals
    a. generally favor activist government policies.
    b. generally favor laissez-faire policies.
    c. believe that frictional unemployment does not exist.
    d. believe that all unemployment is cyclical unemployment.

11. The level of output that would materialize at the target rate of unemployment and the target rate of capital
    utilization is called
    a. nominal output.
    b. actual output.
    c. potential output.
    d. utilized output.

12. Okun's rule of thumb states that
    a. a 1 percentage point change in the unemployment rate will cause income to change in the same direction by
       2.5 percent.
    b. a 1 percentage point change in the unemployment rate will cause income to change in the opposite direction
       by 2.5 percent.
    c. a 2.5 percentage point change in the unemployment rate will cause income to change in the same direction
       by 1 percent.
    d. a. 2.5 percentage point change in the unemployment rate will cause income to change in the opposite
       direction by 1 percent.

13. Using Okun's rule of thumb, if unemployment rises from 5 to 6 percent, one would expect total output of $5 trillion to
    a. rise by $5 billion.
    b. rise by $125 billion.
    c. fall by $125 billion.
    d. fall by $5 billion.

14. A one-time rise in the price level is
    a. inflation if that rise is above 5 percent.
    b. inflation if that rise is above 10 percent.
    c. inflation if that rise is above 15 percent.
    d. not inflation.

15. Food and beverages make up about 20 percent of total expenditure. If food and beverage prices rise by 10 percent while the other components of the price index remain constant, approximately how much will the price index rise?
    a. 1 percent.
    b. 2 percent.
    c. 20 percent.
    d. 25 percent.

16. Real output is
    a. total amount of goods and services produced.
    b. total amount of goods and services produced adjusted for price level changes.
    c. total amount of goods produced, adjusted for services that aren't real.
    d. total amount of goods and services that are really produced as opposed to ones that are resold.

17. If the price level rises by 20 percent and real output remains constant, by how much will nominal output rise?
    a. 1 percent.
    b. 5 percent.
    c. 20 percent.
    d. 40 percent.

18. If inflation occurs when the economy significantly exceeds full employment, it is likely
    a. demand-pull inflation.
    b. cost-push inflation.
    c. commodity price inflation.
    d. consumer price index inflation.

19. If inflation occurs when the economy significantly falls below full employment, it is likely
    a. demand-pull inflation.
    b. cost-push inflation.
    c. commodity price inflation.
    d. consumer price index inflation.

20. A cost of inflation is that
    a. it makes everyone poorer.
    b. it makes the poor poorer but the rich richer.
    c. There are no costs of inflation because inflation does not make the society as a whole poorer.
    d. it reduces the informational content of prices.

Answers

Short-Answer Questions

1. The average rate of real growth in output in the United States from 1890 to the present is 2.5 - 3.5% per year. (158)

2. The average expansion since mid-1945 lasted has lasted 51 months. (163)

3. In the 1980s and 1990s, the target rate of unemployment has been between 5 and 6 percent. (167)

4. The inflation rate in the U.S. before World War II fluctuated and was sometimes positive and sometimes negative. Since World War II the price level has continually risen. (173-174)

5. I would tell them: (1) To promote institutions with incentives compatible with growth. Institutions that encourage hard work will lead to growth. (2) To promote institutions that foster creative thinking and lead to technological development; (3) To be creative in recognizing available resources. Growth requires resources and although it may seem that the resources are limited, available resources depend upon existing technology. New technology is a way of overcoming lack of resources. (4) To invest in capital. This would include not only buildings and machines, but also human and social capital. (5) To encourage entrepreneurship. An economy deficient in the other four areas can still grow if its population can translate vision into reality. Each of these will contribute to growth. (159-161)

6. The four phases of the business cycle are: the peak, the downturn, the trough, and the upturn. They are labeled in the graph to the right. (163)

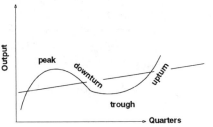

7. Unemployment is calculated by dividing the number of unemployed individuals by the number of people in the civilian labor force, and multiplying the result by 100. (165-169)

8. Those who are not in the labor force and those incapable of working are not employed and are not counted as unemployed. They include students, retirees, homemakers, those incapable of working, and those who choose not to participate in the labor force. (169)

9. Two microeconomic subcategories of unemployment include how people become unemployed and demographic unemployment. Others are duration of unemployment and unemployment by industry. These categories are important to follow because policies affect different types of unemployment differently and sometimes macro policies should be supplemented by micro policies. (172)

10. Potential income is that level of output that will be achieved at the target rate of unemployment. (171)

11. Inflation is a continual rise in the price level. If there were no inflation there would be no difference between real and nominal concepts. A real concept is the nominal concept adjusted for inflation. (176-177)

12. Yes, nominally Maseratis have risen by 166% from 1975 to 1995, but all other prices have risen during that time period too, including wages. You must adjust the rise in the aggregate price level to find out how much Maseratis have risen in real terms. From 1975 to 1995, the price level rose by 156%. (We used the *Economic Report of the President* to find this information.) So, the real price of the Maserati rose by only approximately 10% from 1975 to 1995. (176-177)

13. Cost-push inflation involves a rise in the price level resulting from restrictions on supply due to some sort of legal or social pressure. Demand-pull inflation involves excess demand resulting in price increases. (177-178)

14. Graph (a) demonstrates demand-pull inflation and graph (b) demonstrates cost-pull inflation. Graph (a) shows demand shifting to the right and equilibrium prices rising. Graph (b) shows supply contracting, leading to higher prices. (178)

15. Expected inflation is the amount of inflation that people expect. Unexpected inflation is inflation that is a surprise. (178)

16. Two important costs of inflation are that it redistributes income from people who do not raise their price to people who do raise their price; and it can reduce the amount of information that prices are supposed to convey. (179)

Word Scramble
1. business cycle   2. inflation   3. unemployment rate

Match the Terms and Concepts to Their Definitions
1-p; 2-n; 3-e; 4-t; 5-h; 6-l; 7-r; 8-d; 9-f; 10-m; 11-i; 12-b; 13-g; 14-c; 15-k; 16-o; 17-a; 18-j; 19-s; 20-q.

Problems and Exercises

1. Okun's law states that a 1-percentage point change in unemployment rate will cause income in the economy to change in the opposite direction by 2.5 percent.
   a. Income rises 5 percent. (171)
   b. Income rises 2.5 percent. (171)
   c. Income falls 7.5 percent. (171)

2. a. Cyclical because it is unemployment due to a change in economic activity. (165-166)
   b. Structural because this is a structural change in the economy. (165-166)
   c. Structural because this is a change in labor allocation. (165-166)
   d. Structural because this is a change in social structure. (165-166)
   e. Cyclical because this is unemployment due to a change in economic activity. (165-166)

3. a. Labor force = employed + unemployed = 144 million. (169)
   b. Unemployment rate = (unemployed/labor force)$\times$100 = 6.9%. (169)

4. a. The price of the basket in 1997 is $805 and in 1998 is $900. Since 1997 is the base year, the index must be 100. This is calculated as (price of the basket in 1997)/(price of the basket in 1997) = $805/$805 $\times$ 100=100. (174)
   b. The price index in 1998 is (price of the basket in 1998)/(price of the basket in 1997) = $900/$805 $\times$ 100= 112. Prices rose by 12%. (174)
   c. Some potential flaws are that (1) the basket of goods is small and might not reflect the true basket of goods purchased by Green Bay Packer fans, (2) the basket of goods is fixed (since the price of cheese fell, fans might be buying more cheese and fewer football tickets), (3) the basket does not reflect quality improvements (since the Green Bay Packers won the Super Bowl in 1997, the quality of subsequent games in 1998 might improve, but the tickets are counted as if they were the same as in 1997).

5. a. Nominal GDP in 1995 is $7,297 billion dollars. Calculate this by multiplying real GDP in 1995 by the GDP deflator and dividing by 100. (176)
   b. Real GDP in 1992 dollars in 1975 is $3,8634 billion and in 1985 $5,319 billion. Calculate these by dividing nominal GDP by the GDP deflator and multiplying by 100. (176)
   c. The price level rose by 86% from 1975 to 1985. Calculate this by dividing the change in the GDP price deflator by the base year deflator and multiplying by 100: (78.6 − 42.2)/42.2 $\times$ 100. (176)
   d. Nominal output grew by 156% from 1975 to 1985. Calculate this by dividing the change in nominal GDP from 1975 to 1985 by the base year nominal GDP and multiplying by 100: (4180.7 − 1630.6)/1630.3 $\times$ 100. (176)

6. a. Nominal output increased by 6.1% from 1993 to 1994. Since the GDP deflator rose over that same year, we know that real output increased 3.8% from 1993 to 1994. Subtract inflation from the change in nominal output to get the change in real output: 6.1% − 2.3% = 3.8%. (176)
   b. Real output increased 4.1% from 1992 to 1993. Since the GDP deflator rose 3% over that same year, we know that nominal output increased 7.1% from 1992 to 1993. Add inflation to the change in real output to find the change in nominal output: 3% + 4.1% = 7.1%. (176)

c. Real output fell 2.1% from 1990 to 1991. Since nominal output rose by 2%, we know the price level rose 4.1% from 1990 to 1991. Subtract the change in real output from the change in nominal output to find the inflation rate: 2.0%- (-2.1%) = 4.1%. (176)

7. a. Demand-pull inflation. (177)
   b. Demand-pull inflation. (177)
   c. Cost-push inflation. (177)
   d. Initial cause of inflation is unclear, but turned into demand-pull inflation. (177)

Multiple Choice Questions

1. b. See page 158.

2. d. As more material goods made available by growth are used for antipollution equipment, less is available for personal consumption. The added material goods have already been used. See page 158.

3. d. Strong government may or may not be an important ingredient of growth. The other three definitely are ingredients of growth. See page 158-161.

4. c. Technological change definitely changes the nature of capital, making it more productive; it does not necessarily increase the total amount of capital. It is also possible that one could see technological change as increasing the effective resources, but what it does is to increase *available* resources—resources are fixed. Since d didn't say effective resources, c is the better answer. This is a hard question. When presented with two answer you think might be right, choose the one you are most sure of. See pages 159-160.

5. b. See page 162.

6. d. The others are coincidental indicators. Even if you didn't remember this, you should be able to figure out that the change in inventory predicts what firms think will be happening in the future, whereas the others tell what is happening now. See page 164.

7. c. As discussed on pages 165-166, the fear of hunger was the main deterrent to unemployment. A second deterrent would have been emigration, but that would not be as good an answer. Since d says immigration (the flowing in of people), not emigration, d is definitely wrong.

8. c. See page 167.

9. a. See page 167.

10. b. See page 167.

11. c. As discussed on page 171, the statement that begins the question is the definition of potential output.

12. b. See page 171.

13. c. Total output moves in the opposite direction by 2.5% times $5 trillion, which equals a fall of $125 billion. See page 171.

14. d. As the text points out on page 173, inflation is an *ongoing* rise in the price level, so the use of the term "one-time" should have clued you that d is the answer.

15. b. To determine the price level rise you multiply each component by its price rise. Since only 20% of the total rose, you get 10% times 20% = 2% . See page 174.

16. b. See page 176. A reminder: A service is considered just as much a good and a component of real output as is a physical good.

17. c. If real output remains constant, then the nominal output must also rise by 20%, as discussed on page 176.

18. a. As discussed on page 177, demand-pull inflation occurs above full employment. Commodity price inflation was not discussed in the text, and could be either cost-push or demand-pull inflation.

19. b. As discussed on page 177, cost-push inflation occurs below full employment. Commodity price inflation was not discussed in the text, and could be either cost-push or demand-pull.

20. d. Inflation does not make society richer or poorer, and the distributional consequences of inflations differ, eliminating answers a and b. While the second part of c is true, that doesn't mean that there are no costs of inflation and, as discussed on page 179, one of those costs is the reduction in the informational content of prices.

Chapter 8: National Income Accounting

Chapter at a glance

1. National income accounting enables us to measure and analyze how much a nation is producing and consuming. (184)

   GDP:
   - *(1) Most common measure of a nation's output (income)*
   - *(2) Calculated by either:*
     - *a) expenditures approach, or*
     - *b) income approach*

2a. Gross domestic product (GDP): Aggregate final output of residents and businesses in an economy in a one-year period. (184)

   GDP is total market ($) value of all <u>final</u> goods and services produced in a one-year period.

2b. Gross national product (GNP): Aggregate final output of citizens and businesses of an economy in a one-year period. (184)

   ✔ *GDP is output produced within a country's borders; GNP is output produced by a country's citizens wherever they may be in the world.*

   ✔ *GNP = GDP + Net foreign factor income where: Net foreign factor income => Add the foreign income of one's citizens and subtract the income of residents who are not citizens.*

2c. National income (NI) is the total income earned by citizens and businesses in a country. (188)

   See Appendix A for more details concerning national income accounting.

   Hint: In most "non-technical" discussions of "output" (GDP) and "income" (NI) are used interchangeably—that is, GDP is assumed to be equal to NI for purposes of simplification.

3. To avoid double counting, you must eliminate intermediate goods, either by calculating only final output (expenditures approach), or by calculating only final income (income approach) by using the value added approach. (186)

Know what is and is not included in calculating GDP. <u>*GDP does not include:*</u>
1) *intermediate goods (sold for resale or further processing);*
2) *second-hand sales;*
3) *government transfers, housespouse production or any other non-market activity;*
4) *underground economic activity.*

4. $GDP = C + I + G + (X - M)$ is an accounting identity because it is defined as true. (190)

   The above identity is really the expenditures approach, which states:

   Total output = Total expenditures
   Total output = GDP; Total expenditures=C+I+G+(X − M)

   By substitution: $GDP = C + I + G + (X - M)$
   ✔ *Know what C, I, G, X − M stand for!*

   Also note:
   $X_n = (X - M)$ = *Net exports.*
   If X_n *is positive, then X>M => Trade surplus.*
   If X_n *is negative, then X<M => Trade deficit.*
   If X_n *is zero, then X=M => Trade balance.*

5. A real concept is a nominal concept adjusted for inflation. (193)

   GDP is a price times quantity (P×Q) phenomenon. GDP can ↑ due to an ↑ in P (price level) and/or an ↑ in Q (real quantity of output). Real GDP, in essence, holds prices (P) constant. Hence, real GDP is inflation (or deflation) adjusted.

6. Limitations of national income accounting include: (193)
   1. Measurement problems.
   2. GDP measures national activity, not welfare; and
   3. Subcategories are often interdependent.

   ✔ *GDP is not and was never intended to be a measure of social well-being.*

   See also, Appendix A: "National Income Accounting in Detail."

Short-answer questions

1. What is the purpose of national income accounting? (LO1)

2. What is GDP? (LO2)

3. What is GNP? In words, how does it differ from GDP? (LO2)

4. What is NI? What are the four components that comprise NI? (LO2)

5. Calculate the contribution of Chex cereal (from seeds to consumer) to GDP, using the following information: (LO3)

Participants	Cost of materials	Value of Sales
Farmer	0	200
Chex factory	200	500
Distributor	500	800
Grocery store	800	1000

6.   What are the four components of gross domestic product and why does their sum equal national income? (LO4)

7.   Say the price level rises 10% from an index of 1 to an index of 1.1 and nominal GDP rises from $4 trillion to $4.6 trillion. What is nominal GDP in the second period? What is real GDP in the second period? (LO5)

8.   As pointed out by the quotation that begins the chapter on national income accounting, statistics can be misleading. In what way can national income statistics be misleading? Given your answer, why use them at all? (LO6)

Word Scramble

1. _____ _____   2._____ _____   3._____ _____
     a e l r   D G P   a i l m n n o   DPG   a e l u v   d e a d d

Match the Terms and Concepts to Their Definitions

_____ 1. disposable personal income

_____ 2. gross domestic product

_____ 3. gross national product

_____ 4. intermediate products

_____ 5. national income (NI)

_____ 6. national income accounting

_____ 7. net domestic product

_____ 8. net foreign factor income

_____ 9. nominal concepts

_____ 10. nominal GDP

_____ 11. real GDP

_____ 12. value added

_____ 13. Wealth Accounts

a. National income minus personal taxes plus transfer payments made to individuals.

b. Economic concepts specified in monetary terms (current dollars) with no adjustment for inflation.

c. GDP calculated at existing prices.

d. Aggregate final output of residents and businesses in an economy in a one-year period.

e. Total income earned by citizens and businesses of a country.

f. GDP adjusted to take account of depreciation.

g. Aggregate final output of citizens and businesses of an economy in a one-year period.

h. Income from foreign domestic factor sources minus foreign factor incomes earned domestically.

i. Nominal GDP adjusted for inflation.

j. Products of one firm used in some other firm's production of another firm's product.

k. A balance sheet of an economy's stock of assets and liabilities.

l. The increase in value that a firm contributes to a product or service.

m. A set of rules and definitions for measuring economic activity in the aggregate economy.

Problems and Exercises

1. For each of the following, calculate how much the action described has added to GDP:

   a. A used car dealer buys a car for $3,000 and resells it for $3,300.

   b. A company sells 1,000 disks for $500 each. Of these, it sells 600 to other companies and 400 to individuals.

   c. A company sells 50 computers at a retail price of $1,000 apiece and 100 software packages at a retail price of $50 apiece to consumers. The same company sells 25 computers at $800 and 50 software packages at $30 apiece to wholesalers. The wholesalers then sell the 25 computers at $1,250 apiece and the 50 software packages at $75 apiece.

   d. Fred purchases 100 stock certificates valued at $5 apiece and pays a 10% commission. When the price declines to $4.50 apiece, Fred decides to sell all 100 certificates, again at a 10% commission.

   e. Your uncle George receives $600 in social security each month for one year.

2. Use the following table showing the production of 500 boxes of Wheaties cereal to calculate the contribution to GDP using the value-added approach.

Participants	Cost of materials	Value of sales
Farmer	$ 0	$ 150
Mill	$ 150	$ 250
Cereal maker	$ 250	$ 600
Wholesaler	$ 600	$ 800
Grocery store	$ 800	$ 1,000

a. Calculate the value added at each stage of production.

b. What is the total value of sales?

c. What is the total value added?

d. What is the contribution to GDP for the production of those Wheaties?

3. There are three firms in an economy: X, Y, and Z. Firm X buys $200 worth of goods from firm Y and $300 worth of goods from firm Z, and produces 250 units of output at $4 per unit. Firm Y buys $150 worth of goods from firm X, and $250 worth of goods from firm Z, and produces 300 units of output at $6 per unit. Firm Z buys $75 worth of goods from X, and $50 worth goods from firm Y, and produces 300 units at $2 per unit. All other products are sold to consumers. Answer the following:

a. What is GDP?

b. How much government revenue would a value added tax of 10% generate?

c.   How much government revenue would an income tax of 10% generate?

d.   How much government revenue would a 10% sales tax on final output generate?

4.   Use the following table to answer the questions:

Year	Real output in (billions of 1992 dollars)	Nominal output (billions of dollars)	GDP deflator (1992=100)
1991	6079.0	5916.7	_____
1992	6244.4	6244.4	100.0
1993	6383.8	_____	102.6
1994	_____	_____	105.0
1995	_____	7297.2	108.0

a. What is output for 1995 in 1992 dollars?

b. What is the output in nominal terms in 1993?

c. What is the GDP deflator (1992=100) in 1991?

d. Real output grew by 3.5% from 1993 to 1994. By how much did nominal output grow in 1994?

A1. You have been hired as a research assistant and are given the following data about the economy:
All figures are in billions of dollars.

Transfer payments	$70
Interest paid by consumers	5
Net exports	10
Indirect business taxes	44
Net foreign factor income	3
Corporate income tax	69
Contribution for social insurance	37
Personal tax and non-tax payments	92
Undistributed corporate profits	49
Gross private investment	200
Government purchases	190
Personal consumption	550
Depreciation	65

You are asked to calculate the following:

a. GDP.

b. GNP.

c. NNP.

d. NDP.

e. NI.

f. Personal income.

g. Disposable personal income.

A2. You have been hired as a research assistant and are given the following data about another economy (profits, wages, rents, and interest are measured nationally):

Corporate income tax	$200
Proprietors' income	225
Profits	250
Wages	800
Rents	30
Depreciation	20
Indirect business taxes	110
Undistributed corporate profits	50
Net foreign factor income	-5
Interest	175
Social security contribution	0
Transfer payments	0
Personal taxes	150

Calculate the following:

a. GDP.

b. GNP.

c. NDP.

d. NNP.

e. National income.

f. Domestic income.

g. Personal income.

h. Disposable personal income.

Multiple Choice Questions

1. If inflation is 10 percent and nominal GDP goes up 20 percent, real GDP goes up approximately
   a. 1 percent.
   b. 10 percent.
   c. 20 percent.
   d. 50 percent.

2. To move from GDP to GNP, one must
   a. add net foreign factor income.
   b. subtract inflation.
   c. add depreciation.
   d. subtract depreciation.

3. If a firm's cost of materials is $100 and its value of sales is $500, its value added is
   a. $100.
   b. $400.
   c. $500.
   d. $600.

4. If you, the owner, sell your old car for $600, how much does GDP increase?
   a. By $600.
   b. By the amount you bought it for, minus the $600.
   c. By zero.
   d. By the $600 you received and the $600 the person you sold it to paid, or $1,200.

5. The size of the U.S. federal government budget is approximately $1.7 trillion. The federal government's contribution in the GDP accounts is approximately
   a. $660 billion.
   b. $1 trillion.
   c. $1.7 trillion.
   d. $5.6 trillion.

6. If a woman divorces her housespouse and hires him to continue cleaning her house for $20,000 per year, GDP will
   a. remain constant.
   b. increase by $20,000 per year.
   c. decrease by $20,000 per year.
   d. remain unchanged.

7. The national income identity shows that
   a. the value of factor services is equal to the value of goods plus investment.
   b. the value of factor services is equal to the value of goods plus savings.
   c. the value of factor services is equal to the value of goods sold to individuals.
   d. the value of consumption goods is equal to the value of factor services.

8. The four components of expenditures in GDP are
   a. consumption, investment, government spending, and net exports.
   b. consumption, depreciation, investment, and government expenditures.
   c. consumption, investment, gross exports, and government expenditures.
   d. durable goods, nondurable goods, services, and government expenditures.

9. The largest component of expenditures in GDP is
   a. consumption.
   b. investment.
   c. net exports.
   d. government purchases of goods and services.

10. The largest component of national income is
   a. rents.
   b. net interest.
   c. profits.
   d. compensation to employees.

11. Switching from the exchange rate approach to the purchasing power parity approach for comparing GDP among countries generally
   a. does not make a significant difference for a developing country's GDP relative to a developed country's GDP.
   b. generally increases a developing country's GDP relative to a developed country's GDP.
   c. generally decreases a developing country's GDP relative to a developed country's GDP.
   d. changes the relative GDP of developing country's GDP, but not in a predictable fashion.

12. If the price level rises by 2 percent and nominal GDP increases from $5 trillion to $6 trillion, by approximately how much has real GDP increased?
   a. 0%.
   b. 2%.
   c. 18%.
   d. 48%.

13. If nominal GDP rises
   a. welfare has definitely increased.
   b. welfare has definitely decreased.
   c. welfare may have increased or decreased.
   d. welfare most likely has increased.

14. Estimates of the importance of the underground economy in the United States
   a. are that it is very small—under 1 percent.
   b. are that it's somewhere between 1.5 percent and all the way to 20 percent.
   c. are that it's somewhere between 1.5 percent and all the way to 60 percent.
   d. are that it is as large as the non-underground economy.

A1. The largest component of U.S. consumption expenditures is
   a. durable goods.
   b. nondurable goods.
   c. services.
   d. investment.

A2. Gross investment differs from net investment by
   a. net exports.
   b. net imports.
   c. depreciation.
   d. transfer payments.

A3. GDP differs from net domestic product by
   a. depreciation.
   b. exports.
   c. imports.
   d. consumption.

A4. Whenever investment increases in a country its productive capital
   a. definitely increases.
   b. will likely increase, but may not.
   c. definitely decreases.
   d. will likely decrease, but may not.

Answers

Short-answer questions

1. The purpose of national income accounting is to measure and analyze how much the nation is producing and consuming. National income accounting defines the relationship among the sub-aggregates of aggregate production. (184)

2. GDP is the aggregate final output of *residents* and businesses *in* an economy in a one-year period. (184)

3. GNP is aggregate final output of *citizens* and businesses *of* an economy in a one-year period. GDP is output produced within a country's borders while GNP is output produced by a country's citizens. Add net foreign factor income to GDP to get GNP. (184)

4. NI is total income earned by citizens and businesses of a country. The four components that comprise NI are compensation to employees, rents, interest, and profits. (188-189)

5. $1,000. We could use either the value added approach or the final output approach. Summing the value added at each stage of production — the difference between cost of materials and value of sales —we get $1,000. (186)

Participants	Cost of materials	Value of Sales	Value Added
Farmer	$0	$200	$200
Chex factory	200	500	300
Distributor	500	800	300
Grocery store	800	1000	200
Sum (total output)			1000

6. The four components of gross domestic product are consumption, investment, government expenditures, and net exports. Their sum equals national income because it is an accounting identity — the definitions are chosen so that equality cannot be false. (190)

7. A real value is a nominal value adjusted for inflation. So, nominal GDP in the second period is $4.6 trillion, but real GDP is $4.6 trillion divided by the price index, 1.1, or $4.18 trillion. (193)

8. National income accounting statistics can be misleading. They are subject to measurement error; they are based on samples of data and assumptions about behavior. For example, the measurement of inflation is widely believed to overestimate true inflation. Also, GDP does not include non-market activities such as housework. It measures national activity, not welfare; output could rise but welfare fall. Its subcategories are often interdependent; that is, arbitrary decisions were made when determining what goes in which subcategory. Nevertheless, national income accounting makes it possible to discuss the aggregate economy. It is important to be aware of the limitations of the data in those discussions. (193-196)

Word Scramble   1. real GDP   2. nominal GDP   3. value added

Match the Terms and Concepts to Their Definitions
1-a; 2-d; 3-g; 4-j; 5-e; 6-m; 7-f; 8-h; 9-b; 10-c; 11-i; 12-l; 13-k.

Problems and Exercises

1. a. $300. Only the value added by the sale would be added to GDP, which in this case is the difference between the purchase price and the sale price. (186-187)

b. $200,000. Total output produced is 1,000 × $500 = $500,000. Of this intermediate goods valued at 600 × $500 = $300,000. So, the company's contribution to GDP is ($500,000-$300,000) = $200,000. (186-187)

c. Only that amount that is sold to the consumer is counted in GDP. This is 50×1,000 + 100×50 = $55,000 sold by the first company plus the sales of the wholesaler, which is 25×$1250 + 50×$75 = $35,000. Total contribution to GDP is $90,000. (186-187)

d. Only the commissions of $50 and $45 are counted in GDP. Together they contribute $95. (186-187)

e. Nothing has been added to GDP. Government transfers are not included in GDP. (186-187)

2.

Participants	Cost of materials	Value of sales	Value added
Farmer	$ 0	$ 150	150
Mill	$ 150	$ 250	100
Cereal maker	$ 250	$ 600	350
Wholesaler	$ 600	$ 800	200
Grocery store	$ 800	$ 1,000	200

a. The value added at each stage of production is shown in the table above. (186-187)

b. The total value of sales is $2,800. Find this by adding the rows of the value of sales column. (186-187)

c. The total value added is $1,000. Find this by adding the value added at each stage of production. (186-187)

d. The contribution to GDP for the production of those Wheaties is $1,000. Value added at each stage of production is the contribution to GDP. This avoids double-counting. (186-187)

3. a. $2375: GDP is the sum of the value added by the three firms = 500 + 1,400 + 475. (186-187)

b. $237.50: A 10% value added tax would generate = (.10)($2,375) = $237.50 of revenue. (186-187)

c. $237.50: A 10% income tax would generate the same revenue as a 10% value added tax. (186-187)

d. $340: A 10% sales tax on final output would generate = $340 of revenue: (.10) (1,000 + 1,800 + 600). (186-187)

4. a. $6756.6 billion 1992 dollars: Real output = (Nominal output/deflator) × 100 = 7297.2/108 × 100.

b. $6549.7 billion: Nominal output = (real output × deflator) / 100 = (6383.8 × 102.6)/100.

c. 97.3: Deflator = (Nominal output/real output) × 100 = (5916.7/6079.0) × 100.

d. Real output grew by 3.5% and inflation rose by 2.3%, so nominal output grew by 5.8%.

A1. a. $950: GDP = $C + I + G + (X\text{-}M)$ = 550 + 200 + 190 + 10 = 950. (202)

b. $953: GNP = GDP + net foreign factor income = 953. (184)

c. $888: NNP = GNP − depreciation = 953 − 65 = 888. (203)

d. $885: NDP = GDP − depreciation = 950 − 65 = 885. (202)

e. $844 : NI = NNP − indirect business taxes = 888 − 44 = 844. (203-204)

f. $759: PI = NI + transfers from government − corporate retained earnings − corporate income taxes − social security taxes = 844 + 70 − 49 − 69 −37 = 759. (204)

g. $667: DPI = PI −personal income tax = 759 −92 = 667. (204)

A2. a. $1,615: GDP = NDP + Depreciation = NNP − net foreign factor income + depreciation = NI + indirect business tax − net foreign factor income + depreciation = wages + rents + interest + profits + proprietors' income + indirect business taxes − net foreign factor income + depreciation = 800 + 30 + 175 + 250 - (-5) + 225 + 110 + 20 = 1615. (199-203)

b. $1,610: GNP = GDP + net foreign factor income = 1615+(-5). (184, 199-203)

c. $1,595: NDP = GDP − depreciation = 1615 − 20. (199-203)

d. $1,590: NNP = GNP − depreciation = 1610 − 20. (184, 199-203)

e. $1,480: NI = NNP − indirect business taxes = 1590 − 110. (199-203)

f. $1,485: DI = NI − net foreign factor income = 1480 − (−5) . (199-203)

g. $1,230: PI = NI + transfers − corporate income taxes − undistributed corporate profits − social security contributions = 1480 + 0 − 200 − 50 − 0. (199-203)

h. $1,080: DPI = PI − personal taxes = 1230 − 150. (199-203)

Multiple Choice Questions

1. b. As discussed on page 193, real concepts are nominal concepts adjusted for inflation. As a first approximation you can simply subtract one from the other, giving you 10%.

2. a. As discussed on page 184, GDP + net foreign factor income = GNP.

3. b. Value added equals value of sales minus cost of materials. See page 186.

4. c. As discussed on page 187, sales of used goods do not contribute to GDP except to the degree that they are sold by a second hand dealer. Then the dealer's profit would be the value added.

5. a. It is not $1.7 trillion because the only part of the government budget that goes in GDP accounts is spending on goods and services. The portion of the budget for redistribution is not included in the GDP accounts. See page 187.

6. b. As discussed on page 187, GDP measures market transactions. The divorce-and-hire changes the housecleaning activities from nonmarket to market and hence increases GDP.

7. c. The equality can be seen in Exhibit 3 on page 189. The basis of the equality is the double entry bookkeeping upon which the national income accounts are based.

8. a. See page 190.

9. a. Consumption makes up 69% of expenditures. See Exhibit 5, page 190.

10. d. As you can see in Exhibit 4 on page 189, compensation to employees is the largest percent of national income.

11. b. In developing countries, living expenses are generally lower than in developed countries. Thus moving towards a purchasing power parity approach generally increases GDP in a developing country. In the example of China given on page 192, the switch increased China's GDP by more than 400 percent.

12. c. If nominal GDP has increased from $5 trillion to $6 trillion, it has increased 20%. Real GDP growth equals nominal GDP growth minus inflation, or 20-2=18%. See page 193.

13. c. Nominal GDP must be adjusted by inflation to arrive at real GDP before one can even start to make welfare comparisons. And even if real GDP increases, it is not clear that welfare has increased, as discussed on page 194.

14. b. See page 194.

A1. c. In 1994 services were approximately 57 percent of GDP, compared to much smaller percentages for the others. See Exhibit A3, page 200.

A2. c. See pages 199-201.

A3. a. See page 201.

A4. b. As discussed on page 201, investment is not a perfect measure of increase in productive capital. So of the two possible answers, a and b, the better is b.

Chapter 9: Money, Banking, and the Financial Sector

Chapter at a glance

1. The financial sector is central to almost all macroeconomic debates because behind every real transaction, there is a financial transaction that mirrors it. (208)

   If the interest rate does not perfectly translate savings (flows out of the spending stream) into investment (flows into the spending stream), then the economy will either expand or contract.

2. Money is a financial asset that makes the real economy function smoothly by serving as a medium of exchange, a unit of account, and a store of wealth. (209)

   Money is any financial asset which serves the functions of money.

3. The three functions of money are: (210)
   1. Medium of exchange;

   As long as people are confident that the purchasing power of the dollar will remain relatively stable over time (by the Fed controlling the money supply) then people will continue to swap real goods, services, and resources for money and vice versa.

   2. Unit of account; and

   Money acts as a measuring stick of the relative value (relative prices) of things. Therefore, the value of money itself must remain relatively stable over time.

   3. Store of wealth.

   Money's usefulness as a store of wealth also depends upon how well it maintains its value.

   ✔ *The key is for the Fed to keep the purchasing power of money (and therefore prices) relatively stable over time. Inflation can be a problem!*

4a. M1 is the component of the money supply that consists of cash in the hands of the public plus checking accounts and traveler's checks. (213)

   M1 is the narrowest definition of the money supply. It is also the most liquid.

4b. M2 is the component of the money supply that consists of M1 plus other relatively liquid assets. (213)

   ✔ *M2 is the definition of the money supply most used by the Fed to measure the money supply in circulation. This is because M2 is most closely correlated with the price level and economic activity.*

   ✔ *Anything which changes M2 changes the money supply.*

4c. The broadest definition of the money supply is L (which stands for liquidity). It consists of almost all short-term financial assets. (213)

5. Banks "create" money because a bank's liabilities are defined as money. So when a bank incurs liabilities it creates money. (215)

   Banks "create" money (increase the money supply) whenever they make loans. Whenever a person borrows from a bank they are swapping a promissory note to repay the loan (which is really an IOU; and an individual's IOU is not money because it doesn't meet the criteria of serving the functions of money) in exchange for cash or funds put in his/her checking account. Cash and checking account balances are money! Therefore, the money supply increases.

   Also Note: When a loan is repaid, the money supply (M2) decreases.

6a. The money multiplier is the measure of the amount of money ultimately created by the banking system per dollar deposited. When people hold no cash it equals 1/r, where r is the reserve ratio. (218)

A single bank is limited in the amount of money it may create. The limit is equal to its excess reserves–the maximum amount of funds which it can legally loan out. However, when considering an entire banking system, where any bank's loans, when spent, may end up being deposited back into that bank or another bank, then the entire banking system ends up being able to increase the money supply by a multiple of its initial excess reserves (the initial maximum amount of funds which can legally be loaned out) because of the money multiplier.

Simple money multiplier = 1/r.

(<u>Initial change</u> in money supply) × (money multiplier) = change in the money supply

6b. When people hold cash the approximate money multiplier is 1/ (r + c). (219)

Approximate real-world money multiplier = 1/(r+c), where c is the ratio of money people hold in currency to the money hold as deposits.

The approximate real-world money multiplier is less than the simple money multiplier because some of the funds loaned out are held as cash and therefore do not return to the banks as deposits.

7. Financial systems are based on trust that expectations will be fulfilled. Banks borrow short and lend long, which means that if people lose faith in banks, the banks cannot keep their promises. (221)

✔ *It is important to maintain the public's confidence in the banking system.*

✔ *Government guarantees of financial institutions can have 2 effects:*
  1) *They can prevent the unwarranted fear that causes financial crises.*
  2) *They can also eliminate <u>warranted</u> fears and hence eliminate a market control of bank loans.*

See also,
Appendix A: "The Value of a Financial Asset."
Appendix B: "A Closer Look at Financial Institutions and Financial Markets."
Appendix C: "Creation of Money Using T-Accounts."
Appendix D: "Precise Calculation of the Money Multiplier When People Hold Currency."

Short-answer questions

1. At lunch you and your friends are arguing about the financial sector. One friend says that real fluctuations are measured by real economic activity in the goods market and therefore the financial sector has nothing to do with the business cycle. You know better and set him straight. (LO1)

2. You are having another stimulating lunchtime conversation, this time about money. Your friend says "I know what money is; it's cash, the dollar bills I carry around." What is your response? (LO2)

3. You continue the conversation and begin to discuss why we have money. Your friend states that the function of money is to buy things like the lunch he has just bought. Another friend says that because she has money she is able to compare the cost of two types of slacks. Still another offers that she holds money to make sure she can buy lunch next week. What is the function of money that each has described? Are there any others? (LO3)

4. What are the two most liquid definitions of money? What are the primary components of each? (LO4)

5. What is the broadest measure of money? What does it consist of? (LO4)

6. Your friends are curious about money. At another lunchtime discussion, they ask each other two questions: Is all the money deposited in the bank in the bank's vaults? Can banks create money? Since they are stumped, you answer the questions for them. (LO5)

7. Using the simple money multiplier, what will happen to the money supply if the reserve ratio is 0.2 and high powered money is increased by $100? (LO6)

8. Using the equation for the approximate real-world money multiplier, what will happen to the money supply if the reserve ratio is 0.2, cash to deposit ratio is 0.3, and high powered money is increased by $100? (LO6)

9. How does the interest rate regulate the flow of savings into the flow of expenditures during normal times? (LO7)

10. What would happen if everyone simultaneously lost trust in their banks and ran to withdraw their deposits? (LO7)

11. What is the potential problem with government guarantees to prevent bank-withdrawal panics? (LO7)

Word Scramble

1. _____   2._____   3._____ _____
    e e e r r s s v   e n y o m   v e s r r e e   t r o i a

Match the Terms and Concepts to Their Definitions

___ 1. approximate real-world money multiplier

___ 2. asset management

___ 3. bond

___ 4. excess reserves

___ 5. Federal Reserve Bank (the Fed)

___ 6. L

___ 7. liability management

___ 8. M_1

___ 9. M_2

___ 10. money

___ 11. reserve ratio

___ 12. reserves

___ 13. simple money multiplier

___ 14. spread

a. Broad definition of "money" that includes almost all short-term assets.

b. Cash that a bank keeps on hand that is sufficient to manage the normal cash inflows and outflows.

c. Component of the money supply that consists of M_1 plus savings deposits, small-denomination time deposits, and money market mutual fund shares, along with some esoteric relatively liquid assets.

d. Component of the money supply that consists of cash in the hands of the public, checking account balances, and travelers' checks.

e. Difference between banks' costs plus the interest they pay out and the interest they take in minus bad loans.

f. How a bank attracts deposits and what it pays for them.

g. How a bank handles its loans and other assets.

h. Measure of the amount of money ultimately created by the banking system, per dollar deposited, when cash holdings of individuals and firms are treated the same as reserves of banks. The mathematical expression is $1/(r+c)$.

i. Measure of the amount of money ultimately created by the banking system per dollar deposited, when people hold no cash. The mathematical expression is $1/r$.

j. Ratio of cash or deposits a bank holds at the central bank to deposits a bank keeps as a reserve against withdrawals of cash.

k. Reserves above what banks are required to hold.

l. The U.S. central bank. Its liabilities serve as cash in the United States.

m. A highly liquid financial asset that is generally accepted in exchange for other goods and is used as a reference in valuing other goods and as a store of wealth.

n. A promise to pay a certain amount of money plus interest in the future.

Problems and Exercises

1. For each, state whether it is a component of M_1 or M_2, both, or neither:

a. Money market mutual funds.

b. Savings deposits.

c. Travelers' checks.

d. Stocks.

e. Twenty-dollar bills.

2. Assuming individuals hold no cash, calculate the simple money multiplier for each of the following reserve requirements:

  a.   15%

  b.   30%

  c.   60%

  d.   80%

  e.   100%

3. Assuming individuals hold 10% of their deposits in the form of cash, recalculate the *approximate* real-world money multipliers from question 2.

  a.   15%

  b.   30%

  c.   60%

  d.   80%

  e.   100%

4. While Jon is walking to school one morning, a helicopter flying overhead drops $300. Not knowing how to return it, Jon keeps the money and deposits it in his bank. (No one in this economy holds cash.) If the bank keeps only 10 percent of its money in reserves and is fully loaned out, calculate the following:

  a.   How much money can the bank now lend out?

  b.   After this initial transaction, by how much has the money in the economy changed?

  c.   What's the money multiplier?

   d.   How much money will eventually be created by the banking system from Jon's $300?

A1. Choose which of the following offerings you would prefer having. (Refer to the present value table on page 226.)

   a. $1,500 today or $2,000 in 5 years. The interest rate is 5%.

   b. $1,500 today or $2,000 in 5 years. The interest rate is 10%.

   c. $2,000 today or $10,000 in 10 years. The interest rate is 15%.

   d. $3,000 today or $10,000 in 15 years. The interest rate is 10%.

B1. A bond has a face value of $5,000 and a coupon rate of 10 percent. It is issued in 1997 and matures in 2006. Using this information, calculate the following:

   a.   What is the annual payment for that bond?

   b.   If the bond is currently selling for $6,000, what is its yield?

   c.   If the bond is currently selling for $4,000, what is its yield?

   d.   What do your answers to (b) and (c) tell you about what the bond must sell for, relative to its face value, if the interest rate is 10%? Rises above 10%? Falls below 10%?

B2. For each, state whether a financial asset has been created. What gives each financial asset created its value?

    a.   Your friend promises to pay you $5 tomorrow and expects nothing in return.

    b.   You buy an apple at the grocery store.

    c.   The government sells a new bond with a face value of $5,000, a coupon rate of 8%, and a maturity date of 2006.

    d.   A firm issues stock.

    e.   An existing stock is sold to another person on the stock market.

B3. For each of the following financial instruments, state for whom it is a liability and for whom it is an asset. Also state, if appropriate, whether the transaction occurred on the capital or money market and whether a financial asset was created.

    a.   First Bank grants a mortgage to David.

    b.   First Bank sells David's mortgage to Financial Services, Inc.

    c.   Broker McGuill sells existing stocks to client Debreu.

    d.   An investment broker sells 100 shares of new-issue stock to client Debreu.

e. U.S. government sells a new three-month T-bill to Corporation X.

f. Corporation X sells a 30-year government bond to Sally Quinn.

C1. Assume that Textland Bank Balance Sheet looks like this:

Assets		Liabilities	
Cash	30,000	Demand Deposits	150,000
Loans	300,000	Net Worth	350,000
Phys. Assets	170,000		
Total Assets	500,000	Total Liabilities and net worth	500,000

a. If the bank is not holding any excess reserves, what is the reserve ratio?

b. Show the first three steps in money creation using a balance sheet if Jane Foundit finds $20,000 in cash and deposits it at Textland.

Step #1

Step #2

Step #3

c.   After the first three steps, how much in excess reserves is the bank holding?

d.   Show Textland's balance sheet at the end of the money creation process.

D1. Assuming individuals hold 10% of their money in the form of cash, calculate the actual money multiplier for each of the following reserve requirements.

a.   15%

b.   30%

c.   60%

d.   80%

e.   100%

Multiple Choice Questions

1. For every financial asset
    a. there is a corresponding financial liability.
    b. there is a corresponding financial liability if the financial asset is financed.
    c. there is a real liability.
    d. there is a corresponding real asset.

2. Using economic terminology, when an individual buys a bond, that individual
    a. is investing.
    b. is saving.
    c. is buying a financial liability.
    d. is increasing that individual's equities.

3. Which of the following is not a function of money?
    a. Medium of exchange.
    b. Unit of account.
    c. Store of wealth.
    d. Equity instrument.

4. Rational individuals
    a. would hold no money, because it pays no interest.
    b. would prefer to change all their money into bonds, which pay interest.
    c. would prefer to hold all money and no bonds.
    d. would prefer a combination of bonds and money.

5. Which of the following is not included in the M_1 definition of money?
    a. checking accounts.
    b. currency.
    c. traveler's checks.
    d. savings accounts.

6. Which of the following components is not included in the M_2 definition of money?
    a. M_1.
    b. savings deposits.
    c. small-denomination time deposits.
    d. bonds.

7. In an advertisement for credit cards, the statement is made, "Think of a credit card as smart money." An economist's reaction to this would be
    a. a credit card is not money.
    b. a credit card is dumb money.
    c. a credit card is simply money.
    d. a credit card is actually better than money.

8. Using a credit card creates
    a. a financial liability for the holder and a financial asset for the issuer.
    b. a financial asset for the holder and a financial liability for the issuer.
    c. a financial liability for both the holder and issuer.
    d. a financial asset for both the holder and issuer.

9. Modern bankers
    a. focus on asset management.
    b. focus on liability management.
    c. focus equally on asset management and liability management.
    d. are unconcerned with asset and liability management and instead are concerned with how to make money.

10. Assuming individuals hold no cash, the reserve requirement is 20 percent, and banks keep no excess reserves, an increase in an initial $100 of money will cause an increase in total money of
    a. $20.
    b. $50.
    c. $100.
    d. $500.

11. Assuming individuals hold no cash, the reserve requirement is 10 percent, and banks keep no excess reserves, an increase in an initial $300 of money will cause an increase in total money of
    a. $30.
    b. $300.
    c. $3,000.
    d. $30,000.

12. Assuming the ratio of money people hold in cash to the money they hold in deposits is .3, and the reserve requirement is 20 percent, and that banks keep no excess reserves, an increase in an initial $100 of money will cause an increase in total money of _____. (Use the approximate real world money multiplier.)
    a. $50.
    b. $100.
    c. $200.
    d. $500.

13. If banks hold excess reserves whereas before they did not, the relative money multiplier
    a. will become larger.
    b. will become smaller.
    c. will be unaffected.
    d. might increase or might decrease.

14. A sound bank will
    a. always have money on hand to pay all depositors in full.
    b. never borrow short and lend long.
    c. never borrow long and lend short.
    d. keep enough money on hand to cover normal cash inflows and outflows.

15. FDIC is an acronym for
    a. major banks in the United States.
    b. major banks in the world.
    c. U.S. government program that guarantees deposits.
    d. types of financial instruments.

16. The textbook author's view of government guarantees of deposits is
    a. they don't make sense.
    b. stronger ones are needed.
    c. it depends.
    d. it should be a private guarantee program.

A1. If the interest rate falls, the value of a fixed interest rate bond
    a. rises.
    b. falls.
    c. remains the same.
    d. cannot be determined as to whether it rises or falls.

B1. A secondary financial market is a market in which
    a. minor stocks are sold.
    b. minor stocks and bonds are sold.
    c. previously issued financial assets can be sought and sold.
    d. small secondary mergers take place.

B2. If you are depositing money at a bank, the bank is likely
    a. an investment bank
    b. a commercial bank.
    c. a municipal bank.
    d. a government bank.

B3. Liquidity is
    a. a property of water stocks.
    b. the ability to turn an asset into cash quickly.
    c. the ability to turn an asset into liquid quickly.
    d. a property of over-the-counter markets.

B4. A financial market in which financial assets having a maturity of more than one year are bought and sold is called a
    a. money market.
    b. capital market.
    c. commercial paper market.
    d. commercial bank market.

B5. Two bonds, one a 30-year bond and the other a 1-year bond, have the same interest rate. If the interest rate in the economy falls, the value of the
    a. long-term bond rises by more than the value of the short-term bond rises.
    b. short-term bond rises by more than the value of the long-term bond rises.
    c. long-term bond falls by more than the value of the long-term bond falls.
    d. short-term bond falls by more than the value of the long-term bond falls.

C1. The demand deposits in a bank would go on
    a. the asset side of its balance sheet.
    b. the liabilities side of its balance sheet.
    c. the net worth part of its balance sheet.
    d. on both sides of its balance sheet.

C2. The cash that a bank holds would go on
    a. the asset side of its balance sheet.
    b. the liabilities side of its balance sheet.
    c. the net worth part of its balance sheet.
    d. on both sides of its balance sheet.

D1. Using the precise complex money market multiplier, determine how much total money will increase if there is an increase of $1,000 in high-powered money when people hold cash, c equals 20 percent, and r equals 30 percent.
    a. $1,200.
    b. $2,400.
    c. $2,600.
    d. $2,800.

D2. Using the precise complex money market multiplier, determine how much total money will increase if there is an increase of $1,000 in high-powered money when people hold cash, c equals 30 percent, and r equals 20 percent.
    a. $1,200.
    b. $2,400.
    c. $2,600.
    d. $2,800.

Answers

Short-answer questions

1. The financial sector is important to the business cycle because the financial sector channels the flow of savings out of the circular flow back into the circular flow either as consumer loans, business loans, or government loans. If the financial sector did not translate enough of the savings out of the spending stream back into the spending stream, output would decline and a recession might result. Likewise, if the financial sector increased flows into the spending stream (loans) that exceeded flows out of the spending stream (savings) an upturn or boom might result and inflation might rise. It is this role of the financial sector that Keynesians focused on to explain why production and expenditures might not be equal, resulting in fluctuations in output. (208-209).

2. In one sense your friend is right; cash is money. But money is more than just cash. Money is a highly liquid financial asset that is accepted in exchange for other goods and is used as a reference in valuing other goods. It includes such things as CDs and traveler's checks. (209-210)

3. The first friend has described money as a medium of exchange. The second has described money as a unit of account. And the third has described money as a store of wealth. These are the three functions of money. There are no others. (210-212)

4. The two most liquid definitions of money are M_1 and M_2. M_1 consists of currency, checking accounts, and traveler's checks. M_2 consists of M_1 plus savings deposits, small-denomination time deposits, money market mutual funds, and a few esoteric financial instruments not discussed in the text. (213)

5. The broadest measure of money is L. L consists of almost all short-term financial assets. (213-214)

6. No, banks do not hold all their deposits in the vault. They keep a small percentage of it for normal withdrawal needs and lend the remainder out. This maintenance of checking accounts is the essence of how banks create money. You count your deposits as money since you can write checks against them and the money that is lent out from bank deposits is counted as money. Aha! The bank has created money. (215-219)

7. The equation for the simple money multiplier is $(1/r)$ where r is the reserve ratio. Plugging in the values into the equation, we see that the money multiplier is 5, so the money supply increases by $500. (218)

8. The equation for the approximate real-world money multiplier is $1/(r+c)$ where r is the reserve ratio and c is the ratio of cash to deposits. Plugging the values into the equation, we see that the money multiplier is 2, so the money supply increases by $200. (219-220)

9. Just as price equlibrates supply and demand in the real sector, interest rates equilibrate supply and demand for savings. The supply of savings comes out of the spending stream. The financial sector transforms those savings back into the spending stream in the form of loans that are then used to purchase consumer or capital goods. (208-209)

10. If everyone lost their trust in banks, a financial panic could occur. The bank holds only a small portion of total deposits as reserves so that if everyone withdraws their money, the bank cannot meet its promises. (222-221)

11. The potential problem with government guarantees to prevent bank-withdrawal panics is that guarantees might lead to unsound lending and investment practices by banks. Also, depositors have less of a reason to monitor the practices of their banks. (222)

Word Scramble   1. reserves   2. money   3. reserve ratio

Match the Terms and Concepts to Their Definitions

1-h; 2-g; 3-n; 4-k; 5-l; 6-a; 7-f; 8-d; 9-c; 10-m; 11-j; 12-b; 13-i; 14-e.

Problems and Exercises

1. a. M_2. (213)
   b. M_2. (213)
   c. Both. (213)
   d. Neither. (213)
   e. Both. (213)

2. a. 6.67. multiplier = (1/.15). (218)
   b. 3.33. multiplier = (1/.30). (218)
   c. 1.67. multiplier = (1/.6). (218)
   d. 1.25. multiplier = (1/.8). (218)
   e. 1. multiplier = (1/1). (218)

3. a. 4 = 1/(.10+.15). (220)
   b. 2.5 = 1/(.1+ .3). (220)
   c. 1.43 = 1/(.1+ .6). (220)
   d. 1.11 = 1/(.1+ .8). (220)
   e. 0.91. In reality a multiplier less than one would be highly unlikely. Recall that this is the approximate real-world multiplier. In Appendix D the precise complex multiplier is given. See pages 242-244.

4. a. $270. (217-219)
   b. $570: the initial $300 in new deposits plus .9×300 in loans that are then deposited. (217-219)
   c. 10: 1/r = 1/.1. (217-219)
   d. $3,000: money multiplier×initial deposit = 10×300. (217-219)

A1. Using the table to calculate the present value of $100 to be received in the future, we find that the better value is
   a. $2,000 in 5 years, valued today at $1,568. (226)
   b. $1,500 today. $2,000 in 5 years when the interest rate is 10% is worth only $1,242 today. (26)
   c. $10,000 in 10 years, valued at $2,470 when the interest rate is 15%. (226)
   d. $3,000 today. $10,000 in 15 years when the interest rate is 10% is worth only $2,390 today. (226)

B1.a. The annual payment for that bond is $5,000×.10 = $500 annually. (237-238)
   b. If the bond is currently selling for $6,000, its yield is $500/$6,000 = 8.3%. (237-238)
   c. If the bond is currently selling for $4,000, its yield is $500/$4,000 = 12.5%. (237-238)
   d. My answers to (b) and (c) tell me that the bond must sell for its face value if interest rate is 10%, less than face value if interest rates rise above 10%, and more than face value if interest rates fall below 10%. (237-238)

B2.a. A financial asset has been created. Your friend's promise to pay you $5 is what gives that asset its value. (228)
   b. No, a financial asset has not been created, although a financial transaction did occur. (228)
   c. Yes, a financial asset has been created. The government's promises to pay you $5,000 at maturity and $400 each year until then are what give that asset its value. (228)
   d. Yes, a financial asset has been created. A claim to future profits is what gives that asset its value. (228)
   e. No, a financial asset has not been created. The financial asset already existed. (228)

B3.a. The mortgage is an asset for First Bank and a liability for David. The transaction occurred on the capital market. A financial asset was created. (228-232)
   b. The mortgage is an asset for Financial Services, Inc., and a liability for David. The transaction occurred on the capital market. A financial asset was not created. (228-232)
   c. The stocks are an asset for client Debreu and a liability for the broker's firm. The transaction occurred on the capital market. A financial asset was not created. (228-232)
   d. The stocks are an asset for client Debreu and a liability for the firm. The transaction occurred on the capital market. A financial asset was created. (228-232)
   e. The T-bill is a liability for the U.S. government and an asset for Corporation X. The transaction occurred on the money market. A financial asset was created. (228-232)
   f. The bond is a liability for the U.S. government and an asset for Sally Quinn. The transaction occurred on the capital market. A financial asset was not created. (228-232)

C1.a. .2: cash/deposits = 30,000/150,000. (242-244)
   b. Step 1: Increase of $20,000 in demand deposits and cash:

Assets		Liabilities	
Cash	30,000	Demand Deposits	150,000
Cash from Jane	20,000	Jane's deposit	20,000
Total cash	50,000	Total deposits	170,000
Loans	300,000	Net Worth	350,000
Phys. Assets	170,000		
Total Assets	520,000	Total Liabilities and net worth	520,000

Step 2: Assuming the reserve ratio is .2 as calculated in (a), the bank can now lend out 80% of the $20,000 received in cash. It lends $16,000 to Sherry: (242-244)

Assets		Liabilities	
Cash	50,000	Demand Deposits	170,000
Cash to Sherry	16,000		
Total cash	34,000		
Begin. Loans	300,000	Net Worth	350,000
Loan to Sherry	16,000		
Total loans	316,000		
Phys. Assets	170,000		
Total Assets	520,000	Total Liabilities and net worth	520,000

Step 3: Sherry uses the loan to purchase a car from John. John deposits the cash in the bank (242-244):

Assets		Liabilities	
Cash	34,000	Demand Deposits	170,000
Cash from John	16,000	Deposit from John	16,000
Total cash	50,000	Total Deposits	186,000
Begin. Loans	316,000	Net Worth	350,000
Phys. Assets	170,000		
Total Assets		536,000 Total Liabilities and net worth	536,000

c. The bank is holding $12,800 in excess reserves. Required reserves for $186,000 in deposits is .2*186,000 = $37,200. The bank has $50,000 in reserves, $12,800 higher than required. (242-244)

d. The ending balance sheet will look like this (242-244):

Assets		Liabilities	
Cash	50,000	Demand Deposits	250,000
Loans	380,000	Net Worth	350,000
Phys. Assets	170,000		
Total Assets	600,000	Total Liabilities and net worth	600,000

D1. We use the equation from the money multiplier found in Appendix D. (242-244)

a. $4.4 = (1+.1)/(.1+.15)$.   b. $2.75 = (1+.1)/(.1+.30)$.   c. $1.57 = (1+.1)/(.1+.60)$.

d. $1.22 = (1+.1)/(.1+.80)$.   e. $1 = (1+.1)/(.1+1.00)$.

Multiple Choice Questions

1. a. The very fact that it is a financial asset means that it had a financial liability, so the qualifier in b is unnecessary. See pages 208-209.

2. b. In economic terminology, buying a financial asset, which is what buying a bond is, is a form of saving. Investing occurs when a firm or an individual buys a real asset. See page 209.

3. d. See pages 210-211.

4. d. Even though money does not pay interest, it is useful as a medium of exchange. Thus, only d is acceptable. See page 210.

5. d. See page 213 and Exhibit 2 on page 214.

6. d. See page 213 and Exhibit 2 on page 214.

7. a. A credit card is not money and thus a would be the best answer. A credit card replaces money, making the same amount of money able to handle many more transactions. See page 214.

8. a. One is borrowing money when one uses a credit card, thereby incurring a financial liability. See page 214.

9. c. As discussed on page 215, banks are concerned with both asset management and liability management. The second part of answer d is obviously true, but it's through management of assets and liabilities that they make money, so the first part is wrong.

10. d. The simple money multiplier is $1/r=1/.2=5$, which gives an increase in total money of $500. See page 218.

11. c. The simple money multiplier is $1/r=1/.1=10$ which gives an increase of total money of $3,000. See page 218.

12. c. The approximate real-world money multiplier is $1/(r+c)=1/.5=2$, which gives an increase in total money of $200. See pages 219-220.

13. b. Holding excess reserves would be the equivalent to increasing the reserve requirement, which would decrease the multiplier. See pages 217-218.

14. d. Banks earn income by managing their assets and liabilities. To follow any policy other than d would cost them income. See page 217.

15. c. FDIC stands for Federal Deposit Insurance Corporation. See page 221.

16. c. For this textbook author, just about everything depends; you can't get him to take a firm position on anything. See page 223.

A1. a. The present value formula tells us that the value on any fixed interest rate bond varies inversely with the interest rate in the economy. See page 226.

B1. c. See page 230.

B2. b. Investment banks don't take deposits, and who knows what the last two types of banks are; we certainly don't. See page 229.

B3. b. Answers a and c are total gifts to you — water stocks; give us a break — and it's unclear what d means. The b option is the definition given on page 231.

B4. b. See page 232.

B5. a. Since bond values vary inversely with interest rate changes, the answer must be a or b. Judging between a and b will be hard for you at this point unless you have studied present value in another course. However, based on the discussion in the text on pages 237 and 238, you can deduce that since a long-term bond is not paid back for a long time, it will be much more strongly affected by interest rate changes.

C1. b. Demand deposits at banks are liabilities for those banks and hence go on the liability side. (241)

C2. a. The cash that banks hold is an asset for them; hence it goes on the asset side. See page 240.

D1. b. The precise complex money multiplier is $(1+c)/(r+c)$ or $1.2/.5 = 2.4$, so the increase in total money is $2,400. See pages 242-243.

D2. c. The precise complex money multiplier is $(1+c)/(r+c)$ or $1.3/.5 = 2.6$, so the increase in total money is $2,600. See pages 242-243.

Chapter 10:
The Modern Macroeconomic Debate

Chapter at a glance

1. The historical development of macro has involved a debate between laissez-faire and activist economists. Laissez-faire economists oppose government intervention. Activist economists generally favor government intervention. (247)

   Laissez-faire economists are sometimes referred to as Classical economists and activist economists are sometimes referred to as Keynesian economists. However, don't overemphasize the difference between these two camps. There is more agreement among them than disagreement. Moreover, few economists today fall solidly into either camp.

2. Say's Law—supply creates its own demand. (248)

   Say's law implies that any savings (leakage out of the spending stream—the circular flow of spending) would be re-injected back into the spending stream in the form of investment by businesses. Therefore, underspending is very unlikely and there would be no change in the level of economic activity. Moreover, if wages (and prices) are allowed to adjust, any unemployment would not last long because real wages would fall. This Classical reasoning implies there is virtually no role for government in the economy—Classicals advocate a laissez-faire approach.

   The 2 pillars of the Classical Model are:
   1. *Say's Law, and*
   2. *The Quantity Theory of Money:*
   (Say's law analysis determines real output and the quantity theory determines the price level)

   According to Clasicals: MV=PQ
   a) *Velocity (V) is constant*
   b) *Real output (Q) is independent of the money supply (M). Moreover, Q is relatively constant and would exist at full employment (potential Q) because of flexible wages and prices*
   c) *Causation runs from M to P (an increase in M causes an increase in P)*

   ✔ *Therefore, $\overset{\Uparrow}{M}\overline{V} = \overset{\Uparrow}{P}\overline{Q}$.*
   The experience of the Great Depression cast much doubt on the Classical Theory. Keynesian analysis began gaining favor.

   Keynesians argue:
   a) *There is no guaranteed equality between savings and investment (the leakages and injections in the spending stream)*
   b) *Given the institutional realities of relatively fixed prices and wages if people stopped spending as much, firms would decrease their production, creating some unemployment, which would cause a further decline in spending, production, and still more unemployment...*

   ✔ *Therefore, government should increase its spending or cut taxes (fiscal policy), or increase the money supply (monetary policy) to combat unemployment. Keynesians argue for activist government policy.*

3a. The slope of the AED curve is determined by the international effect and the wealth effect (among others) and the repercussions these effects cause. (254)

   As the price level falls, the cash people hold is worth more, making people richer, so they buy more (wealth effect). Also, as the price level in the United States falls (assuming the exchange rate does not change), the price of U.S. goods relative to foreign goods goes down. U.S. exports increase and U.S. imports decrease. That is, the quantity of U.S. goods demanded rises (the international effect). Repercussions of these effects are called multiplier effects (and make the AED curve flatter than otherwise).

3b. Five important initial shift factors of the AED curve are: (256)

   1. Changes in foreign income.
   A rise in foreign income leads to an increase in U.S. exports and an increase (outward shift) of the U.S. AED curve.

   2. Changes in expectations.
   Positive (optimistic) expectations about the future state of the economy could cause an outward shift of the AED curve.

   3. Changes in exchange rates.
   A decrease in the value of the dollar relative to other currencies shifts the AED curve outward to the right.

4. Changes in the distribution of income.
Typically, as the real wage increases, the AED curve increases (shifts out).

5. Changes in government aggregate demand policy.
Expansionary macro policy (an increase in government spending and/or a decrease in taxes—fiscal policy; or an increase in the money supply—monetary policy) increases the AED curve, shifting it outward to the right.

✔ *Note: Anything that affects autonomous components of aggregate expenditures (AE or "total spending") is a shift factor of AED (aggregate equilibrium demand). (Recall that AE = C + I + G + X − M). These components are autonomous consumption (C), investment (I), government spending (G), and net exports (X − M). Any change in these components of total spending is multiplied by the multiplier effect shifting the AED curve by a multiple of the original change in spending.*

4a. The AS path has three ranges: (260)

1. A fixed-price range,
The flat (horizontal) portion; often referred to as "Range A" or the "Keynesian range."

2. A partially flexible price range, and
The upward sloping portion; often referred to as "Range B" or the "intermediate range." Most economists see the economy in this range.

3. A perfectly flexible price range.
The vertical portion; often referred to as "Range C" or the "Classical range."

These ranges are determined by empirical observations.

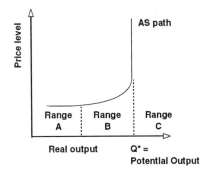

4b. The horizontal portion of the AS path can shift up or down due to nominal price level shocks. The vertical portion of the AS path can shift left or right due to changes in productive capacity. (263)

Anything which significantly increases (decreases) costs of production or prices of goods will shift the horizontal (and upward sloping) portion of the AS path upward (downward). An increase (decrease) in perceived or actual productive capacity shifts the vertical portion of the AS path to the right (left).

5. Activist Keynesians see the economy in the fixed-price range of the AS path. Laissez-faire Classicals see the economy in the perfectly-flexible range of the AS path. (262)

Most economists are somewhere between committed Keynesians and committed Classicals; they see the economy in the intermediate range—Range B, where real output changes some, and the price level changes some as the AED curve shifts.

6. Shifts in aggregate equilibrium demand and the aggregate supply path can affect the price level and real output. How it does so depends upon the shift as well as where the economy is before the shift. (267)

Start at some point of intersection between the AED curve and the AS path. Given a shift of either the AED curve or AS path, simply find the new point of intersection. However, note that any initial change in the AED curve is magnified because of the multiplier effect. The impact on P and Q depends on which range of the AS path we started in and the extent of the shift. ("Problems and Applications" exercise #3 allows you to practice some of this.)

7. Knowing where potential output is and dealing with structural change are just two reasons why macro policy is more complicated that the model makes it look. (268)

We have no way of precisely determining for sure what range the economy is in, or precisely where the correct target level of potential output is, and therefore of precisely knowing by how much we should shift the AED curve (with the use of macro—fiscal and monetary—policy). Hence, the debate between Keynesians and Classicals can be expected to remain quite lively. However, most economists are neither committed Keynesians nor committed Classicals and therefore see the economy in the intermediate range.

See also, Appendix A: "The Foundations of the Macro Policy Model."

Short-answer questions

1. What was the main difference between Classical and Keynesian economists? (LO1)

2. How does the Keynesian explanation of the Great Depression differ from the Classical explanation? (LO1)

3. What is Say's law and what is the reasoning behind Say's law? (LO2)

4. What is the quantity theory of money? (LO2)

5. What effects determine the slope of the AED curve? (LO3)

6. List some of the important initial shift factors of the AED curve. (LO3)

7. Define the aggregate supply path. What the three ranges of the AS path? (LO4)

8. What will shift the horizontal portion of the AS path up or down? What shifts the vertical portion of the AS path right or left. (LO4)

9. Why do Keynesians believe that activist policies are effective while Classicals believe they are not? Explain using the macro policy model. (LO5)

10. Show graphically the effect of increased government expenditure on real output when the economy is in the fixed price-level range and when it is in the perfectly flexible price-level range of the AS path. (LO6)

11. State two reasons why the macro policy model is more complicated than the model makes it look. (LO7)

Word Scramble

1. _____ _____ _____   2. _____ _____   3. _____ _____
   g a r e t g a g e   u l p y s p   a t p h   c a r o m   l y o i p c   d m l o e   y ' s S a   a w l.

Match the Terms and Concepts to Their Definitions

____1. aggregate equilibrium demand curve

____2. aggregate supply path

____3. disinflation

____4. equilibrium income

____5. international effect

____6. macro policy model

____7. multiplier effect

____8. potential income

____9. quantity-adjusting markets

____10. quantity theory of money

____11. real business cycle theory

____12. real wage

____13. Say's law

____14. structural readjustment

____15. wealth effect

a. Supply creates its own demand.
b. Phenomenon of the economy trying to change from what it had been doing to doing something new, not to repeat what it did in the past.
c. The level of income that the economy technically is capable of producing without generating accelerating inflation.
d. A curve that shows how a change in the price level will change aggregate equilibrium demand after all the dynamic interactive effects between production and expenditures are taken into account.
e. All changes in the economy are real shifts—shifts in potential income—that reflect real causes such as technological changes or shifting tastes.
f. Markets in which firms modify their supply to bring about equilibrium instead of changing prices.
g. A curve that tells us how changes in aggregate equilibrium demand will be split between real output changes and price level changes.
h. The level of income toward which the economy gravitates in the short run because of the cumulative circles of increasing and decreasing production.
i. Model that demonstrates the effects of macro policy on output and prices.
j. Wage level relative to the price level.
k. As the price level falls, people are richer, so they buy more.
l. As the price level in a country falls the quantity of that country's goods demanded by foreigners and residents will increase.
m. Repercussions that the change in aggregate expenditures has on production and subsequently on income and expenditures.
n. The price level varies in response to changes in the quantity of money.
o. A fall in the rate at which the price level is rising.

Problems and Exercises

1. State the equation of exchange. With that equation answer the following questions:

   a. GDP is $2,000, the money supply is 200. What is the velocity of money?

   b. The velocity of money is 5.60, the money supply is $1,100 billion. What is nominal output?

    c.   Assuming velocity is constant and the money supply increases by 6%, by how much does nominal output rise?

2.   What will likely happen to the shape or position of the *AED* curve in the following circumstances?

    a.   A rise in the price level does not make people feel poorer.

    b.   Income is redistributed from poor people to rich people.

    c.   The country's currency depreciates.

    d.   The exchange rate changes from fixed to flexible.

    e.   Expectations of future rises in the price level develop without any current change in the price level.

3.   State what range of the aggregate supply path you think the economy is in, given the following information:

    a.   The economy is significantly below potential. Downward shifts in aggregate equilibrium demand do not result in falls in the price level.

    b.   Increases in aggregate equilibrium demand result in little change in real output and large increases in the price level.

c.   Increases in aggregate equilibrium demand seem to be split roughly equally between increases in real output and increases in the price level.

4.   Graphically demonstrate the effect of each of the following on the position of the *AS* curve. Be sure to label all axes.

a.   Businesses find that they are able to produce more output without having to pay more wages nor increase their costs of capital.

b.   A severe snow storm paralyzes most of the United States.

c.   The country's currency appreciates dramatically.

5.   What will happen to the position of the *AS* path in the following circumstances?

a.   Available inputs fall.

b.   A hurricane destroys productive capital.

c.   The relative price of oil drops by half.

6.   The government of Germany wants to expand its economy through increased spending. Show the likely effects of an activist policy in the following three cases.

a.   Economists believe that the economy is in the fixed price-level range.

b.   There are some supply bottlenecks appearing in the economy and most economists think the economy is in the partially flexible price-level range.

c.   Most economists think that the high unemployment figures in Germany reflect structural unemployment.

7.   The Japanese economy has some supply bottlenecks and most economists think it is operating in the partially flexible price-level range on the aggregate supply path. Now suppose the Japanese yen appreciates.

a.   If there is no inflation in the Japanese economy (any shift in the AED is deflationary) what would the likely equilibrium price and output level be after the appreciation?

b.   If there has been inflation in the Japanese economy (any shift in the AED is disinflationary) what would the likely equilibrium price and output level be after the appreciation?

A1.   Show the difference between the Classical and the Keynesian adjustment mechanism if the aggregate equilibrium demand falls.

Multiple Choice Questions

1.   Classical economists
   a. generally favor government intervention.
   b. generally oppose government intervention.
   c. believe the economy is primarily directed by the invisible handshake.
   d. think unions are not responsible for unemployment.

2.   Say's law states that
   a. demand creates its own supply.
   b. supply creates its own demand.
   c. supply and demand are not related.
   d. there is no such thing as a free lunch.

3. When people save, Say's law
   a. is invalidated.
   b. remains true because saving has nothing to do with Say's law.
   c. remains true as long as saving is translated back into investment.
   d. is false because saving creates unemployment.

4. Classical economists believed all the following except
   a. frictional unemployment could exist.
   b. structural unemployment could exist.
   c. cyclical unemployment could be caused by a shortage of aggregate demand.
   d. cyclical unemployment could be caused by inflexible wages.

5. The equation of exchange is
   a. $MP = VQ$.
   b. $MQ = VP$.
   c. $MV = PQ$.
   d. $PV = QM$.

6. In its simplest terms, the quantity theory of money states that
   a. the price level varies in response to changes in the quantity of money.
   b. the equation of exchange is true.
   c. if you count the money you can tell how much unemployment there will be.
   d. the only function of money is as a medium of exchange.

7. If $M = 200$, $V = 4$, P = 2, then $Q =$ _____.
   a. 50.
   b. 100.
   c. 200.
   d. 400.

8. Classical economists believed the equation of exchange should be read from
   a. left to right.
   b. right to left.
   c. top to bottom.
   d. bottom to top.

9. To move from the equation of exchange to the quantity theory, all the following assumptions are needed
   except
   a. Velocity is constant.
   b. Real output is independent of the money supply.
   c. Causation goes from money supply to prices.
   d. Velocity varies in relation to the change in the money supply.

10. The Classical economists' solution to the Great Depression was
    a. reduce the wage rate.
    b. increase aggregate demand.
    c. increase the money supply.
    d. decrease the money supply.

11. Keynes's major problem with the Classical model was that
    a. it focused too much on money.
    b. it was a short-run model.
    c. it lacked a reasonable disequilibrium adjustment mechanism.
    d. it would assume the price level constant.

12. A decrease in foreign income
    a. would likely shift the United States' AED in.
    b. would likely shift the United States' AED out.
    c. would likely make the United States' AED flatter.
    d. would likely make the United States' AED steeper.

13. Suppose there is an increase in the expected future prices in the U.S. This would likely
    a. shift the AED in.
    b. shift the AED out.
    c. make the AED flatter.
    d. make the AED steeper.

14. In the middle of 1985, the value of the Japanese yen rose. This likely:
    a. shifted its AED in.
    b. shifted its AED out.
    c. made its AED flatter.
    d. made its AED steeper.

15. The aggregate supply path is
    a. another name for the short-run aggregate supply curve.
    b. another name for the long-run aggregate supply curve.
    c. a curve based upon institutional realities.
    d. another name for the aggregate demand curve.

16. If the economy is significantly below its potential output, the aggregate supply path is generally considered to be
    a. flat.
    b. upward sloping.
    c. backward sloping.
    d. perfectly vertical.

17. If the economy is at its highest potential output, the aggregate supply path is generally considered to be
    a. flat.
    b. upward sloping.
    c. backward sloping.
    d. perfectly vertical.

18. The Keynesian range of the aggregate supply path is
    a. horizontal.
    b. vertical.
    c. upward sloping.
    d. backward bending.

19. Germany has some of the world's highest wage rates. It also has nationwide unions. If the government managed to lower labor wages by 12 percent, the aggregate supply path in Germany would likely:
    a. move right.
    b. move left.
    c. move up.
    d. move down.

20. A major technological improvement would likely cause the aggregate supply path of a country to:
    a. move right.
    b. move left.
    c. move up.
    d. move down.

21. Assuming the interdependency between expenditure and production decisions discussed in the text exists, if the economy is in the fixed price-level range and there is an increase in aggregate expenditures, aggregate output will
    a. increase by a multiple of the shift.
    b. decrease by a multiple of the shift.
    c. remain the same.
    d. increase by the amount of the shift.

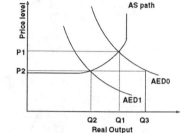

22. Suppose the AED curve shifted in from AED_0 to AED_1. If there had been inflation and the price level axis is interpreted as inflation relative to expectations, i.e., the shift was disinflationary, the resulting price and output level would be at:
    a. P_1, Q_1.
    b. P_2, Q_1.
    c. P_2, Q_2.
    d. P_1, Q_3.

23. When an economy is in Range B of the aggregate supply path, policy making is difficult because:
    a. output cannot be increased by government action.
    b. output can be increased but the cost is price-level stability.
    c. it is impossible to reach potential output or Range C.
    d. trying to do anything might put the economy on a downward spiral.

A1. If a country changes from fixed to flexible exchange rates, one would expect the aggregate demand curve to be
    a. flatter.
    b. unaffected.
    c. steeper.
    d. backward sloping.

A2. If the price level changes one would expect
    a. the aggregate demand curve to shift to the right.
    b. the aggregate demand curve to shift to the left.
    c. the aggregate demand curve to remain unchanged.
    d. the aggregate demand curve to become flatter.

A3. The AED curve includes which of the following that the AD curve does not?
    a. the wealth effect.
    b. the price-level interest rate effect.
    c. the multiplier effect.
    d. the international effect.

A4. The graph to the right shows the first two interactive shifts in the Keynesian AS/AD model. As a result of a decline in aggregate demand, the final Keynesian equilibrium will be at point:
    a. A.
    b. B.
    c. C.
    d. None of the above.

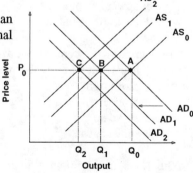

Answers

Short-Answer Questions

1. Classical economists opposed government intervention in the economy whereas Keynesian economists advocated it. (247)

2. Classical economists focused on the real wage. They explained that unemployment would decline if the real wage were allowed to decline. Political and social forces were keeping the real wage to high. Keynesians focused on insufficient aggregate expenditures that resulted in a downward spiral. The economy was at a below-potential-income equilibrium. (247-252)

3. Say's Law states that supply creates its own demand. According to Say's Law people work because they want goods; thus supply creates its own demand. Even if people save, supply still creates its own demand because savings leads to investment. (248-249)

4. The quantity theory of money holds that increases in the money supply cause increases in the price level, and that real output is independent of the money supply and hence the price level. (249-250)

5. The wealth effect, the international effect, and the repercussions these effects cause, i.e., the multiplier effect, determine the slope of the AED curve. (253-254, 256)

6. Five important initial shift factors of the AED curve are: 1. Changes in the world income. 2. Changes in expectations. 3. Changes in exchange rates. 4. Changes in the distribution of income. 5. Changes in government aggregate demand policy. (256)

7. The aggregate supply path is a curve that tells us how changes in aggregate equilibrium demand will be split between real output changes and price level changes. Its three ranges are the fixed price-level range, the partially flexible price-level range, and the perfectly flexible price-level range. (260)

8. The horizontal portion of the AS path could shift up or down due to nominal price level shocks. The vertical portion of the AS path could shift right or left due to changes in actual or perceived productive capacity. (264)

9. Activist Keynesians see the economy in the fixed price-level range of the aggregate supply path. So, the economy can be expanded through activist policies without causing any change in the price level. The Classicals believe the economy to be in the perfectly flexible price-level range of the aggregate supply path. Activist policies would only succeed in changing the price level. Real output would remain unchanged. (262)

10.

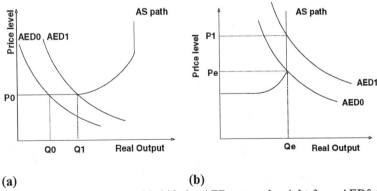

(a)   (b)

Increased government expenditures would shift the AED out to the right from AED0 to AED1 in (a). In the fixed price-level range, the price level would remain the same at P0 but real output would increase from Q0 to Q1. In the perfectly flexible price-level range, the real output would remain unchanged at Qe but the price level would rise from Pe to P1 in (b). (267)

11. Knowing where the potential output of the economy is and coping with structural changes in the economy are two reasons why the macro policy model becomes very complicated. (268)

Word Scramble   1. aggregate supply path   2. macro policy model.   3. Say's law.

Match the Terms and Concepts to Their Definitions

1-d; 2-g; 3-o; 4-h; 5-l; 6-i; 7-m; 8-c; 9-f; 10-n; 11-e; 12-j; 13-a; 14-b; 15-k.

Problems and Exercises

1. $MV = PQ$ where M = quantity of money, V = velocity of money, P = price level, Q = quantity of real output. (249)
   a. $V = 10$: $MV = PQ$; $200V = \$2,000$; $V = 10$. (249)
   b. \$6,160 billion: $MV = PQ$; $(5.6)(1,100) = \$6,160$ billion. (249)
   c. By 6%.

2. a. This would cause the wealth effect to become inoperative and the AED curve will become steeper. (254)
   b. Assuming the marginal propensity to consume of rich people is less than that of poor people, the AED curve will shift to the left. (257)
   c. As the exchange rate depreciates, exports will rise and imports will fall. This shifts the AED curve out. (257)
   d. If the exchange rate were originally assumed to be fixed and became flexible, increases in the price level will be offset by changes in the exchange rate and the international effect becomes inoperative. The *AED* curve will be steeper. (257)
   e. Expectations of future price increases without changes in the current price level will tend to cause the *AED* curve to shift to the right. (256)

3. a. Fixed price-level range. (260-261)
   b. Upwardly flexible price-level range. (260-261)
   c. Partially flexible price-level range. (260-261)

4.

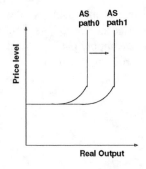 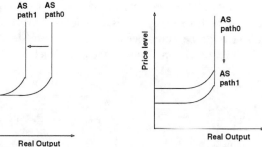

(a)   (b)   (c)

   a. The aggregate supply path shown in (a) shifts to the right from AS path0 to AS path1, because businesspeople are finding that their productive capacity is larger than they had thought. (263-264)
   b. The aggregate supply path shown in (b) shifts to the left from AS path0 to AS path1 because bad weather will hinder production. (263-264)
   c. The aggregate supply path shown in (c) above shifts down from AS path0 to AS path1, because businesses will benefit from the declining import prices to the extent that imports are used in production. The fall in input prices is passed through to the goods market. (263-264)

5. a. A decrease in available inputs shifts the *AS* path to the left. (263-264)
   b. Destruction of productive capital and will cause a shift in the AS path to the left. (263-264)
   c. Initially, to the degree that the fall in the relative price of oil causes the price level to fall, the AS path will shift down. (263-264)

6.

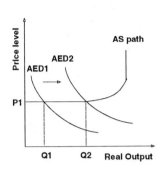

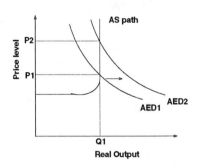

(a)   (b)   (c)

a. The economy is in the fixed price-level range of the aggregate supply path as shown in (a) above. As the AED curve shifts out, the price level remains unchanged at P1, and output increases to Q2. Government activism in this range is very effective. (263-267)

b. The economy is in the partially flexible price-level range of the aggregate supply path as shown in (b) above. As the AED curve shifts out, the price level rises from P1 to P2 and output increases from Q1 to Q2. Government activism in this range is less effective than in Range A. In this range, real output rises by less than in (a) and the economy experiences some demand-pull inflation. (263-267)

c. The economy is in the perfectly flexible price-level range of the aggregate supply path as shown in (c) above. As the AED curve shifts out, the output remains unchanged at Q1 and only the price level increases from P1 to P2. Government activism in this range is ineffective. (263-267)

7. a. The exchange rate appreciation will shift the AED curve back from AED1 to AED2. If there is no inflation in the economy the price level will remain fixed at P1 and output will fall to Q3. (263-267)

b. In this case, we interpret the vertical axis as a deviation from the expected rate of inflation. If there is inflation in the economy the price level relative to expected inflation will fall to P2 and output will fall only to Q2. (263-267)

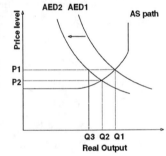

A1.   In the Keynesian model, effective aggregate demand and aggregate supply are interdependent and the AS path is assumed flat. The shift in demand causes a shift in supply and the shift in supply causes a shift in demand. Since the price level is assumed constant, the adjustment path is along arrow A in graph (a) below. In the Classical model, aggregate demand and supply are not interdependent and wages and the price level are flexible. A drop in demand will lead to a fall in prices while output remains constant as shown in graph (b) below. (277-278)

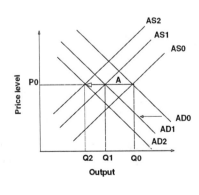

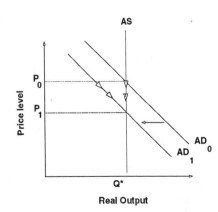

(a)   (b)

Multiple Choice Questions

1. b. See page 247.

2. b. See page 248.

3. c. See pages 249, especially Exhibit 2. The financial sector translates savings into investment.

4. c. See page 249.

5. c. See page 249.

6. a. The correct answer is the definition given in the text on page 249. The "equation of exchange" is a tautology and is true by definition; thus b can't be an answer. The quantity theory of money adds assumptions about the variables in the equation of exchange.

7. d. Since $MV=PQ$; 200 times 4 equals 800, so Q equals 800 divided by 2 or 400. See page 249.

8. a. By reading it from left to right they saw changes in the money supply *causing* changes in prices. See page 250.

9. d. Velocity is constant in the quantity theory. See page 250.

10. a. See page 250. They knew this was unpopular, but it was what their theory said.

11. c. As discussed on pages 251-252, Keynes felt the Classicals had no reasonable explanation of how the aggregate economy adjusted to equilibrium.

12. a. A decrease in foreign income would mean that foreign countries would import less from the U.S., shifting its AED in. See page 256.

13. b. An increase in expected future prices would mean that people would tend to buy more immediately instead of waiting to buy. This would likely shift the AED out. See pages 256-257.

14. a. A rise in the exchange rates would decrease exports and increase imports. This likely shifted the AED in. See page 257.

15. c. See page 258, including Exhibit 4.

16. a. See page 260.

17. d. See page 261.

18. a. See Exhibit 6, page 261.

19. d. Because of the nominal price fall, the aggregate supply path is likely to move down. See page 263.

20. a. Because productive capacity would increase, the aggregate supply path would shift to the right. See pages 263-264.

21. a. Since the price level wouldn't change at all at this range, an increase in aggregate equilibrium demand will cause aggregate output to increase by a multiple of the shift of the initial change in aggregate expenditures. See pages 266-267.

22. c. The deviation from expected inflation will fall to P_2 and the output will fall to Q_2. See pages 265-266.

23. b. Expansionary activist policy could increase income, but the price level will rise as this happens. See page 266

A1. c. The change from fixed to flexible exchange rate means that the international effect is reduced. Since the international effect is one of the reasons the AD curve slopes downward, its elimination makes the AD curve steeper. See pages 273-274.

A2. c. The change in the price level causes a movement along the existing AD curve; it does not change the slope or the position of the aggregate demand curve. See pages 272-273.

A3. c. The AED curve takes into account the interactive effects between aggregate supply and demand. See page 274.

A4. d. According to Keynes the shifts in the effective aggregate demand and the effective aggregate supply curve would continue beyond point C because of the interdependencies between expenditures and production. See pages 277-278.

Chapter 11:
The Macro Debate in Reference to the Aggregate Production/Aggregate Expenditures Model

Chapter at a glance

1. Autonomous expenditures are unrelated to income; induced expenditures are directly related to income. (284)

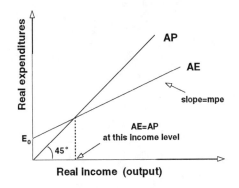

E_0 (autonomous expenditures) can change (shift the AE curve) if there is an autonomous change in any component of aggregate expenditures (AE).

Note: $AE = C + I + G + (X - M)$.

2. To determine income graphically in the Keynesian AP/AE model, you find the income level at which aggregate expenditures equal aggregate production. (287)

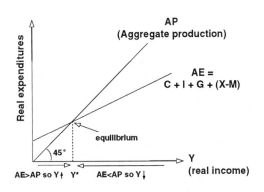

3. To determine income using the Keynesian equation you determine the multiplier and multiply it by the level of autonomous expenditures (289)

$Multiplier = 1/(1 - mpe) = 1/mpw.$
$Y = (multiplier)(Autonomous\ expenditures)$
$\Delta Y = (multiplier)(\Delta Autonomous\ expenditures)$

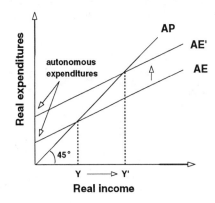

4. The multiplier process works because when expenditures don't equal production, businesspeople change planned production, which changes income, which changes expenditures, which.... (289)

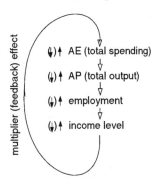

✔ This is the income adjustment process—the multiplier effect on income given a change in spending.

5a. A mechanistic Keynesian model sees the model as a direct guide for policy; it tells you what policy to follow. An interpretive Keynesian model sees the model as a guide to one's common sense; highlighting important dynamic interdependencies. Before applying the model, one must consider other interdependencies.

The interpretive approach is best. It's the approach taken in the textbook.

The Keynesian model is applied by making policy recommendations (prescriptions) to try to smooth out the business cycles. But all "medicine" should be taken with common sense.

5b. A mechanistic Classical sees the Classical model as a direct guide for policy; an interpretive Classical sees the Classical model as an aid in understanding complicated disequilibrium dynamics with interdependencies. (299)

The Classical model, like the Keynesian model, cannot be applied mechanistically; it is only a guide to common sense.

6. The macro policy model dynamics and the AP/AE model dynamics are equivalent when the price level is fixed. The AED curve can be derived from the AP/AE model. (299)

When the price level is constant (we are in Range A of the AS path) the AP/AE model tells us precisely how much the AED curve will shift when autonomous expenditures shift by a specified amount. The difference between the shift in autonomous expenditures (the AE curve) and the AED curve is due to the multiplier.

See also, Appendix A: "An Algebraic Presentation of the Expanded Keynesian Model."

Short-answer questions

1. What is the difference between induced and autonomous expenditures? (LO1)

2. Draw an AP and AE curve and show how the level of income is graphically determined in the Keynesian aggregate production/aggregate expenditures model. Describe the forces that are set in motion when income levels are above and below equilibrium? (LO2)

3. In the Keynesian model, if autonomous expenditures were $200 and the *mpe* were 0.75, what is equilibrium income? (LO3)

4. Explain the process by which the economy reaches a new equilibrium income if autonomous expenditures increase by $100. The marginal propensity to expend is 0.5. (LO4)

5. Suppose an economist appears before Congress and states that his model has estimated the *mpe* in the U.S. to be 0.75. Given this estimate he tells the Congress that the $200 reduction in government spending will result in a decline in output of $800 billion. Another economist also testifying before Congress says that the first economist's answer is in the right direction, but too precise. She states that the U.S. economy is complicated and a simple model cannot capture the complicated disequilibrium dynamics of the U.S. economy. How would you characterize the Keynesian model used by each economist and why? (LO5)

6. Suppose a decrease in the price level causes the AE curve to shift up. How do you show this shift in the macro policy model? (LO6)

7. What happens to output in the AP/AE model if there is perfect price-level flexibility when the AE curve shifts up due to a shift in autonomous expenditures? (LO6)

Word Scramble

1. _____   2._____   _____
      u t r p m l l i i e   a e e i K n n s y   u t q o n i e a

3._____   _____
      u t s p o o n n m i c   c f i n n o t u

Match the Terms and Concepts to Their Definitions

___1. aggregate expenditures

___2. aggregate production curve

___3. Aggregate Production/Aggregate Expenditures (AP/AE) Model

___4. autonomous expenditures

___5. expenditures function

___6. income adjustment mechanism

___7. induced expenditures

___8. interpretive Keynesian model

___9. Keynesian equation

___10. marginal propensity to expend

___11. multiplier

___12. path-dependent equilibrium

___13. permanent income hypothesis

___14. real business cycle theory

a. Chase between aggregate production and aggregate expenditures.
b. The hypothesis that expenditures are determined by permanent or lifetime income.
c. Expenditures that change as income changes.
d. The theory that fluctuations in the economy reflect real phenomena—simultaneous shifts in supply and demand, not simply supply responses to demand shifts.
e. Equation that tells us that income equals the multiplier times autonomous expenditures.
f. Equilibrium that is influenced by the adjustment process to that equilibrium.
g. A number that tells us how much income will change in response to a change in autonomous expenditures.
h. In the Keynesian model, the total level of expenditures in an economy, the summation of all four components of expenditures: aggregate consumption, investment, spending by government, and net foreign spending on U.S. goods. It is expressed by the equation $AE = C + I + G + (X - M)$.
i. In the Keynesian model, the 45° line on a graph with real income measured on the horizontal axis and real production on the vertical axis. Alternatively called the aggregate income curve.
j. The ratio of a change in expenditures, to a change in income.
k. Expenditures that are unaffected by changes in income.
l. Keynesian model that is an aid in understanding complicated disequilibrium dynamics.
m. Representation of the relationship between expenditures and income as a mathematical function ($E = E_0 + mpeY$, where E = expenditures, E_0 = autonomous expenditures, mpe = marginal propensity to expend, Y = income).
n. Keynesian model giving "aggregate supply" the name "aggregate production" and focusing on total production changes, not on changes in output caused by price level changes, and emphasizing the difference between the Keynesian focus and the Classical focus on quantity of aggregate supply and demand changes resulting from changes in the price level.

Problems and Exercises

1. Answer the following questions about the aggregate production curve.

   a. Draw an aggregate production curve. Label all axes.

b.   What is the slope of the aggregate production function?

c.   Why is the slope as you have drawn it?

2.   You are given the following information about the economy:

Income	Expenditures
0	100
500	500
1000	900
2000	1700
3000	2500
4000	3300

a.   What is the level of autonomous expenditures?

b.   What is the marginal propensity to expend?

c.   What expenditures function (an equation) corresponds to the table?

d.   What is the *mpw*? Explain why it is important.

3.   Putting expenditures and production together:

a.   Graph the expenditures function from question 2 on the aggregate production curve from question 1.

b.   What is the slope of the expenditures function?

4.   Given the following equation, answer the questions: $AE = C_0 + .6Y + I + G + (X - M)$ where $C_0 = 1000$, $I = 500$, $G = 300$, $X = 300$, $M = 400$.

   a.   Draw the aggregate expenditures curve.

   b.   What is the slope of the curve?

   c.   What is the vertical axis intercept?

   d.   Add the aggregate production curve.

   e.   What is the multiplier?

   f.   What is equilibrium income? Label that point A on the graph.

g. What is the effect of an increase in autonomous consumption of $200 on equilibrium income? Demonstrate your answer graphically.

h. What is the effect on equilibrium income of a change in the *mpe* from .6 to .8? Demonstrate your answer graphically. How does your answer to (g) change with the new *mpe*?

5. Calculate the multiplier in each case.

a. *mpe* = .7

b. *mpw* = .4

6. For each of the following, state what will happen to equilibrium income.

a. The *mpe* is 0.9 and autonomous government expenditures just rose $200 billion. Graph your analysis.

b. The *mpe* is 0.65 and autonomous investment just fell $70 billion. Graph your analysis.

A1. You've just been appointed chairman of the Council of Economic Advisers in Textland. The *mpc* is .8, and all nonconsumption expenditures and taxes are exogenous.

    a.   How can the government increase output by $400 through a change in expenditures?

    b.   Oops! There's been a mistake. Your research assistant tells you that taxes are actually not exogenous, and that there is a marginal tax rate of .1. How can the government change expenditures to increase income by $400?

    c.   There's more new news which your research assistant just found out. She tells you that not only is there a marginal tax rate of .1; there's also a marginal propensity to import of .2. You have to change your solutions now. How can the government change expenditures to increase income by $400?

Multiple Choice Questions

1.   In the Keynesian model the aggregate production curve is
    a. a horizontal line.
    b. a vertical line.
    c. a 45° line.
    d. a downward slope line.

2.   Autonomous expenditures are
    a. expenditures that are automatically created by income.
    b. expenditures that are unrelated to income.
    c. expenditures that change as income changes.
    d. expenditures that automatically change as income changes.

3.   The equation for the expenditures function is
    a. $E = E_0 - mpeY$.
    b. $E = E_0 \times mpeY$.
    c. $E = E_0 + mpeY$.
    d. $E = E_0 + mpe + Y$.

4.   The marginal propensity to expend is the
    a. change in expenditures times change in income.
    b. change in expenditures divided by the change in income.
    c. change in expenditures divided by income.
    d. expenditures divided by the change in income.

5. *Mpe* plus *mpw* equals
   a. zero.
   b. one.
   c. ten.
   d. unknown (cannot be determined).

6. If the *mpe* is .8, what is the size of the multiplier in the Keynesian model?
   a. .5.
   b. 5.
   c. 1.
   d. 10.

7. As the *mpe* rises, the multiplier
   a. increases.
   b. decreases.
   c. remains the same.
   d. sometimes rises and sometimes falls.

8. In the Keynesian *AE/AP* model, if autonomous expenditures are $5,000 and the *mpe* equals .9, what is the level of income in the economy?
   a. $5,000.
   b. $10,000.
   c. $20,000.
   d. $50,000.

9. In the Keynesian *AE/AP* model, if autonomous exports falls by 40 and the *mpe* is .5, what happens to the income?
   a. income rises by 20.
   b. income falls by 20.
   c. income rises by 80.
   d. income falls by 80.

10. In the Keynesian *AE/AP* model if autonomous investment falls by 20 and the *mpe* is .75, what happens to the income?
    a. income rises by 15.
    b. income falls by 15.
    c. income rises by 80.
    d. income falls by 80.

11. In the Keynesian *AE/AP* model, if autonomous consumption increases by 10 and the *mpe* is .8, what happens to the income?
    a. income rises by 8.
    b. income falls by 8.
    c. income rises by 50.
    d. income falls by 50.

12. In the Keynesian *AE/AP* model, if government spending falls by 20 and the *mpe* is .66, what happens to the income?
    a. income rises by 60.
    b. income falls by 60.
    c. income rises by 126.
    d. income falls by 126.

13. In the Keynesian *AE/AP* model, if autonomous imports fall by 40 and the *mpe* is .5, what happens to the income?
    a. income rises by 20.
    b. income falls by 20.
    c. income rises by 80.
    d. income falls by 80.

14. In the Keynesian *AE/AP* model, if autonomous exports falls by 40 and government spending increases by 20, and the *mpe* is .8, what happens to the income?
    a. income rises by 25.
    b. income falls by 25.
    c. income rises by 100.
    d. income falls by 100.

15. The term paradox of thrift refers to the process by which
    a. individuals attempt to save less, but in doing so spend less causing income to decrease, ending up much less than they desired.
    b. individuals attempt to save less, but in doing so spend more causing income to decrease, ending up saving much less than desired.
    c. individuals attempt to save more, but in doing so spend less causing income to decrease, ending up saving less.
    d. individuals attempt to save more, but in doing so spend more causing income to decrease, ending up saving less.

16. The hypothesis that expenditures are determined by permanent or lifetime income (making the mpe close to zero) implies that the AE curve will be close to
    a. a flat line.
    b. a vertical line.
    c. an upward sloping 45^0 line.
    d. something economists cannot determine.

17. When the price level falls
    a. the aggregate expenditures curve remains constant.
    b. the aggregate expenditures curve shifts down.
    c. the aggregate expenditures curve shifts up.
    d. the slope of the aggregate expenditures curve changes.

18. To derive the aggregate equilibrium demand curve from the Keynesian *AE/AP* model, one must
    a. relate the initial autonomous shifts caused by price level changes on the *AE* curve to the *AED* curve.
    b. relate the *AE/AP* equilibria at different price levels to the *AED* curve.
    c. relate the *AE/AP* equilibria at different quantity levels to the *AED* curve.
    d. relate the initial autonomous shifts caused by price level changes on the *AP* curve to the *AED* curve.

19. If there is partial price-level flexibility
    a. the Keynesian *AE/AP* model is no longer relevant.
    b. the results of the Keynesian *AE/AP* model will be reversed.
    c. the results of the Keynesian *AE/AP* model will be modified but the central point will remain the same.
    d. the Keynesian *AE/AP* model will turn into a Classical model.

20. A path-dependent equilibrium
    a. is an equilibrium that one arrives at in a supply/demand model.
    b. cannot exist since the economy would always be on a path.
    c. the type of equilibrium the Classical model arrived at.
    d. an equilibrium in which the adjustment process influences the final equilibrium.

21. The interpretive Keynesian macro model differs from the mechanistic Keynesian model in that
    a. the interpretive Keynesian model is essentially a Classical model.
    b. the interpretive model sees the Keynesian model as a guide, not a definitive result.
    c. the interpretive Keynesian model integrates the quantity theory into the *AE/AP* model.
    d. the interpretive Keynesian model integrates the quantity theory into both the Keynesian *AS/AD* and the *AE/AP* models.

22. Which group is most likely to believe that a model using autonomous expenditures is relevant?
    a. Keynesians.
    b. Classicals.
    c. Keynesians and Classicals would be equal in their belief.
    d. Neither Keynesians nor Classicals would see a model using autonomous elements as relevant.

23. In the real business cycle theory, business cycles occur because of
    a. changes in the real price level.
    b. changes in real income.
    c. technological and other natural shocks.
    d. changes in the money supply.

24. In the modern Keynesian model, Keynesians see
    a. the real business cycle as totally irrelevant.
    b. the real business cycle as expanded beyond what people desire because of TANSTAFFL.
    c. the real business cycle as exaggerated beyond what people desire because of dynamic externalities.
    d. the real business cycle as true.

A1. If the marginal tax rate increases, what would happen to the general expenditures multiplier?
    a. It would increase.
    b. It would decrease.
    c. It would remain the same.
    d. One cannot say.

A2. In the Keynesian *AE/AP* model, if a country has a very large marginal propensity to import
    a. expansionary fiscal policy would be extremely effective in expanding domestic income.
    b. expansionary fiscal policy would not be very effective in expanding domestic income.
    c. The size of the marginal propensity to import has no effect on the effectiveness of expansionary fiscal policy.
    d. The Keynesian *AE/AP* model is not relevant to a country with a very large marginal propensity to import.

A3. Assuming the marginal propensity to import is .1, the tax rate is .2, and the marginal propensity to expend is .6, the multiplier will be approximately
    a. 0.
    b. 1.2.
    c. 1.6.
    d. 2.6.

A4. Assume the marginal propensity to import is .1, the tax rate is .25, the marginal propensity to expend is .8, and that the government wants to increase income by 100. In the Keynesian model you would suggest increasing government spending by
    a. 10.
    b. 35.7.
    c. 50.
    d. 100.

A5. Assume the marginal propensity to import is .3, the tax rate is .2, the marginal propensity to expend is .5, and that the government wants to increase income by 200. In the Keynesian model you would suggest increasing government spending by
    a. 87.5.
    b. 100.
    c. 180.
    d. 200.

Answers

Short-answer questions

1. Induced expenditures depend upon the level of income. Autonomous expenditures are independent of income. (284)

2. The *AP* curve is a 45 degree line through the origin. At all points on the *AP* curve, output equals income. The *AE* curve is an upward-sloping line with a slope less than one that intersects the expenditures axis at the level of autonomous expenditures. These curves are shown in a graph to the right. Equilibrium income is where the two curves intersect. At points to the left, aggregate expenditures exceed aggregate production and businesses are finding their inventories running down faster than desired. They increase production, which increases income and expenditures, moving income toward equilibrium. At points to the right, aggregate expenditures are less than aggregate production and businesses see their inventories accumulating. They cut production, which cuts income and expenditures, moving income toward equilibrium. (287)

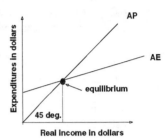

3. To determine equilibrium income multiply the sum of all autonomous expenditures by the multiplier. In this case the multiplier is $1/(1-.75) = 4$, so equilibrium income is $800. (289)

4. The initial shock is $100. This increase in expenditures causes aggregate production to increase also by $100, which creates an additional $100 in income. Consumers spend $50 of this additional income on additional goods. Once again aggregate production rises by the same amount as the $50 increase in aggregate expenditures. Subsequent increases in aggregate expenditures and aggregate production are determined in a similar fashion, each time getting smaller and smaller. Equilibrium income is $200 higher at the end of this multiplier process. This is determined by calculating the multiplier, $1/(1-mpe) = 2$ and multiplying it by the initial rise in aggregate expenditures, $100. (289)

5. The first economist is following a mechanistic Keynesian model while the second is following an interpretive Keynesian model. The mechanistic Keynesian sees the model as a direct guide for policy. An interpretive Keynesian sees the model as a guide to one's common sense, highlighting important dynamic interdependencies. (299)

6. A decline in the price level will shift the AE curve up. This is shown as a movement down along the AED curve connecting the output and price levels corresponding to equilibrium output in the AE/AP model at the two prices. (299-300)

7. In the AP/AE model, a change in autonomous expenditures will be offset entirely by a change in the price level that shifts the AE curve in a direction opposite to the initial shift. If the initial shift causes the AE curve to shift up, prices will rise sufficiently to shift the AE curve back to its initial position. (300)

Word Scramble   1. multiplier   2. Keynesian equation   3. consumption function

Match the Terms and Concepts to Their Definitions
1-h; 2-i; 3-n; 4-k; 5-m; 6-a; 7-c; 8-l; 9-e; 10-j; 11-g; 12-f; 13-b; 14-d.

Problems and Exercises

1. a. The aggregate production curve is a 45 degree line shown on the right. Production is on the vertical axis and real income is on the horizontal axis. (282-283)
    b. The slope is 1. (282-283)
    c. The slope is one because the aggregate production curve represents the identity that aggregate production must equal aggregate income. That can only be represented by a straight line through the origin with slope one. (282-283)

2. a. Autonomous expenditures are $100. It is that amount that is independent of income. (284-289)

   b. The marginal propensity to expend is 0.8: This is calculated as the change in expenditures/change in disposable income = 400/500. (284-289)

   c. The expenditures function that corresponds to the table is $E = 100 + .8Y$. The 100 comes from the level of consumption when income is zero and the .8 is the *mpe*. (284-289)

   d. The *mpw* is 0.2. It is important because it tells us how much of the income escapes the circular flow each round of increases or decreases in income. It is because of the leakages that income changes by a multiple of a change in autonomous expenditures. (290-291)

3. a. The graph of the expenditure function from question 2 and the aggregate production from question 1 are shown together on the right. (287)

   b. The slope of the expenditure function is the *mpe,* or 0.8. (285-286)

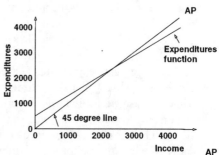

4. a. The aggregate expenditures curve is drawn on the right. The slope of the *AE* curve is the *mpe* and the vertical intercept is autonomous expenditures. (287-290)

   b. The slope of the curve is .6. It is the *mpc.* (288-290)

   c. The vertical axis intercept is 1000+500+300+(300-400) = 1700. The vertical axis intercept is the level of autonomous expenditures. (288-290)

   d. The aggregate production curve is shown in the graph to the right. It is a 45 degree line through the origin. (288-290)

   e. The multiplier is 2.5. It is 1/(1-*mpe*). (288-290)

   f. Equilibrium income is $4,250: autonomous expenditures × multiplier, $1,700/(1-.6). This is shown as point A on the graph. (288-290)

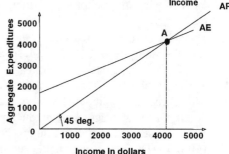

   g. An increase in autonomous expenditures of $200 will increase equilibrium income by $500. This is calculated by multiplying $200 by the multiplier, 2.5. This is shown to the right as a shift up in the AE curve by 200. New equilibrium income is point B on the graph to the right. (288-290)

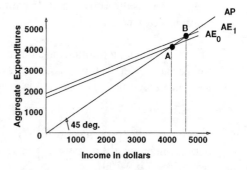

   h. The *AE* curve becomes steeper with a slope of .8. The multiplier is now 5 and equilibrium income is now $8,500. This is shown as point C in the graph on the right. Equilibrium income is calculated by multiplying autonomous expenditures, $1,700, by the multiplier. Since the multiplier is larger, an increase of $200 in autonomous expenditures now increases equilibrium income by $1,000. (289-290)

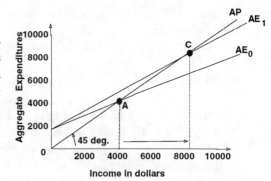

5. a. Multiplier is 3.33: 1/(1-.7). (288-290)

   b. Multiplier is 2.5: 1/(.4). (288-290)

6. a. Income rises by $2 trillion: 200/(1-0.9). In this case the aggregate expenditures curve has a slope of 0.9 as shown in the graph to the right. The increase in government expenditures shifts the *AE* curve up from AE_0 to AE_1 and income increases by a multiple of that amount, in this case by a multiple of 10. (291-292)

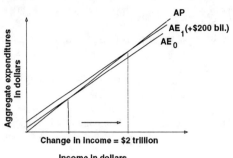

Change in Income = $2 trillion

Income in dollars

b. Income falls by $200 billion: $70/.35. In this case the aggregate expenditures curve has a slope of .65 as shown in the graph to the right. The decrease in investment shifts the *AE* curve down from AE_0 to AE_1 and income decreases by a multiple of that amount, in this case by a multiple of 2.86. (291-292)

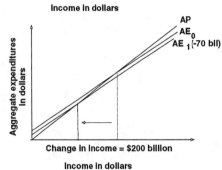

Change in Income = $200 billion

Income in dollars

A1. Given an *mpc* of .8:
   a. Increase expenditures by $80. The multiplier is $1/(1-mpc) = 1/(1-.8) = 5$. Therefore, to increase GDP by $400, government spending has to increase $80. (304-305)
   b. Increase expenditures by $112. The multiplier is $1/(1- mpc+ t \times mpc) = 1/(1-.8+.1 \times .8) = 3.57$. Therefore, to increase GDP by $400, government spending has to increase by $112. (304-305)
   c. Increase expenditures by $193. The multiplier is $1/(1- mpc + t \times mpc + mpm) = 1/(1-.8+.1 \times .8+.2) = 2.08$. Therefore, to increase GDP by $400, government spending has to increase by $192. (304-305)

Multiple Choice Questions

1. c. See pages 282-293, including Exhibit 2.

2. b. See page 284.

3. c. See page 285.

4. b. See page 285.

5. b. See page 290.

6. b. The multiplier equals $1/(1-.8)=1/.2=5$. See pages 288-289.

7. a. You can determine this by substituting into the formula. See page 289.

8. d. The multiplier is 10 so the answer is 10 times $5,000, or $50,000. See page 288.

9. d. The multiplier is 2 so the answer is 2 times -40, or minus 80. See pages 291-292.

10. d. The multiplier is 4 so the answer is 4 times -20, or minus 80. See pages 291-292.

11. c. The multiplier is 5 so the answer is 5 times 10, or 50. See pages 291-292.

12. b. The multiplier is 3 so the answer is 3 times -20, or minus 60. See pages 291-292.

13. c. The multiplier is 2 so the answer is 2 times - (-40), or plus 80. Imports falling is expansionary. See pages 291-292.

14. d. The multiplier is 5 so the answer is 5 times (-40 + 20), or minus 100. See pages 291-292.

15 c. See page 294.

16. a. If the mpe is close to zero it would mean that the slope of the AE curve would also be zero, making it flat. See page 297.

17. c. Since a lower price level makes the cash people hold worth more, people feel wealthier and the *AE* curve shifts up. See page 299.

18. b. As discussed on pages 299-301, especially Exhibit 12, one considers the effect of different price levels on the *AE* curve to derive an *AED* curve.

19. c. If you could follow that complicated Exhibit 12(c and d) on page 301 you would see that the results are modified. If you are following that, you're doing great. Have you thought of becoming an economist?

20. d. As discussed on pages 297-298, in a path-dependent equilibrium the adjustment process influences the final equilibrium. The supply/demand and Classical models are definitely not path-dependent models.

21. b. As discussed on page 298, the interpretive Keynesian model views the Keynesian model as an aid in understanding. It might integrate the Keynesian model with other models but that is not what is distinctive about it.

22. a. Keynesians see policy as useful because some aspects of expenditures are autonomous. Classicals see everything as induced, making government policy useless. See pages 297-299.

23. c. See page 297.

24. c. As discussed on page 297, modern Keynesians see externalities in the adjustment process that lead to outcomes which do not reflect people's desires.

A1. b. This is a hard question since it requires some deduction. The marginal tax rate is one of the components of the marginal propensity to expend. It is a leakage from the circular flow, so it makes the multiplier smaller. See pages 304-305.

A2. b. A large marginal propensity to import reduces the size of the multiplier since the marginal propensity to import is one of the components of the marginal propensity to expend. See pages 304-305.

A3. c. The multiplier for the full model is $1/(1-b+bt+m)$. Substituting in gives $1/(1-.6+.1+.12)$ or $1/.62$ or a multiplier of about 1.6. See pages 304-305.

A4. c. First you determine the multiplier. The multiplier for the full model is $1/(1-b+bt+m)$. Substituting in gives $1/(1-.8+.1+.2)$ or $1/.5$ or a multiplier of 2. Dividing 100 by 2 gives an increase of government spending of 50. See pages 304-305.

A5. c. First you determine the multiplier. The multiplier for the full model is $1/(1-b+bt+m)$. Substituting in gives $1/(1-.5+.3+.1)$ or $1/.9$ or a multiplier of about 1.11. Dividing 200 by 1.11 gives an increase of government spending of about 180. The multiplier is very small because the *mpc* is low and the *mpm* is high. See pages 304-305.

Chapter 12:
Demand Management, Fiscal Policy, and the Debate about Activist Demand Management Policy

Chapter at a glance

1. Expansionary fiscal policy involves decreasing taxes or increasing government spending. Contractionary fiscal policy involves increasing taxes or decreasing the government spending. (307)

✔ Use *expansionary fiscal policy* to combat cyclical unemployment and slow growth *during a recession* (a downturn in the business cycle).

✔ Use *contractionary fiscal policy* to combat demand-pull inflation *during an upturn* in the business cycle.

2a. Expansionary fiscal policy stimulates autonomous expenditures, which increases people's income, which increases people's spending even more. (309)

Any increase in autonomous C, I, G or (X-M) times the multiplier [1/(1 - mpe)] equals the change in income

2b. Expansionary fiscal policy shifts the aggregate equilibrium demand curve up. The effect on prices and output depends upon where the economy is on the aggregate supply path. (310)

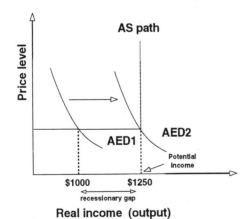

Real income (output)

In the graph above, the AS path is simplified with only two ranges, Range A and Range C. If the multiplier is

5 and there is a recessionary gap of $250, government must increase expenditures by $50 (since $50 × multiplier of 5 = $250) to arrive at potential income. If the AS path had a Range B, the effect of the shift in the AED curve (and the multiplier effect) would be split between increases in real output and increases in the price level.

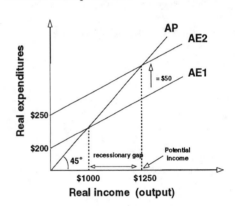

Real income (output)

Here is the story using the AP/AE model: In the graph above, initial autonomous AE is $200 and the mpe is 0.8. The multiplier is 1/(1−0.8) = 5. Equilibrium income is $1000. Since there is a recessionary gap of $250, government increases expenditures by $50 (since $50 × multiplier of 5 = $250). This depends upon the economy being in the Keynesian range of the AS path.

Keynesians argue the economy is usually operating in Range A (the horizontal portion of the AS path). Classicals think the economy is usually operating in Range B (upward sloping portion) or Range C (vertical portion), where any increase in aggregate expenditures results in a much smaller increase in income and a much larger increase in the price level.

3. Three alternatives to fiscal policy are directed investment policies, trade policies, and autonomous consumption policies. (315)

   Anything which government can do to alter components of AE (I, X-M, and C) will have a multiple impact on Y (the income-output level in the macroeconomy) because of the multiplier. For example, Rosy Scenarios, bank guarantees, reduction in interest rates, export-led growth policies, and increases in consumer credit availability could increase AE and stimulate the economy.

4. A structural deficit is a deficit that would exist at potential income. A passive deficit is the deficit that exists because income is below or above potential income. (319)

   A structural deficit can be a problem because the economy cannot "grow" out of it. Passive deficits are not as much a problem because we can grow out of them. Passive deficits are expected to occur during recessions because of the automatic stabilizers.

5. Six assumptions of the model that could lead to problems with fiscal policy are: (323)

   1. Financing the deficit doesn't have any offsetting effects.
   In reality, it often does (e.g., the crowding-out effect).

   2. The government knows what the situation is.
   In reality the government must estimate what the situation is.

   3. The government knows the economy's potential income.
   In reality the government may not know what this level is.

   4. The government has flexibility in terms of spending and taxes.
   In reality, the government cannot change them quickly.

   5. The size of the government debt doesn't matter.
   In reality, the size of the debt often does matter.

   6. Fiscal policy doesn't negatively affect other government goals.
   In reality, it often does.

6. Crowding out is the offsetting effect on private expenditures caused by the government's sale of bonds to finance expansionary fiscal policy. (325)

   Increases in the deficit financed by borrowing (selling bonds) leads to increases in interest rates (which increases the cost of borrowing). This leads to lower investment (business spending on capital) which offsets the rise in government spending.

   ✔ *So, increased deficit spending may be partially or totally offset by decreases in other spending components.*
   ✔ *The size of the crowding-out effect is debatable.*

7. An automatic stabilizer is any government program or policy that will counteract the business cycle without any new government action. (328)

   Automatic stabilizers include:
   1. *Welfare payments*
   2. *Unemployment insurance, and*
   3. *Income tax system.*

   Assume a recession which is caused by too little total spending. Government expenditures automatically rise (because of increased welfare payments and unemployment claims). Taxes automatically decrease (because fewer people are earning income). The deficit increases and AE (total spending) increases. This passive deficit is good for the economy because it automatically stimulates AE which is needed during a recession. The opposite occurs during an upturn in the business cycle. <u>Automatic stabilizers help smooth out the business cycle.</u>

Short-answer questions

1. The intial policy proposal by U.S. Keynesian economists was to introduce public works programs. How did that proposal work and what was added to that policy by subsequent Keynesian policymakers? (LO1)

2. Suppose you are the featured speaker at a primer for the first-year Congresspeople. You have been asked to speak about fiscal policy. A Congressperson asks what fiscal policy tools Congress has to affect the economy, and what effect they have on the level of output. You tell her. (LO1)

3. What are contractionary and expansionary fiscal policies? (LO1)

4. How does fiscal policy affect the economy? Demonstrate an expansionary fiscal policy graphically using the macro policy model. (LO2)

5. The first-year Congresspeople are worried about how your answer to question 2. They feel they are politically unable to implement those policies. What three alternatives to fiscal policy can you offer? (LO3)

6.   First-year Congresspeople are eager to pass a balanced budget amendment that will make deficits unconstitutional. You warn them about the effects of this amendment by explaining the difference between a structural deficit and a passive deficit. (LO4)

7.   How do the six problems of fiscal policy limit its use? (LO5)

8.   You are speaking at the Congressional conference. A Congressperson wonders whether the funding of fiscal policy by selling bonds will change the direct effect of fiscal policy. You tell her that it might and explain how. (LO6)

9.   Some Classical economists argue that crowding out totally undermines the Keynesian view of fiscal policy. Explain their argument. (LO6)

10. A country has just removed its unemployment insurance program and is experiencing a recession. How will this recession differ from earlier recessions? (LO7)

Word Scramble

1. _____ _____   2._____ '_ _____   3._____ _____
    a c f i l s   y p o l i c   u s O n k   a l w   a a f i i l n n o r t y   a p g

Match the Terms and Concepts to Their Definitions

___ 1. aggregate demand (expenditure) management policy

___ 2. automatic stabilizer

___ 3. crowding in

___ 4. crowding out

___ 5. exchange rate policy

___ 6. export-led growth policy

___ 7. fine tuning

___ 8. fiscal policy

___ 9. inflationary gap

___ 10. Okun's law

___ 11. passive deficit

___ 12. recessionary gap

___ 13. Rosy Scenario policy

___ 14. structural deficit

a. Any policy that increases autonomous exports or decreases autonomous imports, thereby increasing autonomous expenditures.

b. Any government program or policy that will counteract the business cycle without any new government action.

c. Countercyclical fiscal policy designed to keep the economy always at its target or potential level of income.

d. Deliberate change in either government spending or taxes to stimulate or slow down the economy.

e. Deliberately affecting a country's exchange rate in order to affects its trade balance.

f. Government policy of making optimistic predictions and never making gloomy predictions.

g. Portion of the deficit that exists because the economy is operating below its potential level of output.

h. Positive effects of government spending on other components of spending.

i. Proportion of the budget deficit that would exist even if the economy were at its potential level of income.

j. Rule of thumb economists use to translate the unemployment rate into changes in income. "A one percentage point fall in the unemployment rate equals a 2.5 percent increase in income."

k. The offsetting effect on private expenditures caused by the government's sale of bonds to finance expansionary fiscal policy.

l. The difference between equilibrium income and potential income when equilibrium income exceeds potential income.

m. The difference between equilibrium income and potential income when potential income exceeds equilibrium income.

n. Policy aimed at changing the level of income in the economy by a combination of a change in autonomous expenditures and the multiplied induced expenditures resulting from that change.

Problems and Exercises

1. You are hired by the president who believes that the economy is operating at a level $300 billion beyond potential output. You are told that the marginal propensity to expend is 0.5.

   a. The president wants to use taxes to close the gap. What do you advise? Show your answer using the AP/AE model. (Read the Added Dimension on page 315 for a hint).

   b. The president wants to compare your plan in (a) to a plan using spending to close the inflationary gap. What do you advise? Show your answer graphically using the macro policy model.

c.   Advisers from the council realize that the marginal propensity to expend is 0.75. Recalculate your answer to (b) and show using the macro policy model.

2.   You are called by the president to close a recessionary gap of $1,000. You are told that the mpe is 0. You estimate that the economy is in Range B of the AS path. Show why the expenditures needed to close the gap if the economy were in Range A are insufficient to close the gap when the economy is in Range B.

3.   Calculate the structural deficit and the passive deficit for each of the following:

a.   Suppose potential income is $6 trillion and actual income is $5.7 trillion. The actual deficit is $200 billion and the marginal tax rate is .25.

b.   Suppose potential income is $5 trillion and actual income is $4.5 trillion. The actual deficit is $400 billion and the marginal tax rate is .15.

c.   Suppose potential income is $10 trillion and actual income is $9 trillion. The actual deficit is $500 billion and the marginal tax rate is .3.

4.   Suppose the government wants to increase income by $250 billion. The *mpe* is .6.

a.   Assuming the economy is in Range A of the AS path, by how much must government increase spending to reach its goal? Show the effect of this action, using the macro policy model.

b. Suppose government finances this increase in spending with the sale of bonds. As a result, interest rates increase. How does this affect the analysis? Demonstrate using the AE/AP model.

5. Congratulations. You have just been appointed economic adviser to Dreamland. For each of the following, advise the president.

a. The president wants to reduce unemployment from 8 to 6 percent. Income is $40,000 and the *mpe* is .4. What spending policy would you advise?

b. The president wants to reduce unemployment from 8 to 6 percent. Income is $50,000 and the *mpe* is .75. What fiscal spending policy would you advise?

6. In 1995, national income was $7 trillion and unemployment was 6%. Assume the tax rate is 25%.

a. Suppose the Chairman of the Council of Economic Advisers believed that the natural rate of unemployment was 5% while the Chairman of the Fed believed that natural rate was 5.5%. Calculate the difference in the underlying estimates of potential income.

b. Which Chairman would estimate a lower structural deficit?

c. What spending policy would each recommend to close the recessionary gap, assuming the *mpe* is .5?

Multiple Choice Questions

1. Expansionary fiscal policy involves
   a. increasing taxes.
   b. increasing the money supply.
   c. increasing government spending.
   d. changing the exchange rate.

2. The macro policy that followed from the Keynesian *AE/AP* and macro model is generally called
   a. aggregate supply management.
   b. aggregate demand management.
   c. price-level policy.
   d. exchange rate policy.

3. In the graph on the right, actual income is below potential income. The government is planning to use expansionary fiscal policy. This will
   a. shift the *AP* curve up.
   b. shift the *AE* curve up.
   c. shift the *AP* curve down.
   d. shift the *AE* curve down.

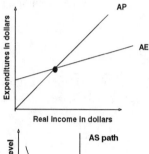

4. In the graph on the right, autonomous imports have just increased. This will cause
   a. the aggregate supply path to shift down.
   b. the aggregate supply path to shift up.
   c. the aggregate equilibrium demand curve to shift to the right.
   d. the aggregate equilibrium demand curve to shift to the left.

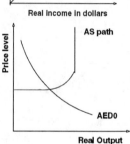

5. The economy has a fixed price level, an *mpe* of .5, and a recessionary gap of 240. Using the Keynesian *AE/AP* model, an economist would advise government to
   a. increase autonomous expenditures by 120.
   b. increase autonomous expenditures by 240.
   c. increase autonomous expenditures by 480.
   d. increase autonomous expenditures by 620.

6. The economy is in Range A of the aggregate supply path, the *mpe* is .8, and there is a recessionary gap of 600. Using the macro policy model, an economist would advise government to
   a. increase autonomous expenditures by 120
   b. increase autonomous expenditures by 480
   c. increase autonomous expenditures by 600.
   d. increase autonomous expenditures by 3000.

7. The economy has a fixed price level, an *mpe* of .66, and a recessionary gap of 900. Using the Keynesian *AE/AP* model, an economist would advise government to
   a. increase autonomous expenditures by about 30.
   b. increase autonomous expenditures by about 300.
   c. increase autonomous expenditures by about 600.
   d. increase autonomous expenditures by about 2700.

8. The economy has an inflationary gap in the macro policy model at point A. In the graph on the right, the government should shift
   a. the *AS* path up.
   b. the *AS* path down.
   c. the *AED* curve to the right.
   d. the *AED* curve to the left.

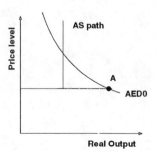

9. Which of the following is true in the late 1990s?
    a. Keynesian economists support fine tuning.
    b. Classical economists support fine tuning.
    c. Both Keynesian and Classical economists generally support fine tuning.
    d. Both Keynesian and Classical economists generally oppose fine tuning.

10. Expansionary aggregate demand policy includes all of the following except
    a. increasing government spending.
    b. increasing autonomous expenditures.
    c. increasing imports.
    d. decreasing taxes.

11. Contractionary aggregate demand policy includes all of the following except
    a. decreasing autonomous investment.
    b. decreasing imports.
    c. decreasing exports.
    d. decreasing government spending.

12. Exchange rate policy is
    a. increasing the size of the government deficit.
    b. deliberately affecting the country's exchange rate in order to affect its trade balance.
    c. deliberately affecting the country's money supply in order to affect its trade balance.
    d. deliberately affecting the country's tax rate in order to affect its trade balance.

13. When there are induced elements of taxes and imports and an expansionary fiscal policy of 100 is run, at the new equilibrium
    a. the government deficit will increase by precisely 100.
    b. the budget deficit will increase by less than 100.
    c. the government deficit will increase by more than 100.
    d. there will be no budget deficit.

14. In an economy the trade deficit is 20. When there are induced elements of taxes and imports and an expansionary fiscal policy is run, at the new equilibrium
    a. the trade deficit will be more than 20.
    b. the trade deficit will be less than 20.
    c. the trade deficit will remain at 20.
    d. the trade deficit will be zero.

15. The portion of the budget deficit that would exist even if the economy were at its potential level of income is called the
    a. structural deficit.
    b. passive deficit.
    c. primary deficit.
    d. secondary deficit.

16. Crowding out occurs when
    a. the government runs a deficit and sells bonds to finance that deficit.
    b. the government prints money.
    c. the government runs a surplus and sells bonds and the people who buy those bonds sell their older bonds to the government.
    d. the tendency for new workers to replace more expensive older workers is a factor.

17. Generally, the U.S. economy is in
    a. a Keynesian range of the price-level flexibility curve.
    b. a Classical range of the price-level flexibility curve.
    c. the intermediate range of the price-level flexibility curve.
    d. an unemployment rate of over 25 percent.

Answers

Short-Answer Questions

1. Keynes's policy proposals worked by starting the multiplier process that got the economy in a low income equilibrium in reverse. It increases aggregate expenditures. Businesses produce more to meet the additional demand which creates additional income. The additional income results in a further increase in ependitures. The process continues until a new equilibrium level of income is reached. Later Keynesians added to that policy: (1) another way to stimulate the economy by reducing taxes, (2) a way to slow down the economy when called for by decreasing spending or increasing taxes, (3) policies to change the money supply as a way of controlling the economy, and (4) general policies to influence components of aggregate expenditures. (307-309)

2. The tools of fiscal policy are changing taxes and changing government spending. Increasing taxes and lowering spending contract the economy; decreasing taxes and expanding spending expand the economy. (307)

3. Contractionary fiscal policies involve increasing taxes or decreasing government spending. Expansionary fiscal policies involve decreasing taxes or increasing government spending. (309-314)

4. Fiscal policy affects the economy by changing aggregate expenditures, which changes people's incomes, which increases people's spending even more. Expansionary fiscal policy shifts the aggregate equilibrium curve to the right by a multiple of the increase in government spending, as shown in the accompanying diagram. The change in income equals the multiplier times the change in government expenditures. (308-309, 311)

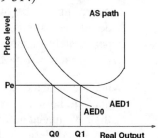

5. Three alternatives to fiscal policy are directed investment policies, trade policies, and autonomous consumption policies. Directed investment policies include talking up the economy so that businesses will invest in expectation of better days and protecting the financial system by guarantees. Trade policies would include government assistance to promote exports. Autonomous consumption policies would include creating institutions conducive to easy credit. (315)

6. A structural deficit is a deficit that would exist at potential income. A passive deficit is the part of the deficit that exists because income is below potential income. (319)

7. The six problems with fiscal policy limit its use in the following ways: (1) Financing the deficit might have offsetting effects, reducing the net effect. (2) The government doesn't always know the current state of the economy and where it is headed, meaning these must be forecast; if you don't know the state of the economy you don't know what fiscal policy to use. (3) The government doesn't know what potential income is, meaning it must be estimated; if you estimated it wrong, you get the wrong fiscal policy. (4) The government cannot implement policy easily; if you can't implement it you can't use it. (5) The size of the debt might matter and since deficits create debt, you might not want to use it. And (6) fiscal policy often negatively affects other government goals; if it does you might not use the policy even though it would change the economy in the direction you want. The bottom line is: In extreme cases, the appropriate fiscal policy is clear, but in most cases, the situation is not extreme. (323-327)

8. This first-year Congressperson is sharp! What she has described is crowding out. Crowding out is the offsetting effect on private expenditures caused by the government's sale of bonds to finance expansionary fiscal policy. If the government finances expansionary fiscal policy through the sale of bonds, interest rates will tend to rise. This will cause investment to decline, offsetting the initial stimulus. (323-325)

9. If crowding out is so strong that the reduced investment totally offsets the expansionary effect of fiscal spending, the net effect of fiscal policy can be zero. (325)

10. Unemployment insurance is an automatic stabilizer, a government program that counteracts the business cycle without any new governtment action. If the income falls, automatic stabilizers will increase aggregate expenditures to counteract that decline. Likewise with increases in income: when income increases, automatic stabilizers decrease the size of the deficit. Eliminating unemployment insurance will eliminate this stabilization aspect of the policy and will contribute to making the recession more severe than it otherwise would have been. However, it would also make people more likely to accept lower wages and search harder for a job, thereby reducing the amount of unemployment. As usual, the answer depends. (328)

Word Scramble   1. fiscal policy   2. Okun's law   3. inflationary gap

Match the Terms and Concepts to Their Definitions
1-n; 2-b; 3-h; 4-k; 5-e; 6-a; 7-c; 8-d; 9-l; 10-j; 11-g; 12-m; 13-f; 14-i.

Problems and Exercises

1. a. The spending multiplier is 2, $1/(1-.5)$, but only a fraction of the increase in taxes reduces spending. Taxes must be increased by $300 to reduce income by $300 billion. We calculate this by solving the following for change in taxes: change in taxes $\times mpe \times 1/(1-mpe)) = $300 billion. (312-315)

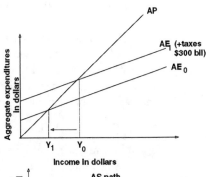

   b. The spending multiplier is 2. Spending must be decreased by $150 to reduce income by $300 billion. We calculate this by solving the following for change in government spending: change in government spending $\times (1/(1-mpe)) = -300$ billion. This is shown in the graph on the right. (312-315)

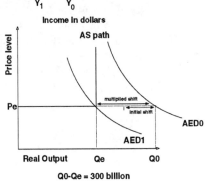

   c. The spending multiplier is now 4, $1/(1-.75)$. Government spending must be decreased by $75 billion to reduce income by $300 billion. We calculate this by solving the following for change in government spending: change in government spending $\times 4 = -300$ billion. This is shown in the graph to the right. Notice that the initial shift in the AED curve is smaller than in (b). If (b) and (c) had been shown using the AE/AP model, the *AE* curve in (c) would be steeper than the AED curve for (b). (312-315)

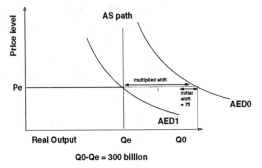

2. To close the recessionary gap in Range A, government expenditures need to rise by the full amount of the gap because the multiplier is 1. This is shown as a shifting from AED0 to AED1. However, given that the economy is in Range B, the same shift of $1000 from AED1 to AED2 will not close the gap because the increase in expenditures is split between an increase in the price level and an increase in output. When expenditures rise by $1,000, a recessionary gap of Q3-Q2 remains. (312-315)

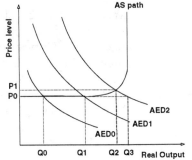

3. a. There is an income shortfall of $300 billion ($6 - $5.7 trillion). If the economy were at potential, tax revenue would be $75 billion higher and the deficit would be $125 billion. The structural deficit is $125 billion. The $75 billion (.25×300 billion) is the passive deficit. (319-320)

   b. There is an income shortfall of $500 billion ($5 - $4.5 trillion). If the economy were at potential, tax revenue would be $75 billion higher and the deficit would be $325 billion. The structural deficit is $325 billion. The $75 billion (.15×500 billion) is the passive deficit. (319-320)

   c. There is an income shortfall of $1 trillion ($10 - $9 trillion). If the economy were at potential, tax revenue would be $300 billion higher and the deficit would be $200 billion. The structural deficit is $200 billion. The $300 billion (.3×1 trillion) is the passive deficit. (319-320)

4. The spending multiplier is 2.5 (1/(1-.4). (310-314)

   a. Assuming the economy is in range A of the AS path government must increase spending on goods and services by $100 billion to increase income by $250 billion. This is shown to the right as a rightward shift in the *AED* curve of $100 billion from AED_0 to AED_1. Income increases by a multiple of that amount, by 2.5×100 = $250 billion. If the economy is in range B, the increase in expenditures will be split between increases in real output and the price level. To increase income by $250, expenditures must increase by some amount more than $100 billion. (310-314)

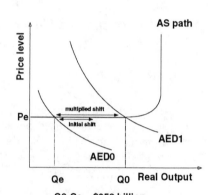

   b. Again, we're assuming the economy is in Range A of the AS path. Since interest rates have risen, investment declines and the *AE* curve shifts down, partially offsetting the initial increase in aggregate expenditures. The net effect of the spending increase is smaller than $250 billion. This is shown by a shift down in the *AE* curve from AE_1 to AE_2 resulting in income Y_2, lower than Y_1. (310-314, 323-324)

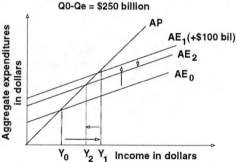

5. a. Increase spending by $1,200. According to Okun's Law, to decrease unemployment by 2 percent income must rise 5 percent, which in this case is $2,000. With an *mpe* of .4 and thus a multiplier of 1.67, the government needs to increase spending by $2,000/1.67 or $1,200 (325-326)

   b. Increase spending $625. According to Okun's Law to decrease unemployment by 2 percent income must rise 5 percent, which is $2,500. With an *mpe* of .75 and thus a multiplier of 4, the government needs to increase spending by $2,500/4 or $625. (325-326)

6. a. Since a 1 percent decrease in the unemployment rate means an increase in income of 2.5%, or, in 1995, $175 billion, the difference in their estimates of potential is $87.5 billion (.5×175). The Chairman of the CEA believed potential income was $7.175 trillion while the Chairman of the Fed believed potential income was $7.0875 trillion. (319-320, 325-326)

   b. Since the Chairman of the CEA believed the natural rate of unemployment was lower, his estimate of the structural deficit would be lower by $21,875 million. According to the Chairman of the CEA, the shortfall in income was $175 billion. According to the Chairman of the Fed, the shortfall in income was $87.5 billion. The difference in these shortfalls times the tax rate, 25%, is the amount by which their estimates differed. (319-320, 325-326))

   c. The spending multiplier is (1/(1-*mpe*)) = 2. The Chairman of the CEA would suggest an increase in spending of $175/2 = $87.5 billion while the Chairman of the Fed would suggest an increase in spending of $87.5/2 = $43.75 billion. (319-320, 325-326))

Multiple Choice Questions

1. c. See page 309.

2. b. See page 309.

3. b. See Exhibit 1, page 310.

4. d. See Exhibit 1, page 310. Also remember from earlier chapters that an increase in imports is a decrease in autonomous expenditures.

5. a. To determine how much to increase expenditures in the Keynesian *AE/AP* model to reach potential income, you divide the recessionary gap of 240 by the multiplier of 2. See pages 311-312.

6. a. To determine how much to increase expenditures in the macro policy model in Range A of the AS path, you divide the recessionary gap, 600, by the multiplier, 5. See pages 311-312.

7. b. To determine how much to increase expenditures in the Keynesian *AE/AP* model to reach potential income, you divide the recessionary gap of 900 by the multiplier of 3. See pages 311-312.

8. d. Aggregate demand management policies do not affect the AS, so a and b are out. With an inflationary gap you want to decrease output, so the answer is d. See Exhibit 3 on page 313.

9. d. As discussed on page 314, while earlier Keynesian economists supported fine tuning, modern Keynesian economists do not.

10. c. Increasing imports is contractionary. See pages 312-314.

11. b. Decreasing imports is expansionary. See pages 312-314.

12. b. See page 318.

13. b. When there are induced elements of taxes, the increase in income will bring in more taxes, reducing the actual deficit at the new equilibrium. See page 319.

14. a. When there are induced elements of imports, the increase in income will increase imports, increasing the trade deficit at the new equilibrium. See page 319.

15. a. See page 319.

16. a. See page 323. Answer c, if you could follow it, is nonsensical.

17. c. When it is not in this range there is a consensus of action that brings it back into this range. See page 329.

Chapter 13: Monetary Policy and the Debate about Macro Policy

Chapter at a glance

1. Monetary policy is a policy that influences the economy through changes in the money supply and available credit. (333)

   Expansionary (contractionary) monetary policy shifts the AED curve to the right (left). The effect on real income depends upon the range of the AS path the economy is operating in.

2a. The Fed is a semiautonomous organization composed of 12 regional banks. It is run by the Board of Governors. (335)

   The Fed (Federal Reserve Bank) is in charge of monetary policy (changing the money supply, credit availability, and interest rates).

2b. Congress gave the Fed six explicit duties. The most important is conducting monetary policy. (336)

   6 Functions of the Fed:
   1. *Conducting monetary policy (influencing the supply of money and credit in the economy).*
   2. *Supervising and regulating financial institutions.*
   3. *Serving as a lender of last resort to financial institutions.*
   4. *Providing banking services to the U.S. government.*
   5. *Issuing coin and currency.*
   6. *Providing financial services (such as check clearing) to commercial banks, savings and loan associations, savings banks, and credit unions.*

3. The three tools of monetary policy are: (338)

   1. Changing the reserve requirement;
   This is the least-used tool. It is a potentially very powerful tool (could be a case of overkill) because it changes (1) banks, excess reserves and (2) the money multiplier.

   2. Changing the discount rate; and
   The discount rate is the interest rate the Fed charges banks for loans. It is the least powerful tool.

   ✔ *Banks don't usually like to borrow from the Fed any more than we do from our parents.*

   3. Executing open market operations.
   Open market operations are the Fed's buying and selling of U.S. government securities. This is the most frequently used and most important tool to change the money supply.

   ✔ *Assume a recession:*
   The Fed should increase the money supply (pursue an expansionary monetary policy) by doing any one or more of the following:
       1. Decrease the reserve requirement.
       2. Decrease the discount rate.
       3. Buy government securities.

4. The Federal funds rate is the interest rate banks charge one another for overnight bank reserve loans. The Fed determines whether monetary policy is loose or tight depending upon what's happening to the Fed funds rate. The Fed funds rate is an important intermediate target. (343)

   The Fed targets a range for the Fed funds rate. If the Fed funds rate goes above (below) that target range, it buys (sells) bonds. These are "defensive" actions by the Fed.

5. In the Keynesian model, monetary policy works as follows: (344)
       Contractionary monetary policy:
       $M\downarrow \Rightarrow i\uparrow \Rightarrow I\downarrow \Rightarrow Y\downarrow$
   Used during an upturn in the economy to close an inflationary gap.

       Expansionary monetary policy:
       $M\uparrow \Rightarrow i\downarrow \Rightarrow I\uparrow \Rightarrow Y\uparrow$
   Used during a downturn in the economy to close a recessionary gap.

To increase the money supply (M2), the Fed must first increase banks' excess reserves and therefore bank loans.

Keynesians emphasize interest rates because it is changes in interest rates (i) which change investment (I) and eventually change income (Y).

6. In the Classical model, monetary policy works through the quantity theory: $MV = PQ$. It has short-run effects on real output, Q, but in the long run it affects only the price level, P. (346)

Three assumptions Classicals make in the quantity theory of money:
1. *Velocity (V) is constant.*
2. *Real output (Q) is independent of the money supply (M).*
3. *Causation goes from money (M) to prices (P). That is, an increase (decrease) in M causes an increase (decrease) in P.*

Classicals argue:
1. *The short-run impact of changes in M are unpredictable because of the effects on inflationary expectations, and therefore interest rates.*
2. *In the long run we're already at full employment, so Q is fixed. Because V is constant any increase in M will only increase P (the price level).*

✔ *The short-run effects of monetary policy are uncertain. The long-run effect is negative. So don't change M. Keep M constant, or increase it at a constant rate equal to the potential annual growth rate of the economy. That is, follow a monetary rule.*

7. Five problems of monetary policy: (345)

1. Knowing what policy to use.
Need to know the potential income level first.

2. Understanding what policy you're using.
Fed only indirectly controls M.

3. Lags in monetary policy.
It takes time to work.

4. Political pressure.
Fed is not totally insulated from political pressures.

5. Conflicting international goals.
We live in a global economy. The desired domestic policy may adversely affect the exchange rate value of the dollar and our trade balance.

See also,
Appendix A: "The Effect of Monetary Policy Using T-Accounts."
Appendix B: "Keynesian and Classical Theories of interest and Their Implications for Monetary Policy."

Short-answer questions

1. You have been asked to speak to the first-year Congresspeople. Your talk is about the Fed. They want to know what monetary policy is. You tell them. (LO1)

2. To clarify your answer to question 1 tell when the Fed was created and what its specific duties are. (LO2)

3. Another Congressperson asks what monetary policy actions the Fed can take. You answer. (LO3)

4. You are asked to elaborate on your answer to question 3. Now that you have listed each of the tools of monetary policy, how does each work? (LO3)

5. One Congressperson realizes that the Fed does not have complete control over the money supply. She states that people could demand more cash, which will reduce the money supply. How does the Fed know whether its buying and selling of bonds is having the desired effect? You answer by explaining the Fed's intermediate target. (LO4)

6. Another Congressperson asks how monetary policy can keep the economy from overheating. You reply from a Keynesian perspective. (LO5)

7. Suppose the economy is below potential output. Now how can monetary policy boost output? You reply again from a Keynesian perspective. (LO5)

8. Someone from the audience speaks up after your answers to the last two questions. "That's not what I remember from my college economics course." After some discussion you realize that her professor was a Classical economist. You explain to everyone how your answers to 6 and 7 change if answered from a Classical perspective. (LO6)

9. You take one final question at the conference and it is a difficult one: "It doesn't seem that the Fed is doing a good job. I read in the paper that the Fed has followed too contractionary a policy and has caused a recession or that it is not even sure what policy it is following." How do you respond to those concerns? (LO7)

Word Scramble

1. _____ _____   2._____ _____   3._____ _____ _____
    a e m n o r t y   c y p o l i   e F d   p o n e   a e k m r t   t s r p o o n i e a

Match the Terms and Concepts to Their Definitions

___ 1. central bank

___ 2. contractionary monetary policy

___ 3. discount rate

___ 4. equation of exchange

___ 5. expansionary monetary policy

___ 6. Federal Open Market Committee (FOMC)

___ 7. Federal funds rate

___ 8. monetary base

___ 9. nominal interest rate

___ 10. open market operations

___ 11. quantity theory of money

___ 12. real interest rate

___ 13. reserve requirement

___ 14. veil of money assumption

___ 15. velocity of money

a. The theory that the price level varies in direct response to change in the quantity of money.

b. Interest rate you actually see and pay.

c. Interest rate adjusted for expected inflation.

d. Assumption that holds that real output is not influenced by changes in the money supply.

e. Rate of interest the Fed charges on loans it makes to banks.

f. The Fed's day-to-day buying and selling of government securities.

g. The number of times per year, on average, a dollar goes around to generate a dollar's worth of income.

h. The percentage the Federal Reserve System sets as the minimum amount of reserves a bank must have.

i. A banker's bank; it conducts monetary policy and supervises the financial system.

j. The vault cash plus reserves that banks have at the Fed.

k. Monetary policy aimed at raising the money supply and raising the level of aggregate demand.

l. Monetary policy aimed at reducing the money supply and reducing the level of aggregate demand.

m. The Fed's chief policy making body.

n. The interest rate banks charge one another for Fed funds.

o. An equation for "quantity of money times velocity of money equals the price level times the quantity of real goods sold."

Problems and Exercises

1. The Fed wants to change the reserve requirement in order to change the money supply (which is currently $3,000). For each situation below, calculate the current reserve requirement and the amount by which the Fed must change the reserve requirement to achieve the desired change in the money supply. Assume no cash holdings.

    a. Money multiplier is 3 and the Fed wants to increase money supply by $300.

    b. Money multiplier is 2.5 and the Fed wants to increase the money supply by $300.

c. Money multiplier is 4 and the Fed wants to decrease the money supply by $500.

d. Money multiplier is 4 and the Fed wants to increase the money supply by $1,000.

2. How do your answers change for 1 (a) - (d) if instead of changing the reserve requirement, the Fed wants to use an open market operation to change the money supply? Assume the reserve requirement remains unchanged. What should the Fed do to achieve the desired change? (The multiplier and desired change in money supply for each are listed.)

a. Money multiplier is 3 and the Fed wants to increase money supply by $300.

b. Money multiplier is 2.5 and the Fed wants to increase the money supply by $300.

c. Money multiplier is 4 and the Fed wants to decrease the money supply by $500.

d. Money multiplier is 4 and the Fed wants to increase the money supply by $1000.

3. Instead of changing the reserve requirement or using open market operations, the Fed wants to change the discount rate to achieve the desired change in the money supply. Assume that for each 1 percentage point fall in the discount rate, banks borrow an additional $20. How do your answers change to from answers 1 (a)-(d)? (The multiplier and desired change in money supply for each are listed.)

a. Money multiplier is 3 and the Fed wants to increase money supply by $300.

b. Money multiplier is 2.5 and the Fed wants to increase the money supply by $300.

c. Money multiplier is 4 and the Fed wants to decrease the money supply by $500.

d. Money multiplier is 4 and the Fed wants to increase the money supply by $1,000.

4. a.   What are the three assumptions that translate the equation of exchange into the quantity theory of money?

    b.   State the equation of exchange and show how the three assumptions lead to the conclusion that inflation is always and everywhere a monetary phenomenon.

5. Answer the following questions about the quantity theory of money: Assume the money supply is $1,200 billion, the price level is $1.25, and the velocity of money is 6.

    a.   What is the level of real output?

    b.   What is the level of nominal output?

    c.   Assuming the velocity of money remains at 6, what will nominal output be if the money supply increases by 7%?

    d.   Assuming the velocity of money remains at 6, by how much will prices rise if the money supply increases by 7%?

6. Fill in the blanks in the following table:

	Inflation rate	Nominal Interest Rate	Real Interest rate
a.	5%	10%	_____
b.	_____	15%	7%
c.	-3%	_____	9%
d.	4%	_____	10%

7. Suppose the Fed decides to pursue an expansionary monetary policy. The money supply is currently $1 billion. Assume people hold no cash, the reserve requirement is 10 percent, and there are no excess reserves.

   a. By how much must the Fed change the reserve requirement to increase the money supply by $100 million?

   b. What would the Fed do to increase the money supply by $100,000 through open market operations?

8. The money supply is currently $1 billion. Assume people hold 25 percent of their money in the form of cash balances, the reserve requirement is 25 percent, and there are no excess reserves.

   a. By how much must the Fed change the reserve requirement to increase the money supply by $200 million?

   b. What would the Fed do to increase the money supply by $200 million through open market operations?

A1. Suppose the money multiplier is 2.5 and there are no cash holdings. Textland Bank is the only bank in the country. The Fed wants to decrease the money supply by $10,000. The initial balance sheet is shown below.

Initial Balance Sheet

Assets		Liabilities	
Cash	20,000	Demand Deposits	50,000
Loans	120,000	Net Worth	100,000
Phys. Assets	10,000		
Total Assets	150,000	Total Liabilities and net worth	150,000

a. What open market operations must the Fed execute to reduce the money supply by $10,000?

b. Using T-accounts show the first two steps of the effects of the Fed open market operation reducing the money supply by $10,000.

Step #1

Assets	Liabilities

Step #2

Assets	Liabilities

c. Show the final balance sheet for Textland bank.

Final Position

Assets	Liabilities

A2. Using T-accounts, show the effect of a decrease in the reserve ratio from .2 to .1 given the following initial position of Textland. Again, Textland is the only bank, no one holds cash, and there are no excess reserves. Show the first two steps and the then the final position.

Initial Position

Assets		Liabilities	
Cash	40,000	Demand Deposits	200,000
Loans	230,000	Net Worth	100,000
Phys. Assets	30,000		
Total Assets	300,000		
		Total Liabilities and net worth	300,000

Step #1

Assets	Liabilities

Step #2

Assets	Liabilities

Final Position

Assets	Liabilities

Multiple Choice Questions

1. The central bank of the United States is
    a. the Treasury.
    b. the Fed.
    c. the Bank of the United States.
    d. Old Lady of Threadneedle Street.

2. Monetary policy is
    a. a variation of fiscal policy.
    b. undertaken by the Treasury.
    c. undertaken by the Fed.
    d. the regulation of monetary institutions.

3. There are seven Governors of the Federal Reserve, who are appointed for terms of
    a. 5 years.
    b. 10 years.
    c. 14 years.
    d. 17 years.

4. Explicit functions of the Fed include all the following except
    a. conducting monetary policy.
    b. conducting fiscal policy.
    c. providing banking services to the U.S. government.
    d. serving as a lender of last resort to financial institutions.

5. FOMC stands for
    a. Federal Open Money Committee.
    b. Federal Open Market Committee.
    c. Fixed Open Market Commitments.
    d. Federation of Open Monies Committee.

6. Tools of monetary policy include all the following except
    a. changing the reserve requirement.
    b. changing the discount rate.
    c. executing open market operations.
    d. running deficits.

7. Assuming $c = .2$ and $r = .1$, the approximate real-world money multiplier would be
    a. 1.33.
    b. 2.33.
    c. 3.33.
    d. 4.33.

8. The discount rate refers to
    a. the lower price large institutions pay for government bonds.
    b. the rate of interest the Fed charges for loans to banks.
    c. the rate of interest the Fed charges for loans to individuals.
    d. the rate of interest the Fed charges for loans to government.

9. The primary tool of monetary policy is
    a. open market operations.
    b. changing the discount rate.
    c. changing the reserve requirement.
    d. imposing credit controls.

10. The Fed wants to increase the money supply.
    a. It should buy bonds.
    b. It should sell bonds.
    c. It should pass a law that the interest rates rise.
    d. It should pass a law that the interest rates fall.

11. When the Fed sells bonds, the money supply is
    a. expanded.
    b. contracted.
    c. Selling bonds does not have any effect on the money supply.
    d. sometimes raised and sometimes lowered

12. An open market purchase
    a. raises bond prices and reduces interest rates.
    b. raises both bond prices and interest rates.
    c. reduces bond prices and raises interest rates.
    d. reduces both bond prices and interest rates.

13. The Federal funds rate is
    a. the interest rate the government charges banks for Fed funds.
    b. the interest rate the Fed charges banks for Fed funds.
    c. the interest rate the banks charge individual investors for Fed funds.
    d. the interest rate the banks charge each other for Fed funds.

14. If the Fed undertakes expansionary monetary policy the effect will be to
    a. shift the AED curve to the right.
    b. shift the AED curve to the left.
    c. shift the AS path up.
    d. shift the AS path down.

15. If the Fed undertakes contractionary monetary policy the effect will be to
    a. shift the AED curve to the right.
    b. shift the AED curve to the left.
    c. shift the AS path up.
    d. shift the AS path down.

16. Which of the following is the path through which contractionary monetary policy works?
    a. money down implies interest up implies investment down implies income down.
    b. money down implies interest down implies investment down implies income down.
    c. money down implies interest up implies investment up implies income down.
    d. money down implies interest down implies investment up implies income down.

17. In the Classical model, monetary policy works through the quantity theory, which is designed around the equation of exchange. This equation of exchange is
    a. $MV = PM$.
    b. $MV = PQ$.
    c. $AE = AP$.
    d. $MF = CE$.

18. In 1997 nominal GDP in the U.S. was approximately $7.5 trillion, and the money supply was approximately $3.75 trillion. The velocity of money was
    a. 1/2
    b. 2
    c. $7.5 \times $3.75
    d. cannot be determined.

19. An economist has just said she favors "steady as you go" monetary policy. This economist
    a. is most likely a Keynesian.
    b. is most likely a Classical.
    c. could equally be either a Keynesian or a Classical.
    d. must be neither a Keynesian nor a Classical, since neither group favors such a policy.

20. Expected inflation is 4 percent; nominal interest rates are 7 percent; the real interest rate is
    a. 1 percent.
    b. 2 percent.
    c. 3 percent.
    d. 7 percent.

21. The real interest rate is 3 percent; the nominal interest rate is 7 percent. It is likely that one could deduce an
    expected inflation rate of
    a. 1%.
    b. 2%.
    c. 3%.
    d. 4%.

22. The Fed most directly controls
    a. M_1.
    b. M_2.
    c. the monetary base.
    d. the amount of credit in the economy.

B1. The Keynesian theory of the interest rate says that the interest rate is determined primarily in the
    a. money market.
    b. saving/investment market.
    c. real economy.
    d. exogenously.

B2. The Classical theory of the interest rate says that the interest rate is determined primarily in the
    a. money market.
    b. saving/investment market.
    c. foreign exchange market
    d. exogenously.

Answers

Short-answer questions

1. Monetary policy is a policy that influences the economy through changes in the money supply and available credit. The Fed conducts U.S. monetary policy. (333)

2. The Fed was created in 1913. Its six explicit duties are (1) conducting monetary policy, (2) regulating financial institutions, (3) serving as a lender of last resort, (4) providing banking services to the U.S. government, (5) issuing coin and currency, and (6) providing financial services to financial institutions. (336-337)

3. The three tools of monetary policy at the disposal of the Fed are (1) changing the reserve requirement, (2) changing the discount rate, and (3) executing open market operations (buying and selling bonds). (338)

4. Changing the reserve requirement changes the amount of reserves the banks must hold and thus changes the amount of loans they can make. This changes the money supply. Changing the discount rate changes the willingness of banks to borrow from the Fed to meet reserve requirements, thus changing the amount of loans they are willing to make. This changes the money supply. Open market operations change the reserves banks hold by directly increasing or decreasing cash held by banks and simultaneously decreasing or increasing their holdings of government bonds. This changes the amount of loans banks can make and changes the money supply. (338-341)

5. Economists and policymakers keep a close eye on the Fed funds rate, the rate banks charge one another for loans of reserves, as an intermediate target to determine the effect of an open market operation—whether it indeed was expansionary or contractionary. An expansionary action will lower the Fed funds rate and contractionary action will raise the Fed funds rate. In effect, the Fed chooses a range for the Fed funds rate and buys and sells bonds to keep the Fed funds rate within that range. If the Fed funds rate is below (above) the target, the Fed sells (buys) bonds. (343)

6. Contractionary monetary policy in the Keynesian model increases interest rates, lowers investment, and reduces income. (344)

7. Expansionary monetary policy in the Keynesian model decreases interest rates, raises investment, and increases income. (344)

8. Contractionary monetary policy in the Classical model works through the quantity theory of money, $MV = PQ$. Classicals believe that V is relatively constant, Q is determined by forces outside the model, and causation goes from MV to PQ. In the short run, it can lead to decreases in output, but in the long run, it only leads to decreases in the price level. Expansionary monetary policy in the Classical model works through the quantity theory of money, $MV = PQ$. In the short run, it can lead to increases in output, but in the long run, it only leads to inflation. (346-349)

9. You tell the Congressperson that conducting monetary policy is difficult. Five problems often encountered in conducting monetary policy are: (1) Knowing what potential income is. No one has the magic number. It must be estimated. (2) Knowing whether the policy you are using is contractionary or expansionary. The Fed does not directly control the money supply. (3) There are significant lags in the effect of monetary policy in the economy. (4) The Fed is subject to political pressure. And (5) often domestic goals differ from international goals when deciding which policy to follow. (350-351)

Word Scramble   1. monetary policy   2. Fed   3. open market operations

Match the Terms and Concepts to Their Definitions

1-i; 2-l; 3-e; 4-o; 5-k; 6-m; 7-n; 8-j; 9-b; 10-f; 11-a; 12-c; 13-h; 14-d; 15-g.

Problems and Exercises

1. a. Current $r = 1/3$; New $r = .3$, so it must be changed by .03. To find the reserve requirement solve $1/r = 3$ for r. $r = 1/3$. These calculations are based on the formula $M = (1/r) \times MB$, where M is the money supply, r is the reserve ratio, and MB is the monetary base (here it equals reserves). We first find out the cash (monetary base) that supports \$3,000 money supply with a money multiplier of 3. It is \$1,000. We want the money supply to be \$3,300. So the multiplier we want is \$3,300/1,000= 3.3. Again solving $1/r = 3.3$ we find r must be 0.3. (339)

    b. To find the reserve requirement solve $1/r = 5/2$ for r. $r = .4$. Cash must be \$1,200 to support money supply of \$3,000. The Fed must reduce the reserve requirement to .3636 to increase the money supply by \$300. Use the method described in (a) to find the answer. (339)

    c. To find the reserve requirement solve $1/r = 4$ for r. $r = .25$. Cash must be \$750 to support money supply of \$3,000. The Fed must increase the reserve requirement to .3 to decrease the money supply by \$500. Use the method described in (a) to find the answer. (339)

    d. To find the reserve requirement solve $1/r = 4$ for r. $r = .25$. Cash must be \$750 to support money supply of \$3,000. The Fed must reduce the reserve requirement to .1875 to increase the money supply by \$1,000. Use the method described in (a) to find the answer. (339)

2. These calculations are based on the formula $M = (1/r) \times MB$, where M is the money supply, r is the reserve ratio, and MB is the monetary base (here it equals reserves).

    a. The Fed should buy bonds to increase reserves in the system by \$100. We find this by dividing the desired increase by the money multiplier. (338-339, 341)

    b. The Fed should buy bonds to increase reserves in the system by \$120. We find this by dividing the desired increase by the money multiplier. (338-339, 341)

    c. The Fed should sell bonds to decrease reserves in the system by \$125. We find this by dividing the desired increase by the money multiplier. (338-339, 341)

    d. The Fed should buy bonds to increase reserves in the system by \$250. We find this by dividing the desired increase by the money multiplier. (338-339, 341)

3. These calculations are based on the formula $M = (1/r) \times MB$, where M is the money supply, r is the reserve ratio, and MB is the monetary base (here it equals reserves). Find out how much reserves must be changed and divide by 20 to find how much the discount rate must be lowered (if reserves are to be raised) or increased (if reserves are to lowered).

    a. To increase reserves in the system by \$100, the discount rate should be reduced by 5 points. We find how much reserves must be increased by dividing the desired increase in the money supply by the money multiplier. We find how much the discount rate must be lowered by dividing the desired increase in reserves by 20 (the amount reserves will increase with each percentage point decline in the discount rate). (339-340)

    b. To increase reserves in the system by \$120, the discount rate should be reduced by 6 points. See introduction to answer number 3 for how to calculate this. (339-340)

    c. To decrease reserves in the system by \$125, the discount rate should be increased by 6.25 points. See introduction to answer number 3 for how to calculate this. (339-340)

    d. To increase reserves in the system by \$250, the discount rate should be reduced by 12.5 points. See introduction to answer number 3 for how to calculate this. (339-340)

4. a. 1. Velocity is constant, 2. Real output is independent of the money supply, 3. Causation goes from money supply to prices. (346-348)

    b. $MV = PQ$ is the equation of exchange. Since V is constant and Q exogenous, the only remaining variables that change within the system are M and P. Since the causation runs from M to P, to keep the equation balanced, a rise in M must lead to a rise in P (and only P since Q is exogenous). (346-348)

5. a. \$5,760 billion: $MV = PQ$; $6 \times 1200 = 1.25Q$. Solve for Q. (346-348)

    b. \$7,200 billion: $MV = PQ = 6 \times 1200$. (346-348)

    c. \$7,704: $MV = PQ = 6 \times 1284$. (346-348)

    d. 7%. (346-348)

6.

Inflation rate	Nominal Interest Rate	Real Interest rate	
a. 5%	10%	5% :	Real rate = nominal - inflation. (349)
b. 8%	15%	7%:	Inflation = nominal - real rate. (349)
c. -3%	6%	9%:	Nominal = inflation + real. (349)
d. 4%	14%	10%:	Nominal = inflation + real. (349)

7. These calculations are based on the formula $M = (1/r) \times MB$, where M is the money supply, r is the reserve ratio, and MB is the monetary base (here it equals reserves).
   a. The money multiplier is $1/r = 10$. Reserves must be $100 million to support a money supply of $1 billion. The reserve ratio to support $1.1 billion money supply with $100 million reserves is about 9.1%. We find this by dividing reserves by the desired money supply. (339-343)
   b. The Fed would have to buy $10,000 worth of bonds to increase the money supply by $100,000. Calculate this by dividing the desired increase in the money supply by the money multiplier. (339-343)

8. In this case, the approximate real-world money multiplier is $1/(r + c) = 1/(.25+.33) = 1.72$. The cash-to-deposit ratio is .33 since people hold 25% of their money in cash and the remainder, 75%, in deposits.
   a. The reserve requirement must be lowered to about 15%. We find this by first calculating the monetary base: $1 billion /1.72 = $580 million (Money supply/ multiplier). For the money supply to increase to $1.2 billion, the money multiplier must be $1.2/.580 = 2.07. To find the new reserve ratio solve $1/(r+c) = 2.07$ for r. We find that $r = .15$. (339-343)
   b. The Fed must buy $116,280,000 in bonds to increase the money supply by $200 million Calculate this by dividing the desired increase in the money supply by the money multiplier: $200 million / 1.72. (339-343)

A1. This calculations are based on the formula $M = (1/r) \times MB$, where M is the money supply, r is the reserve ratio, and MB is the monetary base (here it equals reserves).
   a. The Fed must sell bonds worth $4,000 to reduce reserves by $4,000. We calculate this by dividing the desired reduction in the money supply by the money multiplier. (354-355)
   b. Step 1: An individual or group of individuals buy $4,000 in Treasury bonds from the Fed. Individuals withdraw the funds from the bank. (354-355)

Assets		Liabilities	
Cash	20,000	Demand Deposits	50,000
Payment to individuals	(4,000)	Withdrawals	(4,000)
Total cash	16,000	Total demand deposits	46,000
Loans	120,000	Net Worth	100,000
Phys. Assets	10,000		
Total Assets	146,000	Total Liabilities and net worth	146,000

Step 2: Reserves are now too low to meet the reserve requirement of .4. (We calculated the reserve requirement by solving the equation $1/r = 2.5$ for r.) The bank must call in $2,400 in loans ($46,000 \times .4 - 16,000$). This shows up as loans repaid. But the individuals repaying the loans must get the money from somewhere. Since no one holds cash and Textland bank is the only bank, the individuals must withdraw the $2,400 from the bank. This is shown as a withdrawal on the liability side and a payment to individuals on the asset side. Again reserves are too low, this time by $1,440. (354-355)

Assets		Liabilities	
Cash	16,000	Demand Deposits	46,000
Loans repaid	$2,400	Withdrawals	(2,400)
Payment to inds.	(2,400)	Total demand deposits	43,600
Total cash	16,000		

Loans	120,000	Net Worth	100,000
loans called in	(2,400)		
Loans	117,600		
Phys. Assets	10,000	Total Liabilities	
Total Assets	143,600	and net worth	143,600

c. Final balance sheet: Banks continue to call in loans to meet reserve requirements until the multiplier process is finished. The money supply is now $10,000 less. At last, the balance sheet is as shown: (354-355)

Assets		Liabilities	
Cash	16,000	Demand Deposits	40,000
Loans	114,000	Net Worth	100,000
Phys. Assets	10,000		
Total Assets	140,000	Total Liabilities	
		and net worth	140,000

A2.   Step 1: The bank makes $20,000 in new loans. This money is spent and then deposited into Textland by other individuals. (354-355)

Assets		Liabilities	
Cash	40,000	Demand Deposits	200,000
Payments out	(20,000)	New deposits	20,000
Payments in	20,000	Total deposits	220,000
Total cash	40,000		
Loans	230,000	Net Worth	100,000
New loans	20,000		
Total loans	250,000		
Phys. Assets	30,000	Total Liabilities	
Total Assets	320,000	and net worth	320,000

Step 2: Textland still has excess reserves (40,000/220,000 > .1) by $18,000 so it makes $18,000 in new loans. Calculate excess reserves by reserves - total deposits×reserve ratio. (354-355)

Assets		Liabilities	
Cash	40,000	Demand Deposits	220,000
Payments out	(18,000)	New deposits	18,000
Payments in	18,000	Total deposits	238,000
Total cash	40,000		
Loans	250,000	Net Worth	100,000
New loans	18,000		
Total loans	268,000		
Phys. Assets	30,000		
Total Assets	338,000	Total Liabilities	
		and net worth	338,000

Final position: The previous steps continue until the money creation process ends as shown below. (354-355).

Assets		Liabilities	
Cash	40,000	Demand Deposits	400,000
Loans	430,000	Net Worth	100,000
Phys. Assets	30,000		
Total Assets	500,000	Total Liabilities and net worth	500,000

Multiple Choice Questions

1. b. See pages 333-335.

2. c. The correct answer is "policy undertaken by the Fed." The last answer, d, involves regulation, which is also done by the Fed, but such regulation generally does not go under the name "monetary policy." Given the accuracy of answer c, answer d should be avoided. See pages 333-334, 336-337.

3. c. See page 335.

4. b. Fiscal policy is definitely not a function of the Fed. See pages 336-337.

5. b. See the text, Exhibit 2, page 336, and page 338.

6. d. Deficits are a tool of fiscal policy. See page 338.

7. c. The approximate real-world money multiplier is $1/(r + c) = 1/.3=3.33$. See page 339.

8. b. The Fed makes loans only to other banks, and the discount rate is the rate of interest the Fed charges for these loans. See page 335, 340.

9. a. See pages 338-341.

10. a. The last two answers, c and d, cannot be right, because the Fed does not pass laws. When the Fed buys bonds, it lowers the interest rate but it does not lower interest rates by law. Therefore, only a is correct. See page 341.

11. b. People pay the Fed for those bonds with money—FED IOUs-—so the money supply in private hands is reduced. See page 341.

12. a. As the Fed buys bonds and reduces their supply, their price rises. Since bond prices and interest rates are inversely related, interest rates will fall. See pages 341-342.

13. d. See page 342.

14. a. See pages 334 and 342.

15. b. Contractionary monetary policy increases interest rates which reduces investment, a component of aggregate expenditures. The AED curve shifts to the left by a multiple of the decline in investment. See pages 334 and 342.

16. a. Contractionary monetary policy increases interest rates which decreases investment, thereby decreasing income by a multiple of that amount. See pages 344, 342, and 344.

17. b. See page 346.

18. b. Velocity of money equals nominal GDP divided by the money supply (7.5/3.75). See page 347.

19. b. While it could be either, it is most likely a Classical; Keynesians tend to favor more activist policy. See page 348.

20. c. To determine real interest rate, you subtract expected inflation from nominal interest rates. 7-4=3. See page 349.

21. d. To determine expected inflation you subtract real interest rates from nominal interest rates. 7-3=4. See page 349.

22. c. The monetary base is the vault cash and the reserves banks have at the Fed. It is the one variable the Fed can directly control. See page 350.

B1. a. The Keynesian theory of the interest rate focuses on the supply and demand for money. See page 356.

B2. b. See page 356.

Pretest II
Chapters 7 - 13

Take this test in test conditions, giving yourself a limited amount of time to complete the questions. Ideally, check with your professor to see how much time he or she allows for an average multiple choice question and multiply this by 33. This is the time limit you should set for yourself for this pretest. If you do not know how much time your teacher would allow, we suggest 1 minute per question, or about 35 minutes.

1. The secular trend growth rate in the United States is approximately
   a. 1 to 1.5 percent per year.
   b. 2.5 to 3.5 percent per year.
   c. 5 to 5.5 percent per year.
   d. 7 to 7.5 percent per year.

2. In the 1980s and 1990s the target rate of unemployment generally has been
   a. between 2 and 3 percent.
   b. between 3 and 5 percent.
   c. between 4 and 6 percent.
   d. between 7 and 8 percent.

3. Okun's rule of thumb states that
   a. a 1 percentage point change in the unemployment rate will cause income to change in the same direction by 2.5 percent.
   b. a 1 percentage point change in the unemployment rate will cause income to change in the opposite direction by 2.5 percent.
   c. a 2.5 percentage point change in the unemployment rate will cause income to change in the same direction by 1 percent.
   d. a. 2.5 percentage point change in the unemployment rate will cause income to change in the opposite direction by 1 percent.

4. Real output is
   a. total amount of goods and services produced.
   b. total amount of goods and services produced adjusted for price level changes.
   c. total amount of goods produced, adjusted for services that aren't real.
   d. total amount of goods and services that are really produced as opposed to ones that are resold.

5. If inflation is 10 percent and nominal GDP goes up 20 percent, real GDP goes up approximately
   a. 1 percent.
   b. 10 percent.
   c. 20 percent.
   d. 50 percent.

6. If you, the owner, sell your old car for $600, how much does GDP increase?
   a. By $600.
   b. By the amount you bought it for, minus the $600.
   c. By zero.
   d. By the $600 you received and the $600 the person you sold it to paid, or $1,200.

7. The four components of expenditures in GDP are
   a. consumption, investment, government spending, and net exports.
   b. consumption, depreciation, investment, and government expenditures.
   c. consumption, investment, gross exports, and government expenditures.
   d. durable goods, nondurable goods, services, and government expenditures.

8. The largest component of national income is
   a. rents.
   b. net interest.
   c. profits.
   d. compensation to employees.

9. For every financial asset
   a. there is a corresponding financial liability.
   b. there is a corresponding financial liability if the financial asset is financed.
   c. there is a real liability.
   d. there is a corresponding real asset.

10. Assuming individuals hold no cash, the reserve requirement is 20 percent, and banks keep no excess reserves, an increase in an initial $100 of money will cause an increase in total money of
    a. $20.
    b. $50.
    c. $100.
    d. $500.

11. If banks hold excess reserves whereas before they did not, the relative money multiplier
    a. will become larger.
    b. will become smaller.
    c. will be unaffected.
    d. might increase or might decrease.

12. A sound bank will
    a. always have money on hand to pay all depositors in full.
    b. never borrow short and lend long.
    c. never borrow long and lend short.
    d. keep enough money on hand to cover normal cash inflows and outflows.

13. Classical economists
    a. generally favor government intervention.
    b. generally oppose government intervention.
    c. believe the economy is primarily directed by the invisible handshake.
    d. think unions are not responsible for unemployment.

14. When people save, Say's law
    a. is invalidated.
    b. remains true because saving has nothing to do with Say's law.
    c. remains true as long as saving is translated back into investment.
    d. is false because saving creates unemployment.

15. If $M = 200$, $V = 4$, P = 2, then $Q =$ _____.
    a. 50.
    b. 100.
    c. 200.
    d. 400.

16. A decrease in foreign income
    a. would likely shift the United States' AED in.
    b. would likely shift the United States' AED out.
    c. would likely make the United States' AED flatter.
    d. would likely make the United States' AED steeper.

17. If the economy is significantly below its potential output, the aggregate supply path is generally considered to be
    a. flat.
    b. upward sloping.
    c. backward sloping.
    d. perfectly vertical.

18. Suppose the AED curve shifted in from AED_0 to AED_1. If there had been inflation and the price level axis is interpreted relative to expectations, i.e., the shift was disinflationary, the resulting price and output level would be at:
    a. P_1, Q_1.
    b. P_2, Q_1.
    c. P_2, Q_2.
    d. P_1, Q_3.

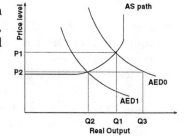

19. The marginal propensity to expend is the
    a. change in expenditures times change in income.
    b. change in expenditures divided by the change in income.
    c. change in expenditures divided by income.
    d. expenditures divided by the change in income.

20. If the *mpe* is .8, what is the size of the multiplier in the Keynesian model?
    a. .5.
    b. 5.
    c. 1.
    d. 10.

21. In the Keynesian *AE/AP* model, if autonomous exports falls by 40 and the *mpe* is .5, what happens to the income?
    a. income rises by 20.
    b. income falls by 20.
    c. income rises by 80.
    d. income falls by 80.

22. In the Keynesian *AE/AP* model, if autonomous exports falls by 40 and government spending increases by 20, and the *mpe* is .8, what happens to the income?
    a. income rises by 25.
    b. income falls by 25.
    c. income rises by 100.
    d. income falls by 100.

23. To derive the aggregate equilibrium demand curve from the Keynesian *AE/AP* model, one must
    a. relate the initial autonomous shifts caused by price level changes on the *AE* curve to the *AED* curve.
    b. relate the *AE/AP* equilibria at different price levels to the *AED* curve.
    c. relate the *AE/AP* equilibria at different quantity levels to the *AED* curve.
    d. relate the initial autonomous shifts caused by price level changes on the *AP* curve to the *AED* curve.

24. Which group is most likely to believe that a model using autonomous expenditures is relevant?
    a. Keynesians.
    b. Classicals.
    c. Keynesians and Classicals would be equal in their belief.
    d. Neither Keynesians nor Classicals would see a model using autonomous elements as relevant.

25. The economy has a fixed price level, an *mpe* of .5, and a recessionary gap of 240. Using the Keynesian *AE/AP* model, an economist would advise government to
    a. increase autonomous expenditures by 120.
    b. increase autonomous expenditures by 240.
    c. increase autonomous expenditures by 480.
    d. increase autonomous expenditures by 620.

26. Expansionary aggregate demand policy includes all of the following except
    a. increasing government spending.
    b. increasing autonomous expenditures.
    c. increasing imports.
    d. decreasing taxes.

27. The portion of the budget deficit that would exist even if the economy were at its potential level of income is called the
    a. structural deficit.
    b. passive deficit.
    c. primary deficit.
    d. secondary deficit.

28. Crowding out occurs when
    a. the government runs a deficit and sells bonds to finance that deficit.
    b. the government prints money.
    c. the government runs a surplus and sells bonds and the people who buy those bonds sell their older bonds to the government.
    d. the tendency for new workers to replace more expensive older workers is a factor.

29. Explicit functions of the Fed include all the following except
    a. conducting monetary policy.
    b. conducting fiscal policy.
    c. providing banking services to the U.S. government.
    d. serving as a lender of last resort to financial institutions.

30. Tools of monetary policy include all the following except
    a. changing the reserve requirement.
    b. changing the discount rate.
    c. executing open market operations.
    d. running deficits.

31. Assuming $c = .2$ and $r = .1$, the approximate real-world money multiplier would be
    a. 1.33.
    b. 2.33.
    c. 3.33.
    d. 4.33.

32. When the Fed sells bonds, the money supply is
    a. expanded.
    b. contracted.
    c. Selling bonds does not have any effect on the money supply.
    d. sometimes raised and sometimes lowered

33. An economist has just said she favors "steady as you go" monetary policy. This economist
    a. is most likely a Keynesian.
    b. is most likely a Classical.
    c. could equally be either a Keynesian or a Classical.
    d. must be neither a Keynesian nor a Classical, since neither group favors such a policy.

Answers

1. b (7:1)	12. d (9:14)	23. b (11:18)
2. c (7:8)	13. b (10:1)	24. a (11:22)
3. b (7:12)	14. c (10:3)	25. a (12:5)
4. b (7:16)	15. d (10:7)	26. c (12:10)
5. b (8:1)	16. a (10:12)	27. a (12:15)
6. c (8:4)	17. a (10:16)	28. a (12:16)
7. a (8:8)	18. c (10:22)	29. b (13:4)
8. d (8:10)	19. b (11:4)	30. d (13:6)
9. a (9:1)	20. b (11:6)	31. c (13:7)
10. d (9:10)	21. d (11:9)	32. b (13:11)
11. b (9:13)	22. d (11:14)	33. b (13:19)

Key: The figures in parentheses refer to multiple choice question and chapter numbers. For example (1:4) is multiple choice question 1 from chapter 4.

Chapter 14:
Inflation and Its Relationship to Unemployment and Growth

Chapter at a glance

1. High inflation rates are inevitably accompanied by high money growth and high inflationary expectations. The reason is that the velocity of money generally cannot increase enormously and people's expectations of the future are determined in large part by what is occurring now. (359)

   Inflation can either be cost-push or demand-pull and these can feed on each other because of adaptive expectations.

2. The long-run Phillips curve is vertical; it takes into account the feedback of inflation on expectations of inflation. The short-run Phillips curve does not take this feedback into account. (364)

   In the long run when expectations of inflation are met, changes in the rates of inflation have no effect on the level of unemployment. Classicals believe the long-run Phillips curve is fixed at the natural rate of unemployment. This is shown as LR in the accompanying graph.

   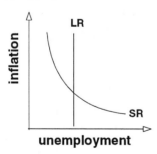

   The short-run Phillips curve reflects the empirically observed trade-off between inflation and unemployment. Expectations of inflation are constant along the short-run (SR) Phillips cuve. Increases (decreases) in inflationary expectations shift the short-run Phillips curve to the right (left).

Classicals believe that inflation undermines long-run growth and that there is an inverse relation between inflation and long-run growth.

In the long run we have more time to adjust our expectations to actual inflation. In the short run we may be fooled–we may expect less (more) inflation than actually occurs when inflation is accelerating (decelerating).

3. The Classical theory of inflation is summarized by the sentence: Inflation is everywhere and always a monetary phenomenon. (367)

   $$Long\ Run: M\overset{\uparrow}{\overline{V}} = \overset{\uparrow}{P}\overline{Q}$$

   Note: The price level rises because the money supply rises.

   Short Run: An increase in the money supply may also increase real output (employment and income), but only for awhile–for as long as people are fooled into thinking increases in nominal income are increases in their real income.

4. Classical economists favor a monetary rule because they believe the short-run effects of monetary policy are unpredictable and the long-run effects of monetary policy are on the price level, not on real output. (369)

   Monetary Rule: Increase the money supply by a constant rate year after year equal to the potential annual growth rate in real GDP (about 2.5-3.5%).

5. The Keynesian theory of inflation holds that institutional and structural aspects of inflation, as well as increases in the money supply, are important causes of inflation. (370)

    The "insider" versus "outsider" situation creates imperfect markets. Imperfect markets provide an opportunity for "insiders" to increase their wages and prices even when unemployment and excess capacity exists in the overall economy, thereby creating inflation.

6a. Classicals view the long-run Phillips curve as vertical; the short-run trade-off is only a temporary illusion. (370)

    The Classical view of the Phillips curve trade-off centers around the natural rate of unemployment. Any attempts to maintain unemployment at a rate below the natural rate is unsustainable because doing so would cause accelerating inflation.

✔   *To stop an inflation, Classicals say the Fed must reduce the rate of growth of the money supply.*

6b. Keynesians believe that institutional factors play a major role in determining inflation, and that expected inflation need not precisely equal actual inflation. Within a range of output levels, a trade-off is possible. (372)

    So, whenever inflation is not really out of control then there is a long-run trade-off between inflation and unemployment (the Phillips curve is downward sloping).

✔   *To stop an inflation, Keynesians favor contractionary monetary policy along with a combination of other policies that directly slow down inflation such as an incomes policy. Exhibit 6 shows how an incomes policy works.*

    In sum, Keynesians see inflation as an institutional phenomenon; Classicals see it as a monetary phenomenon.

Short-answer questions

1. If there is a high inflation, most economists are willing to accept that a rough approximation of the quantity theory holds true. Why? (LO1)

2. Which of the two curves in the graph on the right is a short-run Phillips curve, and why? (LO2)

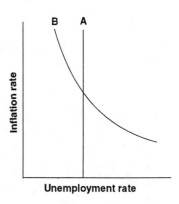

3. What is the Classical view of inflation and how does it relate to long-run growth? (LO3)

4. Are Classical economists or Keynesian economists more likely to favor a monetary rule? Why? (LO4)

5. How does the Keynesian theory of inflation differ from the Classical theory of inflation? (LO5)

6. Would Keynesians or Classicals be more likely to see a long-run trade-off between inflation and unemployment? Why? (LO6)

7. Why would a Keynesian be more likely to support the introduction of an incomes policy than a Classical would be? (LO6)

Word Scramble

1. _____   2._____   _____   3._____
        tonnliifa   sPplliih   vurec   ttsonligfaa

Match the Terms and Concepts to Their Definitions

____ 1. adaptive expectations

____ 2. cost-push inflation

____ 3. demand-pull inflation

____ 4. expectations of inflation

____ 5. incomes policy

____ 6. inflation

____ 7. just-noticeable difference

____ 8. long-run Phillips curve

____ 9. monetary rule

____ 10. natural rate of unemployment

____ 11. Phillips curve

____ 12. short-run Phillips curve

____ 13. stagflation

a. A threshold below which our senses don't recognize that something has changed.

b. A prescribed monetary policy to be followed regardless of what is happening in the economy.

c. A representation of the relation between inflation and unemployment.

d. A policy placing direct pressure on individuals to hold down their nominal wages and prices.

e. A curve showing the trade-off between inflation and unemployment when expectations of inflation are constant.

f. A curve showing the trade-off (or complete lack thereof) between inflation and unemployment when expectations of inflation equal actual inflation.

g. Classical term for the unemployment rate in long-run equilibrium when expectations of inflation equal the actual level of inflation.

h. Combination of high and accelerating inflation and high unemployment.

i. Expectations of the future based on what has been in the past.

j. Inflation where money supply increases cause price increases.

k. Inflation where price increases cause money supply increases.

l. The rise in the price level that the average person expects.

m. A continuous rise in the price level.

Problems and Exercises

1. Suppose the economy is operating at potential output. Inflation is 3% and expected inflation is 3%. Unemployment is 5.5%.

   a. Draw a long-run Phillips curve and a short-run Phillips curve consistent with these conditions.

   b. The government implements an expansionary monetary policy. As a result, unemployment falls to 4.5% and inflation rises to 6%. Expectations do not adjust. Show where the economy is on the graph you drew for 1(a). What happens to the short-run Phillips curve? Inflation? Unemployment?

   c. Expectations now fully adjust. Show this on the graph drawn for 1(a). What happens to the short-run Phillips curve?

2.   Redraw the long-run Phillips curve and a short-run Phillips curve consistent with the conditions of the economy described in question #1 above and explain the effect of the following on inflation and unemployment using the curves you have drawn.

   a.   The government implements a contractionary monetary policy. As a result, unemployment rises to 6.5% and inflation falls to 0%. Expectations do not adjust.

   b.   Expectations now fully adjust.

3.   For each of the following points that represents the economy on the Phillips curve, make a prediction for unemployment and inflation.

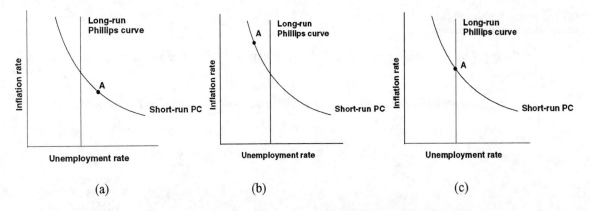

                (a)   (b)   (c)

4.   Suppose inflation is 12% and unemployment is 5.5% and the natural rate of unemployment is 5.5%. The president believes inflation and unemployment are both too high.

   a. Assume you are a Classical economist. What policy would you recommend to improve the situation?

   b. Show the short-run effect of this policy on unemployment and inflation using the Phillips curve analysis. Will the president be satisfied? What is your response?

    c. Show the long-run effect of this policy on unemployment and inflation using the Phillips curve analysis. Will the president be satisfied? What is your response? (In that response, discuss the issue of long-run growth).

Multiple Choice Questions

1. Assuming velocity is relatively constant and real income is relatively stable, an increase in the money supply of 40 percent will bring about an approximate change in the price level of
   a. 4 percent.
   b. 40 percent.
   c. 80 percent.
   d. zero percent.

2. When there is cost/push inflation
   a. price increases tend to lead the money supply increases.
   b. price increases tend to lag the money supply increases.
   c. price increases tend to have no relation to the money supply increases.
   d. price increases sometimes lead and sometimes lag the money supply increases.

3. The Phillips curve represents a relationship between
   a. inflation and unemployment.
   b. inflation and real income.
   c. money supply and interest rates.
   d. money supply and unemployment.

4. The short-run Phillips curve shifts around because of
   a. changes in the money supply.
   b. changes in expectations of employment.
   c. changes in expectations of inflation.
   d. changes in expectations of real income.

5. The slope of the long-run Phillips curve is thought by many economists to be
   a. horizontal.
   b. vertical.
   c. downward sloping.
   d. backward bending.

6. An economist has just said, "Inflation is everywhere and always a monetary phenomenon." You would deduce this economist
   a. is likely to be a Keynesian economist.
   b. is likely to be a Classical economist.
   c. could be either a Keynesian economist or a Classical economist.
   d. must be neither a Keynesian economist nor a Classical economist, because neither of these groups would ever say that.

7. Classicals generally favor a monetary rule that has
   a. money supply not changing at all.
   b. money supply increasing by a predetermined percentage of about 3 percent.
   c. money supply increasing by a predetermined percentage of about 10 percent.
   d. monetary policy tied to whether the economy is in a recession or a boom.

8. Classicals see the economy gravitating towards
    a. the stagflation rate of unemployment.
    b. the natural rate of unemployment.
    c. the inflation rate of unemployment.
    d. the Phillips rate of unemployment.

9. If the economy is at Point A in the Phillips curve graph to the right, what prediction would you make for inflation?
    a. It will increase.
    b. It will decrease.
    c. It will remain constant.
    d. It will explode.

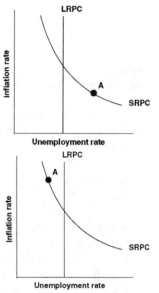

10. If the economy is at Point A in the Phillips curve graph to the right, what prediction would you make for inflation?
    a. It will increase
    b. It will decrease.
    c. It will remain constant.
    d. It will immediately fall to zero.

11. Stagflation is
    a. a combination of low and decelerating inflation and low unemployment.
    b. a combination of low and decelerating inflation and high unemployment.
    c. a combination of high and accelerating inflation and low unemployment.
    d. a combination of high and accelerating inflation and high unemployment.

12. An economist has just made the statement that institutional and structural aspects of inflation are important. You would deduce that this economist
    a. is likely a Keynesian economist.
    b. is likely a Classical economist.
    c. could be either a Keynesian economist or a Classical economist.
    d. must not be an economist, since no economist would make such a statement.

13. One explanation of why the long-run Phillips curve might not be perfectly vertical is
    a. the just noticeable difference explanation.
    b. the supply shock explanation.
    c. the demand shock explanation.
    d. the monetary explanation.

14. An individual has said that she favors an incomes policy. She
    a. is likely a Keynesian economist.
    b. is likely a Classical economist.
    c. could be either a Keynesian economist or a Classical economist.
    d. is not an economist, because no economist could ever support an incomes policy.

15. Classicals generally see supply price shocks
    a. as a cost-push pressure.
    b. as a demand-pull pressure.
    c. as a relative price change.
    d. as an institutional change.

Answers

Short-answer questions

1. The quantity theory is based on the equation of exchange, *MV=PQ*. The quantity theory adds the following assumptions: (1) that velocity is relatively constant; (2) that real output is relatively constant; and (3) that changes in money supply cause changes in prices. In reality, velocity and real output can change sufficiently to make it questionable whether this theory is useful. However, when there is significant inflation—say 100% or more—the relative changes in velocity and real output that are reasonable to assume possible are much smaller than that 100%, leaving a rough correlation between changes in the money supply and changes in the price level.

    The debate between economists does not concern the relationships between money growth and inflation; it concerns the direction of causation. Classicals tend to believe that the causation goes from money to prices, and hence they are willing to accept the existence of a long-run vertical Phillips curve. Keynesians tend to believe that the causation goes from changes in prices and expectations of prices to changes in the money supply—the government is accommodating the higher prices. Thus they favor more institutionally-oriented theories of inflation. (367-372)

2. The Phillips curve represents a trade-off between inflation and unemployment. It is an empirically determined phenomenon, and based on that empirical evidence economists generally believe that the downward sloping curve (curve B) represents the short-run Phillips curve: Whenever unemployment decreases, inflation increases, and vice versa. They explain that this empirical occurrence is due to slowly adjusting expectations and institutions. In the long run, expectations and institutions can change and hence the reason for the trade-off is eliminated, making the vertical line represent the long-run Phillips curve—it represents the lack of a trade-off between inflation and unemployment in the long run. (362-365)

3. The Classical view of inflation is best summarized by the phrase "Inflation is everywhere and always a monetary phenomenon." Essentially, it is that increases in the money supply are the cause of inflation, and all other supposed causes are simply diversions from the key monetary cause. They see a long-run inverse relationship between inflation and growth. (367-370)

4. Classical economists are more likely to favor a monetary rule, because they see the economy gravitating toward a natural rate of unemployment regardless of monetary policy. Thus expansionary monetary policy can lead only to inflation. A monetary rule will limit the government's attempt to expand the economy with monetary policy and hence will achieve the natural rate of unemployment and low inflation. Keynesian economists are less likely to see the economy gravitating toward the natural rate of unemployment, so they would favor some discretionary policy to improve the operation of the macro economy. (368-370, 372)

5. The Keynesian theory of inflation differs from the Classical in that it is more likely to include institutional and social aspects as part of the theory. The insider/outsider model is a Keynesian model of inflation. Another way of stating the difference is that the Keynesian theory of inflation sees the equation of exchange as being read from right to left, rather than from left to right. (370-372)

6. Keynesian economists see institutional and social aspects of the price setting process as more important than do Classicals. They also see individuals as having a cost of rationality, so individuals may not notice small amounts of inflation. These aspects of the Keynesian theory make it more likely that there is a long-run trade-off between inflation and unemployment since, in their absence, we would expect that money is essentially a veil and real forces predominate. (372-374)

7. An incomes policy is a policy designed to put direct downward pressure on the nominal price setting process. Keynesian economists see institutional and social aspects of the price setting process as more important than do Classicals. It is these social aspects of the price setting process which place a direct upward pressure on the price level that will require an incomes policy to offset. Therefore, Keynesians are more likely to support an incomes policy. (374-375)

Word Scramble   1. inflation   2. Phillips curve   3. stagflation

Match the Terms and Concepts to Their Definitions

1-i; 2-k; 3-j; 4-l; 5-d; 6-m; 7-a; 8-f; 9-b; 10-g; 11-c; 12-e; 13-h.

Problems and Exercises

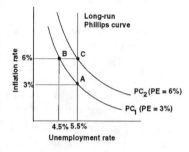

1. a. The long-run Phillips curve is vertical at the rate of unemployment consistent with potential output, here at 5.5%. The short-run Phillips curve is the downward sloping curve shown in the graph to the right as PC_1. In this case, we drew a short-run Phillips curve where expected inflation equals 3%, actual inflation. It intersects the long-run Phillips curve at 5.5% unemployment and 3% inflation. The economy is at point A. (362-365)
   b. The economy moves along the short-run Phillips curve up and to the left to point B. The short-run Phillips curve does not shift since inflation expectations have not changed. At point B, inflation is 6% and unemployment rate is 4.5%. (362-365)
   c. Now that expectations fully adjust, the short-run Phillips curve shifts to the right to PC_2 so that it intersects the long-run Phillips curve at inflation rate of 6%. The unemployment rate returns to 5.5% and inflation remains at 6%. (362-365)

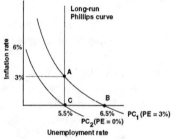

2. a. The economy moves along the short-run Phillips curve down and to the right to point B. The short-run Phillips curve does not shift since inflation expectations have not changed. At point B, inflation is 0% and unemployment rate is 6.5%. (362-365)
   b. Now that expectations fully adjust, the short-run Phillips curve shifts to the left to PC_2 so that it intersects the long-run Phillips curve at inflation rate of 0%. The unemployment rate returns to 5.5% and inflation remains at 0%. (362-365)

3. a. Inflation is below expected inflation and unemployment is higher than the natural rate of unemployment. As expectations adjust, the short-run Phillips curve shifts to the left and both unemployment and inflation will fall. (362-365)
   b. Inflation is above expected inflation and unemployment is lower than the natural rate of unemployment. As expectations adjust, the short-run Phillips curve shifts to the right and both unemployment and inflation will rise. (362-365)
   c. Inflation equals expected inflation and unemployment equals the target rate of unemployment. Inflation and unemployment will not change. (362-365)

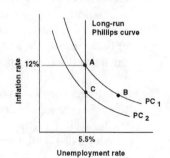

4. a. I assume that in the long run, only inflation can be improved, so I ignore the higher-than-desired rate of unemployment and focus on fighting inflation. A contractionary monetary policy will improve the inflation rate. (368-370)
   b. The economy begins at point A, where unemployment is 5.5% and inflation is 12%. Inflation expectations equal actual inflation. This is shown to the right. With contractionary monetary policy, the economy moves along the short-run Phillips curve down and to the right to point B. The short-run Phillips curve does not shift since inflation expectations have not changed. At point B, inflation is lower than 12% and the unemployment rate is higher than 5.5%. The president will be happy that inflation is lower, but disappointed that unemployment is higher. I tell him that in the short run there is a trade-off between the two. Just wait for expectations of inflation to adjust and we will return to 5.5% unemployment. (368-370)

    c. Now that expectations fully adjust, the short-run Phillips curve shifts to the left to PC_2 so that it intersects the long-run Phillips curve at inflation rate of below 12% at point C. The unemployment rate returns to 5.5% . The president is now pleased because inflation is lower and unemployment returned to 5.5%. But he wanted the unemployment rate to be below 5.5%. I tell him that 5.5% is the natural rate. If he were to follow an expansionary policy, unemployment would fall in the short run, but would return to 5.5% in the long run and inflation would be higher than it currently is. The higher inflation would undermine the economy's long-term growth. (368-370)

Multiple Choice Questions

1. b. Using the equation of exchange, $MV=PQ$, given these assumptions there is a close relationship between changes in M and changes in P. See page 359.

2. a. As the text discusses on page 359, in most cost/push inflation, price increases cause money supply increases, and therefore they lead them. The other answers are possible, but a is clearly the best.

3. a. See page 360.

4. c. The short-run Phillips curve holds expectations of inflation constant. Therefore, it shifts because changes in expectations of inflation cause everybody to build those expectations into their nominal price requests. See pages 362-363.

5. b. As discussed on pages 363-364, the long-run Phillips curve is vertical. Actually, there is some debate about whether it is downward sloping, but the text focuses on the vertical nature of the curve so that is the answer that should be given. Remember, one is choosing the best answer relative to what is presented in the text.

6. b. As discussed on page 367, that phrase is a mantra of Classical economists.

7. b. Classicals generally favor increasing the money supply at a rate of about 3% per year. That, they believe, would allow for real growth without inflation. See page 369.

8. b. The Classical view of the Phillips curve is that all forces push toward the natural rate of unemployment. See pages 368-369.

9. b. Since Point A is to the right of the long-run Phillips curve, actual unemployment exceeds the natural rate of unemployment. Therefore we would expect inflationary expectations to be decreasing, and hence inflation to be decreasing. See page 370, especially Exhibit 5.

10. a. Since Point A is to the left of the long-run Phillips curve, actual unemployment is below the natural rate of unemployment. Therefore we would expect inflationary expectations to be increasing, and hence inflation to be increasing. See pages 369-370, especially Exhibit 5.

11. d. See definition of stagflation on page 362.

12. a. As discussed on pages 369-370, Keynesian economists emphasize institutional and structural aspects of inflation.

13. a. As the text discusses on page 373, the just noticeable difference, which is the threshold below which our senses don't recognize that something has changed, provides a possible explanation of why, even when there is inflation, people will not change their behavior and, instead, blend that inflation into their price-setting decisions.

14. a. As discussed on page 374, an incomes policy is a Keynesian policy designed to offset structural causes of inflation.

15. c. As discussed on pages 375-376 price shocks are relative price changes which do not lead to price level changes. As long as the government does not raise the money supply, other prices will fall to offset the price shock.

Chapter 15:
International Dimensions of Monetary and Fiscal Policies

Chapter at a glance

1a. There is significant debate about what U.S. international goals should be because exchange rates have conflicting effects and, depending on the state of the economy, there are arguments for high and low exchange rates. (381)

A high exchange rate (strong value of the $) helps hold down the prices of imports and therefore inflation. However, it creates a trade deficit and that has a depressing effect on aggregate demand and therefore the income level.

1b. Running a trade deficit is good in the short run but presents problems in the long run; thus there is debate about whether we should worry about a trade deficit or not. (382)

Trade deficit => imports > exports.

Short-run benefit: We are able to consume more than we would otherwise be able to do.

Long-run cost: We have to sell off U.S. assets because we are consuming more than we are producing. All the future interest and profits on those assets will thus go to foreigners, not U.S. citizens.

2. Domestic goals generally dominate international goals because (1) international goals are ambiguous, and (2) international goals affect a country's population indirectly and, in politics, indirect effects take a back seat. (382)

Often a country responds to an international goal only after the international community pressures it to do so.

3a. Monetary policy affects exchange rates through the interest rate path, the income path, and the price-level path, as shown in the diagram on pages 384 and 385. (384-385)

Expansionary monetary policy (increasing the money supply) lowers exchange rates. It decreases the relative value of a country's currency. Contractionary monetary policy has the opposite effect.

Be able to explain why!

3b. Monetary policy affects the trade balance through the income path, the price level path, and the exchange rate path, as shown in the diagram on page 386. (385-386)

Expansionary monetary policy makes a trade deficit larger.

Contractionary monetary policy makes a trade deficit smaller.

Be able to explain why!

4a. Fiscal policy affects exchange rates through the income path, the interest rate path, and the price-level path, as shown in the diagram on page 387. (386-387)

The net effect of fiscal policy on exchange rates is ambiguous.

Be able to explain why!

4b. Fiscal policy affects the trade deficit though the income path and the price-level path, as shown in the diagram on page 388. (387-388)

Expansionary fiscal policy increases a trade deficit.

Contractionary fiscal policy decreases a trade deficit.

Be able to explain why!

5. Governments try to coordinate their monetary and fiscal policies because their economies are interdependent. (389)

Each country will likely do what's best for the world economy as long as it is also best for itself.

6. While internationalizing a country's debt may help in the short run, in the long run it presents potential problems, since foreign ownership of a country's debts means the country must pay interest to those foreign countries and that debt may come due. (390)

We have been internationalizing our debt since the early 1980s which means that we must, at some point in the future, export more than we import (consume less than we produce) to pay for this.

Short-answer questions

1. What should U.S. international goals be? (LO1)

2. Which dominate for a country: domestic or international goals? Why? (LO2)

3. If a country runs expansionary monetary policy, what will likely happen to the exchange rate? (LO3)

4. If a country runs contractionary monetary policy, what will likely happen to the trade balance? (LO4)

5. If a country runs expansionary fiscal policy, what will likely happen to the exchange rate? (LO4)

6. If a country runs contractionary fiscal policy, what will likely happen to the trade balance? (LO4)

7. Given the difficulty of doing so, why do countries try to coordinate their monetary and fiscal policies with other countries? (LO5)

8. The United States in recent years has run a large capital account deficit and has become the world's largest debtor nation. What are some of the potential problems that this presents? (LO6)

Word Scramble

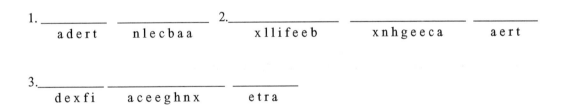

1. _____ _____ 2._____ _____ _____
   a d e r t   n l e c b a a   x l l i f e e b   x n h g e e c a   a e r t

3._____ _____ _____
   d e x f i   a c e e g h n x   e t r a

Match the Terms and Concepts to Their Definitions

___ 1. exchange rate

___ 2. fixed exchange rate

___ 3. flexible exchange rate

___ 4. partially flexible exchange rate

___ 5. trade balance

a. Exchange rate that is set by a country's government, with the commitment to buying and selling that currency at the set rate.

b. The difference between a country's exports and its imports.

c. Exchange rate set by market forces (supply and demand for a country's currency).

d. Exchange rate where the government sometimes buys and sells currencies to influence the price directly and at other times simply accepts the exchange rate determined by supply and demand forces.

e. The rate at which one country's currency can be traded for another country's currency.

Problems and Exercises

1. You observe that over the past decade, a country's competitiveness has improved, reducing its trade deficit.

   a. What monetary or fiscal policies might have led to such results? Why?

   b. You also observe that interest rates have steadily fallen along with a fall in the exchange rate. What monetary or fiscal policies might have led to such results?

2. You have been hired as an adviser to Fantasyland, a country with perfectly flexible exchange rates. State what monetary and fiscal policies you might suggest in each of the following situations. Explain your answers.

   a. You want to increase domestic income and to reduce the exchange rate.

   b. You want to reduce interest rates, reduce inflation, and reduce the trade deficit.

   c. You want lower unemployment, lower interest rates, a lower exchange rate, and a lower trade deficit.

Multiple Choice Questions

1. An exchange rate is
   a. the rate the Fed charges commercial banks for loans.
   b. the rate the Fed charges individuals for loans.
   c. the rate at which one country's currency can be exchanged for another country's currency.
   d. the speed at which exchange occurs.

2. If a country has fixed exchange rates
   a. the government need not worry about the exchange rate.
   b. governments are committed to buying and selling currencies at a fixed rate.
   c. the exchange rate is set by law.
   d. the exchange rate has a fixed component and a flexible component.

3. If a country has a flexible exchange rate, the exchange rate
   a. is determined by flexible government policy.
   b. is determined by market forces.
   c. fluctuates continuously and will always change by at least 1 percent per year.
   d. fluctuates continuously and will always change by at least 10 percent per year.

4. Countries prefer
   a. a high exchange rate.
   b. a low exchange rate.
   c. sometimes a low and sometimes a high exchange rate.
   d. a fixed exchange rate.

5. Countries prefer
   a. a trade deficit.
   b. a trade surplus.
   c. sometimes a trade deficit and sometimes a trade surplus.
   d. a trade equilibrium.

6. Expansionary monetary policy has a tendency to
   a. push interest rates up and exchange rates down.
   b. push interest rates down and exchange rates down.
   c. push income down and exchange rates down.
   d. push imports down and exchange rates down.

7. Contractionary monetary policy has a tendency to
   a. push interest rates up and exchange rates down.
   b. push interest rates down and exchange rates down.
   c. push income down and imports down.
   d. push imports down and exchange rates down.

8. If the exchange rate has gone up, it is most likely that the government ran
   a. an expansionary monetary policy.
   b. a contractionary monetary policy.
   c. an expansionary fiscal policy.
   d. a contractionary fiscal policy.

9. If the trade deficit has gone up, it is most likely that the government ran
   a. an expansionary monetary policy.
   b. a contractionary monetary policy.
   c. a contractionary fiscal policy.
   d. an expansionary monetary policy and a contractionary fiscal policy

10. Expansionary monetary policy tends to
    a. push prices up and the trade deficit down.
    b. push prices down and the trade deficit down.
    c. push income up and the trade deficit down.
    d. push income up and the trade deficit up.

11. Expansionary fiscal policy tends to push
    a. income up and exchange rates up.
    b. income up and exchange rates down.
    c. income up and imports up.
    d. income up and imports down.

12. If the exchange rate has gone up, it is most likely that the government ran
    a. an expansionary fiscal policy.
    b. a contractionary fiscal policy.
    c. Who knows?
    d. an expansionary monetary policy.

13. Contractionary fiscal policy tends to push
    a. income down and imports up.
    b. income down and the trade deficit up.
    c. prices down and the trade deficit down.
    d. prices down and imports up.

14. Assume the United States would like to raise its exchange rate and lower its trade deficit. It would pressure
    Japan to run
    a. contractionary monetary policy.
    b. contractionary fiscal policy.
    c. expansionary monetary policy
    d. expansionary fiscal policy.

15. According to the textbook, generally, when international goals and domestic goals conflict
    a. the international goals win out.
    b. the domestic goals win out.
    c. sometimes it's a toss-up which will win out.
    d. international monetary goals win out but international fiscal goals lose out.

16. When a country runs a large capital account surplus, the amount of crowding out that occurs because of fiscal
    policy is
    a. increased.
    b. decreased.
    c. unaffected.
    d. sometimes increased and sometimes decreased.

Answers

Short-answer questions

1. By "international goals" economists usually mean the exchange rate and the trade balance that policy makers should shoot for. There is significant debate in the United States about what our international goals should be, and there are arguments for both high and low exchange rates, and for both trade deficits and trade surpluses. The argument for a high exchange rate is that it lowers the cost of imports; the argument against it is that it raises the price of exports, making U.S. goods less competitive. The argument in favor of a trade deficit is that it allows a country to consume more than it produces; the argument against is that that trade deficit will have to be paid off at some point. (380-382)

2. Generally, domestic goals dominate for two reasons. (1) International goals are often ambiguous, as discussed in answer 1 above and page 382 of the textbook, and (2) international goals affect a country's population indirectly and, in politics, indirect effects take a back seat. (382)

3. Expansionary monetary policy tends to push income and prices up and interest rates down. All these phenomena tend to push the exchange rate down. Contractionary monetary policy has the opposite effect. (384-385)

4. Contractionary monetary policy tends to push income and prices down and interest rates up. The strongest effect of these phenomena on the trade balance in the short run is the effect on income, which causes a fall in imports and a fall in the trade deficit. (385-386)

5. Expansionary fiscal policy pushes interest rates, income, and prices up. The higher income and higher prices increase imports and put downward pressure on exchange rates. The higher interest rate pushes exchange rates in the opposite direction so the net effect of fiscal policy on exchange rates is unclear. (386-387)

6. Contractionary fiscal policy pushes income and prices down. This tends to decrease imports and increase competitiveness, decreasing a trade deficit. (387-388)

7. The policies of one country affect the economy of another. So it is only natural that they try to coordinate their policies. It is also only natural that since voters are concerned with their own countries, that coordination is difficult to achieve unless it is in the interest of both countries. (389)

8. While internationalizing a country's debt may help in the short run, in the long run it presents potential problems, since foreign ownership of a country's debts means the debtor country must pay interest to those foreign countries, and also, that debt may come due. (390-391)

Word Scramble   1. trade balance   2. flexible exchange rate   3. fixed exchange rate

Match the Terms and Concepts to Their Definitions
1-e; 2-a; 3-c; 4-d; 5-b.

Problems and Exercises

1. a. An increase in competitiveness and a decrease in the trade deficit are probably due to contractionary fiscal policy. Contractionary fiscal policy reduces inflation, improves competitiveness, and decreases income which reduces imports. Improved competitiveness and decreased income both work to reduce the trade deficit. Contractionary monetary policy would also reduce the trade deficit, but its effect on competitiveness is ambiguous. (382-388)
   b. If interest rates have also fallen, it is likely that fiscal policy has been very contractionary because contractionary monetary policy would have led to higher interest rates and a higher exchange rate value of the dollar. (382-388)

2. a. Expansionary monetary policy will reduce the exchange rate through its effect on interest rates and will increase domestic income. Expansionary fiscal policy will increase domestic income. The increase in income will increase imports which will tend to decrease the exchange rate, but higher interest rates will tend to lead to a higher exchange rate. The effect of expansionary fiscal policy on exchange rates is ambiguous. (382-388)

   b. Contractionary fiscal policy will tend to reduce inflation and interest rates. The reduction in inflation will improve competitiveness and a reduction in income will reduce imports. Both work to reduce the trade deficit. (382-388)

   c. Expansionary monetary policy will reduce unemployment and reduce interest rates. Lower interest rates will tend to make exchange rates fall. Expansionary monetary policy, however, will make the trade deficit higher. Expansionary fiscal policy will also reduce unemployment. Interest rates, however, will rise and so will the trade deficit. This mix of goals is difficult to attain. (382-388)

Multiple Choice Questions

1. c. See page 381.

2. b. To keep the exchange rate at the stated amount governments must be willing to buy and sell currencies so that the quantity supplied and quantity demanded are always equal at the fixed rate. See page 381.

3. b. There are no predetermined levels of change with a flexible exchange rate. See page 381.

4. c. The answer is "sometimes a low and sometimes a high exchange rate" because, as discussed on page 381. there are rationales for both.

5. c. The domestic economy's needs change over time and as they do, so does the country's preferred trade situation. Both a deficit and a surplus have their advantages and disadvantages. See pages 381-382.

6. b. See the diagram on page 384.

7. c. See the diagram on page 385.

8. b. As discussed on page 385 the b answer is definitely correct. As discussed on page 387, fiscal policy has an ambiguous effect on exchange rates.

9. a. Both expansionary monetary policy and expansionary fiscal policy increase the trade deficit. Thus only a fits. See the discussion and charts on pages 385-388.

10. d. See the discussion on pages 385-386 and the diagram on page 386.

11. c. The effect of expansionary fiscal policy on exchange rates is ambiguous, which eliminates a and b. Increased income increases imports, not decreases them. (386-387)

12. c. The effect of expansionary fiscal policy on the exchange rate is ambiguous, as shown on the diagram on page 387, eliminating a and b. As discussed on pages 382-384, an expansionary monetary policy pushes the exchange rate down, eliminating d, leaving only c.

13. c. See diagram on page 388 and the discussion on pages 386-388.

14. c. The effect of fiscal policy on the exchange rate is ambiguous, so the only sure option is c. See Exhibit 1 on page 389.

15. b. As discussed in the text on page 389, usually, because of political considerations, domestic goals win out.

16. b. Since there is a capital account surplus, capital must be flowing into the country. That capital usually ends up buying some government debt, which reduces crowding out, as discussed on page 390.

Chapter 16:
Open Economy Macro: Exchange Rate and Trade Policy

Chapter at a glance

1a. The balance of payments is a country's record of all transactions between its residents and the residents of all foreign countries. (395)

Is broken down into the:
1. *current account*
2. *capital account*
3. *official transactions account.*

✔ *Remember: If it is a minus (plus) sign, money is going out (coming in). Moreover, if foreigners are buying our goods, services, or assets, that represents a demand for the dollar (an inflow) in international exchange rate markets. If we buy foreign goods, services, or assets, that represents a supply of dollars (an outflow).*

1b. The balance on goods and services is the difference between the value of goods and services a nation exports and the value of goods and services it imports. (396)

> *The balance of trade is often discussed in the popular press as a summary of how the U.S. is doing in international markets. However, it only includes goods exported and imported—not services. Trade in services is just as important as trade in merchandise, so economists pay more attention to the combined balance on goods and services.*

1c. Since the balance of payments consists of both the capital account and the trade account, if the capital account is in surplus and the trade account is in deficit, there can still be a balance of payments surplus. (397)

The capital account measures the flows of payments between countries for assets such as stocks, bonds, and real estate. The current (or trade) account measures the flows of payments for goods and services.

1d. A deficit in the balance of payments means that the private quantity supplied of a currency exceeds the private quantity demanded. A surplus in the balance of payments means the opposite. (399)

Whenever the exchange rate is <u>above equilibrium</u> (below equilibrium) then the country will experience a balance of payments <u>deficit</u> (surplus).

2. Three important fundamental determinants of exchange rates are prices, interest rates, and income. (399)

<u>A decrease in the value of a currency can be caused by:</u>

1. *<u>An increase in the nation's inflation rate</u> (because this causes the relative price of the nation's goods to rise, domestic consumers will import more, increasing the supply of the nation's currency, while at the same time they export less, decreasing the demand for the currency—an increase in supply and a decrease in demand decreases the relative price of the nation's currency).*

2. *<u>A decrease in the nation's interest rates</u> (because this will decrease foreign demand for domestic assets, decreasing the demand for domestic currency, while at the same time domestic citizens will look abroad for higher rates of return, thereby increasing the supply of the currency—a decrease in demand and an increase in supply will decrease the relative price of the nation's currency).*

3. *<u>An increase in the nation's income</u> (because this will increase the demand for imports, increasing the supply of the nation's currency to buy those imports—an increase in supply decreases the relative price of the currency).*

3. A country fixes the exchange rate by standing ready to buy and sell its currency anytime the exchange rate is not at the fixed exchange rate. (401)

It is easier for a country to maintain a fixed exchange rate below equilibrium. All it has to do is to print and sell enough domestic currency to hold the value down.

However, if a country wants to maintain a fixed exchange rate above long-run equilibrium then it can do so only as long as it has the foreign currency (official) reserves to buy up its currency. Once it runs out of official reserves, it will be unable to intervene, and must either borrow, use indirect methods (domestic fiscal and monetary policies), ask other countries to buy its currency (to sell their currency), or devalue its currency.

In reality, because a country has a limited amount of official reserves, it only uses strategic currency stabilization (not a fixed exchange rate policy).

4. Purchasing power parity is a method of calculating exchange rates such that various currencies will each buy an equal basket of goods and services. Those exchange rates may or may not be appropriate long-run exchange rates. (403)

Long-run equilibrium exchange rates can only be estimated. The PPP (Purchasing Power Parity) is one method of doing so. However, for many economists, it has serious problems. They contend that the current exchange rate is the best estimate of the long-run equilibrium rate.

5a. Three exchange rate régimes are:
   1. Fixed exchange rate: The government chooses an exchange rate and offers to buy and sell currencies at that rate.
   2. Flexible exchange rate: Determination of exchange rates is left totally up to the market.
   3. Partially flexible exchange rate: The government sometimes affects the exchange rate and sometimes leaves it to the market. (404)

   Which is best is debatable.

5b. Fixed exchange rates provide international monetary stability and force governments to make adjustments to meet their international problems. (This is *also* a disadvantage.) If they become unfixed, they create monetary instability. (405)

✔ *Know these advantages and disadvantages!*

5c. Flexible exchange rate régimes provide for orderly incremental adjustment of exchange rates rather than large sudden jumps, and allow governments to be flexible in conducting domestic monetary and fiscal policy. (This is *also* a disadvantage.) They are, however, susceptible to private speculation. (406)

✔ *Know these advantages and disadvantages!*

5d. Partially flexible exchange rate régimes combine the advantages and disadvantages of fixed and flexible exchange rates. (406)

Most countries have opted for this policy. However, if the market exchange rate is below the rate the government desires, and the government does not have sufficient official reserves (to buy and increase the demand for its currency), then it must undertake policies that will either increase the private demand for its currency or decrease the private supply. Doing so either involves using traditional macro policy— fiscal and monetary policy—to influence the economy, or using trade policy to affect the level of exports and imports.

6. Some important international trade restrictions include tariffs, quotas, voluntary restraint agreements, and regulatory trade restrictions. (409)

Know the difference between these different trade restrictions as well as embargoes and nationalistic appeals!

7. Economists generally support free trade because trade restrictions lower aggregate output, reduce international competition, and often result in harmful trade wars that hurt everyone. (412)

The costs of trade restrictions (which include, among other things, higher prices domestic consumers must pay) almost always outweigh the benefits (which include protection from foreign competition that provides higher short-run profits and greater short-run job security to the protected domestic industries).

However, strategic trade policies (threats to implement trade restrictions on another country if it doesn't reduce its trade barriers) can be used to promote free trade (if these threats are credible and the other country reduces its trade restrictions).

See also,
   Appendix A: "The J-Curve"
   Appendix B: "Why Exchange Rate Determination Is More Complicated than the Model Would Suggest"
   Appendix C: "History of Exchange Rate Systems"

Short-answer questions

1. Distinguish between the balance of payments and the balance of trade. (LO1)

2. How can a country simultaneously have a balance of payments deficit and a balance of trade surplus? (LO1)

3. How does each part of the balance of payments relate to the supply and demand for currencies? (LO1)

4. What are the three fundamental determinants of exchange rates? (LO2)

5. If the demand and supply for a country's currency depends upon demand for imports and exports, and demand for foreign and domestic assets, how can a country fix its exchange rate? (LO3)

6. How do market exchange rates differ from exchange rates using the purchasing power parity concept? (LO4)

7. Define fixed exchange rates. (LO5)

8. Define flexible exchange rates. (LO5)

9. Define partially flexible exchange rates. (LO5)

10. Which are preferable, fixed or flexible exchange rates? (LO5)

11. What are a few of the most important international trade restrictions? (LO6)

12. Why do economists generally support free trade? (LO7)

Word Scramble

1. _____ ____ _____   2. _____ _____   3._____
   n l e c b a a   f o   a d e r t   c e n r r t u   u t o n c c a   f a r f i s t

Match the Terms and Concepts to Their Definitions

____ 1. balance of payments

____ 2. balance of trade

____ 3. capital account

____ 4. current account

____ 5. exchange rate intervention

____ 6. fixed exchange rate

____ 7. flexible exchange rate

____ 8. free trade

____ 9. official transactions account

____ 10. partially flexible exchange rate

____ 11. purchasing power parity

____ 12. strategic trade policies.

____ 13. tariffs

____ 14. voluntary restraint aggreement

a. A method of calculating exchange rates that attempts to value currencies at a rate so that each will buy an equal basket of goods.
b. Agreements in which countries voluntarily restrict their exports.
c. A country's record of all transactions between its residents and the residents of all foreign countries.
d. Taxes governments place on internationally traded goods, generally imports.
e. An exchange rate established by a government that sometimes affects the exchange rate and sometimes leaves it to the market.
f. An exchange rate established by a government that chooses an exchange rate and offers to buy and sell currencies at that rate.
g. An exchange rate the determination of which is left up to the market.
h. Threatening to implement tariffs to bring about a reduction in tariffs or some other concession from the other country.
i. Policy of allowing unrestricted trade among countries.
j. Government policy of buying and selling a currency to affect its price.
k. The difference between the value of goods a nation exports and the value of goods it imports.
l. The part of the balance of payments account that records the amount of a currency or other international reserves a nation buys or sells.
m. The part of the balance of payments account that lists all long-term flows of payments.
n. The part of the balance of payments account that lists all short-term flows of payments.

Problems and Exercises

1. State for each whether the transaction shows up on the balance of payments current account or the balance of payments capital account or neither.

   a. An American buys 100 stocks of Mercedes Benz, a German company.

   b. A Japanese businessperson buys Ameritec, an American bank.

   c. An American auto manufacturer buys $20 million in auto parts from a Japanese company.

   d. An American buys 100 shares of IBM stock.

e. Saturn exports 10,000 cars to Germany.

f. Toyota Motor Corporation, a Japanese firm, makes a $1 million profit from its plant in Kentucky, USA.

2. For each of the following, state who is demanding and who is supplying what currency:

a. A French person buys a set of china from a U.S. firm.

b. A U.S. tourist in Japan buys a Japanese kimono from a department store.

c. An Italian exchange rate trader believes that the exchange rate value of the dollar will rise.

d. A Swiss investor in Germany.

3. Draw supply and demand curves for British pounds, showing equilibrium quantity and price. Price is shown by price of pounds in dollars.

a. What is the demand for dollars in this case?

b. Explain a movement up along the supply curve.

c. Explain a movement down along the demand curve.

d. What would be the effect on the price of pounds of an increase in demand for pounds by the British? Show this graphically.

e. What would be the effect on the price of pounds of an increase in demand for dollars by the British? Show this graphically.

4. For each of the following, show graphically what would happen to the market for British pounds. Assume there are only two countries, the United States and Britain.

a. Income in the Britain rises.

b. Income in the United States rises.

c. The prices of goods in the United States increases.

d. Interest rates rise in Britain.

e. The value of the pound is expected to fall.

A1. At an exchange rate of Can$0.6 to US$1, Canada is exporting 20 million pounds of wheat to the United States at US$2 a pound. It is importing 8,000 cars from the United States at US$10,000 apiece. Now say that the value of the Canadian dollar falls to Can$0.80 to US$1. Canada's exports of wheat rise to 22 million pounds of wheat while car imports fall to 7,800 cars.

    a.   What is the original trade balance in Canadian dollars?

    b.   What has happened to the trade deficit?

    c.   What will likely happen in the long run?

B1. What buy or sell recommendations for U.S. dollars would you make in response to the following news?

    a.   U.S. monetary policy is expected to contract.

    b.   Inflation in Japan is expected to accelerate.

    c.   Growth in the United States is expected to be higher.

    d.   German interest rates rise.

    e.   The German central bank reduces its discount rate.

Multiple Choice Questions

1. If a country has perfectly flexible exchange rates and is running a current account deficit, it is running
    a. a capital account surplus.
    b. a capital account deficit.
    c. an official transactions surplus.
    d. an official transactions deficit.

2. In the balance of payments accounts, net investment income shows up in
    a. the current account.
    b. the capital account.
    c. the official transactions account.
    d. It is not an entry in the balance of payments.

3. If the official transactions account is significantly in surplus, the country is
    a. trying to hold up its exchange rate.
    b. trying to push down its exchange rate.
    c. trying to have no effect on its exchange rate.
    d. sometimes trying to increase and sometimes trying to decrease its exchange rate.

4. In recent years, the United States has generally
    a. run a balance of trade surplus.
    b. run a balance of trade deficit.
    c. had sometimes a balance of trade surplus and sometimes a balance of trade deficit.
    d. had a balance of trade equality.

5. In recent years, the United States generally
    a. has run a capital account surplus.
    b. has run a capital account deficit.
    c. has sometimes run a capital account surplus and sometimes run a capital account deficit.
    d. has run a capital account equality.

6. If there is a black market for a currency, the country probably has
    a. nonconvertible currency.
    b. a fixed exchange rate currency.
    c. a flexible exchange rate currency.
    d. a partially flexible exchange rate currency.

7. The graph on the right is of the supply and demand for French francs. If the French demand for U.S. imports increases
    a. the supply curve will shift to the right.
    b. the supply curve will shift to the left.
    c. the demand curve will shift to the right.
    d. the demand curve will shift to the left.

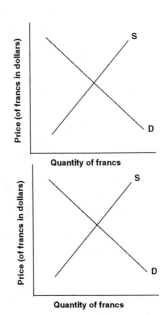

8. The graph on the right is of the supply and demand for French francs. If the U.S. demand for French imports increases
    a. the supply curve will shift to the right.
    b. the supply curve will shift to the left.
    c. the demand curve will shift to the right.
    d. the demand curve will shift to the left.

9. The graph on the right is of the supply and demand for French francs. If U.S.
    income increases
    a. the supply curve will shift to the right.
    b. the supply curve will shift to the left.
    c. the demand curve will shift to the right.
    d. the demand curve will shift to the left.

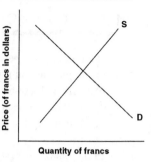

Quantity of francs

10. If there is a rise in the U.S. interest rate, one would expect the price of French francs in terms of dollars to
    a. rise.
    b. fall.
    c. remain unchanged.
    d. sometimes rise and sometimes fall.

11. If there is a rise in the U.S. price level, one would expect the price of French francs in terms of dollars to
    a. rise.
    b. fall.
    c. remain unchanged.
    d. sometimes rise and sometimes fall.

12. If a country runs expansionary monetary policy, in the short run one would expect the value of its exchange
    rate to
    a. rise.
    b. fall.
    c. be unaffected.
    d. sometimes rise and sometimes fall.

13. Say the Bangladeshi taka is valued at 42 taka to $1. Also say that you can buy the same basket of goods for 10
    taka that you can buy for $1. In terms of dollars the purchasing power parity of the taka is
    a. overvalued.
    b. undervalued.
    c. not distorted.
    d. non convertible.

14. Compared to a fixed exchange rate system, a flexible exchange rate system
    a. allows countries more flexibility in their monetary policies.
    b. allows countries less flexibility in their monetary policies.
    c. has no effect on monetary policies.
    d. allows countries more flexibility in their industrial policies.

15. Tariffs are
    a. quantity limits placed on imports.
    b. agreements in which countries voluntarily restrict their exports.
    c. taxes governments place on internationally traded goods—generally imports.
    d. an all-out restriction on the import or export of a good.

16. Which of the following is *not* generally a reason for economists' opposition to trade restrictions?
    a. they lower aggregate output.
    b. they reduce international competition.
    c. they often result in harmful trade wars that hurt everyone.
    d. they increase output of foreign countries relative to the domestic country.

A1. According to the empirical phenomenon of the J-curve, when a country's exchange rate falls its
    a. trade deficit usually become larger initially, then decreases.
    b. trade deficit usually becomes smaller initially, then increases.
    c. capital account usually becomes larger initially, then decreases
    d. capital account usually becomes smaller initially, then increases.

B1. A currency trader will make a larger total profit from trading
    a. if the spread is larger.
    b. if the spread is smaller.
    c. The spread could be either larger or smaller.
    d. The spread will have no relationship to profits.

C1. The gold standard is a type of
    a. fixed exchange rate.
    b. partially flexible exchange rate.
    c. flexible exchange rate.
    d. nonconvertible exchange rate.

C2. The gold specie flow mechanism works primarily by flows of
    a. money from one country to another.
    b. services from one country to another.
    c. merchandise from one country to another.
    d. exchange rates from one country to another.

C3. Under the gold standard, if a country has a balance of payments deficit
    a. gold would flow out of the country.
    b. gold would flow into the country.
    c. the country's exchange rate would rise.
    d. the country's exchange rate would fall.

C4. SDRs refers to
    a. Specie Draft Rights.
    b. Specie Drawing Rights.
    c. Special Drawing Rights.
    d. Special Draft Rights.

Answers

Short-answer questions

1. The balance of payments is a country's record of all transactions between its residents and the residents of all foreign nations. It is divided into the current account, the capital account, and the official transactions account. The balance of trade is one part of the balance of payments—specifically that part dealing with goods. It is not all that satisfactory a measure of the country's position in international markets since it does not include services. Generally, economists pay more attention to the combined balance on goods and services account. (395-398)

2. As discussed in question 1, the balance of trade is one part of the balance of payments. Thus, if other parts of the international payments —for example, the capital account—are in deficit, the balance of trade could be in surplus. (395-396)

3. The balance of payments records the flow of a currency in and out of a country (1) in order to buy and sell goods and services in the current account, (2) in order to buy and sell assets along with payments resulting from previous purchases of assets in the capital account, (3) in order to affect the value of a country's currency in the official transactions account. To buy foreign goods and assets one must supply domestic currency and demand foreign currency. Therefore, the balance of payments records the demand and supply of a country's currency during a given period of time. (395-398)

4. Three fundamental determinants of the value of a country's exchange rate are (1) domestic income, (2) domestic price level and (3) domestic interest rates. (399)

5. The current account and capital account reflect private demand and supply of a country's currency. If the official transactions account were zero, then the currency's value is market determined. If a country wants to fix the value of its currency to maintain its value at the fixed value, the government must buy and sell its currency using official reserves. Buying (selling) one's own currency shows up as a positive (negative) in the official transactions account.   (395-398, 400-401)

6. Market exchange rates are determined by the demand and supply of a country's currency. Since not all goods, services and assets produced in a country can be traded internationally, the value of an exchange rate may not reflect the relative prices in each country. The purchasing power parity concept adjusts the value of a country's currency by determining that rate at which equivalent baskets of goods can be purchased in each country. (403-404)

7. A fixed exchange rate is an exchange rate that the government chooses and then holds at the chosen rate, by standing ready to buy and sell at that rate. (404)

8. Flexible exchange rates are exchange rates that are determined by the market without government intervention. (404)

9. Partially flexible exchange rates are exchange rates that are determined by the market but are affected by government intervention. (404)

10. It depends. Each has its advantages and disadvantages. Flexible exchange rates give a country more control over domestic policy, but it can experience large fluctuations, hurting trade. (404-405)

11. The most important international trade restrictions include tariffs, quotas, voluntary restraint agreements, and regulatory trade restrictions. (409-410)

12. Economists generally support free trade because restrictions in trade lower output, reduce international competition (raising prices to consumers), and often result in harmful trade wars that hurt everyone. (411-412)

Word Scramble   1. balance of trade   2. current account   3. tariffs

Match the Terms and Concepts to Their Definitions
1-c; 2-k; 3-m; 4-n; 5-j; 6-f; 7-g; 8-i; 9-l; 10-e; 11-a; 12-h; 13-d; 14-b.

Problems and Exercises

1. a. Capital account. This is a long-term outflow. (395)
    b. Capital account. This is a long-term inflow. (395)
    c. Current account. This is merchandise imports, a short-term flow. (395)
    d. Neither. It is a domestic transaction. (395)
    e. Current account. This is merchandise exports, a short-term flow. (395)
    f. Current account. This is net investment income. (395)

2. a. The French person supplies francs and demands dollars because the French person sells francs to get U.S. dollars to purchase the china. (398-399)
    b. The U.S. tourist supplies dollars and demands Japanese yen because the tourist has to sell dollars to get yen. (398-399)
    c. The Italian trader will supply Italian lire and demand U.S. dollars because the trader wants to purchase that exchange that is believed to rise, the dollar. The trader must sell lire to get the dollars. (398-399)
    d. The Swiss investor will supply Swiss francs and demand German marks because the Swiss investor needs German marks to invest in Germany. (398-399)

3. A market for British pounds is shown to the right. Price of pounds in U.S. dollars is on the vertical axis and quantity of pounds is on the horizontal axis. Equilibrium price and quantity is determined by where they intersect. (398-401)

    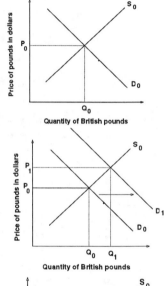

    a. If only two countries exist, the United States and Britain, the demand for dollars is the supply of pounds. (398-401)
    b. As the dollar value of the pound rises, individuals will supply more pounds. (398-401)
    c. As the dollar value of the pound declines, individuals will demand more pounds. (398-401)
    d. An increase in the demand for pounds by the British would shift the demand for pounds as shown on the graph to the right. The price of pounds in dollars would rise. (398-401)

    e. An increase in the demand for dollars by the British is equivalent to an increase in the supply of pounds. The supply curve for pounds would shift to the right as shown on the graph below. The price of pounds in dollars would fall. (398-401)

    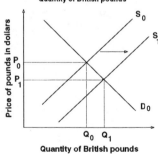

4. a. Demand for imports by the British rises; hence demand for dollars (supply of pounds) rises. This is shown in graph (a) below. (398-401)
    b. Demand for imports by Americans rises; hence demand for pounds rises. This is shown in the graph (b) below. (398-401)
    c. Demand for imports by the British falls; hence demand for dollars (supply of pounds) falls. This is shown in graph (c) below. (398-401)
    d. Demand for British assets will rise; hence the demand for the pound rises. This is shown in graph (d) below. (398-401)
    e. The demand for the pound falls. This is shown in graph (e) below. (398-401)

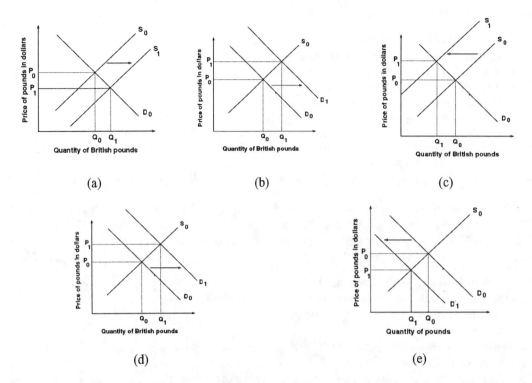

(a)   (b)   (c)

(d)   (e)

A1.a. Can$24 million trade deficit. Exports were Can$24 million (20 million × $US2 × exchange rate). Imports were Can$48 million (8,000 × $US10,000 × exchange rate). The trade balance is imports minus exports. (416-417)

  b. The deficit has risen to Can$27.2 million. Exports are Can$35.2 million (22 million × $US2 x exchange rate). Imports are Can$62.4 million (7,800 × $US10,000 × exchange rate). The trade balance is imports minus exports. (416-417)

  c. In the long run the quantity effects tend to dominate over the price effects and the trade deficit will be smaller than Can$24 million. (416-417)

B1.a. A contractionary U.S. monetary policy would tend to increase interest rates there. This will tend to increase the value of the dollar. We would recommend buying U.S. dollars. (417-420)

  b. As goods in Japan become more expensive, the demand for the Japanese yen will fall. This will tend to reduce the value of the yen. We would recommend selling Japanese yen (buying U.S. dollars). (417-420)

  c. Higher growth in the U.S. will increase the demand for imports. This means the supply of dollars will increase. The value of the dollar will fall. We would recommend selling U.S. dollars. (417-420)

  d. Higher interest rates in Germany will tend to increase the demand for German marks. The exchange rate value of the German mark will rise. We would recommend buying German marks (selling U.S. dollars), other things equal. (417-420)

  e. Lower interest rates in Germany will tend to decrease the demand for German marks. The exchange rate value of the German mark will fall. We would recommend selling German marks (buying U.S. dollars). (417-420)

Multiple Choice Questions

1. a. With perfectly flexible exchange rates the balance of payments must sum to zero; thus the capital account must be in surplus if the current account is in deficit. The official transactions account could not be negative because if there are perfectly flexible exchange rates, there are no official transactions. See pages 397-404.

2. a. Although net investment income might seem to many people as if it goes in the capital account, it is a return for a service and is considered part of the current account, as is discussed on page 396.

3. a. A surplus in the official transactions account means the balance of payments would otherwise be in deficit. The country is buying up its own currency. This means it is trying to hold up its exchange rate. See page 397-398.

4. b. See pages 395-396.

5. a. Running a capital account surplus is the other side of the balance sheet from the trade deficit. See pages 395-396.

6. a. All the others allow free exchange of currency and hence would not generate a black market. See page 401.

7. a. The French demand for U.S. imports is the supply of francs since paying for the imports requires supplying francs to buy dollars. See pages 398-399.

8. c. The U.S. demand for French imports is the demand for francs since paying for the imports requires buying francs. See pages 398-399.

9. c. If U.S. income increases, the U.S. demand for French imports will increase, shifting the demand for francs out. See page 399.

10. b. A rise in U.S. interest rates increases the demand for dollars, causing the price of francs in terms of dollars to fall. See page 399.

11. a. A rise in the U.S. price level would decrease the demand for U.S. imports, and hence decrease the supply of francs, causing the price of francs to rise. See page 399.

12. b. This is a review question from the previous chapter. Expansionary monetary policy decreases interest rates and thereby tends to decrease the exchange rate in the short run. See page 399 (this chapter) and page 384 (from the previous chapter).

13. b. Since the purchasing power parity exchange rate is lower than the actual exchange rate, the taka is undervalued. See page 403.

14. a. Under a fixed exchange rate system countries must use their monetary policies to meet international commitments. Thus flexible exchange rate policies allow them more flexibility in their monetary policies. Flexible exchange rates *may* allow them more flexibility in their industrial policies, but flexible exchange rates *definitely* do allow them more flexibility in their monetary policy, so a is the preferred answer. See pages 405-406.

15. c. See page 409 of textbook.

16. d. Trade restrictions hurt all countries. See pages 411-412.

A1. a. The J-curve refers to the trade deficit or surplus, so c and d can be eliminated. Because the price effects often predominate, the trade deficit usually becomes larger initially. See page 416.

B1. c. The larger the spread, the larger the profit per trade, but the smaller the number of trades, so the effect of the spread is impossible to determine in a general sense, although its effect could be determined with respect to a specific trade. See page 418.

C1. a. See page 421.

C2. a. When there is an imbalance of trade in the gold system, gold—which is money—flows from the deficit country to the surplus country, pushing the price level down in the deficit country and up in the surplus country. This process brings about a trade balance equilibrium, eventually. See page 421.

C3. a. See page 421 about the flow of gold. The last two answers could be eliminated since the gold standard involves fixed exchange rates.

C4. c. As discussed on page 422, SDRs refers to Special Drawing Rights.

Chapter 17:
The Art of Traditional Macro Policy

Learning Objectives

1. Conflicting goals of traditional macro policy are low inflation versus low unemployment and high growth and international trade and exchange rate goals versus domestic goals. Too contractionary a policy will cause unemployment and recession. Too expansionary a policy will accelerate inflation and expand trade deficits. (425)

   Government has to walk a tightrope and use monetary and fiscal policy as a balance bar.

2. Economic relationships are not certain, which makes macroeconomic policy an art rather than a science. (425)

   The macroeconomy is extremely complex–especially when we consider the effects of expectations about policy. However, policy makers don't want complexity. They want answers. Unfortunately, those answers often don't exist.

3. Theoretical models are abstract; they try to capture certain aspects of economic behavior that transcend institutions. Policy models combine individuals' actions that transcend institutions and individual actions that depend on institutions; they try to capture empirical regularities. (428)

   Policy models are more dependent upon the <u>current</u> nature of institutions. If insitutions change, then the policy must change.

4. Modern macro policy economists focus on credibility because they see macro policy operating through expectations as much as through the real channels emphasized in the traditional models. (429)

   Credible systematic policies are those that people believe will be implemented regardless of consequences.

5. Both Keynesians and Classicals generally agree that:
   1. Expansionary monetary and fiscal policies have short-run stimulative effects on income.
   2. Expansionary monetary and fiscal policies have potential long-run inflation effects.
   3. Monetary policy is politically easier to implement than fiscal policy.
   4. Expansionary monetary and fiscal policies tend to increase a trade deficit.
   5. Expansionary monetary policy places downward pressure on the exchange rate.
   6. Expansionary fiscal policy has an ambiguous effect on the exchange rate. (433)

   However, their normative value judgements regarding the benefits and costs of government involvement are very different. There's no objective way to determine who's right.

See also,
   Appendix A: "Nonmainstream Approaches to Macro."
   Appendix B: "Earlier History of Macroeconomic Policy."

Short-answer questions

1. The president of Happyland has appointed you Chairman of her Council of Economic Advisers. She tells you she wants unemployment to be 2% and inflation to be zero. How do you respond? (LO1)

2. Why is macroeconomic policy considered an art rather than a science? (LO2)

3. What is the difference between a policy model and a theoretical model? (LO3)

4. In 1995, the U.S. government gave in to the Unabomber and asked newspapers to meet his demand to publish his manifesto about technological society. Does that "giving in" better represent a Keynesian or a Classical approach to problem? Which is the correct approach? (LO4)

5. List six points of agreement between Classicals and Keynesians. (LO5)

Word Scramble

1. _____ _____ _____ _____
   rat   of   carmo   yoilpc

2. _____ _____
   accehiimnst   yssnnmKiieea

3._____ _____
   lraitnao   xetepacinots

Match the Terms and Concepts to Their Definitions

_____ 1.   art of macro policy

_____ 2.   credible systematic policies

_____ 3.   mechanistic Keynesianism

_____ 4.   rational expectations

a.   Policies that people believe will be implemented regardless of consequences.

b.   Expectations about the future based on the best current information, used in theoretical economic work that focuses on building dynamic feedback effects into macro models.

c.   An art practiced by economists who advise governments about real-world macro policy. In the practice of that art, economists recognize that economic relationships are not certain and conducting macroeconomic policy is not a science.

d.   The belief that the simple multiplier models actually describe the aggregate adjustment process and lead to a deterministic solution that policy makers can exploit in a mechanistic way.

Problems and Exercises

1.   Keynesian and Classical economists differ in their vision and approach to issues. These approaches likely carry over to other elements of their lives.

   a.   State which of the following statements was likely made by a Classical and which by a Keynesian.
   1. Life is tough; that's the way it is.

   2. Let them have an ice cream cone just this once.

   3. Dieting is simply a matter of reducing the intake of calories.

   4. Traditions should be followed in almost all cases.

   b.   Explain the general approach for Keynesians and Classicals that underlay the answers you gave above.

Multiple Choice Questions

1.   You have been appointed adviser to the president. He comes in and says he wants very low unemployment, zero inflation, and very high growth. You should
   a. advise him to use expansionary monetary policy.
   b. advise him to use contractionary monetary policy.
   c. tell him it is likely impossible using traditional tools.
   d. advise him to use a combination of expansionary monetary policy and contractionary fiscal policy.

2.   You've been appointed adviser to the president. She wants interest rates to fall and wants to decrease unemployment. You would suggest
   a. expansionary monetary policy.
   b. contractionary monetary policy.
   c. expansionary fiscal policy.
   d. contractionary fiscal policy.

3. You've been appointed adviser to the president. She wants interest rates to rise and wants to decrease unemployment. You would suggest
    a. expansionary monetary policy.
    b. contractionary monetary policy.
    c. expansionary fiscal policy.
    d. contractionary fiscal policy.

4. You've been appointed adviser to the president. She wants interest rates and inflationary pressure fall. You would suggest
    a. expansionary monetary policy.
    b. contractionary monetary policy.
    c. expansionary fiscal policy.
    d. contractionary fiscal policy.

5. Modern Keynesians
    a. tend to be mechanistic Keynesians.
    b. tend to be interpretive Keynesians.
    c. do not exist because no modern economist would be a Keynesian.
    d. tend to be academic cowonomists.

6. An economist is calling for the implementation of credible, systematic policies, but argues that there should still be significant discretionary policy. This economist
    a. is likely a Classical economist.
    b. is likely a Keynesian economist.
    c. would equally likely be a Classical or Keynesian economist.
    d. does not exist because no economist would call for credible, systematic policies.

7. According to the text
    a. Keynesians are generally correct on policy.
    b. Classicals are generally correct on policy.
    c. Both Keynesians and Classicals are correct on policy sometimes.
    d. Both Keynesians and Classicals are incorrect on policy.

8. Keynesians and Classicals are least likely to agree that
    a. expansionary monetary and fiscal policies have significant long-run stimulative effects on real income.
    b. expansionary monetary and fiscal policies have potentially long-run stimulative effects on inflation.
    c. monetary is politically easier to use than fiscal policy.
    d. expansionary monetary and fiscal policy tend to increase the trade deficit.

9. In what range of the graph to the right will expansionary macro policy be most likely to increase real output the most?
    a. A.
    b. B.
    c. C.
    d. It is equally likely in all ranges.

10. In what range of the graph to the right will contractionary aggregate demand policy be most likely to slow inflation?
    a. A.
    b. B.
    c. C.
    d. It is equally likely in all ranges.

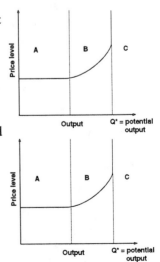

11. The Ricardian equivalence theorem states that
    a. it makes no difference whether one increases the money supply through M_1 or through M_2.
    b. it makes no difference whether government spending is financed by taxes or by a deficit.
    c. it makes no difference whether you use monetary policy or fiscal policy.
    d. it makes no difference whether one is a Keynesian or a Classical.

A1. Economists most likely to support a tax-based incomes policy are
    a. Austrian economists.
    b. Post Keynesian economists.
    c. radical economists.
    d. Classical economists.

A2. Economists most likely to support indicative planning would be
    a. Classical economists.
    b. Austrian economists.
    c. Institutionalist economists.
    d. No economists in their right minds would support indicative planning.

B1. The New Deal
    a. was a program in the 1970s that introduced public works.
    b. was a program in the 1930s that introduced public works.
    c. was an agreement between the Fed and the government on how to finance wartime spending.
    d. involved the introduction of wage and price controls.

B2. October 1979 is an important date in a history of the U.S. economy in that
    a. Keynesian policies were then first adopted.
    b. the Fed suddenly decreased the money supply targets enormously.
    c. the Fed suddenly increased the money supply targets enormously.
    d. rational expectations started to occur in the U.S. economy.

Answers

Short-answer questions

1. Life is tough, and you can't always get what you want. There are trade-offs that must be considered and achieving 2% unemployment and zero inflation is the equivalent to wanting to have kids who do what you tell them without questioning you. And here's my resignation. (425)

2. The study of economic models may be a science but when one translates those models into real-world settings there are ambiguities and judgments must be made that are more artistic than scientific. (425)

3. Theoretical models are deductive models based on first principles; they try to capture aspects of economic behavior that transcend institutions. Policy models are working models; they combine individuals' actions that transcend institutions with individual actions that depend on institutions, and try to capture empirical regularities, whatever the cause. (427-428)

4. Classicals are more likely to stick to rules despite negative short-term consequences, so this was probably a Keynesian response. Which is the correct response? It depends. (428-429)

5. Six points of agreement between Keynesians and Classicals are:

   1. Expansionary monetary and fiscal policies have short-run simulative effects on income.
   2. Expansionary monetary and fiscal policies have potential long-run inflation effects.
   3. Monetary policy is politically easier to use than fiscal policy.
   4. Expansionary monetary and fiscal policies tend to increase a trade deficit.
   5. Expansionary monetary policy places downward pressure on the exchange rate.
   6. Expansionary fiscal policy has an ambiguous effect on the exchange rate. (433)

Word Scramble   1. art of macro policy.   2. mechanistic Keynesianism   3. rational expectations

Match the Terms and Concepts to Their Definitions
   1-c; 2-a; 3-d; 4-b.

Problems and Exercises

1. a. (1) Classical; (2) Keynesian, (3) Classical, (4) Keynesian.
   b. Classicals have a stronger focus on rules and are less likely to consider extenuating circumstances than are Keynesians. (426-433)

Multiple Choice Questions

1. c. As the text makes clear on pages 425-426, there are trade-offs, and good economists are continually pointing out the limits. This combination of goals is, for the most part, unattainable, given current policy options.

2. a. Since you want to decrease unemployment, it will have to be expansionary monetary policy or expansionary fiscal policy, but only expansionary monetary policy will work since the president also wants interest rates to fall. See page 426.

3. c. Since you want to decrease unemployment, it will have to be expansionary monetary policy or expansionary fiscal policy, but only expansionary fiscal policy will work since the president also wants interest rates to rise. See page 426.

4. d.   Since you want to decrease inflationary pressure, it will have to be contractionary monetary policy or contractionary fiscal policy, but only contractionary fiscal policy will work since the president also wants interest rates to fall. See page 426.

5. b.   As discussed on page 427, most Keynesian economists now believe the Keynesian model is simply a guide, not specific, and hence are interpretive Keynesians. The others are throwaway answers.

6. b.   Both Classicals and Keynesians agree that credible, systematic policies are needed. However, the second part, stating that there should still be significant discretionary policy, is a strong sign that this economist is a Keynesian. See page 429.

7. c.   In this text everyone is right some of the time; after all, the author wants to sell the book to all groups. See page 430.

8. a.   Classicals see minimal long-run effects of policy on real income. See pages 426 and 433.

9. a.   When the price-level flexibility curve is flat, expansionary aggregate demand policy will most likely increase real output the most. This range is called the Keynesian range. See Exhibit 4, page 433.

10. c.   When the price-level flexibility curve is vertical, contractionary aggregate demand policy will most likely slow inflation. This range is called the Classical range. See Exhibit 4, page 433.

11. b.   See page 432.

A1. b.   See page 437-439.

A2. c.   See pages 438-439.

B1. b.   See page 440.

B2. b.   The actual event is more complicated than this question allows, but the only answer that is close is b. Actually, the Fed stated that it switched from interest rate targeting to money supply targeting, but most observers believe the desire was simply to provide political cover for reducing money supply growth and squeezing the inflationary expectations out of the economy. See page 444.

Chapter 18: Structural Supply-Side Macro Policies

Chapter at a glance

1. Structural supply-side macro policies are policies that increase the potential output the economy can achieve, thereby allowing a reduction in unemployment, by changing the structure of the economy and the incentives inherent in that structure. (446)

   Structural supply-side policies offer the hope of having it all—growth, prosperity, low fiscal deficits, and low unemployment.

   They are designed to shift the AS path out (not the AED curve), thereby increasing the target level of potential output, and allowing an expansion in output without an increase in inflation.

   Two types of structural policies are activist structural policies that involve <u>more</u> government activity than currently exists (generally favored by Keynesians), and laissez-faire structural policies that involve <u>less</u> government activity than currently exists (generally favored by Classicals).

2. Three general Classical laissez-faire structural supply-side policies are: (1) lowering tax rates; (2) reducing government social welfare spending; and (3) reducing government regulation. (448)

   Lower tax rates, it is argued, create a greater incentive to work, to save, and to invest. Moreover, if the economy is on the downward sloping portion of the Laffer curve, a tax rate cut will decrease a fiscal deficit.

   Reducing need-based social welfare programs, according to Classicals, will increase people's incentive to work, and thereby increase the economy's potential output (income).

   Streamlining, modifying, or eliminating many regulations will reduce the cost of doing busines and encourage new businesses; there will be more competition, and potential output will increase.

3. Much of the discussion of the Laffer Curve has been unfruitful because it does not make clear what time dimension or specific tax opponents and supporters are talking about. (450)

   The effect of a tax cut upon tax revenues depends upon where the economy is along the Laffer curve. Moreover, to make a judgment about whether a tax cut makes sense or not requires a much broader range of judgments than simply what happens to tax revenues. For example, would a tax cut cause government to reduce "wasteful spending"?

4a. Social welfare programs can reduce people's incentive to work, thereby decreasing potential output. (450)

   Many need-based programs involve an incentive to appear needy and to avoid accepting a job. However, eliminating these programs may cause some individuals who were genuinely and unavoidably in need to get less help.

4b. Social welfare programs can increase people's nutrition, and increase society's social cohesion, thereby increasing potential output. (456)

   Ironically, Keynesians see as supply-enhancing some of the same social spending programs that Classicals see as supply-decreasing government programs.

5. Classicals see a much bigger excess burden of taxation than Keynesians do because they see the revenue from taxation as being wasted. Keynesians see it as being transferred to more productive uses. (453)

   Classical economists favor cutting taxes and simultaneously cutting government spending—because they believe the economy can win in both ways.

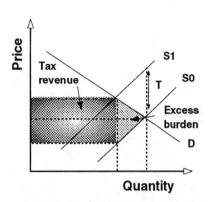

All economists argue that a tax creates excess burden equal to the shaded triangle. Classicals see the revenue to the government as additional excess burden. Keynesians see the revenue to the government as a transfer and thus, not an excess burden.

6. Three Keynesian structural supply-side policies are: (1) productivity-enhancing regulatory reforms; (2) activist industrial policies; and (3) incomes policies. (455)

    Productivity-enhancing regulatory reforms focus, not on cutting social programs and regulations as do the Classical proposals, but on modifying them, improving the positive aspects of the programs while eliminating the negative aspects.

7. An activist industrial policy is a policy under which the government works directly with businesses, providing funds, background research, and encouragement to specific industries It has serious potential political problems. (456)

    Examples include government partnerships with business to encourage exports (like Japan's MITI), strategic trade policy, government-led economic missions, and a targeted employment subsidy policy. A majority of economists argue that the costs outweigh the benefits of a general activist industrial policy. They favor a more informal arrangement.

8. An incomes policy is a policy that is supposed to work by directly holding down nominal wages and price increases, thereby possibly shifting the AS path out. It has serious potential political problems (459-460)

    Ideally, an incomes policy is designed to reduce wages and prices in monopolistic sectors. The politics of an incomes policy renders it extremely unlikely in the near future.

Short-answer questions

1. Once again, you are called to prep freshman Congresspeople. One asks, "The Fed doesn't seem to want to use expansionary monetary policy, and my constituents back home want a balanced budget. That eliminates the two ways you've told us government can get our economy rolling. What other suggestions do you have?" Since you are prepared for this question you tell them about structural supply-side policies and explain how structural macro supply-side policy differs from traditional macro policy. (LO1)

2. The Classical policymakers in the room are wary of your explanation in #1. You tell them three general Classical laissez-faire structural supply-side polices. (LO2)

3. One person in the group remembers that in the 1980s the supply-side policies to reduce taxes based upon the Laffer curve resulted in huge budget deficits. He asks, "What happened to the Laffer curve and why has much of the discussion of the Laffer curve been unfruitful?" (LO3)

4. The laissez-faire Congresspeople want to be armed for a debate about welfare. They ask, "How can reducing government spending on social welfare programs increase potential output?" You tell them. (LO4)

5. How do the Keynesian and the Classical view of the excess burden of taxes differ? (LO5)

6. The Congresspeople who are activist policymakers, listening to your answer to #4, begin to worry. They want to be able to argue in support of welfare. They ask, "How can increasing government spending on social welfare programs increase potential output?" You tell them. (LO6)

7. What are the advantages of an activist industrial policy? (LO7)

8. What sort of practical problems does an incomes policy run into? (LO8)

Word Scramble

1. _____ _____   2._____ _____   3._____ _____

   s x c e e s   u r b n d e   e c o m i n s   o i l c p y   e r a f L f   r c v u e

Match the Terms and Concepts to Their Definitions

___1. activist industrial policy

___2. activist structural supply-side policies

___3. excess burden

___4. incomes policy

___5. industrial policy

___6. Laffer curve

___7. laissez-faire structural policies

___8. military-industrial complex

___9. MITI

___10. need-based social welfare programs

___11. productivity-enhancing social welfare programs

___12. strategic trade policy

___13. structural macro policies

___14. target level of potential output

___15. targeted employment subsidy policy

a. Policies that increase the potential output the economy can achieve, thereby reducing unemployment, by changing the structure of the economy and the incentives inherent in that structure rather than by changing aggregate demand.

b. The highest achievable output level without accelerating inflation.

c. Policies that involve more government activity than currently exists.

d. Policies that involve less government activity than currently exists.

e. A curve that shows the relationship between tax rates and tax revenues.

f. Social welfare programs in which eligibility is determined by need.

g. A loss to producers and consumers that is not gained by anyone else.

h. Social welfare programs that increase productivity and the economy's potential income.

i. The formal policy that government takes toward business.

j. A policy under which government works directly with businesses.

k. Policy under which one country threatens to retaliate unless other countries reduce their explicit or implicit trade barriers.

l. A policy in which government pays business to hire specific groups of workers.

m. A close connection among the armed forces, the industries that manufacture weapons, and members of Congress from states and districts that depend heavily on the defense industry.

n. A policy directly designed to hold down nominal wage and price increases.

o. Japan's Ministry of international Trade and Industry, which guides Japan's activist industrial policy.

Problems and Exercises

1. Suppose you get a need-based payment of $800 a month if you have no income, but you get a need-based payment of $200 if you earn $800 a month. You are deciding whether to take a job at Taco Cabana that pays $5 an hour for 40 hours a week, or $800 a month.

   a. What is your monthly incremental income (the net after you take away the reduction in your need-based payment) after taking the job?

   b. What is the implicit tax rate on your income?

c. What will likely happen to your decision to work because of this implicit tax? Will you work for Taco Cabana or will you decide not to work?

d. Would your answers to a, b, and c affect your supply-side policy proposals? How?

2. The supply and demand curves for bananas are given below. Suppose the government imposes a tax, T, on banana sellers.

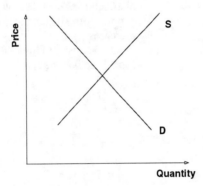

a. What do the Classicals believe to be the excess burden on the graph?

b. What do the Keynesians think the excess burden is on the graph?

3. For each of the following, state whether it is a structural policy or a traditional macro policy, or both. Explain the policy's effect using the macro policy model assuming the economy is in the perfectly flexible price range of the aggregate supply path.

   a. From 1993 to early 1995, the Federal Reserve raised the Fed Funds target from 3% to 6%.

   b. In 1996, a welfare reform bill was passed that limited the time that a person can collect welfare.

   c. In 1982, top marginal tax rates were lowered from 70% to 36%.

   d. In 1997, the Prime Minister of Japan pushed to reduce regulation of business in Japan that will reduce the cost to businesses and consumers an estimated $250 billion a year.

Multiple Choice Questions

1. Structural supply-side policies
    a. shift the AED curve out and increase potential output.
    b. shift the AS path out and increase potential output.
    c. shift both the AED and the AS path out and increase potential output.
    d. shift neither the AED nor the AS path but increase potential output in other ways.

2. Classical methods to create supply-side incentives to increase output include
    a. lowering tax rates, reducing government social welfare spending, and reducing government regulation.
    b. lowering tax rates, reducing government social welfare spending, and increasing government regulation.
    c. lowering tax rates, increasing government social welfare spending, and increasing government regulation.
    d. increasing tax rates, increasing government social welfare spending, and increasing government regulation.

3. The difference between supply-side and Keynesian "tax cutting" policies is that
    a. while the supply-side view holds that tax cuts spur economic growth through the multiplier effect, the Keynesian view does not.
    b. the supply-side view is that "tax cutting" stimulates the economy while the Keynesian view is that it doesn't.
    c. the supply-side view focuses on tax rates and microeconomic incentives while the Keynesian view focuses on tax revenues and aggregate demand.
    d. the supply-side focuses on the effect of tax cuts on aggregate demand while the Keynesian view focuses on the effect of tax cuts on potential income.

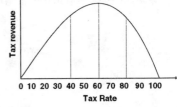

4. Which of the following about the Laffer curve to the right is *false*?
    a. As you increase the tax rate from 40% to 60%, tax revenues will rise.
    b. As you increase the tax rate from 60% to 80%, tax revenues will fall.
    c. As you decrease the tax rate from 80% to 60%, tax revenues will fall.
    d. As you decrease the tax rate from 80% to 60%, tax revenues will rise.

5. The Laffer curve is an inadequate tool to predict the effects of a tax cut because
    a. though it has a time dimension, it does not distinguish between short-run and long-run effects.
    b. though it has a time dimension, it does not talk about any specific tax, which makes it very ambiguous.
    c. it has no time dimension and it does not talk about any specific tax, making it very ambiguous.
    d. it leads to the conclusions that most of the time tax cuts are good but one can't know when to cut taxes because the time dimension is absent from the curve.

6. With which of the following would a Classical economist most likely to agree?
    a. Social welfare programs reduce people's incentives to work and reduce an economy's potential output.
    b. Social welfare programs reduce people's needs and people then have an incentive to appear less needy.
    c. Social welfare programs help maintain social order and cohesion, and thus increase potential income.
    d. Social welfare programs are wasteful in the short-run but are investments in the future.

7. Which of the following is a policy a Classical supply-sider is likely to advocate?
    a. a decrease in the payroll tax.
    b. raise the minimum wage.
    c. institute a targeted employment subsidy policy.
    d. institute an incomes policy.

8. Excess burden is
    a. A loss to consumers that producers gain.
    b. A loss to producers that consumers gain.
    c. A loss to consumers and producers that the government gains.
    d. A loss to consumers and producers that nobody gains.

9. According to the Classicals, which of the following areas represent excess burden due to a tax?
   a. A.
   b. A+B.
   c. A+B+C.
   d. C.

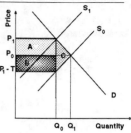

10. If the minimum wage is set at W_{min} the employment level in the economy will be at
   a. Q_D.
   b. Q_E.
   c. Q_S.
   d. zero.

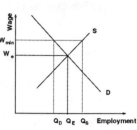

11. The Keynesian view regarding productivity-enhancing social programs is that
   a. the negative incentive effects of these programs make such policies nonviable.
   b. these programs have no negative incentive effects, and have tremendous supply-enhancing effects.
   c. the supply-enhancing effects of these policies often outweigh the negative incentive effects.
   d. although these policies have no supply-enhancing effects, one should support them for moral reasons.

12. An incomes policy is a policy designed to
   a. hold down price increases only.
   b. hold down nominal wage increases only.
   c. hold down nominal wage and price increases.
   d. change relative prices and wages.

13. An incomes policy is supposed to
   a. shift the AED curve out.
   b. shift the AED curve in.
   c. shift the AS path up.
   d. flatten the AS path and shift it out.

Answers

Short-answer questions

1. A structural macro supply-side policy increases the potential output an economy can achieve, thereby reducing unemployment, by changing the structure of the economy and the incentives inherent in that structure, rather than by changing aggregate demand as traditional macro policy does.   See pages 446-447.

2. Three general Classical laissez-faire structural supply-side polices are (1) lowering tax rates, (2) reducing government social welfare spending, and (3) reducing government regulation. See pages 448-452.

3. Much of the discussion of the Laffer curve has been unfruitful because it does not make clear the time dimension under discussion, i.e., it does not make a distinction between short-run and long-run effects. Also, it does not make clear which specific tax is being talking about. Different tax cuts will have different effects on incentives, and talking about some ambiguous tax cut isn't very helpful. See pages 449-450.

4. Social welfare programs that are need-based can make people try to appear more needy than they are and can reduce people's incentive to work because the more they work the less assistance they will get from the government. This set of perverse incentives will decrease potential output. Decreasing such programs can increase the incentives to work, and thus increase potential income. See pages 450-451.

5. Keynesians believe that the excess burden of taxation is lower than what the Classicals believe it to be. Both agree that the red triangle in Exhibit 4 on page 453 represents excess burden. The Classicals see the revenues collected from taxation as wasteful, whereas Keynesians see them as a transfer from one sector to another. See pages 452-454, especially Exhibit 4.

6. Social welfare programs can increase people's nutrition, making them more productive workers, thereby increasing potential output. Also, by increasing social cohesion, they can increase potential output. See page 456.

7. By providing funds, background research and encouragement to specific high-growth industries, activist industrial policies can increase a country's international competitiveness, and so its potential output can be increased. See pages 456-457.

8. Incomes polices have potential political problems. They make distributional issues explicit and by doing so often create more dissension among social groups than existed before. Also, relative prices in a market economy change over time. An incomes policy is not good at determining which relative prices should change and which should not. So incomes policies often work against the market. See pages 459-460.

Word Scramble   1. excess burden   2. incomes policy   3. Laffer curve.

Match the Terms and Concepts to Their Definitions
1-j; 2-c; 3-g; 4-n; 5-i; 6-e; 7-d; 8-m; 9-o; 10-f; 11-h; 12-k; 13-a; 14-b; 15-l.

Problems and Exercises

1. a.   You would be now earning a total of $1000 ($800 from Taco Cabana plus $200 as need-based payment). This is only $200 more than what you would make if you weren't working at all. So, your incremental income is only $200. See page 450.
   b.   The implicit tax rate on your wage is 75%, (600/800), since your need-based payment has dropped by $600 from $800 a month to $200 a month. See pages 450-451.

c. Because of the implicit tax rate your after-tax hourly wage rate will be only $1.25 ($200/160hrs). You would probably find it less attractive to work for Taco Cabana than to receive the $800 payment without working at all. At the same time, you might look for under-the-table work to make some additional income. (450-451)

d. Such calculations suggest that policy makers should recommend policies that take into account the incentive effects of social programs. I would support programs whereby welfare is offered with a time limit and allow people, for a time, to collect both welfare and a salary during that time. Another way to reduce the implicit tax is to offer free childcare if welfare recipients found a job. New state legislation that requires that welfare recipients be actively looking for work has reduced the welfare rolls by eliminating those with under-the-table jobs who don't have time to look for other legitimate jobs. (450-451)

2. a. All economists agree that the area represented by the triangle C is excess burden. Classicals, however, in addition see rectangles A and B (total tax revenue collected by the government) as excess burden since they see the tax revenues as being wasted by the government. (453-454)

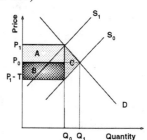

b. Keynesians believe that only triangle C is excess burden generated by taxation. They think that government revenues are being used for productive purposes, and hence don't see rectangles A and B as being excess burden. (453)

3. a. Monetary policy is a traditional macro policy that changes output by shifting the AED curve. The contractionary monetary policy will shift the AED curve to the left and output will not change, prices will rise. See Chapter 13 for a further discussion.

b. A time limit on welfare is both a structural policy and a traditional macro policy. As a structural policy it will increase the number of people who are looking for work. This increases resources available for production, shifting the AS path to the right, leading to higher output and lower price level. As a traditional macro policy it will reduce expenditures, shifting the AED curve to the left leading to a drop in output and a fall in the price level. It depends upon the relative effect of each whether output will rise or fall. (450-451)

c. This is both a structural and a traditional macro policy. To the extent that lower marginal tax rates increase people's willingness to undertake market activity, this is a structural policy that shifts the AS path to the right leading to higher output and a lower price level. To the extent that it results in lower tax payments, it shifts the AED curve to the right leading to even higher output and possibly higher prices. (450-451)

d. Reducing government regulation is a structural policy and a traditional macro policy. To the extent that unfettered businesses will be able to devote more resources to production instead of complying with government regulation, it shifts the AS path to the right leading to greater output and a lower price level. To the extent that government regulation employed government workers who needed supplies to carry out their regulation, this shifts the AED curve to the left lowering output and even lower prices. Whether output rises or falls depends upon the relative effect of each. (450-451)

Multiple Choice Questions

1. b. Structural supply-side policies shift out the AS path, thereby increasing the target level of potential output without an increase in inflation. See pages 446-447.

2. a. See page 448.

3. c. The supply-side view is that lower tax rates work through supply incentives; Keynesians see lower taxes working through aggregate demand. See page 448.

4. c. If you decrease the tax rate from 80% to 60%, tax revenues will rise, not fall. See pages 448-449.

5. c. See pages 449-450.

6. a. Because individuals are guaranteed a certain income, they will have a tendency to shirk work. Thus, potential income will decrease. See page 450.

7. a. Classicals believe that decreasing the payroll tax will encourage businesses to create more jobs and thus increase potential income. The rest are policies that Keynesians would tend to agree with. See pages 452-453.

8. d. See page 453.

9. c. All economists agree that triangle C represents excess burden. Classicals, however, in addition see rectangles A and B (total tax revenue collected by the government) as excess burden since they see tax revenues as being wasted by the government. See page 453-454.

10. a. If the minimum wage is set above the market equilibrium wage rate, there will be unemployment in the economy, and the employment level will be at Q_D. See page 455.

11. c. While Keynesians agree that there are negative incentive effects of social programs, they believe that the supply-enhancing effects make them desirable. See page 456.

12. c. See page 459.

13. d. Incomes polices attempt to flatten out Range B and push the level of full employment out. See page 459.

Chapter 19:
Deficits and Debt

Chapter at a glance

1. A deficit is a shortfall of incoming revenue under outgoing payments. A debt is accumulated deficits minus accumulated payments. (463)

   The deficit is a flow concept, whereas the debt is a stock concept.

   ✔ *Debt is a result of accumulated deficits.*

2. The deficit is simply a summary measure of the financial health of the economy. To understand that summary you must understand the methods that were used to calculate it. (467-468)

   Different accounting procedures yield different figures for both the deficit and the debt.

   When considering debt one should view debt in relation to assets (or GDP). Moreover, government debt is different than an individual's debt. Government is ongoing; government can pay off the debt by printing money; and much of the government debt is internal—owed to its citizens.

3. Since in a growing economy a continual deficit is consistent with a constant ratio of debt to GDP, and GDP serves as a measure of the government's ability to pay off the debt, a country can run a continual deficit. (470)

   GDP serves the same function for government as income does for an individual. The greater the GDP (income); the greater the ability to handle debt.

4. Real deficit = Nominal deficit − (Inflation X Total debt). (471)

   Inflation wipes out debt. Inflation also causes the real deficit to be less than the nominal deficit. However, inflation means a higher percentage of the deficit (or spending) will be devoted to debt service (paying interest on the debt). Moreover, the cost of eliminating the debt through inflation is paid by creditors who do not anticipate the inflation.

5. Even though the real deficit is lower than the nominal deficit, there is still cause for concern because the U.S. budget fails to include many obligations and the government uses many accounting tricks. (475)

   The U.S. government has often used gimmicks to make the deficit look smaller than it is.

6. Because the deficit has many dimensions and each is widely debated, there are many alternative reasonable views about the deficit. (478)

   Economists' views range from:
   1. The wolf-at-the-door group who believe the deficit will bring about imminent doom.

   2. The domesticated-pussycat group who believe the deficit doesn't matter.

   3. The termites-in-the-basement group who believe the deficit will cause serious problems in the long run.

Short-answer questions

1. Distinguish between the terms *deficit* and *debt*. (LO1)

2. How much importance do most economists give to the budget deficit? (LO2)

3. In an expanding economy a government should run a continual deficit. True or false? Why? (LO3)

4. If the nominal interest rate is 6%, the inflation rate is 4%, the nominal deficit is $100 billion, and the debt of the country is $2 trillion, what is the real deficit? (LO4)

5. If the nominal interest rate is 5%, the inflation rate is 5%, the real deficit is $100 billion, and the debt of the country is $1 trillion, what is the nominal deficit? (LO4)

6. If a politician presents you with a plan that will reduce the nominal budget deficit by $40 billion, but will not hurt anyone, how would you in your capacity as an economist likely respond? (LO5)

7. The text presented three general views that economists hold about the deficit. What are those three views, and which one of them is right? (LO6)

Word Scramble

1. _____   2._____   3._____ _____
       t b d e   t i i d c f e   l r e a   t i i f e d c

Match the Terms and Concepts to Their Definitions

___ 1. Budget Enforcement Act of 1990

___ 2. cash flow accounting system

___ 3. debt

___ 4. debt service

___ 5. deficit

___ 6. external government debt

___ 7. funded pension system

___ 8. Gramm-Rudman Hollings Act

___ 9. internal government debt

___ 10. nominal deficit

___ 11. off-budget expenditure

___ 12. policy régime

___ 13. real deficit

___ 14. structural deficit

___ 15. unfunded pension system

a. A federal law establishing mandatory deficit targets for the United States.

b. A federal law establishing a pay-as-you-go test for new spending and tax cuts, along with additional spending limits for government.

c. Accumulated deficits minus accumulated surpluses.

d. An accounting system entering expenses and revenues only when cash is received or paid out.

e. An expenditure that is not counted in the budget as an expenditure.

f. Government debt owed to individuals in foreign countries.

g. Government debt owed to its own citizens.

h. Pension system in which pensions are paid from current revenues.

i. Pension system in which money is collected and invested in a special fund from which payments are made.

j. The nominal deficit adjusted for inflation's effect on the debt.

k. The interest rate on debt times the total debt.

l. The deficit determined by looking at the difference between expenditures and receipts.

m. The deficit that would remain when the cyclical elements have been netted out.

n. The general set of rules, whether explicit or implicit, governing the monetary and fiscal policies a country follows.

o. A shortfall per year of incoming revenue under outgoing payments.

Problems and Exercises

1. Calculate the debt and deficit in each of the following:

   a. Your income has been $30,000 per year for the last five years. Your expenditures, including interest payments, have been $35,000 per year for the last five years.

   b. Your income is $50,000 per year; $15,000 of your $65,000 expenditures are for the purchase of the rights to an invention.

   c. Your wage income is $20,000 per year. You have a bond valued at $100,000 which pays $10,000 per year. The market value of that bond rises to $110,000. Expenses are $35,000 per year. Use the opportunity cost approach in your calculations.

2. For each of the following calculate the real deficit:

    a. Inflation is 5%. Debt is $2 trillion. Nominal deficit is $100 billion.

    b. Inflation is -3%. Debt is $500 billion. Nominal deficit is $20 billion.

    c. Inflation is 10%. Debt is $3 trillion. Nominal deficit is $100 billion.

    d. Inflation is 8%. Debt is $20 billion. Nominal deficit is $5 billion.

3. Assume a country's nominal GDP is $7 trillion, government expenditures less debt service are $1.5 trillion, and revenue is $1.3 trillion. The nominal debt is $4.9 trillion. Inflation is 2% and real interest rates are 5%. Expected inflation is fully adjusted.

    a. Calculate debt service payments.

    b. Calculate the nominal deficit.

    c. Calculate the real deficit.

    d. Suppose inflation rose to 4%. Again, expected inflation is fully adjusted. Recalculate (a) - (c).

4. Assume a country's nominal GDP is $200 billion, government expenditures less debt service are $16 billion, and revenue is $20 billion. The nominal debt is $160 billion. Inflation is falling at a rate of 1% per year and real interest rates are 3%. Expected inflation is fully adjusted.

    a.   Calculate debt service payments.

    b.   Calculate the nominal deficit.

    c.   Calculate the real deficit.

    d.   Suppose inflation rose to 2% per year. Inflation expectations do not adjust. How do your answers to (a) - (c) change?

Multiple Choice Questions

1. A deficit is
   a. the total amount of money that a country owes.
   b. the shortfall of payments under revenues in a particular time period.
   c. the shortfall of revenues under payments in a particular time period.
   d. accumulated debt.

2. Since World War II, nominal U.S. government debt has usually been
   a. rising.
   b. falling.
   c. sometimes rising and sometimes falling.
   d. non-existent because the U.S. government has no debt.

3. Country A has a debt of $10 trillion. Country B has a debt of $5 trillion.
   a. Country A is in a better position than Country B.
   b. Country B is in a better position than Country A.
   c. One cannot say what relative position the countries are in.
   d. Countries A and B are in equal positions.

4. As a percentage of GDP, since World War II
   a. debt in the United States has been rising.
   b. debt in the United States has been falling.
   c. debt in the United States has been sometimes rising, sometimes falling.
   d. the U.S. government has had no debt.

5. If there is growth and the country has decided it wants to keep its ratio of debt to GDP constant
   a. it should run a deficit.
   b. it should run a surplus.
   c. it should run a balanced budget deficit.
   d. the deficit has no effect on debt.

6. The nominal deficit is $100 billion; inflation is 4 percent; total debt is $2 trillion. The real deficit is
   a. zero.
   b. $20 billion.
   c. $80 billion.
   d. $100 billion.

7. The nominal deficit is $200 billion; inflation is 20 percent; total debt is $1 trillion. The real deficit is
   a. zero.
   b. $20 billion.
   c. $80 billion.
   d. $100 billion.

8. The real deficit is $100 billion; inflation is 4 percent; total debt is $2 trillion. The nominal deficit is
   a. zero.
   b. $120 billion.
   c. $180 billion.
   d. $200 billion.

9. Creditors
   a. always lose in an inflation.
   b. always gain in an inflation.
   c. sometimes lose and sometimes gain in an inflation, depending on what happens to real interest rates.
   d. sometimes gain and sometimes lose in an inflation, depending on what happens to the deficit.

10. According to most economists, the deficit
    a. is very important.
    b. is not important at all.
    c. is important primarily as one indicator of the financial health of the economy.
    d. should always be matched by surpluses.

11. Which of the following statements is true?
    a. A funded pension system is preferable to an unfunded pension system.
    b. An unfunded pension system is preferable to a funded pension system.
    c. Whether an unfunded pension system is preferable to an unfunded pension system depends.
    d. An unfunded pension system and a funded pension system are essentially identical.

12. If there is an unfunded pension system with fixed retirement ages and there is a baby boom, when the members of that baby boom retire
    a. the pension system will be in great shape.
    b. the pension system will be in horrendous shape.
    c. the baby boom will have no effect on the pension system.
    d. the pension system will be abandoned.

13. If the U.S. government raised the retirement age to 72 starting in 2010, the current budget deficit would be
    a. reduced.
    b. increased.
    c. unaffected.
    d. eliminated.

14. According to the textbook, most economists
    a. have a wolf-at-the-door view of the deficit.
    b. have a domesticated-pussycat view of the deficit.
    c. have a termites-in-the-basement view of the deficit.
    d. do not even consider the deficit.

Answers

Short-answer questions

1. A deficit is a shortfall of revenues under payments. It is a flow concept that has a time period dimension. A debt is accumulated deficits minus accumulated surpluses. It exists at a moment of time, not over a period of time. (463)

2. While there are differences of opinion, most economists are hesitant to attach too much importance to a deficit. The reason why is that the deficit depends on the accounting procedures used, and these can vary widely. Sometimes a deficit may be of serious concern; at other times it might be of no concern. Thus, only with much more additional information will an economist attribute importance to a deficit. It is financial health—by which is meant the ability to cover costs over the long term—of the economy that most economists are concerned with. (467, 473)

3. It depends. In an expanding economy with no deficits the ratio of debt to GDP will be falling; if the government wants to hold the debt-to-GDP constant it will need to run a continual deficit. If it wants to reduce that ratio, then it need not run a continual deficit. (470)

4. To calculate the real deficit you multiply inflation times the total debt (4% $\times$ $2 trillion), giving $80 billion; then subtract that from the nominal deficit of $100 billion. So in this example the real deficit equals $20 billion. The interest rate does not enter into the calculations. (470-471)

5. To calculate the nominal deficit you multiply inflation times the total debt (5% $\times$ $1 trillion), giving $50 billion, and add that to the real deficit of $100 billion. So in this example the nominal deficit equals $150 billion. There interest rate does not enter into the calculation. (471)

6. TANSTAAFL. I would check to see what accounting gimmick the politician was proposing and what the plan would do to the long-run financial health of the country. (474-477)

7. The three views were the wolf-at-the-door view, the domesticated pussycat view, and the termites-in-the-basement view. Of these, the majority of economists hold the termites-in-the-basement view. The textbook author seems to think the termites-in-the-basement view is the correct view, but since there is disagreement, and I have not studied the issue, I withhold judgment, following the text's line that "It depends." (478-481)

Word Scramble   1. debt   2. deficit   3. real deficit

Match the Terms and Concepts to Their Definitions
1-b; 2-d; 3-c; 4-k; 5-o; 6-f; 7-i; 8-a; 9-g; 10-l; 11-e; 12-n; 13-j; 14-m; 15-h.

Problems and Exercises

1. a. Deficit is $5,000 per year; Debt is $25,000. On page 463, deficit is defined as income less expenditures and debt is defined as accumulated deficits. For each of the past 5 years, you have incurred an annual deficit of $5,000. Total debt is $5,000 times five years, or $25,000. (463)
    b. Deficit is $15,000; Debt is $15,000. Page 465 tells you that what is included as expenses is ambiguous. If you count the purchase of the rights to the invention as a current expenditure, the deficit is $15,000. If you had no previous debt, debt is also $15,000. If, however, you count the purchase of the invention as an investment and include it in your capital budget, then your expenses are only $50,000 and your current account will be in balance. (463, 466)
    c. Surplus of $5,000. Page 466 tells you that using an opportunity cost approach, a person holding bonds should count the rise in the bonds' market value as revenue. Here, wage income is $20,000 per year, interest income is $10,000 and the bond's value has increased by $10,000. Total income is $40,000. Income of $40,000 less expenses of $35,000 per year yields a budget surplus of $5,000. (463, 466)

2. As discussed on page 471, the real deficit is the nominal deficit adjusted for inflation's effect on the debt. The definition of real deficit states: Real deficit = Nominal deficit - (Inflation x Total debt).
   a. $0: $100 billion − .05 × $2 trillion. (471)
   b. $35 billion: $20 billion − (−.03) × $500. (471)
   c. Surplus of $200 billion: $100 billion − .10 × $3 trillion. (471)
   d. $3.4 billion: $5 billion − .08 × $20 billion. (471)

3. a. $343 billion: Debt service payment = nominal interest rate x nominal debt. The nominal interest rate when expected inflation is fully adjusted is the real interest rate plus inflation (5+2). Debt service payment = .07 × $4.9 trillion. (471-473)
   b. $543 billion deficit: The nominal deficit is revenues less government expenditures (including debt service), $1.3 trillion - ($1.5 trillion + $.343 trillion). (471-473)
   c. $445 billion deficit: The real deficit = Nominal deficit − (Inflation ×Total debt) = $.543 trillion − (.02 × $4.9 trillion). (471-473)
   d. Since bondholders must be compensated for the loss in the value of their bonds, they demand a nominal interest rate of 9% (5 + 4). Debt service payment is now $441 billion (.09 × $4.9 trillion). The nominal deficit is higher at $641 billion. ($1.3 trillion − ($1.5 trillion + $.441 trillion)). The real deficit has not changed. It is still $445 billion (The real deficit = Nominal deficit − (Inflation × Total debt) = $.641 trillion − (.04 × $4.9 trillion)). (471-473)

4. a. $3.2 billion: Debt service payment = nominal interest rate x nominal debt. The nominal interest rate when expected inflation is fully adjusted is the real interest rate plus inflation (3+(−1)). Debt service payment = .02 × $160 billion. (471-473)
   b. Surplus of $800 million: The nominal deficit is revenues less government expenditures (including debt service), $20 billion − ($16 billion + $3.2 billion). (471-473)
   c. Deficit of $800 million: The real deficit = Nominal deficit − (Inflation × Total debt) = −.8 billion − (−.01 x $160 billion). (471-473)
   d. The answers to (a) and (b) do not change but the answer to (c) does. Since bondholders do not expect the 2% inflation, they do not have to be compensated for the loss in the value of their bondholdings and the nominal interest rate does not change. Debt service payment is still $3.2 billion; the nominal deficit is still $800 million. The real deficit does, however, change to a real surplus of $4 billion. The real deficit = Nominal deficit − (Inflation × Total debt) = −.8 billion − (.02 × $160 billion). (471-473)

Multiple Choice Questions

1. c. See page 463.
2. a. See Exhibit 1, page 464.
3. c. Debt must be judged relative to assets and to total GDP. See page 467.
4. c. See Exhibit 2, page 469.
5. a. Real growth will reduce the ratio of existing debt to GDP so to hold the ratio constant a continual deficit is necessary. See page 470.
6. b. Real deficit = Nominal Deficit − (Inflation × Total Debt); $100−$80 = $20 billion. See page 471.
7. a. Real deficit = Nominal Deficit − (Inflation × Total Debt); $200−$200 = 0. See page 471.
8. c. Nominal deficit = Real Deficit + (Inflation × Total Debt); $100+$80 = $180 billion. See page 471.
9. c. If the interest rates adjust for the inflation, the creditors will not lose, and if they adjust more than the inflation, creditors will gain. See page 473.
10. c. While there is debate about the deficit, the text argues that the majority of economists take a middle-of-the-road view of the deficit, believing that one should not be concerned about the deficit itself but, rather, about the deficit *as an indicator of the financial health of the economy*, since it is that financial health that should be the real concern. See pages 467and 478.

11. c.   In this text just about everything depends. So when one is given a general question such as this, the "it depends" option is a good one. See pages 475-477 for what the choice depends upon.

12. b.   When members of the baby boom retire there will be few workers and many pensioners. The d option is unlikely because systems usually adapt when forced to do so. See page 476.

13. c.   The U.S. uses a cash flow accounting method, so changes affecting the future are not seen in the current budget. See page 474-476.

14. c.   See page 480.

Chapter 20:
Growth and the Macroeconomics of Developing and Transitional Economies

Chapter at a glance

1. Growth occurs because of an increase in inputs, given a production function; development occurs through a change in the production function. (485)

   Growth is a macro goal because it increases the average absolute standard of living.

2. There are differences in normative goals between developing and developed countries because their wealth differs. Developing countries face true economic needs whereas developed countries' economic needs are considered by most people to be normatively less pressing. (485)

   The main focus of macro policy in developing countries is on how to increase growth through development to fulfill people's basic needs.

3. Economies at different stages of development have different institutional needs because the problems they face are different. Institutions that can be assumed in developed countries cannot necessarily be assumed to exist in developing countries. (487)

   Developed nations have stable governments and market structures which are often lacking in developing countries.

4. "The dual economy" refers to the existence of the two sectors in most developing countries: a traditional sector and an internationally-oriented modern market sector. (488)

   Often, the largest percentage of the population participates in the traditional sector. Tradition often resists change.

5. A régime change is a change in the entire atmosphere within which the government and the economy interrelate; a policy change is a change in one aspect of government's actions. (489)

   A régime change and macro institutional policies designed to fit the cultural and social dimensions of developing and transitional economics are what developing economies need.

6. Central banks recognize that printing too much money causes inflation, but often feel compelled to do so for political reasons. Debate about inflation in developing and transitional countries generally concerns those political reasons, not the relationship between money and inflation. (492)

   Governments in developing and transitional economies risk being thrown out of office unless they run deficits and issue too much money.

7. Full convertibility means one can exchange one's currency for whatever legal purpose one wants. Convertibility on the current account limits those exchanges to buying goods and services. (494)

   Very few developing countries allow full convertibility.

8. The "borrowing circle" concept replaced traditional collateral with guarantees by friends of the borrower. It was successful because the invisible handshake in Bangladesh, where the borrowing circle originated, was very strong. (498)

   This is the creative type of macro institutional policy much needed in developing countries.

Short-answer questions

1. What is the difference between growth and development? (LO1)

2. Why is there often a difference in the normative goals of developed and developing countries? (LO2)

3. Why do economies at different stages of development often have different institutional needs? Explain. (LO3)

4. What is meant by the term "the dual economy"? (LO4)

5. Distinguish between a régime change and a policy change. (LO5)

6. Inflation is simply a problem of central banks in developing countries issuing too much money. Is this true or false? Why? (LO6)

7. What are two types of convertibility? (LO7)

8. The three Cs of Western banking are capital, collateral, and character. If one were describing the Grameen bank's approach to banking how would the three Cs change? (LO8)

Word Scramble

1. _____ _____   2._____   3._____ _____
   eégimr   nhgeca   yttoonnliiidca   wrroonigb   rliecc

Match the Terms and Concepts to Their Definitions

___ 1. balance of payments constraint

___ 2. basic needs

___ 3. borrowing circle

___ 4. conditionality

___ 5. convertibility on the current account

___ 6. developing economy

___ 7. dual economy

___ 8. exchange rate policy

___ 9. full convertibility

___ 10. inflation tax

___ 11. macro institutional policies

___ 12. policy change

___ 13. restructuring

___ 14. soft budget constraint

___ 15. trade credits

a. A change in one aspect of government's actions, such as monetary policy or fiscal policy.

b. Adequate food, clothing, and shelter for the people in a society.

c. The existence in most developing countries of two sectors, a traditional sector and an internationally-oriented modern market sector.

d. An economy that has a low level of GDP per capita and a relatively undeveloped market structure, and has never had an alternative, developed economic system.

e. An implicit tax on the holders of cash and the holders of any obligations specified in nominal terms.

f. Buying and selling foreign currencies in order to help stabilize the exchange rate.

g. Changing the underlying economic institutions of an economy.

h. Limitation on expansionary domestic macro policy due to a shortage of international reserves.

i. Loan system in which collateral is not required. Instead, the borrower must find friends to guarantee the repayment.

j. Loose financial constraints on firms' decisions in centrally-planned economies.

k. Making loans that are subject to specific conditions.

l. Policies to change the underlying macro institutions and thereby increase output.

m. Short-term loans to facilitate inter-firm trade.

n. System that allows people to exchange currencies freely to buy goods and services, but not to buy assets in other countries.

o. System where individuals can change dollars into any currency they want for whatever legal purpose they want.

Multiple Choice Questions

1. The concept "dual economy" refers to
   a. the tendency of developed countries to have a traditional sector and an internationally-oriented sector.
   b. the tendency of both developed and developing countries to have a traditional sector and an internationally-oriented sector.
   c. the tendency of developing countries to have a traditional sector and an internationally-oriented sector.
   d. the fight, or dual, between developed and undeveloped countries.

2. If a country changes its entire approach to policy, that is called
   a. a major policy change.
   b. a policy change.
   c. a régime change.
   d. a constitutional change.

3. The soft budget constraint refers to
   a. the use of government moral suasion on firms.
   b. the use of moral suasion by central banks on firms.
   c. the ability of firms to get loans without significant difficulty.
   d. the use of moral suasion by international agencies on developing countries.

4. The inflation tax is
    a. a tax on those individuals who cause inflation.
    b. a tax on firms who cause inflation.
    c. a tax on both individuals and firms who cause inflation.
    d. a tax on holders of cash and any obligations specified in nominal terms.

5. The revenue of an inflation tax
    a. goes only to government.
    b. goes only to private individuals.
    c. goes to both private individuals and government.
    d. is a meaningless term because there is no revenue from an inflation tax.

6. If you hold a fixed interest rate debt denominated in domestic currency and there is a large inflation, you will
    a. likely lose.
    b. likely gain.
    c. likely experience no effect from the large inflation.
    d. find that the large inflation could cause you either to gain or to lose.

7. If you hold a fixed interest rate debt denominated in a foreign currency, and there is a large domestic inflation, you will
    a. likely lose some.
    b. likely gain some.
    c. likely lose all your debt.
    d. likely experience no direct effect from the large inflation.

8. Conditionality refers to
    a. the U.S. government's policy of only making loans to countries subject to specific conditions.
    b. the IMF's policy of making loans to countries subject to specific conditions.
    c. central banks' policies of making loans to firms only under certain conditions.
    d. the conditions under which inter-firm credit is allowed in transitional economies.

9. According to a World Bank report, the developmental success of the Asian Tigers is in part attributed to
    a. using Keynesian policies.
    b. closing their countries to foreign technology.
    c. opening their economies to foreign technology.
    d. borrowing large amounts of money from abroad.

10. The borrowing circle refers to
    a. a group of countries who borrow from one another.
    b. the tendency of loans to be repaid, thus completing the borrowing circle.
    c. the making of loans to an individual if other individuals agree to repay the loan for the borrower if necessary.
    d. the concept that savings and investment must be equal.

Answers

Short-answer questions

1. Growth occurs because of an increase in inputs, given a production function. Development occurs through a change in the production function. Development involves more fundamental changes in the institutional structure than does growth. (485)

2. Developing countries face true economic needs. Their concern is with basic needs such as adequate clothing, food, and shelter. Developed countries' needs are considered less pressing—for example, will everyone have access to a CD player?(485)

3. Economies at different stages of development have different institutional needs because the problems they face are different. Institutions that can be assumed in developed countries cannot necessarily be assumed to exist in developing countries. For example, developing countries often lack the institutional structure that markets require. (487)

4. Dual economy refers to the existence of the two distinct sectors in most developing countries: a traditional sector and an internationally-oriented modern market sector. (488)

5. A régime change is a change in the entire atmosphere within which the government and the economy interrelate; a policy change is a change in one aspect of government's actions. A régime change affects underlying expectations about what the government will do in the future; a policy change does not. (489)

6. Any simple statement is generally false, and this one is no exception. The reason why this one is false is that while it is true that inflation is closely tied to the developing country's central bank issuing too much money, the underlying problem behind the central bank's actions is often large government deficits that cannot be financed unless the central bank issues debt and then buys the bonds, which requires an increase in the money supply (printing money to pay for the bonds). (492-493)

7. Two types of convertibility are full convertibility and current account convertibility. Full convertibility means you can change your money into another currency with no restrictions. Current account convertibility allows exchange of currency to buy goods but not to invest outside the country. Many developing countries have current account convertibility, but not full convertibility. (494-495)

8. The Grameen Bank introduced the "borrowing circle" approach to banking. It offered to replace collateral with a guarantee by a group of four friends of the borrower. Thus, it reduced the role of two of the Cs (capital and collateral) and put more emphasis on the third C—character. Thus, the Grameen Bank's approach to banking might be described as the Big C (Character) approach. (497-498)

Word Scramble   1. régime change   2. conditionality   3. borrowing circle

Match the Terms and Concepts to Their Definitions
1-h; 2-b; 3-i; 4-k; 5-n; 6-d; 7-c; 8-f; 9-o; 10-e; 11-l; 12-a; 13-g; 14-j; 15-m.

Multiple Choice Questions

1. c. As seen on page 488, c is definition of dual economy. Choice d was put in to throw you off—when the word means "a fight," it is, of course, spelled with an "e"—"duel."

2. c. See page 489.

3. c. See page 490.

4. d. The answer has to be d, as discussed on page 493. The individuals and firms who cause the inflation are gaining from the inflation; they pay no inflation tax.

5. c. The only answer that makes any sense is c. The "revenue" goes from holders of fixed nominal interest rate debt to those who owe that debt. Those who owe the debt include both private individuals and government. See pages 493-494.

6. a. Inflation wipes out the value of fixed interest rate debt. See pages 493-494.

7. d. Because the debt is denominated in a foreign currency, what happens to the domestic price level does not directly affect you. There could be indirect effects but d specifies direct effects. See pages 493-494.

8. b. See page 495.

9. c. As discussed on page 496, the World Bank report says the Asian Tigers got some fundamentals right, one of those fundamentals being opening up their economies to foreign technology.

10. c. See pages 497-498.

Pretest III
Chapters 14 - 20

Take this test in test conditions, giving yourself a limited amount of time to complete the questions. Ideally, check with your professor to see how much time he or she allows for an average multiple choice question and multiply this by 33. This is the time limit you should set for yourself for this pretest. If you do not know how much time your teacher would allow, we suggest 1 minute per question, or about 35 minutes.

1. Assuming velocity is relatively constant and real income is relatively stable, an increase in the money supply of 40 percent will bring about an approximate change in the price level of
   a. 4 percent.
   b. 40 percent.
   c. 80 percent.
   d. zero percent.

2. The short-run Phillips curve shifts around because of
   a. changes in the money supply.
   b. changes in expectations of employment.
   c. changes in expectations of inflation.
   d. changes in expectations of real income.

3. An economist has just said, "Inflation is everywhere and always a monetary phenomenon." You would deduce this economist
   a. is likely to be a Keynesian economist.
   b. is likely to be a Classical economist.
   c. could be either a Keynesian economist or a Classical economist.
   d. must be neither a Keynesian economist nor a Classical economist, because neither of these groups would ever say that.

4. If the economy is at point A in the Phillips curve graph to the right, what prediction would you make for inflation?
   a. It will increase.
   b. It will decrease.
   c. It will remain constant.
   d. It will explode.

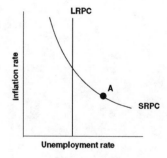

5. An economist has just made the statement that institutional and structural aspects of inflation are important. You would deduce that this economist
   a. is likely a Keynesian economist.
   b. is likely a Classical economist.
   c. could be either a Keynesian economist or a Classical economist.
   d. must not be an economist, since no economist would make such a statement.

6. Classicals generally see supply price shocks
   a. as a cost-push pressure.
   b. as a demand-pull pressure.
   c. as a relative price change.
   d. as an institutional change.

7. If a country has a flexible exchange rate, the exchange rate
    a. is determined by flexible government policy.
    b. is determined by market forces.
    c. fluctuates continuously and will always change by at least 1 percent per year.
    d. fluctuates continuously and will always change by at least 10 percent per year.

8. Expansionary monetary policy has a tendency to
    a. push interest rates up and exchange rates down.
    b. push interest rates down and exchange rates down.
    c. push income down and exchange rates down.
    d. push imports down and exchange rates down.

9. If the trade deficit has gone up, it is most likely that the government ran
    a. an expansionary monetary policy.
    b. a contractionary monetary policy.
    c. a contractionary fiscal policy.
    d. an expansionary monetary policy and a contractionary fiscal policy.

10. Contractionary fiscal policy tends to push
    a. income down and imports up.
    b. income down and the trade deficit up.
    c. prices down and the trade deficit down.
    d. prices down and imports up.

11. According to the textbook, generally, when international goals and domestic goals conflict
    a. the international goals win out.
    b. the domestic goals win out.
    c. sometimes it's a toss-up which will win out.
    d. international monetary goals win out but international fiscal goals lose out.

12. If a country has perfectly flexible exchange rates and is running a current account deficit, it is running
    a. a capital account surplus.
    b. a capital account deficit.
    c. an official transactions surplus.
    d. an official transactions deficit.

13. In the balance of payments accounts, net investment income shows up in
    a. the current account.
    b. the capital account.
    c. the official transactions account.
    d. It is not an entry in the balance of payments.

14. If there is a black market in a currency, the country probably has
    a. nonconvertible currency.
    b. a fixed exchange rate currency.
    c. a flexible exchange rate currency.
    d. a partially flexible exchange rate currency.

15. The graph on the right is of the supply and demand for French francs. If U.S.
    income increases
    a. the supply curve will shift to the right.
    b. the supply curve will shift to the left.
    c. the demand curve will shift to the right.
    d. the demand curve will shift to the left.

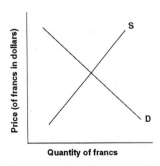

Quantity of francs

16. If a country runs expansionary monetary policy, in the short run one would expect
    the value of its exchange rate to
    a. rise.
    b. fall.
    c. be unaffected.
    d. sometimes rise and sometimes fall.

17. Compared to a fixed exchange rate system, a flexible exchange rate system
    a. allows countries more flexibility in their monetary policies.
    b. allows countries less flexibility in their monetary policies.
    c. has no effect on monetary policies.
    d. allows countries more flexibility in their industrial policies.

18. You have been appointed adviser to the president. He comes in and says he wants very low unemployment,
    zero inflation, and very high growth. You should
    a. advise him to use expansionary monetary policy.
    b. advise him to use contractionary monetary policy.
    c. tell him it is likely impossible using traditional tools.
    d. advise him to use a combination of expansionary monetary policy and contractionary fiscal policy.

19. You've been appointed adviser to the president. She wants interest rates to rise and wants to decrease unem-
    ployment. You would suggest
    a. expansionary monetary policy.
    b. contractionary monetary policy.
    c. expansionary fiscal policy.
    d. contractionary fiscal policy.

20. An economist is calling for the implementation of credible, systematic policies, but argues that there should
    still be significant discretionary policy. This economist
    a. is likely a Classical economist.
    b. is likely a Keynesian economist.
    c. would equally likely be a Classical or Keynesian economist.
    d. does not exist because no economist would call for credible, systematic policies.

21. Keynesians and Classicals are least likely to agree on
    a. expansionary monetary and fiscal policies have significant long-run stimulative effects on real income.
    b. expansionary monetary and fiscal policies have potentially long-run stimulative effects on inflation.
    c. monetary is politically easier to use than fiscal policy.
    d. expansionary monetary and fiscal policy tend to increase the trade deficit.

22. In what range of the graph to the right will expansionary macro policy be most
    likely to increase real output the most?
    a. A.
    b. B.
    c. C.
    d. It is equally likely in all ranges.

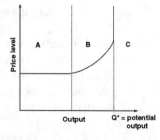

23. Structural supply-side policies
    a. shift the AED curve out and increase potential output.
    b. shift the AS path out and increase potential output.
    c. shift both the AED and the AS path out and increase potential output.
    d. shift neither the AED nor the AS path but increase potential output in other ways.

24. Classical methods to create supply-side incentives to increase output include
    a. lowering tax rates, reducing government social welfare spending, and reducing government regulation.
    b. lowering tax rates, reducing government social welfare spending, and increasing government regulation.
    c. lowering tax rates, increasing government social welfare spending, and increasing government regulation.
    d. increasing tax rates, increasing government social welfare spending, and increasing government regulation.

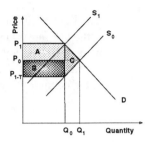

25. According to the Classicals, which of the following areas represent excess burden due to a tax?
    a. A.
    b. A+B.
    c. A+B+C.
    d. C.

26. The Keynesian view regarding productivity-enhancing social programs is that
    a. the negative incentive effects of these programs make such policies nonviable.
    b. these programs have no negative incentive effects, and have tremendous supply-enhancing effects.
    c. the supply-enhancing effects of these policies often outweigh the negative incentive effects.
    d. although these policies have no supply-enhancing effects, one should support them for moral reasons.

27. Country A has a debt of $10 trillion. Country B has a debt of $5 trillion.
    a. Country A is in a better position than Country B.
    b. Country B is in a better position than Country A.
    c. One cannot say what relative position the countries are in.
    d. Countries A and B are in equal positions.

28. The nominal deficit is $100 billion; inflation is 4 percent; total debt is $2 trillion. The real deficit is
    a. zero.
    b. $20 billion.
    c. $80 billion.
    d. $100 billion.

29. According to most economists, the deficit
    a. is very important.
    b. is not important at all.
    c. is important primarily as one indicator of the financial health of the economy.
    d. should always be matched by surpluses.

30. If a country changes its entire approach to policy, that is called
    a. a major policy change.
    b. a policy change.
    c. a régime change.
    d. a constitutional change.

31. The inflation tax is
    a. a tax on those individuals who cause inflation.
    b. a tax on firms who cause inflation.
    c. a tax on both individuals and firms who cause inflation.
    d. a tax on holders of cash and any obligations specified in nominal terms.

32. If you hold a fixed interest rate debt denominated in domestic currency and there is a large inflation, you will
   a. likely lose.
   b. likely gain.
   c. likely experience no effect from the large inflation.
   d. find that the large inflation could cause you either to gain or to lose.

33. Conditionality refers to
   a. the U.S. government's policy of only making loans to countries subject to specific conditions.
   b. the IMF's policy of making loans to countries subject to specific conditions.
   c. central banks' policies of making loans to firms only under certain conditions.
   d. the conditions under which inter-firm credit is allowed in transitional economies.

Answers

1. b (14:1)	12. a (16:1)	23. b (18:1)
2. c (14:4)	13. a (16:2)	24. a (18:2)
3. b (14:6)	14. a (16:6)	25. c (18:9)
4. b (14:9)	15. c (16:9)	26. c (18:11)
5. a (14:12)	16. b (16:12)	27. c (19:3)
6. c (14:15)	17. a (16:14)	28. b (19:6)
7. b (15:3)	18. c (17:1)	29. c (19:10)
8. b (15:6)	19. c (17:3)	30. c (20:2)
9. a (15:9)	20. b (17:6)	31. d (20:4)
10. c (15:13)	21. a (17:8)	32. a (20:6)
11. b (15:15)	22. a (17:9)	33. b (20:8)

Key: The figures in parentheses refer to multiple choice question and chapter numbers. For example (1:4) is multiple choice question 1 from chapter 4.

Chapter 21: Describing Supply and Demand: Elasticities

Chapter at a glance

1. Elasticity is defined as percentage change in quantity divided by percentage change in some variable that affects demand or supply (or quantity demanded or supplied). The most commonly used elasticity concept is price elasticity of demand. (510)

   The price elasticity of <u>demand</u> measures <u>buyer</u> responsiveness to a price change. It equals the percentage change in quantity demanded divided by the percentage change in price. On the other hand, the price elasticity of <u>supply</u> measures <u>seller</u> responsiveness to a price change. It equals the percentage change in quantity supplied divided by the percentage change in price.

2a. To calculate elasticity of a range, economists use the arc elasticity method, calculating the percentage change at the midpoint of the range. (512)

$$E_D = \frac{\left(\dfrac{Change\ in\ Q}{\left(\dfrac{Q_1 + Q_2}{2}\right)}\right)}{\left(\dfrac{change\ in\ P}{\left(\dfrac{P_1 + P_2}{2}\right)}\right)}$$

2b. To calculate elasticity at a point, determine a range around that point and calculate the arc elasticity. (514)

   First create a quantity arc, with the point as the arc's midpoint. Next, determine the price arc relevant for the quantities chosen. Then use the arc elasticity formula to calculate the elasticity at the point. For an example, see Exhibit 2a on page 514.

3. Five elasticity terms are: elastic ($E > 1$); inelastic ($E < 1$); unit elastic ($E = 1$); perfectly elastic ($E = \infty$); and perfectly inelastic ($E = 0$). (515)

   Consider the price elasticity of demand for a good. An elastic demand for a good means buyers are relatively responsive to a price change (the percentage change in the quantity demanded is greater than the percentage change in the price). An <u>in</u>elastic demand for a good means buyers are relatively <u>un</u>responsive to a price change (the percentage change in the quantity demanded is less than the percentage change in the price). When the demand for an item is unit elastic, buyers are neither relatively responsive nor unresponsive—(the percentage change in the quantity demanded equals the percentage change in the price). A perfectly elastic demand curve is a horizontal line. A perfectly inelastic demand curve is a vertical line indicating there is no change in the quantity demanded given a change in the price.

4. The more substitutes, the more elastic the demand and the more elastic the supply. (518)

   The number of substitutes a good has is affected by several factors. Four of the most important determinants of substitutability that give rise to a greater elasticity of demand for a good are:

   1. The larger the time interval considered, or the longer the run.
   2. The less the good is considered a necessity.
   3. The more narrowly the good is defined.
   4. The greater the expenditure is relative to one's income.

   As for the elasticity of supply: the greater the amount of time under consideration, the greater the elasticity of supply (this is because the greater the amount of time, the greater the ability of sellers to respond to the price change).

5. With elastic demands a rise in price decreases total revenue. With inelastic demands a rise in price increases total revenue. (521)

Therefore, firms have a strong incentive to separate out people with a more inelastic demand and charge them a higher price.

6a. Income elasticity of demand shows the responsiveness of demand to changes in income. (523)

It equals the percentage change in demand divided by the percentage change in income. Normal goods have income elasticities greater than zero while inferior goods have negative income elasticities. Moreover, luxuries have an income elasticity greater than 1 while necessities have an income elasticity less than 1 (but still positive).

6b. Cross-price elasticity shows the responsiveness of supply and demand to changes in prices of other goods. (523)

On the demand side: substitutes in consumption have positive cross-price elasticities of demand; complements in consumption have negative cross-price elasticities of demand.

On the supply side it is just the opposite: substitutes in production have negative cross-price elasticities of supply; complements in production have positive cross-price elasticities of supply.

7. Exhibit 11 reviews the effect of shifts in demand and supply with various elasticities. (528)

For example, if demand is highly inelastic and supply shifts in to the left, the price rises significantly while the quantity hardly decreases at all. This is why an inelastic demand creates an enormous incentive for suppliers to get together and look for ways to limit supply (shift the supply curve in to the left).

Also note that the relatively more inelastic the demand or supply, the larger the burden of the tax borne by the demander or supplier. That is, if demand is relatively more inelastic than supply, the larger the burden of the tax paid by the demander; whereas if supply is relatively more inelastic than demand, the larger the burden of the tax paid by the supplier.

Short-answer questions

1. Define the concepts *price elasticity of demand* and *price elasticity of supply.* Explain how they describe the responsiveness of quantity supplied and quantity demanded to changes in price. (LO1)

2. If the price of a good changes by 30 percent and quantity demanded for that same good remains unchanged, what is the price elasticity of demand for that good? (LO2)

3. If price elasticity of supply is 4 and price changes by 10%, by what percent will quantity change? (LO2)

4. Define the terms *elastic, inelastic* and *unit elastic* as applied to points on supply and demand curves. (LO3)

5. What are the four main determinants of the price elasticity of demand? (LO4)

6. What are the main determinants of the price elasticity of supply? (LO4)

7. In each of the following cases, state what will be the effect of a rise in price on total revenue:

    a. Demand is inelastic.

    b. Demand is elastic.

    c. Demand is unitary elastic. (LO5)

8. Define income elasticity of demand. How do the income elasticities of demand differ among normal goods, necessities and luxuries? (LO6)

9. Define cross-price elasticity of demand and cross-price elasticity of supply. (LO6)

10. What is a complementary good? What is a substitute good? (LO6)

11. Explain why elasticity estimates are important to both policy makers and lobbyists. (LO7)

Word Scramble

1. _____   2._____ _____   3._____
   t s p o n m m l e e c   o a n r l m   o d o g   a c e i l s t

Match the Terms and Concepts to Their Definitions

___ 1. complements

___ 2. cross-price elasticity of supply

___ 3. elastic

___ 4. inelastic

___ 5. income elasticity of demand

___ 6. inferior goods

___ 7. jointly produced goods

___ 8. luxury

___ 9. necessity

___ 10. normal goods

___ 11. perfectly elastic

___ 12. perfectly inelastic

___ 13. price elasticity of demand

___ 14. substitutes

___ 15. unit elasticity

a. A measure of the percent change in quantity of goods demanded divided by the percent change in the price of that good.

b. Goods whose consumption decreases when income increases.

c. Goods that can be used in place of one another.

d. Goods that are used in conjunction with other goods.

e. Goods whose consumption increases with an increase in income.

f. Horizontal demand curve. E_d = infinity.

g. Percent (proportional) change in quantity is greater than percent (proportional) change in price. $E_d > 1$.

h. Percent (proportional) change in quantity is less than percent (proportional) change in price. $E_d < 1$.

i. A good that has an income elasticity less than one.

j. For points on curves, the case that the proportional change in quantity is equal to the proportional change in price. E = 1.

k. Vertical demand curve. $E_d = 0$.

l. The percentage change in quantity demanded divided by percentage change in income.

m. The percentage change in supply divided by the percentage change in the price of a related good.

n. Goods in which the production of one good involves, as a byproduct, the production of the other good.

o. A good that has an income elasticity greater than one.

Problems and Exercises

1. Calculate the price elasticity for each of the following. State whether price elasticity of demand is elastic, unit elastic, or inelastic. Will revenue rise, decline, or stay the same with the given change in price?

   a. The price of pens rises 5%; the quantity demanded falls 10%.

   b. The price of a Boston Red Sox baseball game rises from $10 to $12 a game. The quantity of tickets sold falls from 160,000 tickets to 144,000.

   c. The price of an economics textbook declines from $50 to $47.50. Quantity demanded rises from 1000 to 1075.

   d. The price of water beds rises from $500 to $600. Quantity demanded falls from 100,000 to 80,000.

2. Given the demand curve on the right, make the following calculations:

   a. If A were used as a base reference, what is the price elasticity of the arc between A and B?

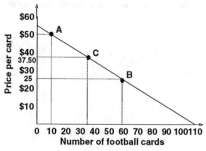

   b. If B were used as a base reference, what is the price elasticity of the arc between B and A?

   c. Using the arc convention, what is the elasticity of point C?

   d. Is elasticity the same along all points? Is the slope of the demand curve the same at all points?

3. Draw the demand curves that correspond to the following price elasticities. What happens to total revenue as price rises in each case?

   a. Demand is perfectly elastic.

   b. Demand is perfectly inelastic.

4. Calculate the price elasticity of the following products. State whether elasticity of supply is elastic, unit elastic, or inelastic.

   a. Cocoa Puffs: The price of a 14-oz. box of Cocoa Puffs rises 4 percent and the quantity supplied rises 15 percent.

   b. Japanese yen: The price of Japanese yen in terms of dollars rises from 100 yen per dollar to 110 yen per dollar. Its quantity supplied rises from 5,000,000 yen to 5,300,000 yen per year.

   c. Jansport backpacks: The price of Jansport backpacks falls from $30 a pack to $25 a pack. The quantity supplied falls from 150,000 to 125,000 per week.

5. Given the supply curve on the right, make the following calculations:

   a. The price elasticity of supply of the arc between points A and B using point A as a reference point.

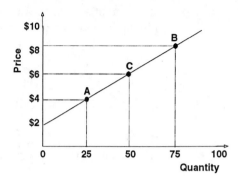

   b. The price elasticity of supply of point C using the arc convention.

   c. What happens to elasticity of supply as you move up this supply curve? State whether all the points along this curve elastic, inelastic, or unit elastic.

6. Calculate the income elasticity of demand for the following goods. State whether each is a luxury, a necessity, or an inferior good.

   a. As average income per student rises from $10,000 to $12,000 a year, demand for ice cream cones increases from 30,000 cones to 37,500 cones per year.

   b. As income decreases from 120,000 to 100,000 French francs per year, demand for margarine increases from 50 to 60 pounds per year.

   c. As income decreases from $20,000 to $18,000 per year, demand for summer cottages in Vermont decreases from 80 to 75.

7.   Determine the cross-price elasticity of demand or supply for the following examples.

   a.   The price of a pizza rises from $9 to $12, and the quantity demanded of Big Macs increases from 3 million to 4 million burgers per year.

   b.   The price of hot dogs falls from $4 a pound to $2 a pound, and the quantity demanded of mustard increases from 15 tons to 20 tons per year.

   c.   The price of wheat in Pakistan rises from 50 rupees a bushel to 75 rupees a bushel. The quantity of rice supplied falls from 10,000,000 to 8,000,000 bushels a year.

8.   What will likely happen to equilibrium price and quantity in the following cases?

   a.   Demand is highly inelastic. The supply curve shifts out.

   b.   Supply is highly inelastic. The demand curve shifts out.

   c.   Supply is highly elastic. The demand curve shifts in.

9. The supply and demand for foreign cars in Bangladesh is shown in the graph on the right. Suppose the government imposes a tax on supply of 10,000 takas per car. The new equilibrium price and quantity is shown in the graph.

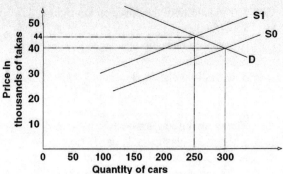

a. What would be the tax paid by consumers? Suppliers? What price is received by suppliers with and without the tax?

b. Demonstrate graphically the tax paid by each.

c. From your answer to (b), what can you conclude about the relative elasticities of the supply and demand curves?

Multiple Choice Questions

1. The definition of price elasticity is
    a. the change in quantity over change in price.
    b. percent change in quantity over percent change in price.
    c. percent change in price over percent change in quantity.
    d. change in price over change in quantity.

2. When the price of a good was raised from $10 to $11, the quantity demanded fell from 100 to 99. The elasticity of demand is approximately
    a. .1.
    b. 1.
    c. 10.
    d. 100.

3. A rise in price has just increased total revenue. One would surmise that the demand for the firm's product is
    a. inelastic.
    b. elastic.
    c. unit elastic.
    d. none of the above.

4. In reference to the graph on the right, which of the following is true?
    a. Point B is more elastic than point A.
    b. Point A is more elastic than point B.
    c. Points A and B have equal elasticity.
    d. One cannot say anything about the elasticities without more information.

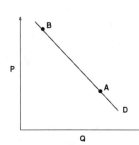

5. The elasticity of the curve on the right is
    a. perfectly elastic.
    b. perfectly inelastic.
    c. unit elastic.
    d. partially inelastic.

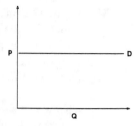

6. The more a good is a necessity
    a. the more elastic its demand curve.
    b. the more inelastic its demand curve.
    c. the more unit elastic its demand curve.
    d. does not matter when discussing demand curves because whether a good is a necessity has nothing to do with the elasticity of its demand curve.

7. The more narrowly a good is defined
    a. the more elastic its demand curve.
    b. the more inelastic its demand curve.
    c. the more unit elastic its demand curve.
    d. does not matter when discussing demand curves because whether a good is narrowly defined has nothing to do with the elasticity of its demand curve.

8. In the long run, the elasticity of demand is generally
    a. more elastic than in the short run.
    b. less elastic than in the short run.
    c. of equal elasticity in the short run.
    d. There is no general relationship between the elasticities in the long run and the short run.

9. Price discrimination is most likely to occur in markets
    a. when all individuals have equal elasticities.
    b. when some individuals have highly inelastic demands and some have highly elastic demands.
    c. in which the elasticity of demand is 1.
    d. in which the elasticity of demand is zero.

10. When price changes from 4 to 5, output supplied changes from 50 to 60. The elasticity of supply is approximately
    a. .5.
    b. .8.
    c. 1.25.
    d. 7.25.

11. In the graph to the right, point A on the supply curve, S_1, is
    a. elastic.
    b. inelastic.
    c. unitary elastic.
    d. unknown because one cannot say from the graph.

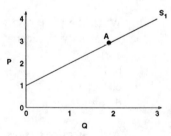

12. In the graph to the right, point A on the supply curve, S_1, is
    a. elastic.
    b. inelastic.
    c. unitary elastic.
    d. unknown because one cannot say from the graph.

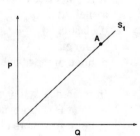

13. The supply curve in the graph at the right is
    a. perfectly inelastic.
    b. perfectly elastic.
    c. unit elastic.
    d. showing that its elasticity changes at various points.

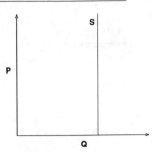

14. A good whose consumption decreases when income increases is generally called
    a. a normal good.
    b. an inferior good.
    c. a substitute good.
    d. a complement good.

15. Pizzas and Big Macs tend to be
    a. substitutes.
    b. complements.
    c. inferior goods.
    d. bounded goods.

16. Hot dogs and mustard tend to be
    a. substitutes.
    b. complements.
    c. inferior goods.
    d. bounded goods.

17. A significant price rise with virtually no change in quantity would most likely be caused by a
    a. highly elastic demand and supply shifts to the right.
    b. highly inelastic supply and a shift in demand to the right.
    c. highly inelastic demand and supply shifts out.
    d. highly elastic supply and demand shifts in.

18. A significant quantity rise with virtually no change in price would most likely be caused by a
    a. highly elastic demand and supply shifts to the right.
    b. highly inelastic supply and demand shifts to the right.
    c. highly inelastic demand and supply shifts to the right.
    d. highly elastic supply and demand shifts to the left.

19. A significant price decline with virtually no change in quantity would most likely be caused by a
    a. highly elastic demand and supply shifts to the right.
    b. highly inelastic supply and demand shifts to the right.
    c. highly inelastic demand and supply shifts out.
    d. highly elastic supply and demand shifts in.

20. A significant quantity decline while virtually no change in price would most likely be caused by a
    a. highly elastic demand and supply shifts to the right.
    b. highly inelastic supply and demand shifts to the left.
    c. highly inelastic demand and supply shifts to the right.
    d. highly elastic supply and demand shifts to the left.

Answers

Short-answer questions

1. *Price elasticity of demand* is the proportional change in quantity demanded relative to the proportional change in price. *Price elasticity of supply* is the proportional change in quantity supplied relative to the proportional change in price. (510)

2. Price elasticity of demand is the percentage change in quantity demanded divided by the percentage change in price. Since the quantity demanded has not changed, the price elasticity of demand is zero. In other words, demand is perfectly inelastic. (510-512)

3. Price elasticity of supply is the percent change in quantity supplied divided by the percent change in price. Thus, if the elasticity of supply is 4 and price changes by 10%, quantity supplied will change by 40%. (512)

4. For elastic points, the proportional change in quantity is greater than the proportional change in price. For inelastic points the proportional change in quantity is less than the proportional change in price. For unit elastic points the proportional change in quantity is equal to the proportional change in price. (515)

5. The four main determinants of price elasticity of demand are (1) the time interval considered, (2) whether the good is a necessity or a luxury, (3) how specifically the good is defined, and (4) its percentage of one's total expenditures relative to one's income. The larger the time interval, the more elastic is demand. The less a good is a necessity, the elastic is demand. The more specifically a good is defined, the more elastic is demand. The greater a percentage of one's expenditures, the more elastic. (518)

6. Price elasticity of supply essentially depends on the time period considered: the longer the time period, the more elastic the supply curve, because there are more options for change. Also, the easier it is to substitute a good, the more elastic the supply curve will be. (518-519)

7. a. If demand is inelastic the percent fall in quantity demanded will be less than the percent rise in price, so a rise in price will increase total revenue. (520-521)
   b. If demand is elastic, the percent fall in quantity demanded will be greater than the percent rise in price, so a rise in price will reduce total revenue. (520-521)
   c. If demand is unit elastic, the percent fall in quantity demanded will equal the percent rise in price, so a rise in price will not change total revenue. (520-521)

8. Income elasticity of demand is the percentage change in demand divided by the percentage change in income. Normal goods have positive income elasticities. Luxury goods have income elasticities greater than one, while necessities have income elasticities less than one. (523-524)

9. Cross-price elasticity of demand is the percentage change in demand divided by the percentage change in the price of another good. Cross-price elasticity of supply is the percentage change in supply divided by the percentage change in the price of another supplied good. (523)

10. A complementary good is a good whose consumption goes down when the price of the other good (for which it is a complement) goes up. A substitute good is a good whose consumption goes up when the price of the other good (for which it is a substitute) goes up. (525)

11. Elasticity estimates are important to policy makers because elasticities will tell them how quantity demanded and quantity supplied will change with various policies that affect price. In the case of price floors or price ceilings it will tell policy makers how much of a surplus or shortage will be created. In the case of taxes, it will tell who will bear the greater burden of the tax. Lobbyists are interested in elasticity estimates for the same reasons. (528-532)

Word Scramble   1. complements   2. normal good   3. elastic

Match the Terms and Concepts to Their Definitions

1-d; 2-m; 3-g; 4-h; 5-l; 6-b; 7-n; 8-o; 9-i; 10-e; 11-f; 12-k; 13-a; 14-c; 15-j.

Problems and Exercises

1. Price elasticity of demand is defined in your text as the percent change in quantity demanded divided by the percent change in price. Demand is elastic if the price elasticity is greater than one; a rise in price will lower total revenue. Demand is inelastic if the price elasticity is less than one; a rise in price will increase total revenue. Demand is unit elastic if the price elasticity is equal to one; a rise in price leaves total revenue unchanged. (For each of the following we use the arc elasticity unless specifically noted.)
   a. Price elasticity of demand is 10%/5% = 2. Since 2 > 1, demand is elastic. Total revenue falls. (510, 515)
   b. Price elasticity of demand is |[(144,000 - 160,000)/152,000]/[(12-10)/11]| = 0.58. Since 0.58 <1, demand is inelastic. Total revenue rises. (510)
   c. Price elasticity of demand is |[(1075 - 1000)/1037.5]/[(47.5 - 50)/48.75]| = 1.41. Since 1.41 > 1, demand is elastic. Total revenue rises. (510)
   d. Price elasticity of demand is |[(80,000 - 100,000)/90,000]/[(600 - 500)/550]| = 1.2. Since 1.2> 1, demand is slightly elastic. Total revenue falls slightly. (510, 515)

2. a. 10. The price elasticity is defined at a point. Thus when you consider a large movement the measure of price elasticity you arrive at changes considerably depending on the point at which you begin. Price elasticity of arc AB measured in reference to point A is |[(60-10)/10]/[(25-50)/50]| = (5)/(.5) = 10. (512)
   b. 0.83. The price elasticity of arc AB measured in reference to point B is |[(10-60)/60]/[(50-25)/25]| = (5/6)/ 1 = .83. This large difference between the answers to a and b is why economists use arc elasticity. (512)
   c. 2.13. The arc elasticity of point C is |[(10-60)/35]/[(50-25)/37.5]| = (1.43)/(.67) = 2.13. (512)
   d. As you can see from the calculations in (a), (b), and (c), elasticity changes along a straight-line demand curve. The slope of the demand curve is calculated as rise over run. It is the same at all points since the demand curve is a straight line. This demand curve has a slope of -0.5. (512)

3. a. When demand is perfectly elastic, the demand curve is horizontal. When prices rise, revenue goes to zero. See the line A in the graph on the right.
   b. When demand is perfectly inelastic, the demand curve is vertical. Revenue rises by the same percentage rise in price. See the line B in the graph on the right.

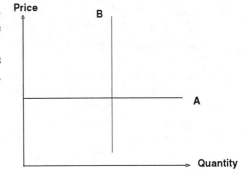

4. a. Price elasticity of supply is 15%/4% = 3.75. Since 3.75 > 1. Supply is elastic. (510-516)
   b. Price elasticity of supply is [5,300,000-5,000,000/5,150,000]/[110-100/105] = 0.61. Since 0.61 < 1, supply is inelastic. (510-516)
   c. Price elasticity of supply is [150,000-125,000/137,500]/[30-25/27.5] = 1. Since 1 = 1, supply is unit elastic. (510-516)

5. a. The price elasticity of supply of arc AB using A as a reference point is [75-25/25]/[8-4/4] = 2. (510-516)
   b. The price elasticity of supply of point C using the arc convention is [75-25/50]/[8-4/6] = 3/2. (510-516)
   c. In an added dimension in the text it is stated that if the supply curve intersects the vertical axis or the price axis, as one goes up along it, the elasticity declines. The entire supply curve is elastic. (510-516)

6. a. The income elasticity of demand is [12,000-10,000/11,000]/[37,500-30,000/33,750] = 0.82. Since 0 < 0.82 < 1, ice cream cones are a necessity. (524)

   b. The income elasticity of demand is [100,000-120,000/11,000]/[60-50/55] = -1. Since -1 < 0, margarine is an inferior good. (524)

   c. The income elasticity of demand is [18,000-20,000/19,000]/[75-80/77.5] = 1.63. Since 1.63 > 1, summer cottages are a luxury good. (524)

7. a. The cross-price elasticity of demand is [4,000,000-3,000,000/3,500,000]/[12-9/10.5] = 1. Since 1 > 0, pizzas and Big Macs are substitutes. (525-526)

   b. The cross-price elasticity of demand is [20 -15/17.5]/[(2 - 4)/3] = -0.43. Since -0.43 < 0, hot dogs and mustard are complements. (525-526)

   c. The cross-price elasticity of supply is [8,000,000 - 10,000,000/9,000,000]/[75-50/62.5] = -0.56. Since -0.56 < 0, wheat and rice are complements. (525-526)

8. a. The price will fall considerably but quantity will not rise significantly, as shown in the graph (a) below. (525-527)

   b. The price will rise considerably but quantity will not rise significantly, as shown in the graph (b) below. (525-527)

   c. The quantity will fall considerably, but price will not fall significantly, as shown in the graph (c) below. (525-527)

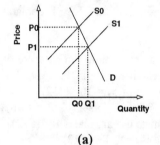

(a)

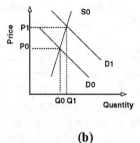

(b)

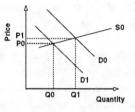

(c)

9. a. The consumers now have to pay 44,000 takas per car which is 4,000 takas more than before. Their tax burden is (4,000 × 250) = 1,000,000 takas. Suppliers now receive 34,000 takas (44,000-10,000) on each car they sell, which is 6,000 takas less per car than before. Their tax burden is (6,000 × 250) = 1,500,000 takas. (529-532)

   b. The graph on the right shows the relative taxes paid by consumers and producers. The upper shaded portion is consumers' tax burden. The lower shaded portion is suppliers' tax burden. (529-532)

   c. Since the supplier's tax burden is greater, the supply curve is less elastic than the demand curve. This is discussed in the textbook. (529-532, especially page 531)

Multiple Choice Questions

1. b. See page 509.

2. a. Substituting in the formula for elasticity gives .01/.1 = .1. See page 510.

3. a. The revenue gain from the increase in price had to exceed the loss from the reduction in quantity, so the demand must be inelastic. See pages 510 and 515.

4. a. The elasticity changes along a straight line demand curve from highly elastic to highly inelastic. See page 513.

5. a. A horizontal demand curve is perfectly elastic because the percentage change in quantity is infinite. See Exhibit 3, page 516.

6. b. Necessities tend to have few substitutes and the fewer the substitutes, the more inelastic the demand curve. See pages 524-525.

7. a. The more narrowly a good is defined, the more substitutes it tends to have. See page 518.

8. a. The longer the run, the greater the possibility of substitution. See page 518.

9. b. Price discrimination requires separating out demanders by their elasticities and charging more to individuals who have inelastic demands. See page 522.

10. b. Elasticity of supply is the percent change in quantity divided by the percent change in price: 20% / 25% = .8. See page 510.

11. a. You can either calculate the elasticity (percent change in quantity divided by the percent change in price) or you can use the trick in the Added Dimension Box (any straight line supply curve that intersects the vertical axis is elastic). (510, 517)

12. c. You can either calculate the elasticity (percent change in quantity divided by the percent change in price) or you can use the trick in the Added Dimension Box (any straight line supply curve going through the origin will have unitary elasticity.) (510, 517)

13. a. For a vertical supply curve the percent change in quantity becomes zero, so the elasticity becomes zero, making it perfectly inelastic. (514)

14. b. See page 524.

15. a. They might be considered by some to be inferior goods but they may not be; consider President Clinton's consumption of both. The answer in economic terms is "substitutes." See page 525.

16. b. This is the classic example of complements. See page 525.

17. b. Since price rose significantly while quantity remained unchanged either demand or supply is inelastic Since price rose, either demand shifted out or supply shifted in. See pages 510, 516.

18. a. Since quantity rose significantly while price remained unchanged either demand or supply is elastic Since quantity rose, either demand shifted out or supply shifted out. See pages 510, 516.

19. c. Since price declined significantly while quantity remained unchanged either demand or supply is inelastic Since price declined, either demand shifted in or supply shifted out. See pages 510, 516.

20. d. Since quantity declined significantly while price remained unchanged either demand or supply elastic Since quantity declined, either demand shifted in or supply shifted in. See pages 510, 516.

Chapter 22:
The Logic of Individual Choice: The Foundation of Supply and Demand

Chapter at a glance

1. The principle of diminishing marginal utility states that, after some point, the marginal utility received from each additional unit of a good decreases with each unit consumed. (538)

   Marginal means "extra."
   Utility means "satisfaction."

2. Principle of rational choice: spend your money on those goods that give you the most marginal utility per dollar. (540)

   If $\dfrac{MU_x}{P_x} > \dfrac{MU_y}{P_y}$ choose to consume an additional unit of good x.

   If $\dfrac{MU_x}{P_x} < \dfrac{MU_y}{P_y}$ choose to consume an additional unit of good y.

   If $\dfrac{MU_x}{P_x} = \dfrac{MU_y}{P_y}$ you're maximizing utility; you cannot increase your utility by adjusting your choices.

   $\dfrac{MU_x}{P_x} = \dfrac{MU_y}{P_y}$ *means the extra satisfaction per last dollar spent on x equals that for y.*

3. When the ratios of the marginal utility to the price of goods are equal, you're maximizing utility (541)

   The equality: $\dfrac{MU_x}{P_x} = \dfrac{MU_y}{P_y}$

   implies a quantity of goods x and y which will maximize your satisfaction given your budget, preferences, and the prices of x and y. No other combination of goods x and y will satisfy you as much.

4. The principle of rational choice states that, to maximize utility, choose goods until the opportunity costs of all alternatives are equal. (545)

The opportunity cost of a forgone opportunity is essentially the marginal utility per dollar you forgo from the consumption of the next-best alternative. To

   say $\dfrac{MU_x}{P_x} > \dfrac{MU_y}{P_y}$ *is to say that the opportunity cost*

   of not consuming good x exceeds that for good y. So you consume x.

5a. According to the principle of rational choice, if there is diminishing marginal utility and the price of a good goes up, we consume less of that good. Hence, the principle of rational choice leads to the law of demand. (544)

   If $\dfrac{MU_x}{P_x} = \dfrac{MU_y}{P_y}$ *and then P_x increases, we get*

   $\dfrac{MU_x}{P_x} < \dfrac{MU_y}{P_y}$, *and we buy more of y and*

   buy less of x.

5b. According to the principle of rational choice, if there is diminishing marginal utility and the price of supplying a good goes up, you supply more of that good. (545)

   Consider labor. As the wage rate goes up, you will be willing to work more hours. Note that the law of supply can be derived from the principle of rational choice.

6. Economists use their simple self-interest theory of choice because it cuts through many obfuscations, and in doing so often captures a part of reality that others miss. (548)

   Approaching problems by asking, "What's in it for the people making the decision?" can be insightful.

   See also, Appendix A: "Indifference Curve Analysis."

Short-answer questions

1. What is marginal utility? (LO1)

2. Suppose you and your friend are studying hard for an economics exam. You have a craving for double cheese pizza. You order a large. Your mouth is watering as you sink your teeth into the first slice. Oh, the pleasure! You eagerly reach for the second slice. The additional pleasure that you get from this slice is less than the first. The third and fourth slice each give you even less pleasure. What principle does this describe? State the principle in general terms. (LO1)

3. Suppose you had $5 to spend. You like going to see Michael Douglas movies a lot, but you like to see John Turturo movies even more. If these were your only choices to spend the $5 on, which movie would you go to see? Show how your choice follows the principle of rational choice. (LO2)

4. What are the formulas that embody the principle of rational choice? (LO2)

5. Explain why you're maximizing utility when the ratios of the marginal utility to the price of goods are equal. (LO3)

6. If the opportunity cost bowling is greater than the opportunity cost of playing tennis, which would a rational person choose? Explain your answer. (LO4)

7. Suppose you are maximizing utility by consuming two Big Macs at $2 apiece and three ice cream cones at $1 apiece. What happens to the number of Big Macs and ice cream cones consumed if the price of ice cream cones rises to $2 apiece? How does this change in consumption account for the law of demand? (LO5)

8. Why might individuals use bounded rationality instead of the rational choice model? (LO6)

9. Why can economists believe there are many explanations of individual choice, but nonetheless focus on self-interest? (LO6)

Word Scramble

1. _____   2._____   _____   _____

   t u i i l t y   m i d i i n s h n i g   g r a m l i n a   t u i i l t y

3. _____   _____

   a t n r a i o l   h i c c e o

Match the Terms and Concepts to Their Definitions

___ 1. bounded rationality

___ 2. diminishing marginal

      utility

___ 3. focal point equilibrium

___ 4. marginal utility

___ 5. principle of rational choice

___ 6. total utility

___ 7. utility

a. As individuals increase their consumption of a good, at some point consuming another unit of the good will simply not yield as much additional pleasure as did consuming the preceding unit.

b. Equilibrium in which goods are consumed, not because the goods are objectively preferred to all other goods, but simply because they have become focal points to which people have gravitated.

c. Rationality based on rules of thumb rather than on the rational choice model.

d. Spend your money on those goods that give you the most marginal utility per dollar.

e. The satisfaction one gets from the consumption of an incremental or additional unit of a product above and beyond what one has consumed up until that point.

f. The satisfaction one gets from one's entire consumption of a product.

g. A measure of the pleasure or satisfaction one gets from consuming a good or service.

Problems and Exercises

1. a. Fill in the blanks for the following table that shows how marginal utility and total utility change as more and more chocolate chip cookies are consumed. (Marginal utility refers to the marginal utility of increasing to that row, e.g., the marginal utility of going from 0 to 1 is 20.)

Number of chocolate chip cookies	Total utility	Marginal utility
1	___	20
2	37	___
3	51	___
4	___	11
5	___	8
6	___	5
7	77	___
8	___	-1

b.   Graph the total utility curve of the table above on the axes to the right.

c.   Graph the marginal utility curve on the axes as for b.

d.   Is the principle of diminishing marginal utility operative in this case? Explain your answer.

e.   At what point does the principle of diminishing marginal utility take effect? At what point does marginal utility become zero?

2.   Using the principle of rational choice, choose the best option in each case:

a.   A $2 slice of pizza giving you 80 utils and a $2 hero sandwich giving you 60 utils.

b.   A $40,000 BMW giving you 200,000 utils and a $20,000 Toyota giving you 120,000 utils.

c.   Taking an economics course that meets 3 times a week for ten weeks giving 900 utils or taking a history course that meets 2 times a week for ten weeks giving 800 utils. Both class periods last 50 minutes. There is no homework or studying.

d.   Taking Tory out for a date to the Four Seasons restaurant in New York City at a cost of $120 which gives you 600 utils and taking Sam out at the corner pizza place at a cost of $15 which gives you 60 utils. (Tory is short for Victoria or Torrence and Sam is short for Samantha or Samuel — you choose which.)

3.   Suppose you are taking courses from two different colleges, both on a part-time basis. One college offers only science courses. The other offers only humanities courses. Each class meets for the same amount of time and you have an unlimited number of hours you can devote to course work, but only $10,500 to devote to tuition. Science courses cost $1,500 a course and humanities courses cost $3,000 a course. You are taking the courses for enjoyment and you have estimated the utility from the consumption of these courses as presented in the following table:

Number of courses	Science Total utility	Humanities Total utility
0	0	0
1	4500	7500
2	7500	12,000
3	9750	15,750
4	11,250	18,750
5	11,750	21,000
6	12,000	22,500

a. How many science courses and how many humanities courses should you take (assuming you follow the principle of rational choice)?

b. Suppose the price of humanities courses falls to $1,000 a course, how would your answer to (a) change?

A1. Suppose you have $10 to spend on pens and note-books. Pen are 50 cents apiece and notebooks are $1 apiece. Draw the budget constraint putting pens on the vertical axis and notebooks on the horizontal axis.

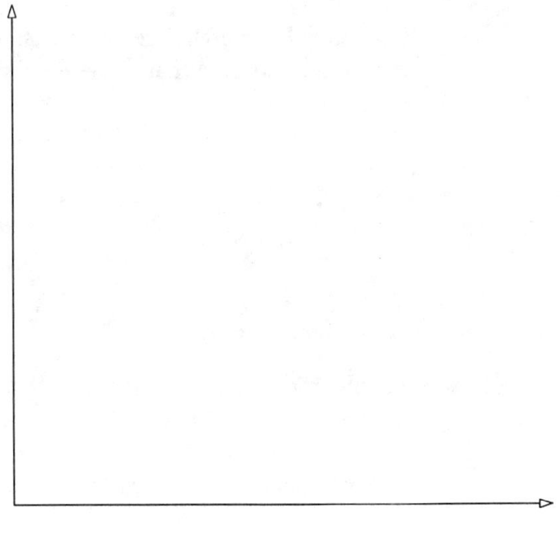

a. What is the slope of the line?

b. What happens to the budget constraint if your income available to spend falls to $8? What is the slope of the new curve? Show this graphically on the graph for (a).

c. Given the new $8 budget constraint, now suppose the price of notebooks rises to $2 apiece. What happens to the budget constraint? Show this graphically using the same axes as in the graph for (a) and (b).

A2. Suppose the following table depicts your indifference between combinations of pens and notebooks:

	Notebooks	Pens
A	12	6
B	8	7
C	6	8
D	5	10
E	4	14

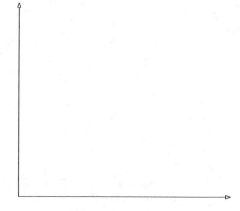

a. Graph the indifference curve on the axes to the right of the table, with pens on the vertical axis and notebooks on the horizontal axis.

b. What is the marginal rate of substitution between combinations C and D?

c. Combine the indifference curve from question A2 with the $10 budget constraint from question A1 on the graph above. What is the combination of goods you will choose using the principle of rational choice?

Multiple Choice Questions

1. The principle of diminishing marginal utility says that
    a. after some point the marginal utility received from each additional unit of a good remains constant with each unit consumed.
    b. after some point the marginal utility received from each additional unit of a good increases with each unit consumed.
    c. after some point the marginal utility received from each additional unit of a good decreases with each unit consumed.
    d. after some point the marginal utility received from each additional unit of a good approaches infinity with each unit consumed.

2. The total utility of the first slice of pizza is 30.
    a. The total utility is greater than the marginal utility.
    b. The total utility is less than the marginal utility.
    c. The total utility and the marginal utility are equal.
    d. There is not enough information to compute the marginal utility.

3. The principle of rational choice specifically states that you choose how to spend additional income based on what gives you
    a. the most total utility per dollar.
    b. the most marginal utility per dollar.
    c. the most average utility per dollar.
    d. the least total utility per dollar.

4. The price of good A is $1; the price of good B is $2. The marginal utility you get from good A is 40; the marginal utility you get from good B is 60. You should
   a. consume more of good A and less of good B.
   b. consume more of good B and less of good A.
   c. keep consuming equal amounts of both goods.
   d. realize that you don't have enough information to answer the question.

5. The price of good A is $2; the price of good B is $2. The marginal utility you get from good A is 40; the marginal utility you get from good B is 60. You should
   a. consume more of good A and less of good B.
   b. consume more of good B and less of good A.
   c. keep consuming equal amounts of both goods .
   d. realize that you don't have enough information to answer the question.

6. The price of good A is $1; the price of good B is $2. The marginal utility you get from good A is 40; the marginal utility you get from good B is 80. You should
   a. consume more of good A and less of good B.
   b. consume more of good B and less of good A.
   c. keep consuming equal amounts of both goods.
   d. realize that you don't have enough information to answer the question.

7. If your marginal utility of additional income is 60 utils, your opportunity cost of working is $5.00 per hour, and you are currently working 10 hours per week at $6.00 per hour, how high a wage will you require to work another hour?
   a. 60 utils
   b. $5.00
   c. $6.00
   d. Insufficient information has been given to answer this question

8. An economist's answer to the question, "Why do people pollute so much?" is likely to be
   a. people haven't been educated about the importance of the environment.
   b. the government has made sufficient rules about pollution.
   c. people are considering average, not marginal, costs of polluting.
   d. people aren't paying enough for their polluting activities.

9. The theory of bounded rationality suggests that
   a. all goods will be normal goods.
   b. all goods will be substitutes.
   c. many of our decisions are based on rules of thumb.
   d. individual tastes will be bounded and hence there will be diminishing marginal utility.

10. A focal point equilibrium is an equilibrium in which
    a. a set of goods is consumed because the goods are subjectively preferred to all other goods.
    b. a set of goods is consumed because the goods are objectively preferred to all other goods.
    c. a set of goods is consumed, not because the goods are necessarily preferred to all other goods, but simply because through luck, or advertising, they have become focal points to which people gravitated.
    d. a set of goods is consumed because through luck, or advertising, they have become focal points to which people gravitated despite the fact that other goods are definitely preferred.

11. The primary explanation of why much more rice is consumed per capita in Japan than in the United States is
    a. price.
    b. custom.
    c. it is impossible to get potatoes in Japan.
    d. relative price.

A1. The budget line (or income constraint) shown in the graph to the right
reflects a relative price of chocolate (in terms of soda) of
a. one-fourth.
b. one-half.
c. one.
d. two.

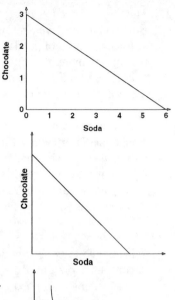

A2. In the graph at the right, if the price of chocolate falls, the income constraint will
a. rotate out and become flatter.
b. rotate in but keep the same slope.
c. rotate in and become steeper.
d. rotate out and become steeper.

A3. The absolute value of the slope of the indifference curve to the right represents
a. the marginal utility of chocolate divided by the marginal utility of soda.
b. the marginal utility of soda divided by the marginal utility of chocolate.
c. the marginal utility of soda times the marginal utility of chocolate.
d. the marginal utility of chocolate divided by price of chocolate.

A4. If chocolate and soda are perfect substitutes, then the indifference curve representing them will be closest to which of the following?
a. A.
b. B.
c. C.
d. D.

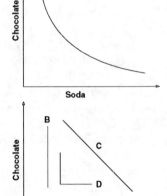

A5. The equilibrium in the indifference curve model in the graph to the right is at
point
a. A.
b. B.
c. C.
d. D.

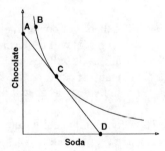

Answers

Short-answer questions

1. Marginal utility refers to the satisfaction one gets from the consumption of an incremental or additional product above and beyond what one has consumed up to that point. (538)

2. The fact that you enjoy each subsequent slice less and less follows the principle of diminishing marginal utility. It states that, after some point, the marginal utility received from each additional unit of a good decreases with each unit consumed. (538)

3. You would choose to see the John Turturo movie because it would give more pleasure for the same amount of money. This decision follows the principle of rational choice which states: Spend your money on those goods that give you the most marginal utility per dollar. (540)

4. The formulas that embody the principle of rational choice are:
If $MU_x/P_x > MU_y/P_y$, choose to consume an additional unit of good x;
If $MU_x/P_x < MU_y/P_y$, choose to consume an additional unit of good y;
If $MU_x/P_x = MU_y/P_y$, you are maximizing utility; you cannot increase your utility by adjusting your choices. (540)

5. If the ratios of the marginal utility to the price of goods are equal, you cannot adjust your spending in any way to increase total utility. Changing your spending will result in additional utility for that good you increased. But that additional utility is less than decrease in utility for that good that you have given up. Thus, the marginal utilities per dollar are no longer equal and total utility has fallen. Total utility is maximized where the ratios of the marginal utility to the price of goods are equal. (541)

6. The opportunity cost of bowling is what is sacrificed to bowl. You would want to minimize your sacrifice. That is, choose that good with the lowest opportunity cost. Since playing tennis has a lower opportunity cost, a rational person would choose tennis over bowling. (545)

7. If you were initially maximizing utility, it must be that $MU_{Big\ Macs}/\$2 = MU_{i.c.}/\$1$. If the price of ice cream cones rise, then you are no longer maximizing utility because $MU_{Big\ Macs}/\$2 > MU_{i.c.}/\$2$. To once again maximize utility you would raise the marginal utility of ice cream cones and lower the marginal utility of Big Macs by choosing to consume more Big Macs and fewer ice cream cones. You would adjust your consumption to the point where the marginal utilities per dollar were once again equal. The relative price of ice cream cones rose and the quantity demanded fell; and the relative price of Big Macs fell and the quantity demanded rose. This is the law of demand. (541-545)

8. In reality, individuals have to make too many choices simultaneously to be able to be rational about every single decision they make. The cost of decision-making is too high. Thus, individuals use bounded rationality, rationality based on rules of thumb ("you get what you paid for," "follow the leader," etc.) rather than using the rational choice model. (546-547)

9. Economists believe there are many explanations of individual choice, but nonetheless focus on self-interest because their simple self-interest theory cuts through many complications and in doing so often captures a part of reality other approaches miss. (548)

Word Scramble   1.utility   2. diminishing marginal utility   3. rational choice

Match the Terms and Concepts to Their Definitions
1-c; 2-a; 3-b; 4-e; 5-d; 6-f; 7-g.

Problems and Exercises

1. a. This question tests the concepts of marginal utility, total utility, and the principle of diminishing marginal utility. Marginal utility is the satisfaction one gets from the consumption of an incremental product. Total utility is the total satisfaction from all products consumed; it is the sum of all marginal utilities of products consumed. (538-539)

Number of chocolate chip cookies	Total utility	Marginal utility
1	20	20
2	37	17
3	51	14
4	62	11
5	70	8
6	75	5
7	77	2
8	76	-1

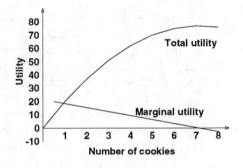

b. The total utility curve is shown on the right. It is bowed downward because the slope of the marginal utility curve is negative. (538-539)

c. The marginal utility curve is shown on the right. Its slope is always negative because the marginal utility of each additional cookie is always declining. (538-539)

d. The principle of diminishing marginal utility is operative in this case. The principle of diminishing marginal utility as explained on page 539 of your text states that as more of a good is consumed, beyond some point, the additional units of consumption will yield fewer utils than the previous units. This is shown in the table by the third column. Its values are always declining. (538-539)

e. The principle of diminishing marginal utility operates from the second cookie on. The second cookie gave less pleasure than the first cookie. This is true throughout, from 2 through 8. Marginal utility becomes zero between 7 and 8 cookies. The marginal utility of the 7th cookie is 2, but the marginal utility of the 8th is -1. (538-839)

2. The principle of rational choice, discussed on page 540, states: Spend your money on those goods that give you the most marginal utility per dollar.

a. Choose the $2 slice of pizza. Marginal utility per dollar of the slice of pizza is 80 utils/$2 = 40 utils per dollar. Marginal utility per dollar of a hero sandwich is 60/ $2 = 30 utils per dollar. 40>30. (539-540)

b. Choose the $20,000 Toyota. Marginal utility per dollar for the Toyota is 120,000 utils/$20,000 = 6 utils per dollar. Marginal utility per dollar for the BMW is 200,000/ $40,000 = 5 utils per dollar. 6>5. (539-540)

c. Choose the history course. Here the two alternatives have a cost in time, not money. The analysis is the same. Just calculate the marginal utility per minute and choose the one with the higher marginal utility per minute. Marginal utility per minute for the economics course is 900 utils/1500 minutes = 0.6 utils per minute. Marginal utility per minute for the history course is 800 utils/ 1000 minutes = 0.8 utils per minute. 0.8 > 0.6. (539-540)

d. Take Tory out for a date to the Four Seasons. Marginal utility per dollar for taking Tory out is 600 utils/ $120 = 5 utils per dollar. Marginal utility per dollar for taking Sam out is 60 utils/ $15 = 4 utils per dollar. 5 > 4. (539-540)

3. This tests the principle of rational choice on page 541 which states that a rational individual will adjust consumption of all goods until the marginal utilities per dollar are equal.

a. 3 science courses and 2 humanities courses. First you must calculate the marginal utilities and marginal utilities per dollar when you are spending all your money. We show the calculations to arrive at the answer in the table below. Following the principle of rational choice, select that combination where the marginal utilities per dollar are equal. Looking only at those combinations where you are spending all your money, this is at the combination of 3 science courses and 2 humanities courses. We figured this out by figuring out different combinations of courses beginning with 6 science courses, calculating how many humanities courses could be purchased with the remaining funds, and comparing marginal utilities per dollar. If the marginal utility per dollar of science courses is lower than that for humanities course, choose one less science course and repeat the calculation. Keep doing this until the marginal utilities per dollar are the same for both. (541-543)

	Science Courses			Humanities Courses		
Number of courses	Total utility	Marginal utility	MU per $	Total utility	Marginal utility	MU per $
0	0	0	0	0	0	0
1	4500	4500	3	7500	7500	2.5
2	7500	3000	2.0	12,000	4500	1.5
3	9750	2250	1.5	15,750	3750	1.25
4	11,250	1500	1	18,750	3000	1.0
5	11,750	500	.33	21,000	2250	.75
6	12,000	250	.17	22,500	1500	.5

b. 3 science courses and 6 humanities courses. First you must calculate the marginal utilities and marginal utilities per dollar. This is shown in the table below. Next, following the principle of rational choice, select that combination where the marginal utilities per dollar are equal and you cannot buy any more courses. This is at the combination of 3 science courses and 6 humanities courses. (541-543)

	Science Courses			Humanities Courses		
Number of courses	Total utility	Marginal utility	MU per $	Total utility	Marginal utility	MU per $
0	0	0	0	0	0	0
1	4500	4500	3	7500	7500	7.5
2	7500	3000	2.0	12,000	4500	4.5
3	9750	2250	1.5	15,750	3750	3.75
4	11,250	1500	1	18,750	3000	3.0
5	11,750	500	.33	21,000	2250	2.25
6	12,000	250	.17	22,500	1500	1.5

A1.   The budget constraint is drawn in figure (A) below. It was constructed by first finding out the y-intercept — how many pens could be bought with the entire $10: 20 pens—and then finding out the x-intercept — how many notebooks could be bought with the entire $10: 10 notebooks. Connect these points to get the budget constraint. (552)

   a.   The slope the budget constraint is $-P_{notebooks} / P_{pens}$ = -$1/0.50 =- 2. (552)

   b.   The budget constraint shifts in, intersecting the pen axis at 16 and notebook axis at 8. To find this, use the process described to find the initial budget constraint. Since relative prices did not change, the slope is still -2. This is shown in figure (B) below. (552)

   c.   Since relative prices changed, the budget constraint rotates. To find the new budget constraint, find first how many notebooks can be bought at their new price: 4. The y-intercept remains at 16 since the price of pens did not change. The budget constraint rotates in along the notebook axis and intersects it at 4 notebooks. Since notebooks became more expensive, the slope became steeper. The slope of the line is $-P_{notebooks} / P_{pens}$ = -$2/0.50 = -4. This is shown in figure (C) below. (552)

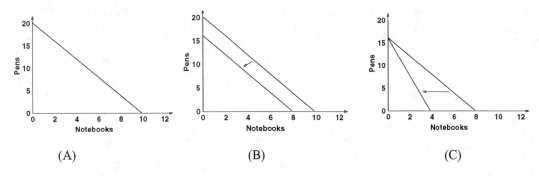

   (A)   (B)   (C)

A2.   a. To graph the indifference curve, plot each set of points which give the same utility. This is done in graph (A) below. (552-553)

   b.   The marginal rate of substitution between the combinations C and D is equal to the slope between C and D, $MU_{notebooks} / MU_{pens}$ = -2. (553-554)

   c.   To find where you maximize utility given the budget constraint, find that point where the slope of the budget constraint equals the marginal rate of substitution between pens and notebooks. This is at points between C and D. At points between C and D, the slope of budget constraint is equal to the marginal rate of substitution: $MU_{notebooks} / MU_{pens}$ = -2 = $-P_{notebooks} / P_{pens}$. (544)

   The budget constraint tangential to the indifference curve at points between C and D implies that any other indifference curve that intersects the budget constraint line gives you less total utility than does the current indifference curve. A rational choice maximizes your own utility. Hence, you should choose combinations represented by points between C and D. (552-554)

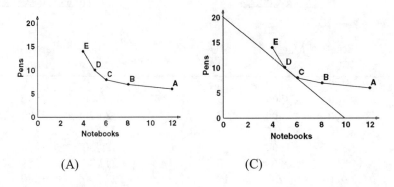

            (A)   (C)

Multiple Choice Questions

1. c. See page 538.

2. c. Because it is the first slice, the total utility and the marginal utility of pizza are equal. See page 538.

3. b. See page 540.

4. a. Applying the rational choice rule, you divide the MU by the price. Increase consumption of the good that gives the greater marginal utility per dollar. 40/1 is greater than 60/2 so increase consumption of A and decrease consumption of B. See pages 539-541.

5. b. Applying the rational choice rule, you divide the MU by the price. Increase consumption of the good that gives the greater marginal utility per dollar. 40/2 is less than 60/2 so increase consumption of B. See pages 539-541.

6. c. Applying the rational choice rule, you divide the MU by the price. Increase consumption of the good that gives the greater marginal utility per dollar. 40/1 equals 80/2 so you consume equal amounts of both goods. See pages 539-541.

7. b. Only the opportunity cost is needed to determine what would be required to get you to work another hour. See page 545.

8. d. Economists tend to believe that actions follow costs so if people pollute a lot it must be because the costs of polluting are too low. See page 549.

9. c. See page 546-547.

10. c. A focal point equilibrium may be the preferred equilibrium but it does not necessarily have to be the preferred equilibrium if individuals had better information. (547)

11. b. The amount of `rice consumed, as discussed on pages 547-548, is governed by Japanese custom, which assigns ceremonial and mystical values to rice and causes it to be eaten at every meal. Relatively, rice is expensive in Japan. (547-548)

A1. d. To get one piece of chocolate you must give up two cans of soda. See page 552.

A2. d. A fall in the price of chocolate means that the same amount of soda will give more pieces of chocolate, so the income constraint rotates up from the intersection of the soda axis, hence becoming steeper. See page 552.

A3. b. A movement down the curve represents the soda needed to compensate the individual—i. e., keep her utility constant—for giving up some chocolate. See pages 552-553.

A4. c. If goods are perfect substitutes, the indifference curve between them will be a downward sloping flat line since at all points the marginal utility needed to compensate the individual for a certain amount of the other good will be constant. See pages 552-553.

A5. c. The equilibrium is where the indifference curve is tangent to the budget line. See page 554.

Chapter 23:
Production and Cost Analysis I

Chapter at a glance

1. A long-run decision is a decision in which the firm can choose among all possible production techniques. A short-run decision is a decision in which the firm is constrained in regard to what production decisions it can make. (559)

    Long run => *all inputs are variable* => *all costs are variable.*

    Short run => *at least one input is fixed* => *some fixed and some variable costs.*

2a. The law of diminishing marginal productivity states that as more and more of a variable input is added to an existing fixed input, after some point the additional output one gets from the additional input will fall. (561)

    Sometimes called "flower pot law." Its existence eventually causes costs of production to rise.

✔ *Study all Exhibits in this chapter!*

2b. As more and more of a variable input is added to a fixed input, the law of diminishing marginal productivity causes marginal and average productivities to fall. As these fall, marginal and average costs rise. (566)

    When productivity curves are falling, the corresponding cost curves are rising. See Exhibit 5 in the textbook on page 567.

3. The most important categories of costs are shown in Exhibit 2. Notice total costs, marginal costs, average fixed costs, average variable costs, and average total costs can be calculated given fixed costs and variable costs at each level of output. (562)

✔ *Also know how to calculate all 7 short-run cost figures! (FC, VC, TC, MC, AFC, and ATC)*

$$TC = FC + VC \, (= ATC \times Q)$$
$$VC = TC - FC \, (= AVC \times Q)$$
$$FC = TC - VC \, (= AFC \times Q)$$
$$MC = \Delta TC/\Delta Q \, (= \Delta TVC/\Delta Q)$$
$$ATC = TC/Q \, (= AFC + AVC)$$
$$AVC = VC/Q \, (= ATC - AFC)$$
$$AFC = FC/Q \, (= ATC - AVC)$$

4. The marginal cost curve goes through the minimum point of the average total cost curve and average variable cost curve; each of these curves is U-shaped. The average fixed cost curve slopes down continuously. (564)

    See Exhibit 4. Know why cost curves are shaped the way they are!

5. When marginal cost exceeds average cost, average cost must be rising. When marginal cost is less than average cost, average cost must be falling. This relationship explains why marginal cost curves always intersect the average cost curve at the minimum of the average cost curve. (568)

    If MC>ATC, then ATC is rising.
    If MC=ATC, then ATC is at its low point.
    If MC<ATC, then ATC is falling.

Short-answer questions

1. Suppose you are the president of a corporation who is designing a 2-year plan of operations and a 10-year plan of operations. How would those plans differ? (LO1)

2. Suppose you are a novice gardener. You plant one seed in a flower pot and watch it grow into a stalk of wheat with plump wheat berries. The next year, you plant two seeds in that pot and harvest double the amount of wheat berries. You deduce that at this rate, you can provide the world's supply of wheat berries in your little pot. Why is this obviously not true? What principle is your answer based upon? (LO2)

3. How does the law of diminishing marginal productivity affect the shape of short-run cost curves? (LO2)

4. What is the algebraic relationship between average total cost, average variable cost and fixed cost? (LO3)

5. What does the marginal cost curve measure? (LO4)

6. What does the average variable cost curve measure? (LO4)

7. What does the average fixed cost curve measure? (LO4)

8. What does the average total cost curve measure? (LO4)

9. Where does the marginal cost curve intersect the average total cost and average variable cost curves? Explain why the relationship between marginal cost and average cost is how you have described it. (LO4, LO5)

10. Draw typical *AFC*, *AVC*, *ATC,* and *MC* curves on the same graph, making sure to maintain the relationships among them from question 10. (LO4)

Word Scramble

1. _____ _____   2._____ _____
      a a g i l m n r   u t r p o d c   n t s a a r c i o t n   t s s o c

3._____ _____
      a a b e i l r v   s t s c o

Match the Terms and Concepts to Their Definitions

___ 1. average total cost

___ 2. average fixed cost

___ 3. average product

___ 4. average variable cost

___ 5. fixed costs

___ 6. law of diminishing marginal productivity

___ 7. long-run decision

___ 8. marginal cost

___ 9. marginal product

___ 10. production function

___ 11. short-run decision

___ 12. total cost

___ 13. transactions costs

___ 14. variable costs

a. A decision in which the firm can choose among all possible production techniques.

b. Additional output forthcoming from an additional input, other inputs constant.

c. As more and more of a variable input is added to an existing fixed input, after some point the additional output one gets from the additional input will fall.

d. Costs of undertaking trades through the market.

e. Costs that are spent and cannot be changed in the period of time under consideration.

f. Equation that describes the relationships between inputs and outputs, telling the maximum amount of output that can be derived from a given number of inputs.

g. Firm is constrained in regard to what production decisions it can make.

h. Fixed cost divided by quantity produced.

i. Sum of the fixed and variable costs.

j. Variable cost divided by quantity produced.

k. The costs of variable inputs; they change as output changes.

l. The cost of changing the level of output by one unit.

m. Total output divided by the quantity of the input.

n. Total cost divided by the quantity produced.

Problems and Exercises

1. Find and graph *TC*, *AFC*, *AVC*, *ATC,* and *MC* for the following table:

Units	FC	VC	TC	MC	AFC	AVC	ATC
0	50	0					
1	50	90					
2	50	120					
3	50	165					
4	50	220					
5	50	290					

2. You are presented with the following table on average productivity. Labor is your only variable cost. The price of labor is $20 per hour, and the fixed cost is $50.

Labor	TP	MP	AP	TC	MC	AVC
1	2					
2	6					
3	15					
4	20					
5	23					
6	24					

a. Derive a table for average product (AP), average variable costs (AVC), marginal product (MP), total cost (TC), and marginal cost (MC) in the space above.

b. Graph the average variable cost curve.

c. Show that the graph you drew in 2(b) is the approximate mirror image of the average productivity curve.

d. Graph the marginal cost and the marginal productivity curves. Show that they are approximate mirror images of each other.

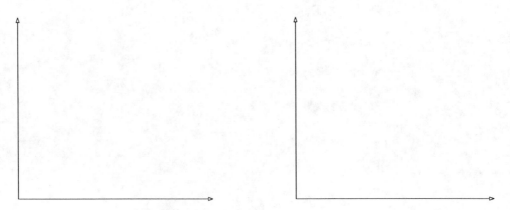

e.   What is the relationship between *MP* and *AP*? *MC* and *AC*?

3.   A firm has fixed cost of $50. Variable costs are as follows:

Units	VC
1	75
2	110
3	150
4	200
5	260
6	335

a.   Graph *AFC*, *ATC*, *AVC,* and *MC* curves on the axes to the right of the table (all on the same graph).

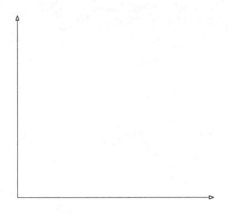

b.   Explain the relationships between the *MC* curve and *ATC* and *AVC*. Between *ATC* and *AVC*.

c.   Suppose fixed costs fall to $20, and graph new *AFC*, *ATC*, *AVC,* and *MC* curves.

d.   Which curves shifted? Why?

4. A box of Wheaties cereal with a wholesale price of $1.60 has the following costs:

Labor:	0.15
Materials:	0.30
Sales cost:	0.30
Advertising:	0.15
Research and Development:	0.15
Rent on factory building and equipment:	0.15
Owner's profit:	0.40

a. Which are likely variable costs?

b. Which are likely fixed costs?

c. If output were to rise, what would likely happen to *ATC*?

Multiple Choice Questions

1. In a short-run decision
   a. a firm has more options than in the long run.
   b. a firm has fewer options than in the long run.
   c. a firm has the same number of options as in the long run.
   d. there is no relation between the number of options a firm has and whether it is a short-run decision or a long-run decision.

2. Five workers are producing a total of 28 units of output. The workers' marginal product
   a. is 5.
   b. is 28.
   c. is 28 divided by 5.
   d. cannot be determined from the information provided.

3. Five workers are producing a total of 28 units of output. The workers' average product
   a. is 5.6.
   b. is 28.
   c. is 140.
   d. cannot be determined from the information provided.

4. In the production function on the right, in the range marked "A" there are
    a. increasing marginal returns.
    b. diminishing marginal returns.
    c. diminishing absolute returns.
    d. diminishing absolute marginal returns.

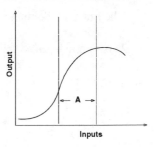

5. When all inputs are changing by equal proportions, the firm notices that when
    it increases workers by 1, output increases by 4. The firm can conclude that
    a. the marginal product of workers is 4.
    b. the average product of workers is 4.
    c. the law of diminishing marginal productivity is holding true.
    d. none of the above.

6. The firm's total fixed costs are 100; total variable costs are 200; and average fixed costs are 20. The firm's
    total costs are
    a. 100.
    b. 200.
    c. 300.
    d. 320.

7. The firm's total fixed costs are 100; total variable costs are 200; and average fixed costs are 20. The firm's
    total output
    a. is 1.
    b. is 5.
    c. is 10.
    d. cannot be determined from the information provided.

8. The firm is producing an output of 24 and has total costs of 260. Its marginal cost
    a. equals 10.83.
    b. equals 8.75.
    c. equals 260.
    d. cannot be determined from the information.

9. The firm is producing an output of 24 and has total costs of 260. Its average total cost
    a. equals 10.83.
    b. equals 8.75.
    c. equals 260.
    d. cannot be determined from the information.

10. The graph at the right
    a. is correct.
    b. is wrong because the average total cost is above the average variable cost.
    c. is wrong because the marginal cost is positioned wrong.
    d. is wrong because the marginal cost and average variable costs are confused.

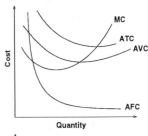

11. The graph at the right
    a. is correct.
    b. is wrong because the average variable cost curve is above the average total cost
       curve.
    c. is wrong because the marginal cost curve is positioned wrong.
    d. is wrong because the marginal cost and average variable cost curves are con-
       fused.

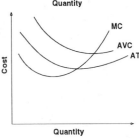

12. The graph at the right
    a. is correct.
    b. is wrong because the average variable cost curve is above the average total cost curve.
    c. is wrong because the marginal cost curve is positioned wrong.
    d. is wrong because the marginal cost and average variable cost curves are confused.

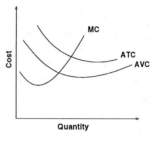

13. The curve at the right is most likely
    a. an average total cost curve.
    b. an average variable cost curve.
    c. an average fixed cost curve.
    d. a total cost curve.

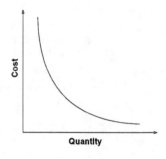

14. When marginal costs are at the minimum point in the short run,
    a. the marginal product of workers is at a maximum.
    b. the marginal product of workers is increasing.
    c. the marginal product of workers is decreasing.
    d. the average product of workers is at a maximum.

15. When the short-run average cost curve is upward sloping,
    a. the average product curve is downward sloping.
    b. the average product curve is upward sloping.
    c. the average product curve may be rising or may be falling.
    d. the average product curve will be flat.

16. If marginal cost is greater than average total cost, then
    a. the average total cost curve is upward sloping.
    b. the average total cost curve is at its low point.
    c. the average total cost curve is downward sloping.
    d. There is no necessary relation between marginal cost and average total costs.

17. If marginal cost is falling, then the average total cost curve
    a. is upward sloping.
    b. is at its low point.
    c. is downward sloping.
    d. There is no necessary relation between marginal cost and average total costs.

Answers

Short-answer questions

1. In a long-run planning decision, a firm chooses among all possible production techniques. In a short-run planning decision, the firm has fewer options. (559)

2. This is obviously not true because each additional seed you are adding will produce fewer and fewer berries. Eventually the yield will even decline as the plants choke one another out. This follows from the law of diminishing marginal productivity: as more and more of a variable input is added to an existing fixed input, after some point the additional output one gets from the additional input will fall. (561)

3. As more and more of a variable input is added to a fixed input, the law of diminishing marginal productivity causes marginal and average productivities to fall. As these fall, marginal and average costs rise. (561-567)

4. ATC = AVC + AFC. (566)

5. A marginal cost curve measures the change in cost associated with a change in output. (567)

6. An average variable cost curve measures variable cost averaged over total output. (566)

7. An average fixed cost curve measures fixed costs averaged over total output. (565-566)

8. An average total cost curve measures total cost (variable plus fixed) averaged over total output. (565)

9. The marginal cost curve intersects the average total and average variable cost curves at their minimum points. The marginal cost curve intersects these average cost curves at their minimum points because when marginal cost exceeds average cost, average cost must be rising; and when marginal cost is less than average cost, average cost must be falling. (565-568)

10. Typical *AFC, AVC, ATC,* and *MC* curves are graphed to the right. Since fixed costs are the same for all levels of output, the *AFC* curve is always falling as the same fixed costs are spread over larger and larger levels of output. The *MC* curve first declines because of increasing marginal productivity but then rises because decreasing marginal productivity eventually sets in. The *MC* curve intersects the *AVC* and *ATC* curves at their minimum points. This is true because if the marginal cost is below average cost, average cost must be falling and if marginal cost is above average cost, average cost must be rising. (565)

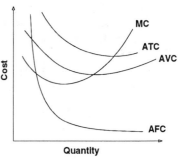

Word Scramble   1. marginal product   2. transaction costs   3. variable costs

Match the Terms and Concepts to Their Definitions

1-n; 2-h; 3-m; 4-j; 5-e; 6-c; 7-a; 8-l; 9-b; 10-f; 11-g; 12-i; 13-d; 14-k.

Problems and Exercises

1. By definition, $TC = FC + VC$, $AFC = FC/Q$, $AVC = VC/Q$, $ATC = AFC + AVC$, and $MC =$ the change in TC. Using this information, we completed the following table. (Marginal cost refers to the marginal cost of increasing output to that row, e.g., the marginal cost of going from 0 to 1 is 90.) (562-569)

Units	TC	MC	AFC	AVC	ATC
0	50	-	-	-	-
1	140	90	50.00	90	140.00
2	170	30	25.00	60	85.00
3	215	45	16.67	55	71.67
4	270	55	12.50	55	67.50
5	340	70	10.00	58	68.00

The total cost curve is shown below on the right. The *AC, AVC, MC,* and *AFC* curves are shown below.

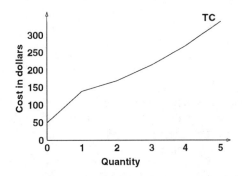

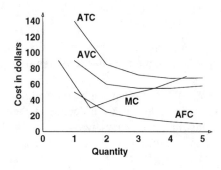

2. $AP = TP/Q$, MP = change in TP, TC is (Labor×\$20) + FC, MC = change in TC per unit change in product. AVC is VC/Q. Using these definitions we completed the following table. (Marginal cost refers to the marginal cost of increasing to that row, e.g., the marginal cost of going from 0 to 1 is 10.) (562-569)

a.

Labor	TP	MP	AP	TC	MC	AVC
1	2	---	2.0	70	---	10.00
2	6	4	3.0	90	5.00	6.67
3	15	9	5.0	110	2.22	4.00
4	20	5	5.0	130	4.00	4.00
5	23	3	4.6	150	6.67	4.35
6	24	1	4.0	170	20.00	5.00

b. The average variable cost curve is shown below. (565)
c. The *AP* and *AVC* curves are shown below. They are the mirror images of one another. The maximum point on the *AP* curve occurs at the minimum point on the *AVC* curve. When *AP* curve is falling, *AVC* is rising, and vice versa. This is because as productivity falls, costs per unit rise, and as productivity increases, costs per unit decrease. (567)

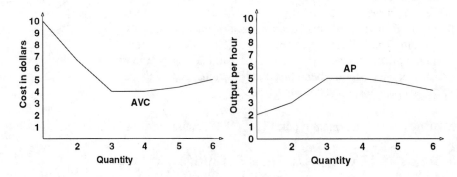

d. The marginal cost and marginal productivity curves are shown on the right. The maximum point on the *MP* curve occurs at the minimum point on the *MC* curve. When the *MP* curve is falling *MC* is rising, and vice versa. This is because as productivity falls, costs per unit rise and as productivity increases, costs per unit decrease. (567)
e. When the *MC* curve is below the *AVC* curve, the *AVC* curve is falling. The *MC* curve intersects with the *AVC* curve at its minimum point. When the *MC* curve is above the *AVC* curve, the *AVC* is rising. The same goes for marginal product and average product. When marginal product is below average product, average product is falling and when marginal product is above average product, average product is rising. (568-569)

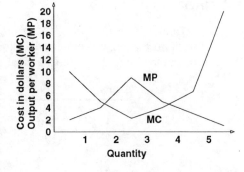

3. a. To graph the *ATC, AFC, AVC,* and *MC* curves, first determine the values of these curves for units 1-6. *TC =* *FC + VC*, *AFC = FC/Q*, *AVC = VC/Q*, *AC = AFC + AVC*, and *MC =* the change in *TC*. Theses values are shown in the table below and the curves are shown on the right. (Marginal cost refers to the marginal cost of increasing to that row, e.g., the marginal cost of going from 0 to 1 is 75.) (563-565)

Units	VC	ATC	AVC	AFC	MC
1	75	125	75	50	75
2	110	80	55	25	35
3	150	66.67	50	16.67	40
4	200	62.5	50	12.5	50
5	260	62	52	10	60
6	335	64.17	55.83	8.33	75

b. The *MC* curve goes through the minimum points of both *ATC* and *AVC* curves, which are rising when they are below the *MC* curve, and which are falling when they are above the *MC* curve. *ATC* and *AVC* curves are both U-shaped. Because of fixed costs, the *AVC* curve is always below *ATC* curve, but the two curves converge as output increases.

c. The curves are shown to the right.

Units	VC	ATC	AVC	AFC	MC
1	75	95	75	20	75
2	110	65	55	10	35
3	150	56.67	50	6.67	40
4	200	55	50	5	50
5	260	56	52	4	60
6	335	59.17	55.83	3.33	75

d. Only the *AFC* and *ATC* curves shifted because they are the only curves that depend upon fixed costs. All the others are based upon only variable costs. Because the fixed cost falls to $20, the average fixed cost must fall as well.

4. a. Labor and material costs are variable costs since they will rise and fall as production of Wheaties rises and falls. (556-557)
   b. Sales, advertising, R & D, and rent on factory building and equipment are fixed cost since they are most likely independent of the level of Wheaties produced. (556-557).
   c. Because fixed cost is high in this production process, almost equal to half of the revenue, an increase in output is likely to reduce *AFC*, and thus, *ATC* would likely fall as well. (556-557)

Multiple Choice Questions

1. b. The longer the time period, the more numerous the options. See page 559.

2. d. To determine marginal product you need to know the change in the product as you add a worker. See page 560.

3. a. To determine average product you divide total output by number of workers (28/5 = 5.6). See pages 560-561.

4. b. A bowed downward production function has marginal product decreasing as output increases. See Exhibit 1, page 560.

5. d. To determine marginal product of one input, the other input must be held constant. This question specifically states that that isn't the case here, so nothing can be said about marginal product. See page 560.

6. c. To determine total costs you add total fixed and total variable costs. See page 563.

7. b. Average fixed costs equal total fixed costs divided by output. If the firm's total fixed costs are 100 and average fixed costs are 20, the quantity must be 100/20 = 5. See pages 563-565.

8. d. To determine marginal costs one must know the change in costs associated with a change in quantity. See page 564.

9. a. Average total costs are determined by dividing total costs by output. 260/24 =10.83. See page 563.

10. a. See Exhibit 4, page 565.

11. b. The average variable cost curve should be below the average total cost curve. See Exhibit 4, page 565.

12. c. The marginal cost curve should go through the minimum point of both the average variable cost curve and the average total cost curve. See Exhibit 4, page 565.

13. c. Only the average fixed cost curve is continuously falling. See Exhibit 4, page 567.

14. a. The marginal product curve is the mirror image of the marginal cost curve. See Exhibit 5, page 567.

15. a. The average product curve is the mirror image of the average cost curve. See Exhibit 5, page 567.

16. a. When marginal costs are above average costs, these additional costs are raising the average costs. See pages 567-569, especially Exhibit 6 on page 568.

17. d. The relative position of the marginal cost curve relative to the average cost curve, not its slope, determines whether the average cost curve is upward or downward sloping. See pages 567-569, especially Exhibit 6 on page 568.

Chapter 24: Production and Cost Analysis II

Chapter at a glance

1. Technical efficiency is efficiency that does not consider costs of inputs. The least-cost technically efficient process is the economically efficient process. (573)

   Firms try to be economically efficient because they want to minimize costs.

2. In the longer run all inputs are variable, so only economies of scale can influence the shape of the long-run cost curve. (575)

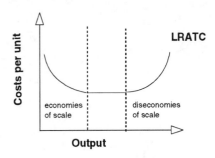

Output

   Note: As quantity of production increases, the firm is using ever larger scales of operation (larger plant or factory sizes).

3. Diminishing marginal productivity refers to the decline in productivity caused by increasing units of a variable input being added to a fixed input. Diseconomies of scale refer to the decreases in productivity which occur when there are equal increases of all inputs. (No input is fixed). (576)

   Diminishing marginal productivity refers to the short run (at least one input is fixed). In the long run all inputs can vary.

✔ *If you double all inputs and <u>per-unit</u> costs fall (rise) then you experience economies (diseconomies) of scale.*

4. The envelope relationship is the relationship explaining that, at the planned output level, short-run average total cost equals long-run average total cost, but at all other levels of output, short-run average total cost is higher than long-run average total cost. (577)

   See Exhibit 3 in the textbook (page 578)

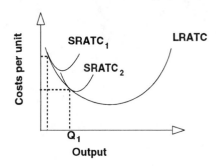

Output

   SRATC$_2$ is the appropriate plant size to produce Q$_1$ because costs per unit are lowest.

5. The difference between the expected price of a good and the expected average total cost of producing it is the supplier's expected economic profit per unit. The expected profit per unit must exceed the opportunity cost of supplying the good for a good to be supplied. (578)

   Potential economic profit motivates entrepreneurs to supply those goods demanded by consumers. The greater demand, the greater the price and profit potential, and the greater the quantity supplied.

✔ *You need to distinguish accounting profit from economic profit!*

6. Some of the problems of using cost analysis in the real world include: (580)
    1. Economies of scope;
    2. Learning by doing and technological change;
    3. Many dimensions;
    4. Unmeasured costs;
    5. Joint costs;
    6. Indivisible costs;
    7. Uncertainty;
    8. Asymmetries; and
    9. Multiple planning and adjustment periods with many different short runs.

7. Marginal cost analysis can be applied to just about every decision facing you. For example, the marginal benefit of reading these marginal notes must exceed the marginal cost, or you shouldn't read them. (585)

    (Marginal => "extra")

    Think on the margin! What's the extra benefit and cost of one additional unit.

    See also, Appendix A: "Isocost/Isoquant Analysis."

Short-answer questions

1. You are consulting for a firm. Through analysis the firm has determined that the best it can do is produce 100 tons of wheat per day with 10 workers and 1 acre of land or 100 tons of wheat per day with 10 acres of land and 1 worker. You are asked to choose the most efficient method of production. What do you advise? (LO1)

2. After having read your report, the executives come running after you. They tell you that they have forgotten to tell you that an acre of land costs $40 an acre per day and workers can be hired for $100 a day. They wonder whether your answer to question 1 changes. (LO1)

3. The cost of developing a typical introductory economics textbook is well over $1 million. Once the textbook is developed and ready to print, the actual print costs for large runs are about $6 per book. How do these facts influence the shape of the long-run average total cost curve of producing textbooks? (LO2)

4. What is the difference between diminishing marginal productivity and diseconomies of scale? (LO3)

5. What is the envelope relationship between short-run cost curves and long-run cost curves? (LO4)

6. Why does an entrepreneur start a business? How are the decisions by the entrepreneur central to all supply decisions? (LO5)

7. Suppose you are giving a talk on costs to decision-makers at firms. You have presented the cost curves as taught to you in this text without caveat. What would be some of the problems your audience might have with your presentation? (LO6)

8. Suppose you bought two stocks: one at $25 and the other at $15. Someone has offered you $30 for either. Which should you sell and why? (LO7)

Word Scramble

1. _____ _____   2. _____ _____   3. _____

  o o n m i e c c   t r p o i f   y o o n m l l i e c c a   t n i i f f e e c   u t r r r p n n e e e e

Match the Terms and Concepts to Their Definitions

____ 1. accounting profit

____ 2. diseconomies of scale

____ 3. economic profit

____ 4. economically efficient

____ 5. economies of scale

____ 6. economies of scope

____ 7. entrepreneur

____ 8. envelope relationship

____ 9. historical cost

____ 10. indivisible setup cost

____ 11. learning by doing

____ 12. minimum efficient level of production

____ 13. technical efficiency

____ 14. technological change

a. A decrease in per-unit cost as a result of an increase in output.

b. An increase in per-unit cost as a result of an increase in output.

c. An increase in the range of production techniques that provides new ways of producing goods.

d. Becoming more proficient at doing something by actually doing it.

e. Cost in terms of money actually spent.

f. Total implicit and explicit revenues minus total implicit and explicit costs.

g. Total revenue minus explicit measurable costs.

h. Individual who sees an opportunity to sell an item at a price higher than the average cost of producing it.

i. The costs of producing products are interdependent so that producing one good lowers the cost of producing another.

j. The level of production run that spreads out setup costs sufficiently for a firm to undertake production profitably.

k. The cost of an indivisible input for which a certain minimum amount of production must be undertaken before the input becomes economically feasible to use.

l. The relationship explaining that, at the planned output level, short-run average total cost equals long-run average total cost, but at all other levels of output, short-run average total cost is higher than long-run average total cost.

m. Using the method of production that produces a given level of output at the lowest possible cost.

n. A situation in which as few inputs as possible are used to produce a given output.

Problems and Exercises

1. Consider the following information about Sarina who has a clothing manufacturing company that sews psychedelic clothing such as Astro turf mini-skirts. Her alternative is working for the designer house DKNY for $160,000 per year. Her revenue is $400,000 per year. Her costs are:

> $60,000 for cloth, thread, and other materials.
> $10,000 for utilities.
> $70,000 for labor.
> $80,000 for rental of equipment.

She has an offer to buy the company for $500,000 which she can otherwise invest with an annual return of 5%.

a. What are her accounting profits? Economic profits?

b. Assuming her only interest is to earn as much as possible, what should she do with her company?

2. The following table represents long-run *TC*:

Q	TC	ATC
1	60	
2	66	
3	69	
4	72	
5	75	
6	90	
7	126	
8	184	
9	297	
10	600	

a. Calculate the average total cost in the space provided.

b. Graph the *ATC* curve in the space to the right of the table.

c. Label the area of economies of scale and the area of diseconomies of scale.

A1. Suppose the following table depicts the combinations of factors of production that results in the production of 100 units of bhindi.

	Labor	Machinery
A	25	4
B	20	5
C	10	10
D	5	20
E	4	25

a. Graph the isoquant curve on axes to the right of the table, with machinery on the vertical axis and labor on the horizontal axis.

b. What is the marginal rate of substitution between combinations C and D?

A2. Suppose you had $120 available to produce the same product (bhindi) as in the previous question. Labor costs are $4 per person and machinery costs are $8 per unit. Draw the isocost curve with machinery on the vertical axis and labor on the horizontal axis.

a.   What is the slope of the line?

b.   What happens to the cost constraint if you frivolously spend $40 of your $120 on entertaining your good for nothing boyfriend Kyle? What is the slope of your new cost constraint? Show this graphically.

c.   Suppose the labor unions manage to raise labor costs to $10 per person. What happens to the isocost line? Show this graphically.

d. Combine the isoquant curve from A1 with the original isocost line from A2. What combination of labor and machinery will you choose for the economically efficient point of production?

Multiple Choice Questions

1. Which of the following is true?
    a. All methods of production that are technically efficient must be economically efficient.
    b. All methods of production that are economically efficient must be technically efficient.
    c. Firms will tend toward technically efficient methods of production but not towards economically efficient methods.
    d. There is no relation between economic efficiency and technical efficiency.

2. If there are economies of scale
    a. there must be diminishing marginal returns.
    b. there must be increasing marginal returns.
    c. There is no relation between economies of scale and marginal returns.
    d. there must be constant marginal return.

3. Indivisible setup costs refer to
    a. the cost of an indivisible input for which a certain minimum amount of production must be undertaken before production becomes economically feasible.
    b. the cost of an indivisible input for which a certain maximum amount of production must be undertaken before production becomes economically feasible.
    c. the cost of an indivisible input whose cost is invisible.
    d. the cost of an indivisible input whose cost of production is lower because an interdependent good is also being produced.

4. In the graph on the right, the section of the long-run average total cost curve marked as A represents
    a. economies of scale.
    b. diseconomies of scale.
    c. diminishing marginal returns.
    d. increasing marginal returns.

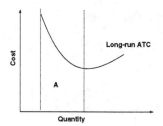

5. Explanations for diseconomies of scale include all of the following *except*
    a. as firm size increases, monitoring costs generally increase.
    b. as size of the firm increases, team spirit or morale generally decreases.
    c. as size of the firm increases, monitoring costs generally decrease, thereby increasing other costs.
    d. All of the above are explanations.

6. The envelope relationship refers to
    a. the fact that the short-run average cost curve forms an envelope around long-run average cost curves.
    b. the fact that the long-run average cost curve forms an envelope around short-run average cost curves.
    c. the fact that the average cost curve forms an envelope around the marginal cost curve.
    d. the fact that the marginal cost curve forms an envelope around the average cost curve.

7. Economies of scope occur when
    a. as firms increase production of a good, that good's cost falls.
    b. as firms increase their long-run vision, costs fall.
    c. the costs of production of one product fall when the firm increases the production of another product.
    d. technological change lowers cost of production.

8. Learning by doing
    a. causes the average cost curve to be downward sloping.
    b. causes the average cost curve to be upward sloping.
    c. causes the marginal cost curve to be downward sloping.
    d. none of the above.

9. Total revenue is 1,000; explicit measurable costs are 500.
    a. Accounting profit is 1,000.
    b. Accounting profit is 500.
    c. Accounting profit is 200.
    d. Accounting profit cannot be determined from the figures given.

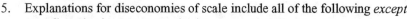

10. Total revenue is 1,000; explicit measurable costs are 500.
    a. Economic profit is 1,000.
    b. Economic profit is 500.
    c. Economic profit is 200.
    d. Economic profit cannot be determined from the figures given.

11. Say you bought two stocks—stock A at $100 and Stock B at $10. You have a chance to sell either stock at $50. Assuming no tax consequences,
    a. you should sell A.
    b. you should sell B.
    c. you should sell equal amounts of each stock.
    d. given the information available, it doesn't matter which you sell.

12. Economists generally
    a. support peak-load pricing because it's based on the relevant marginal costs.
    b. support peak-load pricing because it's based on relevant average costs.
    c. oppose peak-load pricing because it's not based on the relevant marginal costs.
    d. oppose peak-load pricing because it's not based on the relevant average costs.

A1. The absolute value of the slope of the isoquant curve to the right represents
    a. The marginal utility of labor divided by the marginal utility of machinery.
    b. The marginal utility of machinery divided by the marginal utility of labor.
    c. The marginal productivity of labor divided by the marginal productivity of machinery.
    d. The marginal productivity of machinery divided by the marginal productivity of labor.

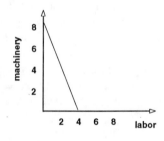

A2. If labor and machinery had to be used in fixed proportions, then the isoquant curve representing them will be closest to which of the following?
    a. A.
    b. B.
    c. C.
    d. D.

A3. The isocost curve shown in the right represents the relative price of machinery (in terms of labor) of
    a. one-eighth
    b. one-fourth
    c. one-half
    d. two.

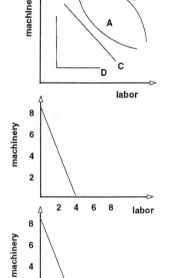

A4. If the price of machinery increases, the isocost curve will
    a. rotate in and become flatter
    b. rotate in and become steeper
    c. rotate out and become flatter.
    d. rotate out and become steeper.

A5. The economically efficient point in the isoquant model in the graph to the right is at point
    a. A.
    b. B.
    c. C.
    d. D.

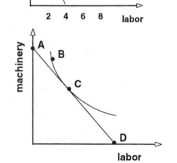

Answers

Short-answer questions

1. You tell them that both methods are of equal technical efficiency, but you cannot determine which is more economically efficient. To make this decision you would need to know the relative prices of each input. (573)

2. You smile and say that is exactly the information you need to tell them the most economically efficient method of production. At these prices, the first method of production costs $1,040 per 100 tons and the second method costs $500 per 100 tons. The second method is the economically efficient method. Technical efficiency means as few inputs as possible are used to produce a given output. It does not consider the costs of inputs. Economic efficiency means using that combination of inputs with the lowest possible cost for a given output. (573-574)

3. Because of the large indivisible setup costs, large economies of scale are possible in printing books. These economies of scale suggest that the long-run average total cost curve is steeply downward sloping. At low levels of production, economies of scale predominate and cost per unit declines. After some point, as output increases, however, diseconomies could set in and cost per unit rise. This would lead to a U-shaped average total cost curve in the long run. (574-576)

4. Diminishing marginal productivity refers to the decline in productivity caused by increasing units of a variable input being added to a fixed input. Diseconomies of scale refer to the decreases in productivity brought about because of equal increases of all inputs. (574-576)

5. The envelope relationship is the relationship explaining that, at the planned output level, short-run average total cost equals long-run average total cost, but at all other levels of output, short-run average total cost is higher than long-run average total cost. (577-578)

6. An entrepreneur will supply a good if the difference between the expected price of the good exceeds the cost of producing it. This difference is the opportunity cost of producing the good, or the entrepreneur's expected profit. It is this profit, or opportunity cost, that underlies production in an economy. (578-580)

7. Since your audience is working with the real world, they will see that actual production processes diverge from textbook analysis. Some of the problems the audience might list are (1) economies of scope; (2) learning by doing and technological change; (3) the supply decision is multidimensional; (4) the relevant costs are not the ones you find in a firm's accounts; (5) joint costs; (6) indivisible setup costs; (7) uncertainty; (8) asymmetries; and (9) multiple planning and adjustment periods with many different short runs. (580-584)

8. I would sell the one whose return I believe would be lower in the future. It does not matter what price I paid for them. The cost of selling a stock is the forgone future income from that stock. The benefit is the price I receive. (585)

Word Scramble   1. economic profit   2. economically efficient   3. entrepreneur

Match the Terms and Concepts to Their Definitions
1-g; 2-b; 3-f; 4-m; 5-a; 6-i; 7-h; 8-l; 9-e; 10-k; 11-d; 12-j; 13-n; 14-c.

Problems and Exercises

1. a. Based on the information given: Accounting profit = Total revenue - explicit measurable cost = $400,000 - $220,000 = $180,000. Economic profit includes implicit costs such as Sarina's opportunity cost ($160,000 forgone salary at DKNY and $25,000 forgone investment income) = Implicit and explicit revenue - implicit and explicit cost = $400,000 - $220,000 - $160,000 - $25,000 = -$5000. (582-583)

b. She should sell the company because she can do better by taking the income from DKNY and investing the $500,000 than from earning negative economic profit of $5,000 per year. (582-583)

3. Before graphing *ATC*, first calculate the figures. *ATC* = *TC/Q*. (575)

a.

Q	TC	ATC
1	60	60
2	66	33
3	69	23
4	72	18
5	75	15
6	90	15
7	126	18
8	184	23
9	297	33
10	600	60

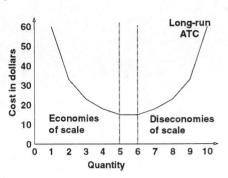

b. The graph shown above plots the values from the table above to show the *ATC* curve. (575)
c. As shown in the figure, economies of scale is to the left of *Q* = 5, where *ATC* is falling. Diseconomies of scale is to the right of *Q* = 6, where *ATC* is rising. (574-576)

A1. a. To graph the isoquant curve plot, each of the combinations of labor and machinery which generate the same (100) units of production of bhindi, as is done in the graph to the right. (588-589)
   b. The marginal rate of substitution between combinations C and D is equal to the absolute value of slope between C and D, $MP_{labor}/MP_{machinery}$ = 2. (589)

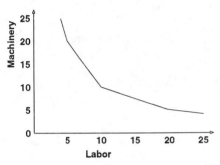

A2. a. The slope of the line is - $P_{labor}/P_{machinery}$ = -4/8 = -1/2. It is shown below in graph (a). (589-591).
   b. The isocost line shifts in as money available for production is reduced to $80. Now maximum 20 units of labor or 10 units of machinery can be purchased. Since the relative price of labor and machinery doesn't change, the slope of the isocost line remains -1/2. It is shown below in graph (b). (589-591)

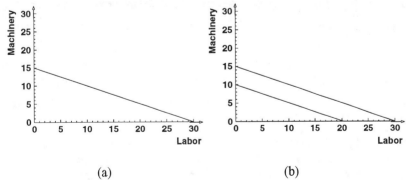

(a)   (b)

   c. Now because relative prices change, the isocost line rotates. To find the new isocost line, find first how many units of labor can be purchased for $120 at the new price $10. The y intercept remains the same at 15 since the price of machinery did not change. The isocost line rotates along the labor axis and intersects it at 12 units of labor. Since labor becomes more expensive, the slope becomes steeper. The slope of the line now is - $P_{labor}/P_{machinery}$ = -10/8 = -5/4. This is shown below in graph (c). (589-591)
   d. To find where you are most economically efficient, find that point where the slope of the isocost curve equals that of the marginal rate of substitution between labor and machinery. This is at points between B and C where -$MP_{labor}/MP_{machinery}$ = -1/2 = -$P_{labor}/P_{machinery}$. The isocost curve tangent to the isoquant curve at points

between B and C implies that any other isoquant curve that intersects the isocost curve is less economically efficient than it. It is shown below in graph (d). (590-591)

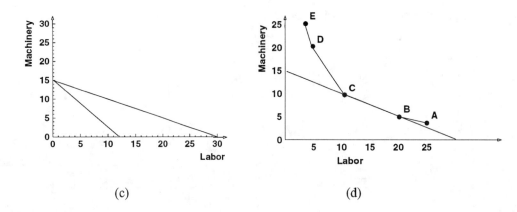

(c)   (d)

Multiple Choice Questions

1. b. An economically efficient production is a technically efficient method of production having the least cost given the current prices of inputs. See page 573.

2. c. Economies of scale refer to changing all inputs equally; marginal returns refer to holding all inputs but one constant. See page 574.

3   a. See pages 574-575.

4. a. The downward sloping portion of the long-run ATC curve represents economies of scale. See Exhibit 1, page 575.

5. c. There is no reason to assume that decreasing monitoring costs will cause other costs to increase. See page 576.

6. b. As discussed on pages 577-578 (including Exhibit 3), the long-run average cost curve forms an envelope around short-run average cost curves.

7. c. As discussed on page 580, c is the definition of economies of scope.

8. d. Learning by doing requires time, and time is not included in the standard model. Learning by doing will shift the average cost curve down, not affect the shape of the cost curve. See page 580-581.

9. b. To determine accounting profits one subtracts explicit measurable costs from total revenue. See page 583.

10. d. Economic profit is defined as explicit and implicit revenues minus explicit and implicit costs. Thus, one does not have enough information to determine economic profit. See page 583.

11. d. Which one you sell depends on what you expect to happen to the price of stocks in the future, not what happened in the past. See page 585.

12. a. Economists see that because of technology, electricity used at different times is different goods, and therefore to conserve energy most efficiently peak-load pricing is required. See pages 581-582.

A1. c. See pages 588-589.

A2. d. If labor and machinery had to be used in fixed proportions, then no substitution is possible. The marginal rate of substitution, the rate at which one adds one factor to compensate for the loss in another factor to keep output constant, is zero. (589-591)

A3. c. To get one unit of machinery one must give up one-half units of labor. (590-591)

A4. a. A rise in the price of machinery means that the same amount of labor will give less machinery, so the isocost line rotates down from the intersection of the labor axis, hence becoming flatter. See pages 589-591.

A5. c. The economically efficient point is where the isoquant curve is tangent to the isocost line. (589-591)

Chapter 25: Perfect Competition

Chapter at a glance

1. Seven conditions for a market to be perfectly competitive are: (593)
   1. Both buyers and sellers are price takers.
   2. Large number of firms.
   3. No barriers to entry.
   4. Homogeneous product.
   5. Instantaneous exit and entry.
   6. Complete information.
   7. Profit-maximizing entrepreneurial firms.

   Compare these with the non-competitive markets (next 2 chapters).

2. If marginal revenue does not equal marginal cost, a perfectly competitive firm obviously can increase profit by changing output. Therefore, profit is maximized when MC = MR = P. (598)

   P = MR for a perfectly competitive firm.

   ✔ *In general, if* $MR > MC \Rightarrow \uparrow Q.$
   $MR = MC \Rightarrow maximizing\ profit.$
   $MR < MC \Rightarrow \downarrow Q.$

3. Because the marginal cost curve tells us how much of a produced good a perfectly competitive firm will supply at a given price, the marginal cost curve is the firm's supply curve. (598)

   The perfectly competitive firm's short-run supply curve is its MC curve above minimum AVC. This is because at any P greater than minimum AVC, a competitive firm will produce where P = MR = MC.

4. The profit-maximizing output can be determined in a table (as in Exhibit 4 on page 600) or in a graph (as in Exhibit 5). (602)

   Just find that output level at which MR = MC. This is shown graphically where the two curves intersect. (Remember: the demand curve facing the firm is also its MR curve).

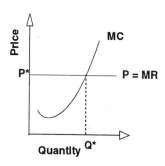

5. Since profits create incentives for new firms to enter, output will increase, and the price will fall until zero profits are being made. (604)

   Over time if economic profits are earned ⇒
   ↑ # of sellers ⇒
   ↑ market supply ⇒
   ↓ market price ⇒
   ↓ firm's profits until economic profits are competed away (zero economic profits — normal profit earned in the long run).

6. Supply and demand curves can be used to describe most real-world events. (609)

   Changes in demand and supply explain changes in market price and quantity.

7. Since the demand curve represents the marginal benefit to society and the supply curve represents the marginal cost to society, a deviation from competitive equilibrium represents a welfare loss to society. Graphically, welfare loss is shown in Exhibit 12. (612)

   A lack of competition results in a higher price and fewer goods produced and consumed. Society is worse off whenever there is a demise of competition (growth of monopoly power). However, perfect competition, may not be so "perfect" either.

Short-answer questions

1. How is competition as a process different from competition as a state? (LO1)

2. What are seven necessary conditions for perfect competition? (LO1)

3. You are advising a vendor of ice cream at a beach. There are plenty of vendors on the beach and plenty more waiting to begin selling. Your client can't seem to change the market price for ice cream, but she still wants to make sure she maximizes profits. What do you advise she do? She knows all her costs of doing business. (LO2)

4. You are given a competitive firm's marginal cost curve and asked to determine the supply curve for that firm. What do you say?   (LO3)

5. On the graph to the right, show the output and short-run profit of a perfect competitor. (LO4)

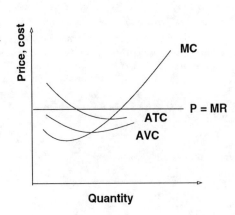

6. Given the following table, what is the output and profit of a perfect competitor? (LO5)

P=MR	Q	FC	VC
35	0	10	0
35	1	10	20
35	2	10	38
35	3	10	50
35	4	10	77
35	5	10	112
35	6	10	156

7. Given the graph on the right, showing a representative firm in a competitive market, what will happen in the long run? Explain using the graph and words. (LO6)

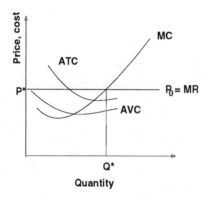

8. Suppose the owners of a small drug store decided to close their store after Wal-Mart opened a store nearby. Assuming the market was competitive before and after Wal-Mart opened its store, show graphically and explain with words the likely conditions for the small drug store before and after Wal-Mart opened. (LO6)

9. What is a Pareto-optimal position? (LO7)

10. The economist, Kenneth Arrow, proved that a perfectly competitive economy would be in a Pareto-optimal position. Still, why do some economists criticize perfect competition as a benchmark? (LO7)

Word Scramble

1. _____   2. _____ _____   3. _____ _____ _____

    tenr   dhnostuw   inopt   rrrieba   ot   yrten

Match the Terms and Concepts to Their Definitions

____ 1.   accounting profit

____ 2.   barriers to entry

____ 3.   consumer surplus

____ 4.   economic profit

____ 5.   homogeneous product

____ 6.   marginal revenue

____ 7.   normal profits

____ 8.   Pareto-optimal position

____ 9.   perfectly competitive market

____ 10. price taker

____ 11. producer surplus

____ 12. rent

____ 13. shutdown point

____ 14. zero profit condition

a.   Firm or individual who takes the market price as given.

b.   Any things that prevent other firms from entering a market.

c.   A product such that each firm's output is indistinguishable from any other firm's output.

d.   The change in total revenue associated with a change in quantity.

e.   The difference between the price at which producers would have been willing to supply a good and the price they actually receive.

f.   Accountants' definition: total revenue minus explicit measurable costs.

g.   Economists' definition: total implicit and explicit revenues minus total implicit and explicit costs.

h.   The returns to the owners of business for the opportunity cost of their implicit inputs.

i.   Point at which the firm will gain more by temporarily shutting down than it will by staying in business.

j.   In the long run, zero profits exist.

k.   An income received by a specialized factor of production.

l.   A position at which no person can be made better off without another being made worse off.

m.   The difference between what consumers would have been willing to pay and what they actually pay.

n.   Market in which economic forces operate unimpeded.

Problems and Exercises

1.   The following table shows the total cost for a product that sells for $20 a unit.

Q	TC
0	30
1	55
2	75
3	85
4	100
5	120
6	145
7	185
8	240
9	310
10	395

a.   What is the output level for a profit-maximizing firm? Use the space to the right of the table to work out your answer.

b. How does your answer change if price rises to $25?

c. Calculate profit in a and b.

d. Should the firm stay in business at $P = \$20$? At $25?

e. Suppose $P = \$15$, what output level maximizes profit? What is the profit? Should the firm stay in business?

2. The cost curves to the right are for a representative firm in a competitive market.

a. Label the minimum point of the ATC and AVC curves as A and B respectively. Explain your answer.

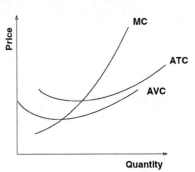

b. Draw the demand curve for this firm on that same graph and explain why you have drawn it this way.

c. Illustrate long-run equilibrium price and quantity for the firm on that same graph. Is the firm earning economic profit? Explain your answer.

3.   Consider the market demand and supply curves on the left and a representative firm's cost curves on the right.

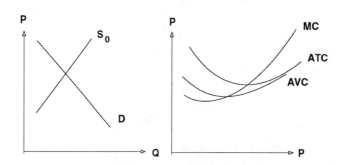

a.   Is this representative firm earning economic profit, loss, or zero profit? Shade the area for profit or loss, or label the point of zero profit.

b.   In the long run, what will happen?

c.   Beginning with the long-run equilibrium in b, show the effect of a decrease in demand on profit. What will happen in long-run to supply, price, and profit?

4.   What is wrong with each of the following graphs?

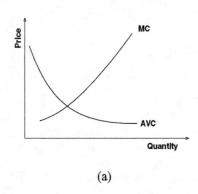

(a)

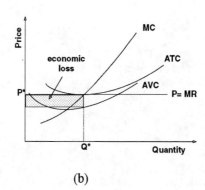

(b)

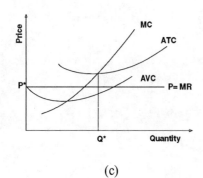

(c)

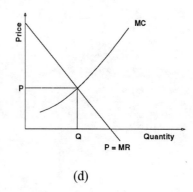

(d)

5. The supply and demand curves for fish in Slovakia are given by the diagram to the right.

   a. What is the consumer surplus in the market?

   b. What is the producer surplus in the market?

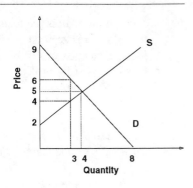

   c. If the government institutes a price floor at 6, by how much does the consumer surplus fall? What is the welfare cost of setting the price floor at 6?

Multiple Choice Questions

1. All the following are requirements of a perfectly competitive market except
   a. buyers and sellers are price takers.
   b. there are no barriers to entry.
   c. there is complete information.
   d. selling firms maximize sales.

2. The perceived demand curve faced by an individual firm in a competitive market is which of the following?
   a. A.
   b. B.
   c. C.
   d. D.

3. In the graph to the right, the market demand curve in a competitive market is which of the following?
   a. A.
   b. B.
   c. C.
   d. D.

4. A competitive firm is producing at output A on the graph on the right.
   a. It could increase profits by increasing output.
   b. It could increase profits by decreasing output.
   c. It cannot increase profits.
   d. One can say nothing about profits from the diagram on the right.

5. A competitive firm is producing at output A on the graph on the right.
   a. It could increase profits by increasing output.
   b. It could increase profits by decreasing output.
   c. It cannot increase profits.
   d. One can say nothing about profits from the diagram on the right.

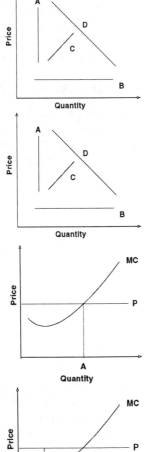

6.   A competitive firm is producing at output A on the graph on the right.
     a. It could increase profits by increasing output.
     b. It could increase profits by decreasing output.
     c. It cannot increase profits.
     d. One can say nothing about profits from the diagram on the right.

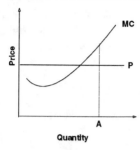

7.   For a firm to determine its profit-maximizing output, it needs to know
     a. marginal cost and marginal revenue.
     b. only marginal cost.
     c. only marginal revenue.
     d. marginal cost, marginal revenue, and average total cost.

8.   Price in a competitive market is $6. The firm's marginal cost is $4 and the marginal cost curve has the normal
     shape. What would you advise the firm to do?
     a. Raise its price.
     b. Increase its output.
     c. Decrease its output.
     d. Lower its price.

9.   In a competitive market which of the following is the firm's supply curve?
     a. The average cost curve.
     b. The marginal cost curve.
     c. The average total cost curve.
     d. The average revenue curve.

10. Normal profits are
     a. approximately 6 percent of costs.
     b. approximately 8 percent of costs.
     c. returns to the owners of business for the opportunity cost of their implicit
        inputs.
     d. generally larger than accounting profits.

11. In the graph on the right, the firm's profit will be measured by
     a. the rectangle ABEF.
     b. the rectangle ACDF.
     c. the rectangle ABHG.
     d. the rectangle BCDE.

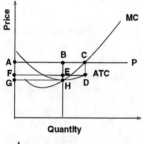

12. What is wrong with the graph on the right?
     a. The equilibrium output is at the wrong point.
     b. The ATC curve has the wrong shape.
     c. The ATC curve is in the wrong position.
     d. Nothing is wrong with it.

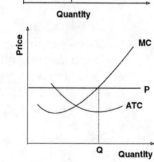

13. In the graph on the right, how low must the price fall before the
        firm will decide to shut down?
     a. Approximately $40.
     b. Approximately $35.
     c. Approximately $18.
     d. Approximately $12.

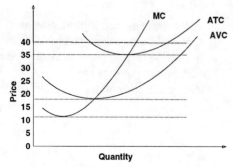

14. In long-run competitive equilibrium
    a. most firms will be going out of business.
    b. most firms will be expanding.
    c. most firms will be making only normal profit.
    d. most firms won't even be making normal profits.

15. In a competitive market for good x, if the price of a complement good falls, what will happen to equilibrium price and quantity of good x?
    a. Equilibrium quantity will increase and equilibrium price will decrease.
    b. Equilibrium quantity will increase and equilibrium price will increase.
    c. Equilibrium quantity will decrease and equilibrium price will increase.
    d. Equilibrium quantity will decrease and equilibrium price will decrease.

16. In a competitive market
    a. the long-run supply curve tends to be more elastic than the short-run supply curve.
    b. the short-run supply curve tends to be more elastic than the long-run supply curve.
    c. the elasticities of the long-run supply curve and the elasticities of the short-run supply curve tend to be equal.
    d. there is no relationship between the long-run elasticities and the short-run elasticities.

17. A Pareto-optimal position is a position from which
    a. no person can be made better off.
    b. no person can be made better off without some other person being made worse off.
    c. Pareto cannot be made better off without making anyone else worse off.
    d. No one else can be made better off without making Pareto worse off.

18. In the graph on the right, what area represents consumer surplus?
    a. A + B + C.
    b. A + B + C + D + E + F.
    c. D + E + F.
    d. A + B + D + F.

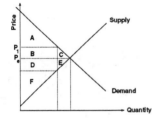

19. In the graph on the right, what area represents producer surplus?
    a. A + B + C.
    b. A + B + C + D + E + F.
    c. D + E + F.
    d. A + B + D + F.

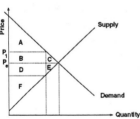

20. In the graph on the right, what area represents the welfare loss from a market charging a price P_1?
    a. B + C + E + D.
    b. B + D
    c. C.
    d. C + E.

21. Which of the following is not a criticism of using perfect competition as a benchmark reference in which to judge the economy?
    a. the Nirvana criticism.
    b. the second-best criticism.
    c. the consumer surplus criticism.
    d. the normative criticism.

Answers

Short-answer questions

1. Competition as a process is a rivalry among firms, with one firm trying to take away market share from another firm. Competition as a state is the end result of the competitive process under certain conditions. (592)

2. The seven conditions necessary for perfect competition are that (1) buyers and sellers are both price takers, (2) the number of firms is large, (3) there are no barriers to entry, (4) firms' products are identical, (5) exit and entry are instantaneous and costless, (6) there is complete information, and (7) selling firms are profit maximizing entrepreneurial firms. (593-594)

3. It is clear that she is in a competitive market. She must take prices as given. I would advise that she calculate her marginal cost at various levels of output and sell the number of ice creams where marginal cost equals price. This will maximize her profit. To see why, for a perfect competitor, producing where $MC = P$ maximizes total profit, you must first understand that $MR = P$ for a perfect competitor. By definition a competitive firm takes price as given, so the incremental revenue, marginal revenue, of selling an additional unit is that unit's price. If we prove that a perfect competitor maximizes profit when $MC = MR$, we simultaneously prove that profit is maximized at output where $MC = P$. If marginal revenue does not equal marginal cost, a firm can increase profit by changing output. If a firm produces where $MC < MR$, it is earning a profit per unit and the firm can increase total profits by producing more until MC is no longer less than MR. If $MC > MR$, the firm is incurring a loss for that last unit; it can increase profits by reducing output until MC is no longer greater than MR. Given these conditions, the firm maximizes profit where $MC = MR$ or $MC = P$. (596-598)

4. The marginal cost curve is the supply curve for a perfectly competitive firm because the marginal cost curve tells us how much of a produced good a firm will supply at a given price. (598)

5. The output of a perfect competitor is shown by the intersection of the marginal cost curve and the marginal revenue curve. On the graph to the right it is at Q^*. Profit for a perfect competitor is the profit per unit, the difference between the price for which each unit is sold and the average cost of each unit, times the number of units sold. Graphically, profit per unit is the vertical distance from the MR curve to the ATC curve. Multiply this by Q^* to get profit. It is the shaded region in the graph. (599-602)

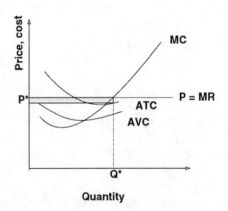

6. To find where the profit- maximizing competitive firm produces, we need to know MR and MC. We know MR. We need to calculate MC, the change in VC. We do this in column 5. To calculate profit we need to know ATC. It is the sum of FC and VC divided by Q and is shown in column 7. (Marginal cost refers to the marginal cost of increasing to that row, e. g.,. the marginal cost of going from 0 to 1 is 40.) (598-600)

P=MR	Q	FC	VC	MC	TC	ATC
35	0	10	---	---	10	---
35	1	10	20	20	30	30
35	2	10	38	18	48	24
35	3	10	50	12	60	20
35	4	10	77	27	87	21.75
35	5	10	112	35	122	24.4
35	6	10	156	44	166	27.67

Looking at the table, we see that $MC = MR$ between $Q=4$ and $Q = 5$. Profit is $(P - ATC) \times Q$ between $Q = 4$ and $Q = 5$. At Q = 5 this is $10.6 \times 5 = 53$. At Q = 4 this is $13.25 \times 4 = 53$. Averaging the two, we estimate profit to be 53.

7. The graph shows that the representative firm in a competitive market is making an economic profit when price is $P*$. Since profits create incentives for new firms to enter, output will increase and the price will fall to P_1 until zero profits are being made. (604)

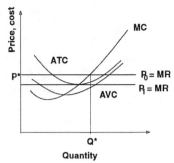

8. Before Wal-Mart opened a store, the small drug store produced $Q*$ given competitive price of $P*$ and earned normal profits. Since Wal-Mart is a discount drug store, opening its store in the market most likely pushed prices down to P_1. Given the new price level, the small drug store now reduced output to Q_1 and incurred a loss. Eventually, all costs are variable and the ATC curve becomes the AVC curve and prices were below the shutdown point. This is shown in the graph on the right. (602-603)

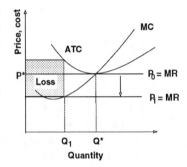

9. A Pareto-optimal position is a position at which no person can be made better off without another being made worse off. (610-611)

10. The critics of perfect competition as a benchmark have three major criticisms: (1) the Nirvana criticism — this is a comparison to something that cannot occur, (2) the second-best criticism — since all seven criteria of perfect competition are rarely met, how do we know whether a movement toward one of those criterion is a movement toward perfect competition?; and (3) normative criticism — a Pareto-optimal position might be undesirable for other reasons. (612-613)

Word Scramble   1. rent   2. shutdown point   3. barrier to entry

Match the Terms and Concepts to Their Definitions

1-f; 2-b; 3-m; 4-g; 5-c; 6-d; 7-h; 8-l; 9-n; 10-a; 11-e; 12-k; 13-i; 14-j.

Problems and Exercises

1. To find the profit-maximizing level of output, first we determine marginal costs for the firm. Here we show the values for a number of costs. We use the formulas for the cost curves: MC = change in total cost, $FC = \$30$ (costs when $Q = 0$); $VC = TC - FC$, $AVC = VC/Q$. (Marginal cost refers to the marginal cost of increasing to that row, e. g., the marginal cost of going from 0 to 1 is 25.) (600)

Q	TC	MC	VC	FC	AVC
0	30	0	0	30	0
1	55	25	25	30	25
2	75	20	45	30	22.5
3	85	10	55	30	18.3
4	100	15	70	30	17.5
5	120	20	90	30	18
6	145	25	115	30	19.2
7	185	40	155	30	22.1
8	240	55	210	30	26.25
9	310	70	280	30	31.1
10	395	85	365	30	36.5

a. A profit-maximizing firm will produce at the output level where $MC = MR$. Since MR = market price for the competitive firm, MR =$20. MC = 20 between 1 and 2 and between 4 and 5. It will not choose to produce between 1 and 2 units because marginal costs are declining and the firm would make additional profit by increasing output above 2. (600)

b. If price rises to $25, so does MR. MC = 25 at between 5 and 6. (600)

c. In (a), profit = total revenue − total costs between 4 and 5: [(5 × $20 − $120) + (4 × $20 − 100)]/2 = -$20, an economic loss. In (b), profit total revenue - total costs between 5 and 6= [(6 × $25 − $145) + (5 x $25 − $120)]/2 = $5. (600)

d. The firm will stay in business at P = $20 or $25, since $MR > AVC$ at both these prices. (600)

e. At P = $15, the profit-maximizing level of output is between 3 and 4 units. The profit in this case is -$40. Since $MR < AVC$ in this case, the firm should temporarily shut down its business. (603-604)

2. a. As shown in the graph on the right, points A and B are the minimum of the ATC and AVC curves. It is where they intersect the MC curve. From an earlier chapter, we know that the MC curve goes through the ATC and AVC curves at their minimum points. (601-603)

b. The demand curve for the representative firm is drawn in the graph to the right. It is a horizontal line because an individual firm in a competitive market is a price taker; the demand for its product is perfectly elastic. (601-603)

c. As illustrated to the right, the long-run equilibrium position occurs when the demand curve is tangential to the ATC curve because it is only at this point that economic profit for the firm is equal to zero. There is no incentive for new firms to enter the market, nor would existing firms exit the market. The long-run equilibrium is reached. (601-603)

3. a. As shown by the shaded region on the graph to the right, the representative firm is earning an economic profit. (601-603)

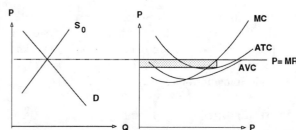

b. More firms will enter the market to share the profit. But as market supply increases from S_0 to S_1, the market price falls which in turn reduces the profit margin for all the firms. This process continues until price falls to P_1 where there is no more economic profit. (601-604)

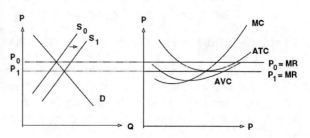

c. As shown on the graphs to the right, a decrease in market demand from D_0 to D_1, results in a fall of market price from P_0 to P_1 which in turn reduces the profit for each firm in the market to a loss. The fall of price will cause some firms to exit the market. Hence, market supply shrinks from S_0 to S_1, until prices rise from P_1 to P_0. In the long run, price returns to the original level while output is reduced. Each firm still has zero economic profit. (601-604)

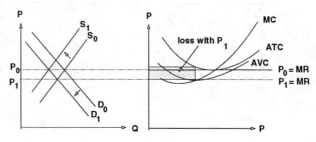

4. a. The curve labeled *AVC* is really an *AFC* curve. The correct *AVC* curve would intersect the *MC* at the minimum point of the *AVC* curve and rise thereafter. (601)

b. Loss is mislabeled in the graph. Loss and profit are measured by the vertical difference between price and average total costs, not average variable costs. Here, there are no economic profits. (601)

c. Output should be where $MC = MR = P$, not where $ATC = MC$. A competitive firm will maximize profits where $MC = MR = P$. (601)

d. A competitive firm faces a horizontal demand curve since it cannot affect prices. Here it is downward-sloping. (601)

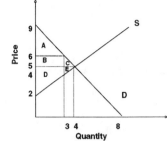

5. a. The consumer surplus is the area A+B+C or $1/2\ [4 \times (9-5)] = 8$. (611)

b. The producer surplus is the area D+E or $1/2\ [4 \times (5 - 2)] = 6$. (611)

c. The new consumer surplus is the area A which is equal to $1/2\ [3 \times (9-6)]$ = 9/2. Therefore, consumer surplus reduces by $7/2\ (8-9/2)$.
The welfare loss is the area C+E or $1/2\ [(6-5) \times (4\text{-}3) + (5-4) \times (4-3)]$ = 1. (611)

Multiple Choice Questions

1. d. In a competitive market selling firms are profit-maximizing, not sales maximizing. See page 593.

2. b. Although the market demand curve is downward sloping, individual firms are so small in relation to the market that they perceive their demand curves as horizontal. See Exhibit 1, page 595.

3. d. The market demand curve is downward sloping. See Exhibit 1, page 595.

4. c. A competitive firm maximizes profit by producing where marginal costs equal price. See page 596, especially Exhibit 2.

5. a. A competitive firm maximizes profit by producing where marginal costs equal price. See page 596, especially Exhibit 2.

6. b. A competitive firm maximizes profit by producing where marginal costs equal price. See page 596, especially Exhibit 2.

7. a. Marginal costs and marginal revenue won't provide information to the firm about what its profit is, but the firm will know what the profit-maximizing output is. See pages 596-597.

8. b. Since marginal cost is below price, it should increase production to increase profit. Changing its price is not an option; a competitive firm is a price taker. See pages 597-598.

9. b. See pages 597-598.

10. c. The text gave no information about what level normal profits are, eliminating answers a and b. Answer d cannot be true because normal profits could be higher or could be lower than accounting profits. (599)

11. b. Output is determined where marginal cost equals price. To determine profit one finds the rectangle formed by ATC at the output and price determined by where marginal cost equals price. See Exhibit 5, page 602.

12. c. The marginal cost curve should go through the minimum point of the ATC curve. See Exhibit 5, page 602.

13. c. The shutdown point is where the marginal cost equals the average variable cost. See Exhibit 7, page 604.

14. c. The zero profit condition discussed in the text includes a normal profit for firms, as discussed on pages 603-604.

15. b. If the price of a complement falls, the demand for x will increase, increasing equilibrium quantity and price. See page 604.

16. a. The long-run supply is always more elastic than the short-run supply because it holds fewer things constant. See pages 608-609, including Exhibits 8 and 9.

17. b. See page 610.

18. a. Consumer surplus is the area under the demand curve above the equilibrium price. See pages 611-612.

19. c. Producer surplus is the area above the supply curve below the equilibrium price. See pages 611-612.

20. d. The loss to consumers is *C* and the loss to producers is *E* so the total loss is $C + E$. See page 611, Exhibit 12.

21. c. The consumer surplus criticism was not even discussed in the text. We haven't the faintest idea what it is. See pages 612-613.

Chapter 26:
Monopoly

Chapter at a glance

1. For a competitive firm, marginal revenue equals price. For a monopolist, it does not. The monopolist takes into account the fact that its decision can affect price. (616)

   The monopolist faces the market demand curve. It must reduce P to sell more. Hence, MR < P.

2. If a monopolist deviates from the output level at which marginal cost equals marginal revenue, profits will decline. (619)

   If $MR > MC \Rightarrow \uparrow Q$.
   ✔ If $MR = MC \Rightarrow$ *maximizing profit (minimizing loss)*
   If $MR < MC \Rightarrow \downarrow Q$.

3a. The monopolist's price and output are determined as follows: (619)

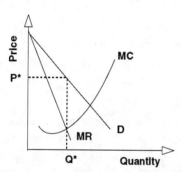

3b. A monopolist's profit is determined by the difference between ATC and price, as in the following diagram: (622)´

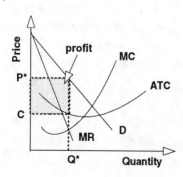

4. A perfectly price-discriminating monopolist does not lose revenue on previously-sold products, so its marginal revenue curve equals its demand curve. Thus, it will produce the same quantity as will a perfectly competitive firm. (624)

   But, the <u>average</u> price a price-discriminating monopolist charges is greater than the competitive price.

5. The welfare loss from monopoly is a triangle as in the graph below. It is not the loss that most people consider. They are often interested in normative losses that the graph does not capture. (626)

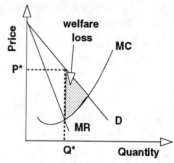

6. If there were no barriers to entry, profit-maximizing firms would always compete away monopoly profits. (628)

   ✔ *Know the different types of barriers to entry.*
   ✔ *The stronger the barriers to entry, the stronger the monopoly power.*

7. Economists generally favor government charging for monopolies because those charges do not raise the price the monopolist charges, and they tend to reduce the rent-seeking expenditures spent to get that monopoly. (630)

   Government charging for a monopoly right would increase only the fixed costs to the monopolist. This charge would not change the monopolist's MC, and therefore would not change the monopolist's output or price.

   See also, Appendix A: "The Algebra of Competitive and Monopolistic Firms."

Short-answer questions

1. What is the key difference between the decisions by monopolists and the collective decisions of competing firms with regard to setting price and production levels? (LO1)

2. The president of Corning Fiberglass comes to you for advice. The firm has patented its pink fiberglass. It seems to be able to set its own price. In fact, you can say it has a monopoly on its shade of pink fiberglass. It wants you to tell it how to maximize profits. What information would you ask the president for, and what would you do with that information?   (LO2)

3. Show a monopolist's price, output, and profit using the graph to the right. (LO3)

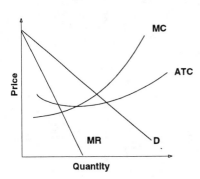

4. Calculate a monopolist's price, output, and profit using the following table: (LO3)

Q	Price	Total cost
0	$36	$47
1	33	48
2	30	50
3	27	58
4	24	73
5	21	89
6	18	113
7	15	153
8	12	209
9	9	289

5.   Why will a perfectly price-discriminating monopolist produce the same output as a perfect competitor? (LO4)

6.   Show graphically the welfare loss from monopoly on the axes to the right. (LO5)

7.   After seeing your answer to question 6, a group of consumers are outraged. "Why," they say, "that doesn't come close to the harm monopolists inflict on us." Why might the welfare loss from monopoly you demonstrated underestimate their view of the loss from monopoly? (LO5)

8.   Why, without barriers to entry, would there be no monopoly? (LO6)

9.   Why do economists generally favor having government charge a fixed fee for monopolies? (LO7)

Word Scramble

1. _____ _____ 2._____ _____ 3._____
    u s r o n m e c   l p r s s u u   e r n t   e e s g k i n   y p o o o n m l

Match the Terms and Concepts to Their Definitions

___ 1. marginal revenue curve

___ 2. monopoly

___ 3. MR = MC

___ 4. natural monopolies

___ 5. patent

___ 6. price discriminate

___ 7. public choice economists

___ 8. rent seeking

___ 9. rent-seeking loss from monopoly

___ 10. Tullock rectangle

___ 11. welfare loss triangle

a. A legal protection of a technical innovation which gives the person holding that protection a monopoly on using that innovation.

b. Attempting to influence the structure of economic institutions in order to create rents for oneself.

c. Economists who integrate an economic analysis of politics with their analysis of the economy.

d. Geometric representation of the welfare cost in terms of the resource misallocation caused by monopoly.

e. Graphical measure of rent-seeking loss from monopoly that results when potential monopolists spend resources to gain monopoly.

f. Graphical measure of the change in revenue that occurs in response to a change in price.

g. The condition under which a monopolist is maximizing profit.

h. Monopolies that exist because economies of scale create a barrier to entry.

i. To charge different prices to different individuals or groups of individuals.

j. Waste caused by people spending money trying to get government to give them a monopoly.

k. A market structure in which one firm makes up the entire market.

Problems and Exercises

1. Consider the following marginal cost, marginal revenue, and demand curves facing a monopolist.

   a. Shade the area that represents the welfare loss of monopoly to society.

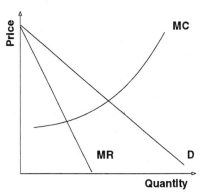

   b. On that same graph draw a marginal cost curve that reflects constant marginal costs that would result in the same quantity and price. Shade the area that represents the welfare loss of monopoly to society.

   c. In which case, (a) or (b), is the welfare loss to society greatest? Why?

2. Suppose a monopolist has the following *MC* curve and faces the following demand and marginal revenue curves.

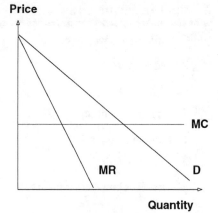

Price

Quantity

MC

MR

D

a. Label the monopolist's price and output Q_m and P_m.

b. What would be price and quantity if the market were competitive?

c. Demonstrate the welfare loss from the monopoly on the graph. Explain your answer.

d. Demonstrate the rent-seeking loss on the graph. Explain your answer.

e. How would your answer to (a) change if government charges the monopolist a per unit tax?

f. What would happen if the monopolist is charged a lump sum tax?

3. The following table represents the market for Corning Fiberglass. Corning is the sole producer of fiberglass.

Q	Price	TC
0	-	60
1	46	65
2	42	81
3	38	111
4	34	145
5	30	189
6	24	249

    a.   Determine the profit-maximizing price and output.

    b.   What is the monopolist's profit?

    c.   Suppose the market is competitive, what is output and price? Would this company stay in business?

A1. Suppose the marginal costs, and therefore the market supply, for Mimi Chocolates in Bhutan is given by $P = Q_s/2 + 3$. The market demand is given by, $Q_d = 10 - 2P$.

    a.   What is the equilibrium price and quantity if the market for chocolates is perfectly competitive?

    b.   If Mimi Chocolates has a monopoly in the markets what will be the price in the market and the quantity produced?

Multiple Choice Questions

1. Monopoly is the market structure in which
   a. one firm makes up the entire market.
   b. two firms make up the entire market.
   c. the market is made up of a few big firms.
   d. firms make a supernormal profit.

2. Which curve is the marginal revenue curve for the demand curve D in the following diagram?
   a. Curve A.
   b. Curve B.
   c. Curve C.
   d. None of the above.

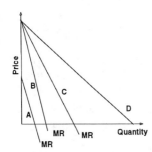

3. In the graph at the right, at what output would a monopolist most likely be operating?
   a. Output A.
   b. Output B.
   c. Output C.
   d. Output D.

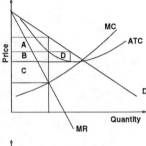

4. If marginal revenue exceeds marginal cost
   a. the monopolist will increase profit by increasing output.
   b. the monopolist will increase profit by decreasing output.
   c. the monopolist is maximizing profit.
   d. nothing can be said about profit.

5. In the graph at the right, which rectangle represents monopolist's profit?
   a. A.
   b. A + B + C.
   c. C + D.
   d. none of the above.

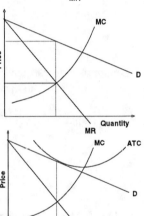

6. In the graph at the right
   a. the monopolist is making a profit.
   b. the monopolist is making a loss.
   c. the monopolist is making zero profit.
   d. It cannot be determined what kind of profit the monopolist is making.

7. In the graph on the right
   a. the monopolist is making a profit.
   b. the monopolist is making a loss.
   c. the monopolist is making zero profit.
   d. it cannot be determined what kind of profit the monopolist is making.

8. When the marginal revenue curve intercepts the quantity axis, the elasticity of demand at that output
   a. is greater than 1.
   b. is less than 1.
   c. is equal to 1.
   d. cannot be determined.

9. In the graph at the right, what area represents the profit of a perfectly discriminating monopolist?
   a. A.
   b. A + B.
   c. A + B + C.
   d. none of the above.

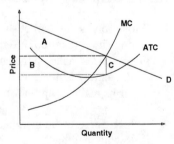

10. A natural monopoly is
    a. a monopoly that exists because of economies of scale.
    b. a monopoly that is created by natural law.
    c. a monopoly where natural legal barriers prevent entry.
    d. a monopoly in which patents exist.

11. In the graph on the right, what areas represent the welfare loss due to a monopolist?

a. A.
b. A + B.
c. B + C.
d. A + B + C.

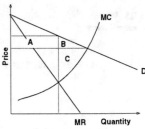

12. In the graph at the right, what area represents the rent-seeking loss from a monopoly?

a. A.
b. B.
c. C.
d. A + B + C.

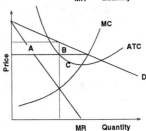

A1. Suppose the marginal costs, and therefore the market supply, for ketchup in Mexico is given by $P = Q_s/2 + 1$. The market demand is given by, $Q_d = 20 - 4P$. If there is a monopoly in the ketchup market the price and the quantity produced is

a. $P = 11/3$, $Q = 16/3$.
b. $P = 11/3$, $Q = 4$.
c. $P = 3$, $Q = 4$.
d. $P = 4$, $Q = 4$.

Answers

Short-answer questions

1. For a competitive firm, marginal revenue equals price regardless of output. But for monopolist, price depends upon output. A monopolist must take into account the fact that its decisions can affect price. Its marginal revenue does not equal the price it charges. (616)

2. You tell the president that the firm needs to know is its marginal costs and its marginal revenues. To maximize profits, it should produce where $MR = MC$. A monopolist produces where $MC = MR$ to maximize total profit for the same reasons a perfectly competitive firm does. If $MC < MR$, it can increase total profits by producing an additional unit. If $MC > MR$, it can increase total profits by decreasing output. It is only where $MC = MR$ that it cannot increase profits by changing output. (619)

3. A monopolist's output is set where $MC = MR$. Extend a line vertically; it sets price where that line intersects the demand curve, here at P^*. Profit is determined by dropping a vertical line from the price the monopolist charges to the ATC curve and multiplying by Q^*. This is the shaded region in the graph to the right. (618-322)

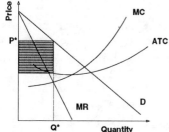

4. To calculate a monopolist's output, first calculate total revenue ($P \times Q$) for each output level. Then calculate marginal revenue (the change in total revenue). Find where $MR = MC$. This is at between 3 and 4 units and a price between $27 and $24. Profit is calculated as total revenue minus total cost between 3 and 4 units: $23. (Marginal cost refers to the marginal cost of increasing to that row, e.g., the marginal cost of going from 0 to 1 is 1. The same goes for marginal revenue.) (617-619)

Q	Price	Total revenue	Marginal revenue	Total cost	Marginal cost
0	$36	0		$47	
1	33	33	33	48	1
2	30	60	27	50	2
3	27	81	21	58	8
4	24	96	15	73	15
5	21	105	9	89	16
6	18	108	3	113	24
7	15	105	-3	153	40
8	12	96	-9	209	56
9	9	81	-15	289	80

5. A perfectly price-discriminating monopolist produces the same output as a perfect competitor because it does not lose revenue on previously-sold products. Its marginal revenue curve equals its demand curve. Thus it will produce the same quantity as will a perfectly competitive firm. (624)

6. Welfare loss from monopoly is shown as the shaded region on the graph to the right. (625)

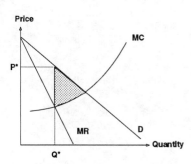

7. You first think that they are wrong. They simply do not understand the model. Upon further reflection, you realize that your model does not capture normative arguments against monopoly. The welfare loss from monopoly shown in question 6 does not capture normative arguments against monopoly such as distributional issues and issues of fairness. (626-627)

8. Without barriers to entry there would there be no monopoly because profit-maximizing firms would always enter to compete away monopoly profits. (627-628)

9. Economists generally favor having government charge for monopolies because charging those prices does not raise the price the monopolist charges for its goods. A government charge also tends to reduce rent-seeking expenditures spent to get the monopoly. (629, 630)

Word Scramble   1. consumer surplus   2. rent seeking   3. monopoly

Match the Terms and Concepts to Their Definitions
1-f; 2-k; 3-g; 4-h; 5-a; 6-i; 7-c; 8-b; 9-j; 10-e; 11-d.

Problems and Exercises

1. a. The area that represents the welfare loss of monopoly to society is shown as the shaded region in the graph on the right. The cost to society of increasing production from the monopolist output to the competitive output is the area under the marginal cost curve between Q_M and Q_C. The benefit to society is the area under the demand curve between Q_M and Q_C. The difference is the net gain to society of eliminating monopoly, or the welfare loss to society from the existence of a monopoly. (625)

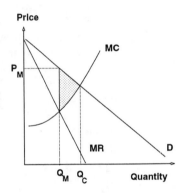

  b. An elastic marginal cost curve intersecting the marginal revenue curve at the same point that the original marginal cost curve intersected marginal revenue curve would keep the same monopolist output and price. This is shown in the figure on the right. (625)
  c. A perfectly elastic marginal cost curve maintaining the same monopolist output and price would decrease the cost to society of increasing output to competitive output. The benefit to society would increase since the competitive output would be higher; the welfare loss to society of the monopoly would increase. This is shown in the figure on the right. You can see that the shaded region includes the entire shaded region in (a) and more. (625)

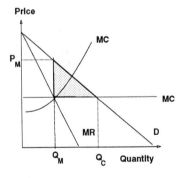

2. a. The monopolist will produce where $MC = MR$, at Q_M, and charge a price, P_M as shown in the graph on the right. (625-630)
  b. If the market were competitive, output would be Q_C and price would be P_C. (625-630)
  c. Welfare loss from monopoly is the geometric representation of the welfare cost of restricting output. In the figure shown on the right, the shaded region is welfare loss and represents the loss in consumer surplus from restricting output. (625)
  d. Rent-seeking loss is the waste caused by people spending money to get a monopoly. It is represented by the shaded region in the graph on the right. (629)

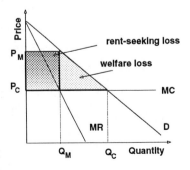

e. If the government charges the monopolist a per unit tax, the *MC* curve will shift up which will cause a fall in *Q* and a rise in *P*. Obviously, this measure will further hurt the consumers. (630)

f. If the government charges the monopolist a fixed fee, the *MC* curve is unaffected. It cuts the monopolist's profit by shifting the *ATC* up, but leaves *P* and *Q* unchanged. This is a way to transfer monopoly profit from the monopolist to government. (630)

3. To answer the following questions, first calculate *MC, MR,* and *AVC*. *MC* is the change in *TC, AVC* is *VC/Q,* and *MR* is the change in *TR,* where *TR* is *P* x *Q*. This is shown below. (Marginal cost refers to the marginal cost of increasing to that row, e.g., the marginal cost of going from 0 to 1 is 5. The same goes for marginal revenue.) (626)

Q	Price	TC	MC	MR	AVC
0	-	60	-	-	0
1	46	65	5	46	5
2	42	81	16	38	10.5
3	38	111	30	30	17.00
4	34	145	34	22	21.25
5	30	189	44	14	25.8
6	24	249	60	-6	31.5

a. Monopolists maximize profits where *MR* = *MC*. *MC* = *MR* between 2 and 3 units. Corning will charge a price between $42 and $38. (617-630)

b. Profit = total revenue minus total costs between 2 and 3, which is $3. (617-620)

c. If the market were competitive, then the firm would choose where *MC* = *P*. So *Q* is between 3 and 4 and *P* = 34. Profit = total revenue - total costs between 3 and 4, which is -$9. The firm will still stay in business since *MR* > *AVC*. (617-320)

A1. a. Rewriting the marginal cost equation with quantity supplied on the left gives: Q_s = 2P - 6. Setting this equal to quantity demanded gives equilibrium price at 4 and quantity at 2. (634-365)

b. Specifying the demand curve in terms of quantity produced gives: P = 5 - Q/2. Multiplying this by Q gives total revenue TR = 5Q - Q²/2. The marginal revenue is the first derivative of this. Thus, MR = 5 - Q. By setting MR = MC and solving for Q we get the quantity that would be produced if the chocolate market were a monopoly. (634-635)

$$5 - Q = Q/2 + 3$$
$$3Q/2 = 2$$
$$Q = 4/3.$$

The monopolist charges the price that consumers are willing to pay for that quantity. Substituting Q = 4/3 into the demand equation gives P = 13/3. You can see that if there is a monopoly in the market, the price charged is higher than the competitive market price; also, the quantity produced is lower. (634-635)

Multiple Choice Questions

1. a. Monopoly means one firm; that firm may or may not make a supernormal profit. See page 616.

2. c. The marginal revenue curve equals the demand curve at the vertical axis and bisects the distance between the demand curve and the vertical axis. See Exhibit 2, page 619.

3. a. The output of a monopolist is determined by the output where marginal revenue equals marginal cost. See page 619, especially Exhibit 2.

4. a. The monopolist's additional revenue from increasing output will exceed its additional costs, so profits will increase. See page 619, especially Exhibit 2.

5. a. Output is determined where marginal revenue equals marginal cost. Profit is determined by the rectangle created by the relevant price and average cost at that output. See Exhibit 4, page 622, and Exhibit 5, 623.

6. d. Since there is no ATC curve, profit cannot be determined. See page 623.

7. c.   The ATC is tangent to the demand, so costs equal price, and there is no profit. See Exhibit 5, page 623.

8. c.   The marginal revenue curve tells us what is happening to total revenue when price is changed. When marginal revenue equals zero, the percentage change in quantity equals the percentage change in price so the elasticity must be unity. See Exhibit 5, page 623.

9. b.   The price discriminating monopolist produces where marginal cost intersects the demand curve. It gets in profit all the consumer surplus plus all the usual monopolist profit. See page 624.

10. a.   In a natural monopoly the barrier to entry is created by economies of scale. No other firm can get a large enough output to secure the economies of scale. See page 628.

11. c.   The welfare loss is represented by the triangle of consumer surplus that is lost to the consumer but not earned in profit by the monopolist. See Exhibit 7, page 625, and Exhibit 8, page 629.

12. a.   The rent-seeking loss is the money spent by the monopolist to secure the monopoly. It is equal to what the profit would have been. See page 629.

A1. d.   Specifying the demand curve in terms of quantity produced gives: $P = 5 - Q/4$. Multiplying this by Q gives total revenue $TR = 5Q - Q^2/4$. The marginal revenue is the first derivative of this. Thus, $MR = 5 - Q/2$. By setting $MR = MC$ and solving for Q we get the quantity produced: $5 - Q/2 = Q/2 + 1$; $Q = 4$. The monopolist charges the price that consumers are willing to pay for that quantity. Substituting $Q = 4$ into the demand equation gives $P = 4$. Thus, d is the correct answer. (634-635)

Chapter 27: Monopolistic Competition, Oligopoly, and Strategic Pricing

Chapter at a glance

1a. A concentration ratio is the percentage of industry output that a specific number of the largest firms have. (638)

A four-firm concentration ratio of 60% means the four largest firms account for 60% of industry sales.

1b. A Herfindahl Index is a method used by economists to classify how competitive an industry is. (638)

(Also used by the Justice Department.)

✔ *Know the 2 advantages it has over a concentration ratio:*
  (1)   takes into account all firms in an industry,
  (2)   gives extra weight to firms with especially large shares of the market.

2. Four distinguishing characteristics of monopolistic competition are: (641)
  1.   Many sellers in a highly competitive market;
  2.   Differentiated products, but firms still act independently;
  3.   Multiple dimensions of competition; and
  4.   Easy entry of new firms in the long run so there are no long-run profits.

✔ *Know these as well as the distinguishing characteristics of all 4 market structures.*

3. The equilibrium of a monopolistic competitor is: (642)

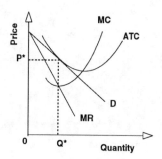

Notice the tangency between the D and ATC curves at output where MR = MC.

Also Note: Only a zero economic profit in the long run (P=ATC). But, because P>MC implies underproduction from society's perspective.

4. If oligopolies can limit the entry of other firms and form a cartel, they increase the profits going to the combination of firms in the cartel. (646)

There is an inherent tendency for collusion (getting together to avoid competing). However, holding firms together is difficult because of a tendency for each of them to cheat.

5. In the contestable market model of oligopoly, pricing and entry decisions are based only on barriers to entry and exit, not on market structure. Thus, even if the industry contains only one firm, it could still be a competitive market if entry is open. (648)

So: 2 extreme models of oligopoly behavior:
1.   Cartel model: Firms set a monopoly price.
2.   Contestable market model: An oligopoly with no barriers sets a competitive price.

Most real-world oligopolies are in between.

6. Exhibit 11 gives a summary of the central differences among the four various market structures. (654)

✔ *Study this exhibit! (It makes for "nice" exam questions.)*

See also, Appendix A: "A Case Study."

Short-answer questions

1. What is the 4-firm concentration ratio for an industry in which 10 firms all have 10% of the market? (LO1)

2. What is a Herfindahl index for an industry in which 10 firms all have 10% of the market? (LO1)

3. The soap industry is characterized by monopolistic competition. There are many types of soap: Ivory, Irish Spring, Lever, and so on. When one firm lowers its price it won't calculate the reaction of the other firms. In the automobile market, which is oligopolistic, GM does worry about how Chrysler prices its cars. Based on level of competition, what distinguishes these two markets? (LO2)

4. Show graphically the equilibrium of a monopolistic competitor. (LO3)

5. Major oil producers in the world have formed a tight cartel, OPEC. At times, the cartel has fallen apart. What are the reasons the major oil producers have a strong desire to keep OPEC strong? (LO4)

6. How does the contestable market theory lead to determining competitiveness by performance rather than structure? (LO5)

7. Fill in the following table, which captures the central differences among various market structures. (LO6)

	Monopoly	Oligopoly	Monopolistic Competition	Perfect Competition
Number of Firms				
Pricing Decisions				
Output Decisions				
Profit				

Word Scramble

1. _____   2._____ _____   3._____ _____
   g i l l o o o p y   a e k m r t   u u t t s r r e c   t t r o o n n n i e c c a   t o i r a

Match the Terms and Concepts to Their Definitions

____ 1. cartel

____ 2. concentration ratio

____ 3. conglomerate

____ 4. contestable market model

____ 5. duopoly

____ 6. market structure

____ 7. game theory

____ 8. Herfindahl Index

____ 9. implicit collusion

____ 10. monopolistic competition

____ 11. oligopoly

____ 12. prisoner's dilemma

____ 13. Standard Industrial Code (SIC)

____ 14. strategic decision making

____ 15. strategic pricing

a. A market structure in which many firms sell differentiated products.

b. A market structure with a few interdependent firms.

c. A well-known game that nicely demonstrates the difficulty of cooperative behavior in certain circumstances.

d. A combination of firms that acts like a single firm.

e. A model that bases pricing and output decisions on entry and exit conditions, not on market structure.

f. The physical characteristics of the market within which firms interact.

g. A method used by economists to classify how competitive an industry is.

h. A large corporation whose activities span various unrelated industries.

i. An oligopoly with only two firms.

j. Firms set their price based upon the expected reactions of other firms.

k. Multiple firms making the same pricing decisions even though they have not consulted with one another.

l. System for classifying industries.

m. Taking explicit account of a rival's expected response to a decision you are making.

n. The application of economic principles to interdependent situations.

o. The percentage of total industry output that a specific number of the largest firms have.

Problems and Exercises

1. For each of the following calculate the four-firm concentration ratio and the Herfindahl index.

   a. 20 firms in the market each having equal shares.

   b. 10 firms in the market. One firm has 91% of market share. The remaining 9 firms share the remaining market equally.

c. The industry's top firm has 31% of the market and the next three have 2% apiece. There are 63 remaining firms, each with a 1% share.

d. 4 firms equally share the market.

e. Rank the markets by how competitive the market is, from more competitive to less competitive, first using the concentration ratio and then the Herfindahl index. Do they differ? Why or why not?

2. Given the following demand curve and marginal revenue curve, add a marginal cost curve.

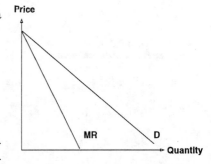

a. Label profit-maximizing price and output for a monopolist. Label profit-maximizing price and output for a monopolistically competitive firm.

b. Add an average total cost curve that is consistent with long-run equilibrium in a market characterized by monopolistic competition. What is the economic profit? Explain your answer.

3. For each of the following graphs state whether it characterizes perfect competition, monopoly, or monopolistic competition in the long run. Explain your answer.

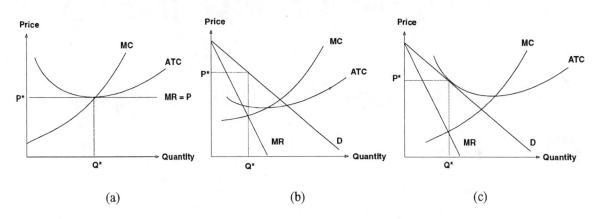

(a)   (b)   (c)

4. Suppose there are two ice-cream stands on opposite sides of the road: Ben's stand and Jerry's stand. Each has identical costs of 25 cents a cone. Each has the option of charging $1 a cone or $1.50 a cone. If Ben and Jerry collude, both charging $1.50 a cone, each will sell 50 cones each day. Ben thinks that he would sell more cones if he sells his at $1 a cone. If he does this, he will sell 80 cones and Jerry will sell 20. Jerry is considering the same strategy. If they both charge $1, each will sell 50 cones per day.

a. Construct a payoff matrix for Ben and Jerry.

b. If the stand is to be in business only one day, what would you advise Ben?

c.   If the stands are to be in business all summer long, what would you advise Ben?

Multiple Choice Questions

1.   In a market there are many firms selling differentiated products. This market is
     a. a competitive market.
     b. a monopolistically competitive market.
     c. an oligopoly.
     d. a monopoly.

2.   Several firms are operating in a market where they take the other firms' response to their actions into account.
     This market is
     a. a competitive market.
     b. a monopolistically competitive market.
     c. an oligopolistic market.
     d. a monopoly.

3.   In the SIC classification system, the broadest classification would be
     a. a two-digit industry.
     b. a three-digit industry.
     c. a four-digit industry.
     d. a five-digit industry.

4.   The top four firms in the industry have 10 percent, 8 percent, 8 percent, and 6 percent of the market. The four-
     firm concentration ratio of this market is
     a. 8.
     b. 32.
     c. 66.
     d. 264.

5.   The top four firms in the industry have 10 percent, 8 percent, 8 percent, and 6 percent of the market. The
     Herfindahl index of this market is closest to which of the following?
     a. 8.
     b. 32.
     c. 66.
     d. 264.

6.   Strategic decision making is most important in
     a. competitive markets.
     b. monopolistically competitive markets.
     c. oligopolistic markets.
     d. monopolistic markets.

7. Equilibrium for monopoly and a monopolistic competitor differs because
   a. the demand curve for a monopoly is more inelastic.
   b. the marginal cost curve of a monopoly is more inelastic.
   c. the demand curve for a monopoly is more elastic.
   d. the average total cost curve of a monopolistically competitive firm is tangent to the demand curve at the quantity produced.

8. At the equilibrium output for a monopolistic competitor
   a. price equals marginal cost equals marginal revenue.
   b. price equals average total cost equals marginal revenue.
   c. marginal cost equals marginal revenue equals average total costs.
   d. price equals average total cost and marginal costs equals marginal revenue.

9. In the graph to the right, which of the following is the output chosen by the monopolistically competitive firm?
   a. Q_1.
   b. Q_2.
   c. Q_3.
   d. The information cannot be gained from the graph to the right.

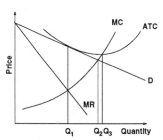

10. In long-run equilibrium, a monopolistically competitive firm
    a. makes a loss.
    b. makes only a normal profit.
    c. makes a monopolistic profit.
    d. may make a loss or a profit.

11. Advertising adds cost to producing a good. Therefore it
    a. increases the average total cost of production.
    b. decreases the average total cost of production.
    c. sometimes increases and sometimes decreases the average total cost of production.
    d. has no effect on the average total cost of production.

12. In the cartel model of oligopoly, the firms would decide how much to produce where
    a. marginal cost equals marginal revenue.
    b. marginal cost equals price.
    c. marginal cost equals average total cost.
    d. where the kink in the demand curve is.

13. The Herfindahl index in an industry is 1500. The economist concludes that the industry is an oligopoly that will charge close to the monopolistic price. This economist is using
    a. the cartel model.
    b. the contestable market model.
    c. the kinked demand curve model.
    d. the strategic pricing model.

14. If there is a kinked demand curve, the marginal revenue curve
    a. also has a kink in it.
    b. is discontinuous.
    c. is steeper than it otherwise would be.
    d. is flatter than it otherwise would be.

15. In a contestable model market model of oligopoly, prices are determined by
    a. costs and barriers to exit.
    b. costs and barriers to entry.
    c. costs, barriers to entry, and barriers to exit
    d. costs alone.

16. There is only one firm in the market. The economist analyzing that market has said she would expect the price to equal the firm's average total costs.
    a. She must be analyzing this market using a contestable market model.
    b. She must be analyzing this market using a game theory model.
    c. She must be analyzing this market using a cartel model.
    d. She must not be an economist, because that answer is clearly wrong.

17. The prisoner's dilemma is a well known game in which
    a. cooperation is costly.
    b. independent action is costly.
    c. firms always cheat.
    d. firms never cheat.

18. A market has the following characteristics: Marginal cost equals marginal revenue; it has the most output restrictions; there is only one firm in the market; and there is a possibility of long-run economic profit. The structure of this market is
    a. monopolistic.
    b. oligopolistic.
    c. monopolistically competitive.
    d. perfectly competitive.

19. The market has the following characteristics: Marginal cost equals marginal revenue; output is restricted somewhat by product differentation; each firm acts independently, and there is no long-run economic profit. This market is
    a. a monopoly.
    b. an oligopoly.
    c. monopolistically competitive.
    d. perfectly competitive.

20. The market has the following characteristics: There is strategic pricing, output is somewhat restricted, there is interdependent decision-making, and some long-run economic profits are possible. This market is
    a. a monopoly.
    b. an oligopoly.
    c. monopolistically competitive.
    d. perfectly competitive.

A1. In the real world most firms
    a. use a cost mark-up pricing system.
    b. use a kinked demand curve pricing system.
    c. price where marginal cost equals price.
    d. price where marginal cost equals marginal revenue.

A2. The mark-up rules of thumb that most firms use in pricing are
    a. inconsistent with the competitive model.
    b. inconsistent with the monopolistic model.
    c. not necessarily inconsistent with any of the models.
    d. inconsistent with the strategic pricing model.

Answers

Short-answer questions

1. A concentration ratio is the percentage of industry output that a specific number of the largest firms have. A 4-firm concentration ratio is calculated by adding together the market shares of the four firms with the largest market shares. In the case given, the 4-firm concentration ratio is 40. (638)

2. A Herfindahl index is a method used by economists to classify how competitive an industry is. It is calculated by summing the squares of the market shares of all the firms in the industry. In this case the Herfindahl index is $10 \times 10^2 = 1000$. (638)

3. The distinguishing characteristics are: (1) In the soap industry there are many sellers in a highly competitive market. In the automobile industry there are about 5 big producers. (2) In the soap industry, the different labels are distinct, but firms still act independently. In the automobile industry, the products are distinct and the firms do not act independently. (3) In the soap industry, there is easy entry of new firms in the long run so there are no long-run profits. In the auto industry entry is not easy. In both industries firms compete on more than price; they also compete on image. (641)

4. The equilibrium of a monopolistic competitor is shown in the graph to the right. A monopolistic competitor earns no economic profit, so the price equals *ATC*. (642)

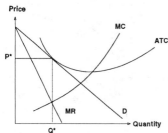

5. Since there are only a few large oil-producing nations, together they are an oligopoly. Oil-producing nations have a powerful desire to keep OPEC strong because as a cartel it can increase the profits going to the combination of oil-producing nations by reducing output. (646)

6. In the contestable market theory, pricing decisions are based on the threat of new entrants into the market, not market share. Thus, even if the industry has only one firm, it could still price competitively. (648)

7. Fill in the following table that captures the central differences among various market structures (650):

	Monopoly	Oligopoly	Monopolistic Competition	Perfect Competition
Number of Firms	1	Few	Many	Almost infinite
Pricing Decisions	MC = MR	Strategic pricing between monopoly and perfect competition	MC = MR	MC = MR = P
Output Decisions	Most output restricted	Output somewhat restricted	Output restricted somewhat by product differentiation	No output restriction
Profit	Possibility of long-run economic profit	Some long-run economic profit possible	No long-run economic profit possible	No long-run economic profit possible

Word Scramble   1. oligopoly   2. market structure   3. concentration ratio

Match the Terms and Concepts to Their Definitions
1-d; 2-o; 3-h; 4-e; 5-i; 6-f; 7-n; 8-g; 9-k; 10-a; 11-b; 12-c; 13-l; 14-m; 15-j.

Problems and Exercises

1. A four-firm concentration ratio is the percentage of the total industry output that the top four firms have. It is calculated by adding together the top four firms' market shares. The Herfindahl index is calculated by adding the squared value of the market shares of all the firms in the industry. (637-639)
    a. Four-firm concentration ratio = 5+5+5+5 = 20. Herfindahl index is $20 \times 5^2 = 500$. (638-639)
    b. Four-firm concentration ratio = 91+1+1+1 = 94. Herfindahl index is $91^2+1^2+1^2+1^2+1^2+1^2+1^2+1^2+1^2+1^2 = 8290$. (638)
    c. Four-firm concentration ratio = 31+2+2+2 = 37. Herfindahl index is $31^2+2^2+2^2+2^2+63 \times 1^2 = 1036$. (638-639)
    d. Four-firm concentration ratio = 25+25+25+25 = 100. Herfindahl index is $25^2+25^2+25^2+25^2 = 2500$. (638-639)
    e. A higher concentration ratio and Herfindahl index indicates that the market is less competitive. The ranking using the four-firm concentration ratio is a (20), c (37), b (94), d (100). Using the Herfindahl index, the ranking is a (500), c (1036), d (2500), b (8290). They differ because the Herfindahl index takes into account all the firms in the market and gives extra weight to a single firm with an especially large share of the market (accounts for difference in the ranking of b). (637-639)

2. a. The graph to the right shows a typical marginal cost curve for a firm. The profit-maximizing level of output for a monopolist is where $MC = MR$. It will set price by extending the quantity line to the demand curve and extending a horizontal line to the price axis. This is the price a monopolist would charge. This is labeled as Q^* and P^* respectively. Profit-maximizing price and output for a monopolistically competitive firm is the same as for a monopolist. (642)

    b. The average total cost curve consistent with long-run equilibrium in a market characterized by monopolistic competition is drawn on the graph to the right. It is tangent to the demand curve at the profit-maximizing price and quantity combination. Economic profit is zero. It is drawn this way because competition implies zero economic profit in the long run. (642)

3. a. This graph depicts perfect competition because the demand curve facing the firm is horizontal and no economic profit is earned. It could also depict a monopolist and a monopolistic competitor in the special case where demand is perfectly elastic. (643)
    b. This graph depicts a monopolist because it faces a downward-sloping demand curve and it is earning economic profit. (654)
    c. This graph depicts a monopolistic competitor because it faces a downward-sloping demand curve and it is not earning any economic profit. It could also depict a monopolist if it so happens that the *ATC* curve is drawn as given. (642)

4. a. The payoff matrix is shown below. Ben's strategies are listed vertically. Jerry's strategies are listed horizontally. The first number in each cell is Ben's profits calculated as quantity times profit per unit. The second number is Jerry's profit calculated in the same way. (652)

		\multicolumn{2}{c}{Jerry's Price}	
		$1.50	$1.00
Ben's Price	$1.50	$62.50/$62.50	$25/$60
	$1.00	$60/$25	$37.5/$37.5

b. If the stand is to be in business only one day I would tell Ben that his profit-maximizing strategy is to charge $1. Expected profit of charging $1.50 is $43.75 ((62.5+25)/2), assuming it is equally likely that Jerry will charge $1.50 or $1.00. Expected profit of charging $1.00 is $48.75 ((60+37.5)/2), assuming it is equally likely that Jerry will charge $1.50 or $1.00. He should charge $1.00. (652)

c. If they were going to sell ice cream all summer long I would recommend that Ben and Jerry develop some level of trust between themselves and collude to charge $1.50 each. This way, they maximize joint profits. (650-652)

Multiple Choice Questions

1. b. See page 636.

2. c. See pages 641, 645.

3. a. In the SIC classification, the more numbers, the greater the particular subdivisions, so the answer is two-digit classification. See page 637.

4. b. The four-firm concentration ratio is the percentage of the market the top four firms hold. See page 638.

5. d. The Herfindahl index adds the squares of the market shares of firms in the industry. Squaring these market shares and adding them gives 264, so the Herfindahl index must exceed that. See pages 638-639.

6. c. It is within oligopolies that firms take other firms' expected reactions into account, so it is oligopoly where strategic decision making is most important. See page 641.

7. d. See page 642, including Exhibit 4.

8. d. The decision where to produce is made by where marginal cost equals marginal revenue. At that output average total costs equals price, but that price does not equal either marginal cost or marginal revenue. See pages 642-643.

9. a. The equilibrium output is determined by where marginal cost equals marginal revenue. See page 642.

10. b. In long-run equilibrium, a monopolistically competitive firm must make zero profit, so that no entry is induced. See pages 642-643.

11. c. The answer is "sometimes increases and sometimes decreases the average total cost of production." Although the ATC curve shifts up, depending on how many economies of scale the advertising allows, economies of scale may increase or decrease average total costs. See Exhibit 6, page 644.

12. a. The cartel model has the oligopoly acting like a monopolist. See page 646-647.

13. a. The only oligopoly model in which the industry charges the monopolistic price is the cartel model. See page 646.

14. b. When the demand has a kink, the marginal curve associated with it is discontinuous. Answer c and answer d are wrong because while parts of the marginal revenue curve are flatter or steeper than they otherwise would have been, the other parts are the opposite, so those answers cannot be correct. See Exhibit 7, page 647.

15. c. Costs determine reference price, and barriers to both entry and exit determine the degree to which price deviates from cost. See pages 648-649.

16. a. In a contestable market model, exit and entry conditions determine the firm's price and output decisions. Thus, if there are no barriers to entry and exit, even if there is only one firm in the industry, the firm will produce where price equals the firm's average total costs. See page 648.

17. b. In the prisoner's dilemma game, cooperation is beneficial for both prisoners, but difficult to achieve. There may or may not be cheating, but the firms expect the other firm to cheat. See pages 649-650.

18. a. See Exhibit 11, page 654.

19. c. See Exhibit 11, page 654.

20. b. See Exhibit 11, page 654.

A1. a. Most firms use a cost mark-up pricing procedure. This doesn't mean that the models you learned are not there—they are behind what the size of the mark-up is. See pages 657-658.

A2. c. The real-world rules of thumb reflect adaptations of economic reasoning to particular situations. They are not necessarily inconsistent with any of the models presented. See pages 657-658.

Pretest IV
Chapters 21 - 27

Take this test in test conditions, giving yourself a limited amount of time to complete the questions. Ideally, check with your professor to see how much time he or she allows for an average multiple choice question and multiply this by 33. This is the time limit you should set for yourself for this pretest. If you do not know how much time your teacher would allow, we suggest 1 minute per question, or about 35 minutes.

1. When the price of a good was raised from $10 to $11 the quantity demanded fell from 100 to 99. The elasticity of demand is approximately
   a. .1.
   b. 1.
   c. 10.
   d. 100.

2. In reference to the graph on the right, which of the following is true?
   a. Point B is more elastic than point A.
   b. Point A is more elastic than point B.
   c. Points A and B have equal elasticity.
   d. One cannot say anything about the elasticities without more information.

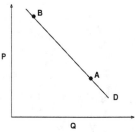

3. Price discrimination is most likely to occur in markets
   a. when all individuals have equal elasticities.
   b. when some individuals have highly inelastic demands and some have highly elastic demands.
   c. in which the elasticity of demand is 1.
   d. in which the elasticity of demand is zero.

4. In the graph to the right, point A on the supply curve, S$_1$, is
   a. elastic.
   b. inelastic.
   c. unit elastic.
   d. unknown because one cannot say from the graph.

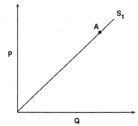

5. Hot dogs and mustard tend to be
   a. substitutes.
   b. complements.
   c. inferior goods.
   d. bounded goods.

6. A significant price decline while virtually no change in quantity would most likely be caused by
   a. Highly elastic demand and supply shifts to the right.
   b. Highly inelastic supply and demand shifts to the right.
   c. Highly inelastic demand and supply shifts out.
   d. Highly elastic supply and demand shifts in.

7. The principle of diminishing marginal utility says that
   a. after some point the marginal utility received from each additional unit of a good remains constant with each unit consumed.
   b. after some point the marginal utility received from each additional unit of a good increases with each unit consumed.
   c. after some point the marginal utility received from each additional unit of a good decreases with each unit consumed.
   d. after some point the marginal utility received from each additional unit of a good approaches infinity with each unit consumed.

8. The price of good A is $2; the price of good B is $2. The marginal utility you get from good A is 40; the marginal utility you get from good B is 60. You should
   a. consume more of good A and less of good B.
   b. consume more of good B and less of good A.
   c. keep consuming equal amounts of both goods .
   d. realize that you don't have enough information to answer the question.

9. An economist's answer to the question, "Why do people pollute so much?" is likely to be
   a. people haven't been educated about the importance of the environment.
   b. the government has made sufficient rules about pollution.
   c. people are considering average, not marginal, costs of polluting.
   d. people aren't paying enough for their polluting activities.

10. Five workers are producing a total of 28 units of output. The workers' marginal product
    a. is 5.
    b. is 28.
    c. is 28 divided by 5.
    d. cannot be determined from the information provided.

11. In the production function on the right, in the range marked "A" there are
    a. increasing marginal returns.
    b. diminishing marginal returns.
    c. diminishing absolute returns.
    d. diminishing absolute marginal returns.

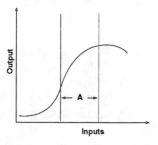

12. The firm is producing an output of 24 and has total costs of 260. Its average total cost
    a. equals 10.83.
    b. equals 8.75.
    c. equals 260.
    d. cannot be determined from the information.

13. The graph at the right
    a. is correct.
    b. is wrong because the average variable cost is above the average total cost.
    c. is wrong because the marginal cost is positioned wrong.
    d. is wrong because the marginal cost and average variable costs are confused.

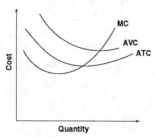

14. If marginal cost is greater than average total cost, then
    a. the average total cost curve is upward sloping.
    b. the average total cost curve is at its low point.
    c. the average total cost curve is downward sloping.
    d. There is no necessary relation between marginal cost and average total costs.

15. Which of the following is true?
    a. All methods of production that are technically efficient must be economically efficient.
    b. All methods of production that are economically efficient must be technically efficient.
    c. Firms will tend toward technically efficient methods of production but not towards economically efficient methods.
    d. There is no relation between economic efficiency and technical efficiency.

16. Explanations for diseconomies of scale include all of the following *except*
    a. as firm size increases, monitoring costs generally increase.
    b. as size of the firm increases, team spirit or morale generally decreases.
    c. as size of the firm increases, monitoring costs generally decrease, thereby increasing other costs.
    d. All of the above are explanations.

17. Total revenue is 1,000; explicit measurable costs are 500.
    a. Accounting profit is 1,000.
    b. Accounting profit is 500.
    c. Accounting profit is 200.
    d. Accounting profit cannot be determined from the figures given

18. Total revenue is 1,000; explicit measurable costs are 500.
    a. Economic profit is 1,000.
    b. Economic profit is 500.
    c. Economic profit is 200.
    d. Economic profit cannot be determined from the figures given.

19. The perceived demand curve of an individual firm in a competitive market is which of the following?
    a. A.
    b. B.
    c. C.
    d. D.

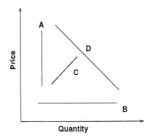

20. A competitive firm is producing at output A on the graph on the right.
    a. It could increase profits by increasing output.
    b. It could increase profits by decreasing output.
    c. It cannot increase profits.
    d. One can say nothing about profits from the diagram on the right.

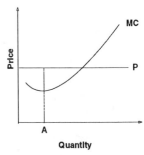

21. In a competitive market which of the following is the firm's supply curve?
    a. The average cost curve.
    b. The marginal cost curve.
    c. The average total cost curve.
    d. The average revenue curve.

22. In the graph on the right, the firm's profit will be measured by
    a. the rectangle ABEF.
    b. the rectangle ACDF.
    c. the rectangle ABHG.
    d. the rectangle ECED.

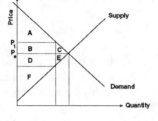

23. In long-run competitive equilibrium
    a. most firms will be going out of business.
    b. most firms will be expanding.
    c. most firms will be making only normal profit.
    d. most firms won't even be making normal profits.

24. In the graph on the right, what area represents the welfare loss from a market
    charging a price P$_1$?
    a. B + C + E + D.
    b. B + D
    c. C.
    d. C + E.

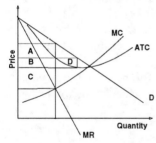

25. In the graph at the right, at what output would a monopolist most likely be
    operating?
    a. Output A.
    b. Output B.
    c. Output C.
    d. Output D.

26. In the graph at the right, which rectangle represents monopolist's profit?
    a. A.
    b. A + B + C.
    c. C + D.
    d. none of the above.

27. When the marginal revenue curve intercepts the quantity axis, the elasticity of demand at that output
    a. is greater than 1.
    b. is less than 1.
    c. is equal to 1.
    d. cannot be determined.

28. In the graph on the right, what areas represent the welfare loss due to a mo-
    nopolist?
    a. A.
    b. A + B.
    c. B + C.
    d. A + B + C.

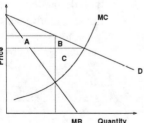

29. In a market there are many firms selling differentiated products. This market is
    a. a competitive market.
    b. a monopolistically competitive market.
    c. an oligopoly.
    d. a monopoly.

30. The top four firms in the industry have 10 percent, 8 percent, 8 percent, and 6 percent of the market. The Herfindahl index of this market is closest which of the following?
    a. 8.
    b. 32.
    c. 66.
    d. 264.

31. In the graph to the right, which of the following is the output chosen by the monopolistically competitive firm?
    a. Q_1.
    b. Q_2.
    c. Q_3.
    d. The information cannot be gained from the graph to the right.

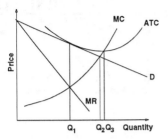

32. The Herfindahl index in an industry is 1500. The economist concludes that the industry is an oligopoly that will charge close to the monopolistic price. This economist is using
    a. the cartel model.
    b. the contestable market model.
    c. the kinked demand curve model.
    d. the strategic pricing model.

33. A market has the following characteristics: Marginal cost equals marginal revenue; it has the most output restrictions; there is only one firm in the market; and there is a possibility of long-run economic profit. The structure of this market is
    a. monopolistic.
    b. oligopolistic.
    c. monopolistically competitive.
    d. perfectly competitive.

Answers

1. a (21:2)	12. a (23:9)	23. c (25:14)
2. a (21:4)	13. b (23:11)	24. d (25:20)
3. b (21:9)	14. a (23:16)	25. a (26:3)
4. c (21:12)	15. b (24:1)	26. a (26:5)
5. b (21:16)	16. c (24:5)	27. c (26:8)
6. c (21:19)	17. b (24:9)	28. c (26:11)
7. c (22:1)	18. d (24:10)	29. b (27:1)
8. b (22:5)	19. b (25:2)	30. d (27:5)
9. d (22:8)	20. a (25:5)	31. a (27:9)
10. d (23:2)	21. b (25:9)	32. a (27:13)
11. b (23:4)	22. b (25:11)	33. a (27:18)

Key: The figures in parentheses refer to multiple choice question and chapter numbers. For example (1:4) is multiple choice question 1 from chapter 4.

Chapter 28:
Competition in the Real World

Chapter at a glance

1. The monitoring problem is that employees' incentives differ from the owner's incentives. Because monitoring these employees is expensive, some economists are studying ways to change the situation. (660)

   An incentive-compatible contract is needed to match the goals of both parties.

2. Corporate takeovers, or simply the threat of a takeover, can improve firms' efficiency. (662)

   The competitive pressures a firm faces limit its laziness and its X-inefficiency.

3. When competitive pressures get strong, individuals often fight back through social and political pressures. Competition is a process—a fight between the forces of monopolization and the forces of competition. (663)

   Everyone applauds competition, except for themselves.

   Competitive markets will exist only if suppliers or demanders don't collude.

4. A natural monopoly is an industry with strong economies of scale so the average cost is continually falling. It can be demonstrated graphically that as the number of firms in a natural monopoly increases, the average cost of producing a fixed number of units also increases. (665)

   Examples of industries that are sometimes considered natural monopolies include local telephone service, cable TV, and electric utilities. Government regulatory boards often regulate the prices charged.

5. Firms protect their monopolies by (1) advertising and lobbying, (2) producing products as nearly unique as possible, and (3) charging low prices. (666)

   Firms will spend money and time to obtain monopoly power until the marginal cost equals the marginal benefit.

6. The economic reasoning process is a useful way to look at many real-world events. (667)

   Economic reasoning involves weighing the marginal benefits against the marginal costs of a course of action.

   See Appendix A: "Economic Reasoning and the Real World: The Example of the Health Care Debate."

Short-answer questions

1. Is the high pay that top-level management receives an example of the monitoring problem? (LO1)

2. What are the implications of the monitoring problem for economics? (LO1)

3. How can corporate takeovers improve firms' efficiency? (LO2)

4. What is meant by the phrase "Competition is a process, not a state"? (LO3)

5. Demonstrate a natural monopoly graphically. (LO4)

6. List three ways in which firms protect their monopoly. (LO5)

7. Economics predicts that third-party payments will increase the quantity demanded of a product and also its price until an alternative effective means of rationing is developed. Explain why. (LO6)

8. Would you expect the funeral home industry to be competitive? Why or why not? (LO6)

Word Scramble

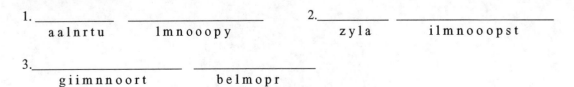

1. _____ _____
     a a l n r t u   l m n o o o p y

2. _____ _____
     z y l a   i l m n o o o p s t

3. _____ _____
     g i i m n n o o r t   b e l m o p r

Match the Terms and Concepts to Their Definitions

___ 1. corporate takeover

___ 2. incentive-compatible contract

___ 3. lazy monopolist

___ 4. monitoring problem

___ 5. natural monopoly

___ 6. patent

___ 7. real-world competition

___ 8. reverse engineering

___ 9. X-inefficiency

a. Problem that employees' incentives differ from the owner's incentives.

b. An agreement in which the incentives and goals of both parties match as closely as possible.

c. Firm that does not push for efficiency, but merely enjoys the position it is already in.

d. Operating less efficiently than technically possible.

e. A firm or a group of individuals issues an offer to buy up the stock of a company to gain control and to install its own managers.

f. A fight between the forces of monopolization and the forces of competition.

g. A legal right to be the sole supplier of a good.

h. Firm buying up other firms' products, disassembling them, figuring out what's special about them, and then copying them within the limits of the law.

i. Industry with strong economies of scale so the average cost is continually falling.

Problems and Exercises

1. Consider the graph on the right representing a firm for a particular industry and answer the following questions.

    a. What sort of monopoly would you characterized this as? Why?

    b. What price would the firm charge if it were unregulated?

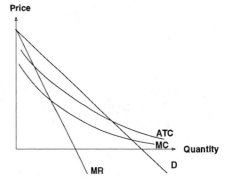

    c. What price would you advise the government the firm should be allowed to charge? Explain your answer.

2. Demonstrate, using the graph on the right, the net gain to producers and the net loss to consumers if suppliers are able to restrict their output to Q_R. What is the net deadweight loss to society?

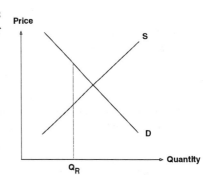

Multiple Choice Questions

1. An incentive-compatible contract is
   a. a contract with sympathetic incentives.
   b. a contract with compatible incentives.
   c. a contract in which the incentive structure corresponds to the firm's goals and managers' goals as much as possible.
   d. a contract that pays bonuses.

2. A firm is making no profit. If there is X-inefficiency, what can we conclude?
   a. The firm is operating economically efficiently.
   b. The firm is operating technically efficiently.
   c. The firm is operating less efficiently than technically possible.
   d. We can say nothing about the efficiency of the firm.

3. The goals of managers are generally
   a. identical to the goals of owners.
   b. identical to the goals of workers.
   c. totally inconsistent with the goals of owners.
   d. somewhat inconsistent with the goals of owners.

4. When there is little competitive pressure, large organizations have a tendency to
   a. make decisions that benefit the consumer.
   b. make decisions that benefit the managers.
   c. make decisions that benefit the owners.
   b. none of the above.

5. Economists would expect that generally
   a. for-profit firms operate more efficiently than nonprofit firms.
   b. nonprofit firms operate more efficiently than for-profit firms.
   c. for-profit firms operate equally efficiently as nonprofit firms.
   d. nonprofit firms cannot exist because they operate so inefficiently.

6. In the graph on the right, if suppliers can restrict output to OL, what area represents the additional amount of revenue the remaining suppliers will receive?
   a. A.
   b. B.
   c. C.
   d. D.

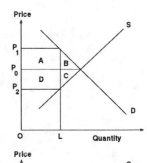

7. In the graph on the right, if demanders can restrict other demanders' purchases to OL, what area represents the additional amount the remaining demanders will receive?
   a. A.
   b. B.
   c. C.
   d. D.

8. In the graph on the right, if suppliers restrict output to OL, what area represents the welfare loss to society?
   a. A + B.
   b. B + C.
   c. C + D.
   d. A + D.

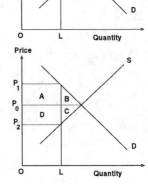

9. A patent is
    a. a type of reverse engineering.
    b. a type of natural monopoly.
    c. a type of corporate takeover.
    d. a type of legal monopoly.

10. If average total costs are decreasing throughout the relevant range of production,
    the industry will be
    a. a natural monopoly.
    b. a prime target for rent-seeking.
    c. a lazy monopolist.
    d. an example of monitoring problems.

11. When firms are allowed to pass on all cost increases to earn a normal profit, they
    a. have a strong incentive to operate efficiently.
    b. have little incentive to operate efficiently.
    c. become a focal point of reverse engineering.
    d. will apply for a patent.

12. Ways in which firms try to protect their monopoly include all the following except
    a. advertising and lobbying.
    b. charging low prices.
    c. making their product unique.
    d. reverse engineering.

13. The fact that funeral homes make high profits on coffins suggests
    a. that the funeral market is not highly competitive.
    b. that the funeral market is highly competitive.
    c. that firms employ price discrimination whenever possible.
    d. that coffins are a unique good.

A1. One of the reasons large companies established employee-related health benefits as a normal job benefit was
    a. the structure of the U.S. tax code, which allowed the cost of those benefits to be deductible.
    b. the structure of the U.S. tax code, which did not allow those costs to be deductible.
    c. the need of employees to cover the expense of their health care.
    d. the need of doctors to be paid for their services.

A2. In health care, cost shifting is
    a. the shifting of costs from the rich to the poor.
    b. the shifting of costs from the poor to the rich.
    c. the shifting of costs from uninsured persons to insured persons.
    d. the shifting of costs from rich uninsured persons to poor insured persons.

A3. In the graph on the right, if there is third-party payment of fees, the quantity
    demanded by individuals will likely be
    a. A.
    b. B.
    c. C.
    d. D.

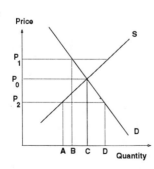

A4. A major advantage of the single-payer health care plan is
    a. simplified administration.
    b. it will avoid all non-price rationing.
    c. it will be financed by government and thus individuals won't have to pay.
    d. it involves only a slight change from the current system.

A5. Under the direct competition plan of reorganizing health care
    a. there would be a single payer.
    b. all health benefits would be made non-taxable.
    c. all health benefits would be made taxable.
    d. the direct competition plan would replace price competition with non-price competition.

Answers

Short-answer questions

1. The monitoring problem is the problem of seeing that self-seeking individuals working for an organization follow the goals of the organization rather than their own goals. The high pay that top-level management gets might be pay for performance, or it might be an example of the monitoring problem. To determine which it is, one would need to consider the specific case and determine whether there are incentive-compatible contracts (probably low base pay and high option bonuses) that make the managers' goals consistent with the goals of the firms' owners. (662)

2. Economics assumes that firms and the economy operate efficiently because firms maximize profits. The monitoring problem undermines that assumption since managers, to some degree, will follow their own goals rather than the profit-maximizing goal. Firms may become lazy monopolists and exhibit X-inefficiency. So the monitoring problem has significant implications. The degree to which firms become lazy monopolists will be limited, however, by competition. (661-663)

3. Answer 2 above pointed out that when there is a monitoring problem a firm can exhibit X-inefficiency—it can have higher costs than necessary. When that happens, the firm's stock price will fall and it may be worthwhile for another firm to come in and take the inefficient firm over, eliminate the inefficiency, and develop better incentive-compatible contracts. Often, these takeovers are financed by large amounts of debt, which means that the resulting firm must make high interest payments. So even if the new firm does not establish incentive-compatible contracts, the high debt can force the firm to operate more efficiently. (661-662)

4. The basic idea of economics is that self-seeking individuals try to do the best they can for themselves—to make life as easy as possible for themselves. One of the important ways in which they can do that is to create a monopoly for themselves. When they do that they create the possibility of profits for other individuals who come in and steal their market—thereby breaking down their monopoly. This process of monopolization and competition breaking down the resulting monopoly is pervasive in our economy and is what is meant by the phrase, "Competition is a process, not a state." (663-665)

5. The graph to the right demonstrates a natural monopoly. It occurs when an industry has sufficiently strong economies of scale so that the average cost is continually falling. The introduction of a second firm will increase the average cost of production. (665)

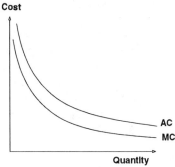

6. Three ways in which firms protect their monopoly are (1) advertising and lobbying; (2) producing products as nearly unique as possible, and (3) charging low prices (a form of limit or stay-out pricing). All these methods cost the firms money in the short run, but increase their monopoly rents in the long run. (666-667)

7. Third party payments separate the payee from the user of the service and unless rationing is imposed upon the user by the payee, economic reasoning predicts that the quantity demanded will increase as demanders move out along their demand curve to the lower price (shown by the movement from point A to Point B in the graph on the right). If suppliers supply that quantity demanded, costs will be pushed up enormously (from C to D) and suppliers will be looking for ways to ration demand of the good among users. This is essentially what is currently happening with the U.S. health care system. These issues are discussed in the appendix. See especially Exhibit A1 and pages 673-678.

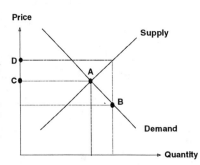

8. As discussed in the text it can be hard to judge competition in a particular market, and funeral homes are no exception. In terms of structure, we tend to see a number of fairly small sellers, so an argument could be made that it is competitive. But the market is one in which information flows are limited, and, when people use the industry, they are not in their most rational state. So probably we would not expect the funeral industry to be highly competitive. (667-669)

Word Scramble   1. natural monopoly   2. lazy monopolist   3. monitoring problem

Match the Terms and Concepts to Their Definitions
1-e; 2-b; 3-c; 4-a; 5-i; 6-g; 7-f; 8-h; 9-d.

Problems and Exercises

1. a. This represents a natural monopoly because average costs are always falling. Natural monopolies exist because certain industries have strong economies of scale. (665-666).

    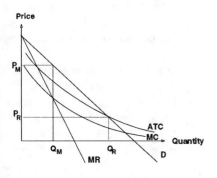

    b. The natural monopolist would produce quantity where $MC = MR$ and charge the price that corresponds to that quantity from the demand curve. This combination is shown on the graph to the right as (Q_M, P_M). (665-666)
    c. I would advise the government that the natural monopolist should be regulated to charge a price where average costs intersects the demand curve. This way, the monopolist earns normal profit. You cannot require that $MC = P$ because $MC < AC$ and the monopolist would not be able to survive under these circumstances. (665-666)

2. As shown on the graph to the right, if suppliers restrict supply to Q_R, they will be able to charge a price of P_R, which is higher than competitive price, P_C. This gives suppliers supplying Q_R additional income, labeled A. Some suppliers are excluded from the market $(Q_C - Q_R)$. They lose area C in producer surplus. Consumers who cannot purchase goods lose consumer surplus represented by area B. Those who can buy goods pay the higher price. Higher expenditures are represented by area A (the additional income to firms). Since A is transferred from consumers to producers, this is not a loss to society. Areas B and C are lost by consumers and producers, respectively, but not transferred to anyone. Those areas are the deadweight loss to society. (661-662)

    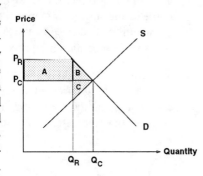

Multiple Choice Questions

1. c. While incentive-compatible contracts could pay bonuses, they do not necessarily have to, which rules out d. The b option doesn't say anything—compatible with what? The c option is the definition found in the text. See page 660.

2. c. Whenever there is X-inefficiency, the firm is operating technically inefficiently. See page 661 and the discussion of efficiency in an earlier chapter.

3. d. Managers' goals are quite inconsistent with the goals of the owners. However, the managers do not want to get fired and the competitive pressures out there mean that managers must make sufficient profits that they don't get fired. To that degree, their goals are consistent with the goals of the owners. See pages 660-661.

4. b. As discussed on pages 660-663, when there are not competitive pressures, organizations have a tendency to make decisions that benefit employees or the decision-makers rather than the owners or consumers.

5. a. While for-profit firms can exhibit inefficiency, the market limits that inefficiency. See pages 661-662.

6. a. The new price will be P_1, so existing suppliers will increase their rents by A. See Exhibit 3, page 664.

7. d. The new price will be P_2, so existing demanders will increase their consumer surplus by D. Notice that when it is demanders that keep other demanders out, the demand falls and the price falls. See Exhibit 3, page 664.

8. b. The welfare loss is the triangle made up of areas B and C. This area represents the producer and consumer surplus lost by both but not gained by the other. The other areas represent transfers. See Exhibit 3, page 664.

9. d. See page 664.

10. a. The a answer is the best. The other answers may fit, but nowhere near as closely. The statement you are asked to complete is essentially the definition of a natural monopoly. See pages 665-666.

11. b. When you can pass on cost increases, why try to hold costs down? See page 666.

12. d. Reverse engineering is a method firms use to try to break down other firms' monopolies. (665)

13. c. Firms have a tendency to try to price discriminate whenever possible. Charging high prices for coffins is a way of doing so; whether the market is competitive or not depends on whether those high prices are offset with low prices on other services the coffin sellers provide. Finally, dying is an expensive proposition but that fact need not be related to the high profits on coffins. See pages 667-669.

A1. a. The answer c is incorrect because while employees definitely like to have the employer cover their health care costs, there is no reason the employer could not pay the employees a high enough wage so that the employees could pay for their own health care. The answer d is incorrect because higher wages paid by employers would allow employees to pay doctors' fees. See page 674.

A2. c. The uninsured rich can afford to pay their medical bills, so hospitals shift some of the costs of caring for uninsured patients to the bills of the rich uninsured patients, because otherwise the hospitals would not get that money for caring for the poor uninsured. Answer b is a possibility, but the rich would complain a lot since they are paying their own bills. It is a third-party payment problems associated with insurance. See page 675.

A3. d. When there are third party payments of fees, individuals will face a lower price, and will increase their quantity demanded. See Exhibit A1 and pages 673-675.

A4. a. While there may be debate about the simplified administration of a single-payer health care plan, there will be considerable savings in the elimination of multiple insurance forms. The others are simply wrong. While government may pay for the plan, individuals will still have to ultimately pay with their taxes. See pages 676-677.

A5. c. One of the reasons we moved away from individuals paying for their own health care was that firms were allowed to deduct medical benefits. To move away from that, all health benefits would have to be made taxable. See page 677.

Chapter 29:
Politics and Economics: The Case of Agricultural Markets

Chapter at a glance

1. In farming, the good/bad paradox is the phenomenon of doing poorly because you're doing well. (680)

   Because of the inelastic demand for farm goods, a good harvest (increase in supply) means revenues (income) to farmers falls.

2. The general rule of political economy states that small groups that are significantly affected by a government policy will lobby more effectively than large groups that are equally affected by that same policy. (683)

   The farm lobby has been successful in generating higher prices and incomes for farmers even though consumers and taxpayers are worse off.

3. In a price support system, the government maintains a higher-than-equilibrium price. (684)

   Because the price support creates a surplus which causes downward pressure on the price, government tries to offset this by various measures.

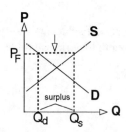

4. Four methods of price support are: (686)
   1. Regulatory methods.
   2. Economic incentives to reduce supply.
   3. Subsidize the sale of the good.
   4. Buying up and storing the good (or giving it away). The distributional effects are shown in Exhibit 3 on page 684.

✔ *Note: #2 is sometimes referred to as an acreage control program or a land bank program. #4 is often referred to as a non-recourse loan program.*

✔ *Know these! Study Exhibit 3! For each of these know who benefits the most and who is hurt the most—evaluate them.*

✔ *The two prevalent farm programs in the U.S. have been:*
   1. *the land bank program and*
   2. *non-recourse loan program (similar to option #4 above and discussed in the textbook).*

5. Many economists are cynical about the recent agricultural policy reform because when one looks carefully at the law that was actually passed, farmers got freedom to produce, but other programs to protect them remain in place and there are doubts that the changes will survive if farmers face difficult times. (689)

   Always keep in mind the general law of political economy. It will likely remain alive and well.

   See also, Appendix A: "History of U.S. Farm Program."

Short-answer questions

1. What is the good/bad paradox in farming? (LO1)

2. What is the underlying cause of the good/bad paradox in farming? (LO1)

3. What is the general rule of political economy in a democracy? (LO2)

4. How does a price support system works? (LO3)

5. What are the four price support options? (LO4)

6.   What are the distributional consequences of the four alternative methods of price support? Use supply and demand curves to support your answers. (LO4)

7.   What made it politically possible for the U.S. government to vote to eliminate aspects of the farm price support program by 2002? (LO5)

8.   Why are many economists cynical about the recent changes in farm price supports? (LO5)

Word Scramble

1._____   _____   2._____ / _____ _____
      x s s e e c   u d b e r n   o o g d   d b a   a a d o p r x

3._____   _____   _____
      c r i p e   s o r t p u p   r r o g p a m

Match the Terms and Concepts to Their Definitions

___ 1. excess burden

___ 2. general rule of political economy

___ 3. good/bad paradox

___ 4. grandfather in

___ 5. price stabilization program

___ 6. price support program

a. Small groups that are significantly affected by a government policy will lobby more effectively than large groups that are equally affected by that same policy.

b. The phenomenon of doing poorly because you are doing well.

c. Program designed to eliminate short-run fluctuations in prices but allow prices to follow their long-term trend line.

d. Program that maintains prices at a level higher than the market prices.

e. To pass a law affecting a specific group but providing that those in the group before the law was passed are not subject to the law.

f. Loss to society caused by a policy introducing a wedge between marginal private and marginal social costs and benefits.

Problems and Exercises

1. Hog farming has become high tech. Companies now house thousands of genetically uniform pigs in large complexes and regulate their environment electronically. The effect of this technological change has been to increase the supply of pigs. The farm lobby is trying to convince government to regulate this industry.

   a. Why would the technological development be troublesome to pig farmers who have small operations? (Hint: use the good/bad paradox). Demonstrate this using supply and demand curves.

   b. Show the effect of regulation when it restricts the development of new agrifirms in order to get back to the original price. Who is hurt? Who is helped?

c. Show the effect of a price support system in which government buys up all the supply that consumers don't buy at the support price equal to the original price. Who is hurt? Who is helped?

d. Show the effect of a price subsidy in which the government buys hogs at the original price, P_0, and then sells the hogs to consumers at P_2 so there is no surplus. Who is hurt? Who is helped?

e. Which would the government favor if it wants to balance its budget without increasing taxes ? Why?

2. Consider the following market demand and supply schedules for peanuts in the U.S.

	Price per ton	Quantity supplied in millions of tons	Quantity demanded in millions of tons
A	$50	-1.0	4.25
B	100	-0.5	4.0
C	150	0	3.75
D	200	0.5	3.5
E	250	1.0	3.25
F	300	1.5	3.0
G	350	2.0	2.75
H	400	2.5	2.5
I	450	3.0	2.25
J	500	3.5	2.0
K	550	4.0	1.75
L	600	4.5	1.5

a. Graph the corresponding demand and supply curves. What is equilibrium price and quantity?

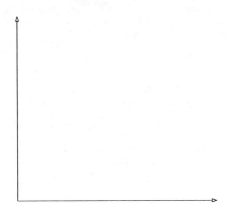

b. Calculate the elasticity of supply from H to G. Calculate the elasticity of demand from H to G. (Use the arc convention).

c. How would you characterize the elasticity of supply and demand calculated in (b)?

d. What would happen to revenue for peanut growers if price fell from H to G?

e. Suppose a technological innovation in peanut growing shifts supply to the following:

	Price per ton	Quantity supplied in millions of tons
A	$50	-.25
B	100	.25
C	150	.75
D	200	1.25
E	250	1.75
F	300	2.25
G	350	2.75
H	400	3.25
I	450	3.75
J	500	4.25
K	550	4.75
L	600	5.25

Demonstrate the effect of this technological innovation on the graph in (a). What is equilibrium quantity and price.

f. As a result of the efforts by the peanut lobby, the government agrees to buy up all the supply that consumer's don't buy at the original equilibrium price. Show this program graphically.

g. Calculate how much consumers benefit or are hurt. Calculate the cost to taxpayers.

Multiple Choice Questions

1. The good/bad paradox exists because there is
   a. an inelastic demand for agricultural goods.
   b. an inelastic supply of agricultural goods.
   c. an elastic demand for agricultural goods.
   d. an elastic supply of agricultural goods.

2. Agriculture is a highly productive industry. This enormous productivity has
   a. caused agriculture to increase in relative importance as a percent of output.
   b. caused agriculture to decrease in relative importance as a percent of output.
   c. caused farmers to be rich and prosperous.
   d. increased the share of the labor force working in agriculture.

3. Say that most apple farmers are having a bad crop, but that in your particular area the weather was great so you are having a great crop. You would
   a. be unhappy because of the good/bad paradox.
   b. favor price controls.
   c. not be hurt by the good/bad paradox.
   d. receive a low price for your apple crop and not be able to sell much of it.

4. In the graph to the right, what area represents the change in income going to farmers from an increase in supply from S_0 to S_1?
    a. A - C.
    b. A + C.
    c. A + B + C.
    d. C - A.

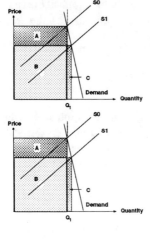

5. In the graph to the right, what area represents the final income going to farmers after the supply shifts out from S_0 to S_1?
    a. A + B.
    b. B + C.
    c. A + C.
    d. A + B + C.

6. Most farmers would
    a. prefer a price stabilization program over a price support program
    b. prefer a price support program over a price stabilization program.
    c. be indifferent between a price support program and a price stabilization program.
    d. oppose both a price support program a price stabilization program.

7. The general rule of political economy in a democracy states
    a. small groups that are significantly affected by a government policy will lobby more effectively than will large groups who are equally affected by that policy.
    b. large groups that are significantly affected by a government policy will lobby more effectively than small groups who are equally affected by that policy.
    c. large groups will always win in majority rule situations
    d. Congress will always be inefficient.

8. In the graph to the right the government imposes quantity restrictions at Q_1 on suppliers. As compared to the free market situation
    a. suppliers' net income will fall by B.
    b. suppliers' net income will rise by A.
    c. suppliers' net income will rise by A - B.
    d. suppliers' net income will be unaffected.

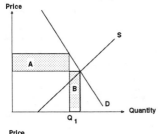

9. In the graph at the right, the government gives enough economic incentives to suppliers to decrease output sufficiently so that the price rises to $5. The area best representing the amount of those incentives is
    a. A.
    b. A + B.
    c. A - B.
    d. A + B + C.

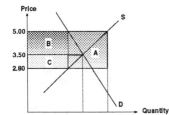

10. In the graph at the right, the government gives enough economic incentives to suppliers to decrease output sufficiently so that the price rises to $5. The area best representing the amount that this program transfers from consumers to suppliers is
    a. A.
    b. B
    c. C
    d. A + B + C.

11. In the graph at the right, if the government sets a price floor of $5 and buys up the surplus, the area best representing the cost to the government is
    a. A.
    b. A + B.
    c. B + C.
    d. A + C.

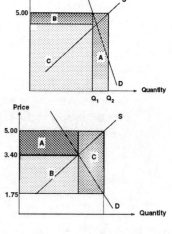

12. In the graph at the right, if the government subsidizes the sale of wheat so that farmers get $5 but the price to consumers is brought down to $1.75, the cost to the government of doing so will be best represented by the area
    a. A.
    b. C.
    c. A +B.
    d. A + B + C.

13. You are the adviser to the president who wants to subsidize the price of wheat so that consumers pay a price of $1.50 per bushel. The current price of wheat is $2 and 100 bushels are being demanded. The president asks you what the program will likely cost. You respond that it will cost
    a. $0.
    b. something, but less than $50.
    c. $50.
    d. more than $50.

14. Economic theory tells us that
    a. farm subsidies are bad policy.
    b. farm subsidies have costs and benefits.
    c. farm subsidies are responsible for the enormous increase in productivity in agriculture.
    d. farm subsidies hurt farmers.

Answers

Short-answer questions

1. The good/bad paradox in farming is the phenomenon of doing poorly because you are doing well. That is, total revenue declines even though crop yield has risen. (680)

2. The underlying cause of the good/bad paradox in farming is that demand for agricultural goods is inelastic so that if the supply of an agricultural good increases, and its price declines, total revenue also declines. (681)

3. The general rule of political economy in a democracy is that small groups that are significantly affected by a government policy will lobby more effectively than large groups that are equally affected by that same policy. (683)

4. In a price support system, the government maintains a higher than equilibrium price. At support price P1, the quantity of goods demanded is only Q_D while the quantity supplied is Q_S. This causes downward pressure on the price, shown by arrow A, which must be offset by government measures shown by arrow B. (684-686)

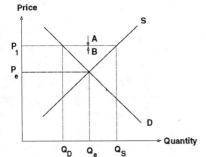

5. The four price support options are (1) regulatory force, (2) economic incentives to reduce supply, (3) subsidizing the sale of goods to consumers, and (4) buying up and giving away, storing, or destroying the good. (684-686)

6. The distributional consequences of the four alternative methods of price support are shown in the four graphs below. (684-687)

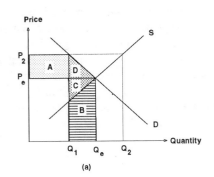

(a)

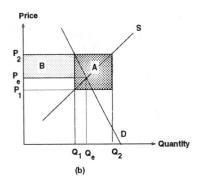

(b)

Graph (a) shows the effect of regulatory measures. Farmers are allowed to produce at Q_1. The farmers who can no longer sell their goods lose areas *B* and *C* but gain back *B* in their other pursuits. Revenue to remaining producers increases by area *A*. Consumers lose areas A and D in consumer surplus. Areas *C* and *D* are lost to society.

Graph (b) shows the effect of providing economic incentives to reduce supply by paying farmers not to produce. It must pay farmers the difference between market price and the support price. The government has to pay farmers area A to reduce the quantity supplied to Q_1. Existing farmers receive payment A from the government and get rectangle B from consumers in the form of higher prices. Consumers pay a higher price for fewer goods.

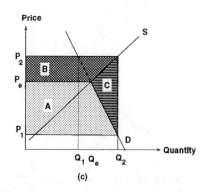

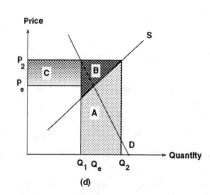

Graph (c) shows the effect of subsidizing the sale of the good. Suppliers supply quantity Q_2 to the government and are paid the price support P_2. Consumers purchase Q_2 at P_1 from the government. They are benefitted by area A, getting more goods at a lower price. Suppliers are benefited by area B, getting a higher price. The taxpayers foot the bill which equals $A + B + C$.

Graph (d) shows the effect of the government buying up the all goods that consumers do not buy at the support price, P_2, and storing or otherwise disposing of the good. The government pays the farmers area $A + B$. The farmers gain area $B + C$. Taxpayers foot the bill of $A + B$. To the extent that the government can get something for the goods it bought, its expenses are lower than area $A + B$. Area C is transferred from consumers to producers.

7. A combination of three forces made it politically possible to eliminate farm support programs: (1) the government deficit, which put pressure on the government to reduce expenditures on costly programs, (2) the ability of U.S. farmers to sell their goods abroad, which reduced the benefits of the existing farm support program, and (3) the general pro-market ideology that gained favor in the 1990s. (689)

8. Many economists are cynical about the recent changes in the farm price support program because although farmers gained the freedom to produce what they choose, other farm support programs remained in place. Three of the programs which most sharply limit production--peanuts, sugar, and dairy products--were left untouched. Secondly, while in a number of areas direct price supports were eliminated, other indirect price support programs were not eliminated. Thirdly, to compensate farmers for the elimination of the price support programs, government has promised to provide direct grants to farmers, regardless of market conditions. Lastly, many economists are concerned that if times become difficult for farmers, there will be a reversal of policy and more beneficial programs to farmers will be introduced. (680, 689)

Word Scramble   1. excess burden   2. good/bad paradox   3. price support program

Match the Terms and Concepts to Their Definitions
1-f; 2-a; 3-b; 4-e; 5-c; 6-d.

Problems and Exercises

1. a. Farmers are upset because demand for pork is relatively inelastic. This is shown in the graph to the right. Before the new technology, price and quantity are P_0 and Q_0. Total income is $P_0 Q_0$. The supply of pigs, however, has shifted to S_1 with the development of agrifirms. Now, equilibrium price is P_1 and quantity is Q_1. Because demand is inelastic, farmers' income has fallen. The lost income, area A, is greater than the gain in income, area C. (680-682)

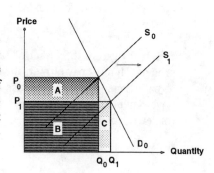

b. In this case, the government would restrict the supply of hogs to Q_0. Farmers' total revenue increases by area A and decreases by areas C and E. There is a net gain in revenue to suppliers. Some suppliers who want to supply $Q_1 - Q_0$ must be excluded from the market. Consumers must pay a higher price, P_0 and get a lower quantity, Q_0. The darkened triangle, areas D and E, represent deadweight loss. It represents a loss to society from the quantity restriction. (684-686)

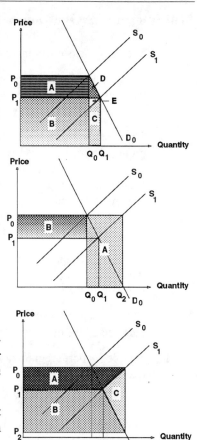

c. Consumers buy Q_0 at P_0. The government buys $Q_2 - Q_0$ at price P_0, paying rectangle A in total. Consumer surplus equal to rectangle B is transferred to hog farmers. Taxpayers are hurt who have to pay rectangle A for goods that most likely cannot be sold elsewhere. Consumers are hurt by having to pay a higher price for fewer goods. (687, 688)

d. In this case, government spends $P_0 Q_2$ to buy the hogs and sells them for $P_2 Q_2$. Consumers benefit from enjoying the lower price P_2 and higher quantity represented by a net gain of area B. Suppliers benefit from a higher price, P_0, a and higher quantity, Q_2. Their net gain is represented by area A. The cost to taxpayers, however, is areas A, B and C, so the net welfare loss is area C. (687, 688)

e. If government wanted to hold government expenditures down, it would favor (b) because the direct cost to government is zero, although there are enforcement and administrative costs. (684-686, 688)

2. a. The corresponding demand and supply curves are shown to the right. Equilibrium quantity and supply is where the two intersect: Quantity is 2.5 million tons at a price of $400 per ton. (681-684)

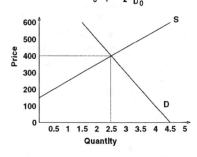

b. $E_S = 1.6$; $E_D = 0.8$. The elasticity of supply is percent change in quantity supplied divided by the percent change in price. From H to G this is $[(2.5\text{-}2)/2.25]/[(400\text{-}350)/375] = .22/.13 = 1.7$. The elasticity of demand is percent change in quantity demanded divided by the percent change in price. From H to G this is $|[(2.5\text{-}2.75)/2.675]/[(400\text{-}350)/375]| = .09/.13 = 0.7$. (681-684)

c. Supply is elastic since $E_S > 1$; Demand is inelastic since $E_D < 1$. (515)

d. Since demand is inelastic between H and G, total revenue would fall. (515)

e. The shift in the supply curve is shown in the graph to the right. Supply shifts from S_0 to S_1. Equilibrium quantity is now 2.75 million tons. Equilibrium price is now $350 per ton. (681-689)

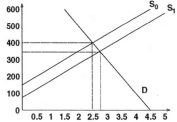

f. This program is shown in the graph to the right. Consumers buy 2.5 million tons at $400 per ton. Government buys 0.75 million tons at $400, spending a total of area A, or $300 million. (684-687)

g. Consumers pay an extra $50 per ton over the $350 they would have paid if the new equilibrium were reached. This means they pay an additional $125 million (2.5 million x 50). This is represented by area B. The cost to taxpayers is area A, or $300 million. (684-687)

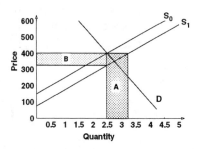

Multiple Choice Questions

1. a. The inelastic demand makes the total revenue vary inversely with shifts in supply. See pages 680-681.

2. b. The high level of productivity has led to falling food prices, and decreases agriculture in relative importance as a percent of the economy's output. This is an example of the long-run good/bad paradox. See pages 680-681.

3. c. The good/bad paradox applies when you are part of a group of farmers that is having a bad year or a group of farmers that is having a good year. In the question, most farmers belong to a group that is having a bad year. In a year like that, if you are an individual who is having a good (or great) year when, generally, most farmers are having a bad year, answer d is wrong because for you the effect is the opposite (you sell a lot and receive a high price for what you sell). Although this case is not explicitly discussed in the text, common sense should have suggested the answer. Remember, don't give up your common sense; sharpen it. See pages 680-682 for the general discussion.

4. d. The increased income from the higher quantity is the area C and the lost income from the lower price is the area $A,$ so the net change in income igoing to farmers the area C-A. It is a loss because the demand is inelastic. See pages 680-682, especially Exhibit 1.

5. b. The revenue or income going to farmers is represented by the rectangle determined by the price they receive and the quantity they sell. See pages 680-682, especially Exhibit 1.

6. b. A price support program raises the price they receive above market price as well as stabilizes their price. See pages 682-683.

7. a. The d option may be true, but it is not the general rule of political economy. See page 683.

8. c. Suppliers will lose the income B because of the quantity restriction, but will gain the area A due to the higher price. See Exhibit 3, page 685.

9. a. To induce farmers not to produce when they can receive a price of $5 for their produce, the government will have to offer enough to offset their opportunity cost, which starts at $2.80 and goes up to $5. If the government could price-discriminate with the incentives, it might be able to pay less, but a is still the best of the options given. See Exhibit 3, page 685.

10. b. Consumers lose the area under the demand curve at the higher price. Of that, producers gain the area B in additional revenue. The triangles are welfare losses. (685)

11. a. With a price floor of $5 the surplus will be Q_2-Q_1, for which the government will have to pay $5. See Exhibit 3, page 685.

12. d. If the price to consumers is held down, at $1.75 the quantity supplied will be Q_2. and subsidy will have to be $3.25. See pages 685 and 687.

13. d. The subsidy will increase the quantity demanded and increase the price farmers get, so the final cost of the subsidy will be more than the 50 cents per bushel that it would cost if nothing changed. See pages 685 and 687.

14. b. Answer a is wrong because economic theory does not tell us anything about policy other than that it has costs and benefits. Theory, combined with value judgments and historical knowledge about the way subsidies have worked out in the past, can mean that most economists oppose farm subsidies, but that judgment is not based solely on theory. See page 690.

Chapter 30:
Microeconomic Policy and Economic Reasoning

Chapter at a glance

1. Economists' views on social policy differ widely because (1) their objective economic analyses are colored by their subjective value judgments; (2) their interpretations of economic issues and of how political and social institutions work vary widely; and (3) their proposals are often based on various models that focus on different aspects of problems. (698)

   Analysis should be as objective as possible.

2. Liberal and conservative economists agree on many policy prescriptions because they use the same models. These models focus on incentives and individual choice. (700)

   There is more agreement among economists than most lay people realize because they all use cost/ benefit analysis.

3. Economists believe many regulations are formulated for political expediency and do not reflect cost/ benefit considerations. (701)

   Economists argue government should keep regulating until marginal benefits of regulation just equal marginal costs of regulating.

4. Cost/benefit analysis is analysis in which one assigns a cost and benefit to alternatives, and draws a conclusion on the basis of those costs and benefits. (701)

   Unfortunately, not all costs and benefits (especially social and political) can be easily quantified.

5. Applying economics is much more than muttering "supply and demand." Economics involves the thoughtful use of economic insights and empirical evidence. (705)

   To be thoughtful requires a careful consideration of all views: mainstream, radical, and conservative.

Short-answer questions

1. What are three reasons why the statement "If you laid all economists end to end, they still wouldn't reach a conclusion" is partly true with regard to social policy? (LO1)

2. Although the quotation in question 1 has some validity, nevertheless liberal and conservative economists often agree in their views on social policy. What is the basis for their agreement? (LO2)

3. When it comes to the actions of politicians, most economists are cynics. Why? (LO3)

4. What is *cost/benefit analysis*? (LO4)

5. Your friend finds you tucked away in a cozy chair in the library studying for an economics exam on policy issues. Your friend says, "Why are you wasting your time? All you have to remember is *supply and demand* and you'll be able to answer any question in economics." How do you respond? (LO5)

Word Scramble

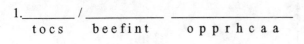

1. _____ / _____ _____
   tocs   beefint   opprhcaa

2. _____ _____ _____
   arpteo   imptloa   solicpie

Match the Terms and Concepts to Their Definitions

___ 1. cost/benefit approach

___ 2. Pareto-optimal policies

a. Approach in which one assigns a cost and benefit to alternatives, and draws a conclusion on the basis of those costs and benefits.

b. Policies that benefit some people and hurt no one.

Problems and Exercises

1. Which of the following regulations would you recommend government implement?

   a. A regulation requiring airline mechanics to check whether all bolts are tightened. This decreases the probability of having an accident by .001. The cost of the average crash is estimated at $200 million for the plane and $400 million in lives. The cost of implementing the program is $16 million.

   b. A regulation requiring all cars have driver-side airbags. This adds $500 to the cost of a car. Having an airbag in a car reduces the chance of dying in a car crash by 1/720. The average individual values his/her life at $500,000.

   c. A regulation stiffening government rules for workplace safety. The cost per worker is $5,000 and the regulations are expected to reduce workplace fatalities by .002. Workers value their lives at an average $2 million.

   d. What are the shortfalls of using the cost/benefit approach to decide (a), (b), and (c)?

Multiple Choice Questions

1. All the following are reasons why economists differ in their views about social policy *except*
   a. policy proposals are based on various models that focus on different aspects of a problem.
   b. policy must be based on imprecise evidence.
   c. some economists can't come to a conclusion.
   d. ideas about social policy are inevitably influenced by subjective value judgments.

2. A Pareto-optimal policy is
   a. a policy that hurts no one.
   b. a policy that benefits all.
   c. a policy that benefits some people and hurts no one.
   d. a policy that benefits more than it hurts.

3. Most economists would advise that real-world governments
   a. follow only Pareto-optimal policies.
   b. primarily follow Pareto-optimal policy.
   c. generally should oppose Pareto-optimal policies.
   d. none of the above.

4. How would a radical economist's analysis of the labor market likely differ from a mainstream neoclassical economist's analysis?
   a. The radical economist's analysis would be more subjective.
   b. The radical economist's analysis would focus on public choice issues.
   c. The radical economist's analysis would focus on tensions among social classes.
   d. The radical economist's analysis would focus more on incentives for the poor.

5. An economist might advise a developing country to turn down the offer of a free dialysis machine because
   a. the marginal cost of using it exceeds the costs of other, more beneficial, life-saving technology.
   b. the average cost of using it exceeds the costs of other, more beneficial, life-saving technology.
   c. there is no such thing as a free machine.
   d. other developing countries may need it more.

6. Say that the implicit value of life people show in their automobile airbag purchases is around $500,000, and is around $5,000,000 in their premium-tire usage. This suggests
   a. that people are not being rational.
   b. that there is a cost of rationality.
   c. that there are other issues involved in the decision, not taken into account in the decision.
   d. any of the above.

7. Suppose that filtering your water at home reduces your chances from dying of giardia (a disease caused by an intestinal parasite) by 1/450. The filter costs you $400 to install. You have chosen to install the filter. Which dollar value best reflects the value you implicitly place on your life?
   a. $180
   b. $1,800.
   c. $18,000.
   d. $180,000.

8. The textbook author would argue that if an initial cost/benefit analysis came out in favor of a project,
   a. the project should be undertaken.
   b. the project should not be undertaken.
   c. that analysis should be used as one dimension in the decision.
   d. none of the above.

9. Thomas Carlyle once said that all you have to do is teach a parrot the words "supply and demand" and you have an economist. According to the textbook author
   a. Carlyle is right, because if you can use the terms properly you can get an A on the exam.
   b. Carlyle is wrong, because applying the supply/demand model involves the thoughtful use of economic insights and empirical evidence.
   c. Carlyle is right as long as one understands the concept of elasticity.
   d. Carlyle is wrong, because economics necessarily involves the use of normative issues that cannot be integrated with supply and demand analysis.

Answers

Short-answer questions

1. The statement is true to the extent that economists sometimes differ in their views on social policy. Three reasons for their differing views are that (1) economists' suggestions are based upon subjective value judgments, (2) economists interpret data and the workings of institutions differently, and (3) economists use different models to explain the problem. (698)

2. Liberal and conservative economists often agree in their views on social policy because they use the same models, which focus on incentives and individual choice. (700)

3. The typical economist views regulations as the result of political expediency, not a reflection of cost/benefit considerations. Most economists believe that decisions should be made on a cost/benefit basis to society instead of on the pressure placed on politicians by special interest groups. (701-704)

4. *Cost/benefit analysis* is an analysis in which one assigns a cost and benefit to alternatives and draws a conclusion on the basis of those costs and benefits. (701-702)

5. You tell a friend to remember the admonition in your textbook: "Teaching a parrot the phrase *supply and demand* does not make it an economist." Elaborating, you tell her that economics involves the thoughtful use of economic insights and empirical evidence. Real-world problems are complex and cannot be explained just with simple models. You are right in taking the time to learn the details. (704-705)

Word Scramble   1. cost/benefit approach   2. pareto-optimal policies

Match the Terms and Concepts to Their Definitions
   1-a; 2-b.

Problems and Exercises

1. For each of these, you calculate the costs and benefits of the regulation. If the cost is higher than the benefit, you would recommend not implementing the program. If the cost is lower than the benefit, you would recommend implementing the program. For each you are assuming you are given all relevant information.
    a. The benefit is saving a plane worth $200 million and saving lives worth $400 million. The regulation reduces the probability of a crash by .001. The marginal benefit is .001 times $600 million = $600,000. The marginal cost is $16 million. Don't implement the program. Marginal cost is more than marginal benefit. (701-702)
    b. The benefit is value of life saved of $500,000 times the increased probability of living, 1/720 = $694. This is greater than the marginal cost to consumers of $500. Implement the program. (702)
    c. The benefit is value of life saved of $2 million times the increased probability of not having a fatal accident, .002 = $4,000. The marginal cost is $5,000 per worker, which is greater than the marginal benefit. Don't implement the program. (702)
    d. The above examples include only quantifiable costs and benefits and involve a huge amount of ambiguity and subjectivity in the calculations. Economists' estimates of the benefit of lives and costs of the program can vary enormously, thus affecting the recommendation enormously. (702-704)

Multiple Choice Questions

1. c. Some economists might not be able to come to a conclusion, but then they would have no view on social policy. Besides, the other three are specifically mentioned on page 698.

2. c. Answer c is the definition given on page 698. It includes both benefiting some people and hurting no one.

3. d. In the real world, policies inevitably hurt some people and help others, so the concept can only be used as a theoretical guide, not as a real-world policy criterion. (698)

4. c. The radical economist's model is designed around class structures whereas mainstream economists do not use class structure. See page 699.

5. a. The a answer is clearly correct, and is discussed on page 700. The c and d answers have some validity but would not be the way an economist would express it. Remember the instructions are to choose the *best* answer consistent with the book.

6. d. Economists are heavily committed to the rationality analysis, and if these numbers are correct, the decision makers in this question are not being rational. All the answers are possible, which leaves d as the best answer. See page 702.

7. d. You implicitly value your life at $(450 \times \$400) = \$180,000$. See page 702.

8. c. As discussed on pages 702-704, the textbook author believes that cost/benefit analyses are not definitive but are simply one part of the analysis. Costs have many dimensions and involve subjectivity and ambiguity; thus, cost/benefit analysis must be used with common sense in which other dimensions of the problem must be added to the consideration. If, after all the costs and benefits were taken into account, cost/benefit analysis came out in favor of a project, the author would probably say it should be undertaken, but there's almost always another cost that hasn't been taken into account.

9. b. This is a question that requires reading between the lines, or a good memory, since b is the answer given on page 705. For the textbook author, getting an A on the exam is not what economics is about, and normative issues can (and must) be integrated with supply and demand analysis.

Chapter 31: The Role of Government in the Economy

Chapter at a glance

1. Two insights behind economists' support of markets are: (1) if people voluntarily trade, that trade must be making them better off; and (2) excess profit generates competition and the price falls. (709)

   But economists agree there are some "market failures." However, they don't agree as to whether government intervention helps more than it hurts.

2. Externalities are effects of decisions not taken into account by the decision makers. (711)

   Externalities can either be negative (have undesirable side effects) or positive (desirable).

3. Four arguments for government intervention are: (713)
   1. Agreements to restrain trade should be restricted.
   2. Informational and rationality problems necessitate government intervention.
   3. When there are externalities, marginal social costs and marginal social benefits should be equalized.
   4. When property rights are unfair, government should intervene to achieve fairness.

   ✔ *Know these!*

4. Four arguments against government intervention are: (716)
   1. Preventing private restraints on trade creates even more restraints.
   2. Correcting informational and rationality problems creates even more problems.
   3. Correcting for externalities creates other problems.
   4. Preventing unfairness creates even more unfairness.

   ✔ *Know these!*

5. Sin taxes are designed to discourage activities society believes are harmful to individuals. Milton Friedman would likely oppose sin taxes because they involve the government trying to direct individuals' behavior. (720)

   Taxes imposed on producers decrease supply, increase market price, and decrease the amount bought and sold in the market.

6. Should government intervene in the market? It depends. (722)

   Need to weight the benefits against the costs on a case-by-case basis and to remain as objective as possible.

   See also, Appendix A: "Aditional Case Studies on the Role of Government."

Short-answer questions

1.   What are two things most economists would say in support of markets? (LO1)

2.   Suppose a steel plant begins production near your home. The resulting smoke pollutes the air you breathe. You bring a complaint to the local town board saying, "I didn't ask for that factory to be built, but I'm having to endure polluted air." The basis of your complaint is an example of what concept in economics? (LO2)

3.   What are four arguments for government intervention in the economy? (LO3)

4.   What are four arguments against government intervention in the economy? (LO4)

5. A tax on liquor is an example of what kind of tax? Explain your answer. (LO5)

6. Why would Milton Friedman likely disapprove of a tax on liquor which is designed to reduce people's drinking? (LO5)

7. Why do economists answer just about every question posed with, "It depends on the costs and benefits"? (LO6)

Word Scramble

1. _____ _____
      i s n   x t a

2. _____
      v t r o n n m g e e

3. _____
      a e e e i i l n r s t t x

Match the Terms and Concepts to Their Definitions

___ 1. consumer sovereignty

___ 2. effluent fees

___ 3. externalities

___ 4. laissez-faire

___ 5. sin tax

a. Effects of decisions not taken into account by the decision makers.

b. Charges imposed by government on pollution.

c. Tax designed to discourage activities society believes are harmful to individuals.

d. The philosophy that government should intervene in the economy as little as possible.

e. The right of the individual to make choices about what is consumed and produced.

Problems and Exercises

1. Secondhand cigarette smoke is believed to have a negative effect on the health of those who inhale the smoke of cigarettes. These people have not chosen to smoke, but nevertheless are negatively affected by the choice by others to smoke. Draw the market for cigarettes showing the marginal cost and marginal social cost of smoking cigarettes if this belief is correct.

a. Label the market price and quantity of cigarettes.

b. Label the efficient level of cigarettes. Explain your answer.

c. Demonstrate graphically the tax the government would have to impose on cigarettes to arrive at the efficient level and price of cigarettes.

d. Demonstrate graphically the tax revenue government would collect from such a tax.

2. Cocaine is an illegal drug in the United States. Still, cocaine is bought and sold.

    a. Demonstrate graphically a market where cocaine is legalized.

    b. Demonstrate the effect of making cocaine illegal. What happens to price and quantity?

    c. Demonstrate the use of a tax to arrive at the same price and quantity.

    d. What is government revenue in (b) and in (c)? What is the effect of (b) and (c) on quantity consumed?

Multiple Choice Questions

1. Laissez-faire is
    a. the philosophy that government should intervene in the economy as little as possible.
    b. the philosophy that government should intervene in the economy as much as possible.
    c. the philosophy that government should not exist.
    d. the philosophy that externalities should be internalized.

2. Reasons for discretionary government intervention include all the following *except*
    a. unfair property rights.
    b. externalities.
    c. informational and rationality problems.
    d. the need for fixed rules.

3. An externality is
    a. the effect of decisions not taken into account by decision makers.
    b. another name for exports.
    c. events that happen that are external to the economy.
    d. the external effect of a government policy.

4. In the graph on the right, the S curve represents the marginal private cost of production, and the D curve represents the marginal private benefit to consumers of the good. If there is a negative externality of production, and one wants to adjust the curves so that the equilibrium demonstrates the appropriate marginal social benefits,
    a. the D curve should be shifted out to the right.
    b. the D curve should be shifted in to the left.
    c. The S curve should be shifted out to the right.
    d. The S curve should be shifted in to the left.

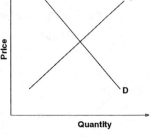

5. In the graph on the right, the S curve represents the marginal private cost of production, and the D curve represents the marginal private benefit to consumers of the good. If there is a positive externality of production, and one wants to adjust the curves so that the equilibrium demonstrates the appropriate marginal social benefits,
    a. the D curve should be shifted out to the right.
    b. the D curve should be shifted in to the left.
    c. The S curve should be shifted out to the right.
    d. The S curve should be shifted in to the left.

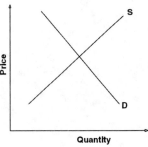

6. A free market advocate would argue that the central problem with government intervention is that
    a. government intervention creates even more problems than it resolves.
    b. government intervention cannot possibly offset positive externalities.
    c. government intervention cannot possibly deal with negative externalities.
    d. the economy on its own is fair.

7. In the graph on the right, if the government were attempting to set an effluent fee, the amount of that effluent fee should be
    a. P_1.
    b. P_2.
    c. P_1-P_0.
    d. P_1-P_2.

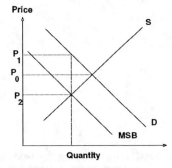

8. Economic theory suggests
    a. we should legalize drugs.
    b. we should not legalize drugs.
    c. we should legalize and tax drugs.
    d. none of the above.

A1. If the information alternative to licensing doctors were introduced, gainers would most likely include
    a. demanders.
    b. existing doctors.
    c. current medical students doing their residency.
    d. none of the above.

Answers

Short-answer questions

1. The two insights that form the basis of most economists' support of markets are (1) if people voluntarily trade, that trade must be making them better off; and (2) if individuals are free to produce whatever goods they want, then the excess profit generated will induce others to enter the market and the price will fall. (709)

2. The pollution that you endure is an example of a negative externality. An externality is an effect of a decision not taken into account by the decision marker. In this case the air pollution is the effect of steel production not taken into account by the firm. (710-712)

3. Four arguments in favor of government intervention in the economy are (1) to defend competition and to prevent the restraint of trade; (2) informational and rationality problems necessitate the need for government intervention; (3) when there are externalities, marginal social costs should be made to equal marginal social benefits; and (4) when property rights are unfair, the government should intervene. (708, 710-713)

4. Four arguments against government intervention in the economy are (1) preventing restraints on trade creates even more restraints; (2) correcting informational and rationality problems creates even more problems; (3) some supposed externalities are not really externalities and even if they were, the government does not have the tools to make marginal social cost equal marginal private costs; and (4) if the government limits people's gains from hard work, then the government will discourage hard work. (713-716)

5. A tax on liquor is an example of a sin tax. A sin tax is a tax designed to discourage an activity that society believes is harmful to individuals. (720)

6. Milton Friedman would likely disapprove of this tax because it is a sin tax. Sin taxes involve the government trying to direct the behavior of individuals. (718-719)

7. Economists answer just about every question posed with "It depends on the costs and benefits" because economists are trained to look at a problem objectively, trying to weigh the benefits and costs. They follow the rule: if the benefits outweigh the costs, do it; if the costs outweigh the benefits, don't do it. (722)

Word Scramble   1. sin tax   2. government   3. externalities

Match the Terms and Concepts to Their Definitions
1-e; 2-b; 3-a; 4-d; 5-c.

Problems and Exercises

1. a. When there is a negative externality, as with the case of secondhand cigarette smoke, the supply curve which represents the marginal private cost, S, is lower than the marginal social cost, MSC. The supply curve represents the opportunity cost of smokers choosing to smoke. The opportunity cost for society is higher, and the marginal social cost is higher, because cigarette smoke hurts those who do not smoke. The demand curve represents marginal social benefits. These curves are drawn on the right. Because the market does not take into account the third-party effects, equilibrium quantity is Q_e and equilibrium price is P_e. (711-712)

   b. The efficient level of cigarettes is where marginal social costs equals marginal social benefits. This is at Q_2 and equilibrium price is P_2. (711)

   c. The tax the government would have to impose on cigarettes to arrive at the efficient level of cigarettes is t equal to $P_2 - P_1$ sufficient to shift the supply curve back to the marginal social cost curve. (720-721)

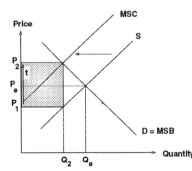

  d.   This is *t* times the quantity of cigarettes in the market. This is shown by the shaded boxed region in the graph above. (720-721)

2.   Cocaine is an illegal drug in the United States. Still, cocaine is bought and sold.

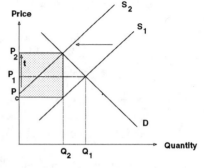

  a.   The market for cocaine given demand, *D*, and supply, S_1, is shown on the right. Equilibrium price and quantity are P_1 and Q_1 respectively. (711-712)

  b.   Making cocaine illegal will shift the supply of cocaine to the left to S_2 to incorporate the costs to suppliers of getting caught selling cocaine. A black market in cocaine will remain. Equilibrium price will rise to P_2 and quantity will fall to Q_2. (711-712)

  c.   A tax equal to *t* will shift the supply curve by the same amount as if cocaine were made illegal, that is, to S_2. This is shown on the graph to the right. (720-721)

  d.   Government revenue in (b) is zero and in (c) is *t* times the quantity of cocaine consumed. Revenue is shown as the shaded region in the graph to the right. Quantity consumed is the same in both cases. (720-721)

Multiple Choice Questions

1.   a.   The "externality" answer has little to do with laissez-faire and would not affect it. Even advocates of laissez-faire agree there is some role for government, so the b answer is wrong. See page 709.

2.   d.   The need for fixed rules would argue against, not in favor of, discretionary government intervention. See pages 708, 713.

3.   a.   See page 711.

4.   d.   A negative externality makes the marginal social cost higher than the marginal private cost of production. See Exhibit 1, page 711.

5.   c.   A positive externality makes the marginal social cost lower than the marginal private cost of production. See Exhibit 1, page 711.

6.   a.   The best of these answers is a. All the others might have some credence but are too strongly put to represent the central problem. See pages 714-715.

7.   d.   The effluent fee should be set to equate marginal social cost with marginal social benefit. See Exhibit 2, page 717.

8.   d.   Economic theory provides insight on problems but does not say which policy is correct. The determination of correct policy concerns institutional and moral issues. As usual in this text, all policy issues depend. See pages 708, 710-711, 721-722.

A1.   a.   Individuals already in the system would be hurt by the introduction of more competition. Demanders would gain by more options and lower prices. It is true that demanders might be overwhelmed by the choices presented to them, but a is by far the best answer. (725-727)

Chapter 32:
Economics and the Environment

Chapter at a glance

1. Four ways in which economists' approach to environmental problems differs from noneconomists' approach include (1) their understanding of the problem, (2) their opposition to explicit regulation, (3) their dubiousness about voluntary solutions, and (4) their methods for paying. (729)

   There's no fundamental difference in terms of beliefs or concerns about the environment. The difference is in approach.

2. Correlation does not necessarily imply causation. (730)

   On hot days people eat more ice cream cones; eating ice cream cones does not necessarily cause hot days. Similarly, modern industrial methods have accompanied a rise in the mean temperature. Modern industrial methods do not necessarily cause the rise in the mean temperature.

3. Economists are likely to oppose direct regulation because it does not achieve the desired end as effectively and as fairly as possible. (733)

   Economists favor market incentive programs (a program that makes the price of the good reflect the negative externality).

4. If a policy isn't optimal, resources are being wasted because the savings from reduction of expenditures on a program will be worth more than the gains that will be lost from reducing the program. (735)

   ✔ *The optimal level of pollution control policy (or any policy) is that amount at which the marginal social benefit (MSB) equals the marginal social cost (MSC).*

   ✔ *If MSB > MSC ⇒ Do more.*
   ✔ *If MSB < MSC ⇒ Do less.*
   ✔ *If MSB = MSC ⇒ Just right!.*

5. Economists believe that a small number of free riders will undermine the social consciousness of many in the society and that eventually a voluntary policy will fail. (736)

   Economists are skeptical of voluntary solutions.

6. If a program requires people to pay a price that reflects the cost of an externality, it will be in their interest to change their behavior until marginal social benefits equal marginal social costs. (737)

   So, economists favor policies that make the price people pay reflect the cost of the externality, as opposed to direct regulation or voluntary conservation.

7. Economists' reasoning involves a general approach to all problems in which a cost/benefit analysis is made and the program with the least cost is chosen. (744)

   Economists search for optimal solutions.

Short-answer questions

1. An economist is on a panel of environmentalists who are not familiar with economic reasoning. She is discussing solutions to environmental problems. What are four ways in which the economist's approach to environmental problems will likely differ from the non-economist's approach? (LO1)

2. Suppose you are a visitor from an alien planet. You observe that on days when many people carry umbrellas, it rains. You report back to your alien colony that on earth carrying umbrellas causes rain. Is your reasoning flawed? How does this differ from economists stating that a fall in prices causes an increase in quantity demanded? (LO2)

3. Suppose the government required that everyone reduce their driving by 20 miles per day to limit carbon monoxide pollution. Why would an economist who nevertheless is a proponent of some form of regulation most likely oppose this particular regulation? (LO3)

4. What would you say to someone who says that society's goal should be a totally pollution-free world? (LO4)

5. Why might voluntary programs to reduce the harmful effects of individuals on the environment not work? (LO5)

6. Why do economists believe that long-term solutions to problems involve making people pay a price that reflects the cost of an externality? (LO6)

7. How would an economist likely approach an environmental problem? (LO7)

Word Scramble

1. _____   2._____   3._____
        Y B I N M   y x t t r n l i e e a   a a c i n o s t u

Match the Terms and Concepts to Their Definitions

___ 1. causation

___ 2. correlation

___ 3. corroboration

___ 4. direct regulation

___ 5. efficiently

___ 6. externality

___ 7. free rider problem

___ 8. global warming theory

___ 9. market incentive program

___ 10. marketable certificate program

___ 11. NIMBY

___ 12. optimal policy

___ 13. optimal level of pollution

___ 14. proven reserves

___ 15. tax incentive program

a. A short way to express "**Not In My Back Yard**" when a community objects to a proposed development in its neighborhood.

b. A result of a decision that is not taken into account by the decision maker.

c. A program that formalizes rights by issuing certificates and allowing trading of those rights.

d. Achieving a desired goal at the lowest possible cost in total resources, without consideration as to who pays those costs.

e. Amount of pollution at which the marginal benefit of reducing pollution equals the marginal cost.

f. Any program in which a tax is used to create incentives for individuals to structure their activities in a way that is consistent with particular desired ends.

g. Policy whose marginal cost equals its marginal benefit.

h. Program in which the amount of a resource people are allowed to use is directly limited by the government.

i. Program that makes the price of a resource reflect the negative externality.

j. Resource reserves that have been discovered, documented to date, and are recoverable with current technology.

k. Term meaning that the data are more consistent with a particular theory than with any other theory, so it makes sense to use the particular theory.

l. Term in statistics meaning that a change in one data point causes another data point to change.

m. Term in statistics meaning the joint movement of data points.

n. The unwillingness of individuals to share in the cost of a public good.

o. The theory that the earth is now going through a period of warming due to the rising level of carbon dioxide gases caused by the burning of fossil fuels.

Problems and Exercises

1. Cars emit pollution in the form of carbon monoxide, affecting the air that all people breathe. Graph the demand and supply of cars below. Given the fact that the air pollution is not taken into account fully by those who purchase cars, draw the marginal social cost of cars purchased on that same graph.

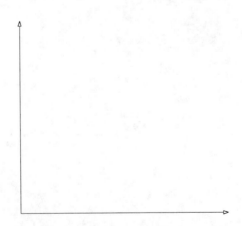

   a. Indicate the market equilibrium and quantity on the graph you drew.

b.   Explain why the marginal social cost of cars is how you drew it.

c.   What is the socially efficient quantity and price?

d.   Show the effects of imposing a tax on cars that would result in the socially efficient quantity of cars.

e.   Show the effects of forcing a percentage reduction in demand for all people that results in the socially efficient quantity of cars.

f.   Which program, (d) or (e), would car makers favor? Why?

2.   Answer the following questions based on the graphs below.

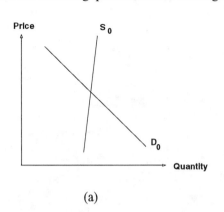
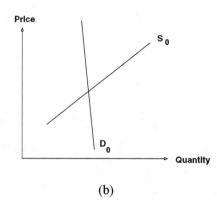

                (a)   (b)

a.   In which case would it take a higher per unit tax to achieve a 10% reduction in quantity demanded?

b.   In which case would a lower equilibrium price result given a 10 % reduction in demand?

Multiple Choice Questions

1.   According to the textbook, four ways in which economists' approach to environmental problems differs from non-economists' approach include all of the following *except*
     a. economists' general opposition to explicit regulation.
     b. economists' concern and dubiousness about voluntary solutions.
     c. economists are likely to have different methods for paying.
     d. economists are likely to be less concerned about the environment.

2.   Looking at the empirical evidence, you notice that whenever the quantity demanded rises, the price falls. Based on this empirical evidence you would conclude that
     a. there is a negative correlation between price and quantity.
     b. there is a positive correlation between price and quantity.
     c. a fall in price causes quantity demanded to decrease.
     d. none of the above.

3. Looking at data for the temperature in a country, you discover that in 1997 the average temperature was identical to the past yearly average temperature for previous years. From this you would definitely conclude
    a. that the country did not have a heat wave in 1997.
    b. that the country did not have a cold wave in 1997.
    c. that the country had neither a heat wave nor a cold wave in 1997.
    d. none of the above.

4. If the public policy goal is to reduce consumption of gasoline, ideally, following an economists' approach
    a. heavy consumers of gasoline would reduce consumption more than light consumers.
    b. light consumers of gasoline would reduce consumption more than heavy consumers.
    c. light consumers of gasoline and heavy consumers of gasoline would make an equal reduction in consumption.
    d. the amount of reduction in consumption of any consumer would depend on the marginal cost of that reduction.

5. Mr. B is using 20 gallons of gas a day and Mr. A is using 10 gallons of gas a day. The marginal cost of reducing gas consumption by 3 gallons a day is $4 for Mr. A and $3 for Mr. B. The government issues a regulation requiring equal reduction so that each has to reduce consumption by 3 gallons a day. Economists would conclude
    a. the reductions are inefficient because they are equal.
    b. the reductions are efficient because they are equal.
    c. the reductions are inefficient because they are based on regulation.
    d. the reductions are inefficient because they do not equalize the marginal costs of reduction.

6. Mr. B is using 20 gallons of gas a day and Mr. A is using 10 gallons of gas a day. The marginal cost of reducing gas consumption by 3 gallons a day is $8 for Mr. A and $4 for Mr. B. The government issues a regulation requiring equal reduction of 3 gallons a day each. Economists would conclude
    a. Mr. A is reducing consumption too much.
    b. Mr. B is reducing consumption too much.
    c. the reductions are inefficient because they are based on regulation.
    d. the reductions are efficient because they equalize the marginal costs of reduction.

7. Mr. B is using 20 gallons of gas a day and Mr. A is using 10 gallons of gas a day. The marginal cost of reducing gas consumption by 3 gallons a day is $8 for Mr. A and $4 for Mr. B. The government places a tax on the use of gasoline. Economists would expect
    a. Mr. A to reduce his consumption by the same amount as Mr. B.
    b. Mr. A to reduce his consumption by more than Mr. B.
    c. Mr. B to reduce his consumption by more than Mr. A.
    d. both to reduce their consumption to zero.

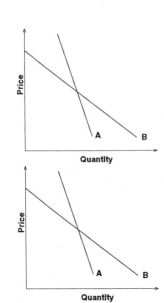

8. In reference to the A and B groups whose demands are shown in the graph on the right, the group most likely to support a marketable permit program to reduce demand as opposed to regulatory solutions is
    a. A.
    b. B.
    c. Neither A nor B is more likely to support a marketable permit solution.
    d. Both A and B are equally likely to support a marketable permit solution.

9. In reference to the A and B groups whose demands are shown in the graph on the right, the group most likely to support regulatory solutions of equal reduction of consumption is
    a. A.
    b. B.
    c. Neither A nor B is more likely to support regulatory solutions.
    d. Both A and B are equally likely to support regulatory solutions.

10. Economists are concerned about the effectiveness of voluntary solutions because, while voluntary solutions may be temporarily successful, in the long run voluntary solutions will experience
    a. free rider problems.
    b. NIMBY problems.
    c. TANSTAAFL problems.
    d. opportunity cost problems.

11. An economist's solution to the NIMBY problem of finding places for landfills would be to
    a. require all places to accept trash.
    b. replace landfills with recycling.
    c. pay areas that accept landfills a sufficiently high amount to make them desire landfills
    d. institute a combination of recycling and high-temperature burners that eliminate most of the trash.

12. In reference to the graph on the right, if there is a severe shortage of land-fills, which of the following might be true?
    a. The price being paid for landfills is currently at 50.
    b. The price being paid for landfills is currently at 200.
    c. The price being paid for landfills is currently at 400.
    d. None of the above.

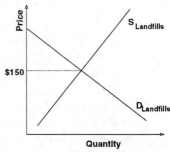

13. The marginal private and social cost of fishing and the demand for fishing are represented by the curves shown in the graph to the right. Assuming perfect competition, there would be
    a. too much fishing.
    b. too little fishing.
    c. the correct amount of fishing.
    d. Based on these curves you cannot answer this question.

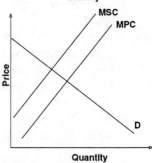

14. In reference to the graph on the right, which shows the marginal private and social cost of fishing and demand for fishing, the socially efficient price of fishing would be
    a. 0.
    b. P_1.
    c. P_2.
    d. P_3.

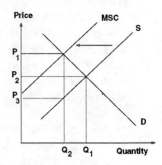

Answers

Short-answer questions

1. The approach by the economist will likely differ from the approach by the non-economist in four ways: (1) Economists understand that correlation does not imply causation and that statistics are often ambiguous. The economist will likely look for other factors that are causing the problems and look critically at the statistics to see any ambiguities. (2) Economists often oppose explicit restrictions and regulation as solutions. Explicit regulations will most likely result in welfare loss. Economists much prefer incentive-based programs. (3) Economists are often dubious of voluntary programs. The voluntary nature of those programs will most likely undermine their success because by nature people act in their own self-interest, not in the interest of society. (4) Economists often prefer market incentive programs instead of direct regulation. (729)

2. Your reasoning is flawed. Based on the other evidence, most people accept models of weather that are not umbrella-dependent. There is a correlation, but you have made the incorrect assumption that correlation implies causation. Although the two phenomena, carrying umbrellas and rain, might move jointly, they might be caused by a third, factor. To determine that, one needs to specify one's theory and test it in a controlled way. Economists have empirically tested their law of demand so their statement that a fall in price causes an increase in the quantity demanded is not subject to that flaw in reasoning. (730, 732)

3. A regulation that requires a reduction in mileage per day for everyone involves direct regulation of behavior. Economists often oppose direct regulation because it does not achieve the desired end as efficiently and as fairly as possible. This approach does not take into account the costs to individuals of reducing mileage. For someone who commutes to work, the cost of reducing driving might mean moving to a town closer to work. Someone who has the option of working at a closer office to comply with the regulations would find the regulation less costly. In fact, if they were simply asked, perhaps some would reduce their daily driving miles even more than required by direct regulation. The fact that this regulation would be more costly than necessary is why an economist would likely oppose it. An economist would prefer a policy that would make the person who has a lower cost of changing consumption choose to do so. (733)

4. I would tell that person that there may be an optimal level of pollution. The savings from the reduction of expenditures on a program to reduce pollution might exceed the gains that are lost from reducing that program. If this is the case, resources are currently being wasted and the level of pollution is less than optimal. (735)

5. Voluntary programs most likely do not work because a small number of free riders will undermine the social consciousness of many in the society and eventually this will lead to the program's failure. (736)

6. Economists believe that long-term solutions to problems involve making people pay a price that reflects the cost of an externality because people do what is in their self-interest. If they must pay a price that reflects the cost of an externality, they will change their behavior in such a way that marginal social benefits equal marginal social costs. (737)

7. Given an environmental issue, an economist would weigh the costs and benefits of the actions that harm the environment and choose that solution with the least opportunity cost. (739-741)

Word Scramble   1. NIMBY   2. externality   3. causation

Match the Terms and Concepts to Their Definitions
1-l; 2-m; 3-k; 4-h; 5-d; 6-b; 7-n; 8-o; 9-i; 10-c; 11-a; 12-g; 13-e; 14-j; 15-f.

Problems and Exercises

1. The supply and demand for cars are shown to the right. Marginal social cost is to the left of supply by the amount of the third-party damage per car sold.

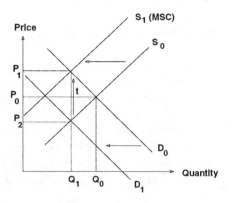

a. Market equilibrium is Q_0, P_0. (733-736, 717)

b. Marginal social cost is above supply because car buyer's opportunity cost of purchasing cars is lower than the opportunity cost to society of purchasing cars because of the pollution cars emit.

c. The socially efficient quantity and price is where marginal social cost equals marginal social benefit, at Q_1, P_1. (733-736, 717)

d. A tax equalling the difference between marginal social cost and supply would result in a socially efficient quantity of cars. Supply shifts from S_0 to S_1 as shown on the right. (733-736, 717)

e. Forcing a reduction in demand shifts the demand curve to the left to D_1. The new equilibrium price, P_2, is lower than initial market price of P_0. (733-736, 717)

f. Car makers are indifferent between the two. In case (d) equilibrium price is P_1, but a tax of t is paid. In case (e) equilibrium price is P_2 which is t less than P_1. (733-736, 717)

2. a. The case with a more inelastic demand, (b), would take a higher per unit tax to achieve a 10% reduction in quantity demanded. This is because a tax shifts the supply curve up. Since demand is inelastic, it would take a greater change in price to elicit the same change in quantity demanded. The supply curve would have to shift up more in (b) to achieve the same reduction in quantity. (734)

b. The case with a more inelastic supply would lower equilibrium price result given a 10 percent reduction in demand. This is because a 10% reduction in quantity demanded shifts both demand curves to the left by the same amount. Since supply is more inelastic in (a), price declines by more when demand falls by 10%. (734)

Multiple Choice Questions

1. d. The author explicitly argues that economists are not less concerned about the environment. The differences include the first three which involve economists' approach to solving problems. See page 729.

2. a. Even though economic theory suggests that c is correct, the observation of the empirical evidence is simply that there is a correlation, and thus a is correct and c is not. See page 730.

3. d. The average temperature is, by definition, the averaging of many things. It could average a major heat wave and a major cold wave together and come up with the identical average, as discussed on page 732.

4. d. The optimal reduction requires equalizing the marginal cost of reduction of consumption. See page 733.

5. d. The optimal reduction requires equalizing the marginal cost of reduction. See pages 733, 735.

6. a. The optimal reduction requires equalizing the marginal cost of reduction of consumption. Assuming increasing marginal costs of reduction, as economists usually do, Mr. A is reducing consumption too much. The fact that the reductions in consumption are determined by regulation does not make them inefficient; the fact that they do not equalize the marginal cost of reduction makes them inefficient. See page 733.

7. c. The amount of reduction will be based on the marginal costs of reduction. Since the marginal costs of reduction are higher for Mr. A, economists would expect Mr. B to reduce his consumption by more. See page 733.

8. a. Regulatory solutions generally impose equal quantity restrictions because any other type of regulatory solution is too difficult to set up and administer. Marketable solutions let people decide. Group A would find it much more costly to reduce because the demand curve for group A is more inelastic than that for group B, so it would be hurt much more by a regulatory solution; therefore it would likely favor the alternative that lets it decide how much to reduce its quantity demanded. See pages 733-735.

9. b. Group B would find it much less costly to reduce consumption an equal amount, so it would be hurt much less by a regulatory solution; therefore it would be more likely to favor the regulatory solution. See pages 733-735.

10. a. Voluntary solutions lead people to supply less effort to contribute to the solution because they will have a tendency to rely on others to do it. Thus, "The free rider problem" is the best answer, even though the other answers may have some validity. See pages 736-737.

11. c. The option c would be most likely to equalize marginal costs and marginal benefits. See page 735.

12. a. If there is a severe shortage, the price being paid for landfills must be below the equilibrium price. See page 741.

13. a. The socially optimal amount of fishing would be where the MSC intersects the demand curve. See pages 735-736 in this chapter of the text and Exhibit 2, page 717, in the chapter on the role of government in the economy.

14. b. The socially efficient price is where the marginal social cost equals the marginal social benefit, which, in absence of any information to the contrary, can be assumed to be represented by the demand curve. See pages 735-736 in this chapter of the text and Exhibit 2, page 717, in the chapter on the role of government in the economy.

Chapter 33:
Antitrust and Industrial Policies

Chapter at a glance

1. Judgement by performance is the view that competitiveness of a market should be judged by the behavior of firms in that market; judgment by structure is the view that competitiveness of a market should be judged by the structure of the market. (747)

   Both criteria have their problems. There are no definitive criteria for judging whether a firm has violated antitrust statutes. However, since 1945, most court decisions have relied on judgment by structure.

2. Public outrage at the formation and activities of trusts such as Standard Oil led to the passage of the Sherman Act, the Clayton Act, and the Federal Trade Commission Act. (748)

✔ *Know what these Acts outlaw.*

3a. The IBM case was dropped by the United States, but the prosecution of the case likely led to some of IBM's problems in the 1990s. It won but it also lost. (754)

   Changes in technology can alter market structure (the degree of competition) rather rapidly.

3b. The AT&T case was settled by AT&T agreeing to be split up into regional companies handling local service, and AT&T itself competing in the long-distance market. (756)

   Up until 1982, AT&T was a regulated monopoly. Telephone services were believed to be a natural monopoly.

3c. The Microsoft case has been halted with a consent decree making Microsoft agree to "be good." The controversy, however, continues. (758)

   Rapid changes in technology can make anti-trust cases moot.

4. Horizontal mergers are companies in the same industry merging together. Vertical mergers are combinations of two companies, one of which supplied inputs to the other's production. Conglomerate mergers are combinations of unrelated businesses. (760)

✔ *Know the differences. Also become familiar with the various terms associated with takeovers.*

✔ *Most antitrust policy has concerned horizontal mergers.*

5. Five reasons why unrelated firms merge include: (761)
   1. To achieve economies of scope;
   2. To get a good buy;
   3. To diversify;
   4. To ward off a takeover bid; and
   5. To strengthen their political-economic influence.

   When unrelated firms merge, this constitutes a conglomerate merger.

6. An industrial policy is a government's formal policy toward business. (764)

   Although the U.S. has always had an industrial policy, recently some argue for an <u>activist</u> policy to help U.S. industry compete in the global economy. This is controversial.

7a. Two arguments for an industrial policy are (1) that it will create gains from cooperation among firms, and (2) that it will channel funds to high-growth industries. (764)

   These are the potential benefits.

7b. Two problems of an industrial policy are (1) graft and (2) the inevitable waste inherent in bureaucracy. (764)

   One needs to weigh the benefits against the costs.

Short-answer questions

1. How does judging competition by structure differ from judging competition by performance? (LO1)

2. What are the two provisions of the Sherman Antitrust Act? What year was it passed by Congress? (LO2)

3. What was the resolution of the IBM antitrust case? (LO3)

4. What was the resolution of the AT&T antitrust case? (LO3)

5. What was the resolution of the Microsoft antitrust case? (LO3)

6. What are horizontal, vertical, and conglomerate mergers? (LO4)

7. What are five reasons why unrelated firms would want to merge? (LO5)

8. What is an *industrial policy*? Does the United States have one? (LO6)

9. Japan's Ministry of International Trade and Industry (MITI) directs activist industrial policy for Japan. How would an advocate of an activist industrial policy say that policy has helped Japan? (LO7)

10. What would the critics of MITI (Japanese Ministry of International Trade and Industry) respond to your answer to question 8? (LO7)

Word Scramble

1._____ 2._____ _____ 3._____ _____ _____
    grmeer   adiilnrstu   cilopy   Srnmhea   utttsrniA   tAc

Match the Terms and Concepts to Their Definitions

____ 1. acquisition

____ 2. antitrust policy

____ 3. conglomerate merger

____ 4. deacquisition

____ 5. co-opetition

____ 6. horizontal merger

____ 7. hostile takeover

____ 8. industrial policy

____ 9. judgment by performance

____ 10. judgment by structure

____ 11. MITI

____ 12. multinational corporation

____ 13. Sherman Antitrust Act

____ 14. takeover

____ 15. vertical merger

a. A company buys another company; the buyer has direct control of the resulting venture, but does not necessarily exercise that direct control.

b. A merger of companies in the same industry.

c. A merger in which one company buys another that does not want to be bought.

d. A government's formal policy toward business.

e. The Japanese agency that conducts Japan's industrial policy.

f. Cooperation among competitors.

g. Combination of unrelated businesses.

h. Combination of two companies, one of which supplies inputs to the other's production.

i. Firm with production facilities and a marketing force in two or more countries.

j. Judging the competitiveness of markets by the number of firms in the market and their market shares.

k. Judging the competitiveness of markets by the behavior of firms in that market.

l. Law passed by the U.S. Congress in 1890 to attempt to regulate the competitive process.

m. One company's sale of parts of another company it has bought.

n. Purchase of a firm by another firm that then takes direct control over its operations.

o. Government's policy toward the competitive process.

Problems and Exercises

1. You're an economist in the Antitrust Division of the Justice Department. In the personal computer market, suppose Compaq has petitioned to merge with AT&T. Compaq currently has 14% of the PC market and AT&T has 3%. The other three large firms in the market, Packard Bell, IBM, and Apple, have 11%, 9%, and 8% of the PC market respectively. In the Windows-based PC market, Compaq has 18% of the market and AT&T has 5%. The other three large firms in the Windows-based PC market, Packard Bell, IBM, and Hewlitt Packard, have 14%, 12%, and 9% of the PC market respectively.

   a. Calculate the approximate Herfindahl and 4-firm concentration ratios for these firms in each industry before the merger and after the merger.

   b. If you were Compaq's economist, which industry definition would you suggest using when making your petition to the Justice Department?

c.   Give an argument why the merger might decrease competition.

d.   Give an argument why the merger might increase competition.

2.   Suppose you are advising a regulatory agency of the Federal govern-
     ment to regulate the prices of a monopolist depicted by the graph
     on the right.

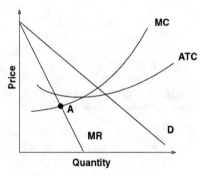

a.   Would you recommend setting prices at point A where $MC =$
     MR? Why or why not?

b.   What would be the minimum price you would recommend? Why?

c.   Does the monopolist still enjoy economic profit at the minimum price you determined in b? If so,
     what are they?

Multiple Choice Questions

1. An important law in the U.S. regulation of markets is
   a. the Standard Oil Antitrust Act of 1890.
   b. the Sherman Antitrust Act of 1890.
   c. the ALCOA Antitrust Act of 1890.
   d. The Lincoln Antitrust Act of 1890.

2. In the Standard Oil and American Tobacco Company antitrust cases in 1911, the Court ruled that
   a. the two companies had a monopolistic structure and therefore should be broken up.
   b. the two companies were guilty of unfair business practices and therefore should be broken up.
   c. the Sherman Antitrust Act did not apply.
   d. the two companies had to be disbanded.

3. In the ALCOA antitrust case in 1945, the Court ruled that
   a. the company had a monopolistic structure and therefore should be broken up.
   b. the company was guilty of unfair business practices and therefore should be broken up.
   c. the Sherman Antitrust Act did not apply.
   d. the two companies had to be disbanded.

4. The resolution of the IBM antitrust case was that
   a. IBM was broken up.
   b. IBM was combined with AT&T.
   c. the government dropped the IBM case.
   d. IBM was allowed to stay in the large-computer market but was kept out of the personal-computer market.

5. The resolution of the AT&T antitrust case of the 1980s was
   a. AT&T agreed to split up into three operating divisions.
   b. AT&T agreed to split up and allow the Baby Bells to be independent.
   c. AT&T was combined with MCI and Sprint.
   d. MCI and Sprint were broken off from AT&T and developed as competitors to AT&T.

6. The resolution of the Microsoft antitrust case of the 1990s was
   a. Microsoft agreed in a consent decree to "be good."
   b. the government dropped the Microsoft case.
   c. Microsoft agreed to government regulation of its prices.
   d. Microsoft was forced to get out of the internet business.

7. When two merging companies are in the same industry their merger is called
   a. a horizontal merger.
   b. a vertical merger.
   c. a conglomerate merger.
   d. a takeover merger.

8. When one of two merging companies supplies one or more of the inputs to the other merging company, the merger is called
   a. a horizontal merger.
   b. a vertical merger.
   c. a conglomerate merger.
   d. a takeover merger.

9. When two companies that are in unrelated industries merge, the merger is called
   a. a horizontal merger.
   b. a vertical merger.
   c. a conglomerate merger.
   d. an unrelated merger.

10. Reasons firms would want to enter into a conglomerate merger include all the following except
    a. to achieve economies of scope.
    b. to diversify.
    c. to strengthen their political and economic influence.
    d. to become a natural monopoly.

11. Antitrust laws in Japan
    a. tend to be weaker than in the United States.
    b. tend to be stronger than in the United States.
    c. tend to be approximately the same strength as antitrust laws in the United States.
    d. do not exist; there are no antitrust laws in Japan.

12. Industrial policy is
    a. a policy of government entering into competition with business.
    b. a policy of government industries entering into competition with business.
    c. a formal policy that government takes towards business.
    d. a laissez-faire policy of government towards business.

Answers

Short-answer questions

1. Judging competition by structure is the view that competitiveness of a market should be judged by the number or firms in the market and their market shares. Judging competition by performance is the view that competitiveness of a market should be judged by the behavior of firms in that market. (747, 749-750, 751)

2. The two provisions of the Sherman Antitrust Act passed in 1890 are (1) every contract, combination, or conspiracy in restraint of trade is illegal and (2) every person who shall monopolize or attempt to monopolize shall be deemed guilty of a misdemeanor. (748)

3. The IBM case was dropped by the United States, but the prosecution likely led to IBM's problems in the 1990s. (753)

4. The AT&T case was settled by AT&T agreeing to be split up into regional companies handling local service and AT&T itself competing in the long-distance market. (754-757)

5. The Microsoft case was halted with a consent decree by Microsoft agreeing to "be good." (757-758)

6. A horizontal merger is a merger between two companies in the same industry. A vertical merger is a firm merging with the supplier of one (or more) of its inputs. A conglomerate merger is a merger between unrelated businesses. (760)

7. Five reasons why unrelated firms would want to merge are (1) to achieve economies of scope, (2) to get a good buy, (3) to diversify, (4) to ward off a takeover bid, and (5) to strengthen political-economic influence. (761-762)

8. An *industrial policy* is a government's formal policy toward business. The United States has always had an industrial policy. What the United States falls short of having is an *activist* industrial policy under which government works directly with businesses, providing funds, background research, and encouragement to specific industries. (764-765)

9. MITI is credited by many economists with engineering Japan's growth over the past 40 years. It has created gains from cooperation among firms such as consulting with banks to encourage loans and has channelled funds to high-growth industries that focussed on international rather than domestic competition. (764-765)

10. MITI's activism has had its problems. Some economists argue that without MITI, Japan would have grown even faster. They point out that MITI often backed losing industries. They also point out that there were significant amounts of dishonest actions by politicians to acquire money from firms and that MITI's bureaucratic involvement has been accompanied by the inevitable waste inherent in bureaucracy. (764-766)

Word Scramble   1. merger   2. industrial policy   3. Sherman Antitrust Act

Match the Terms and Concepts to Their Definitions

1-a; 2-o; 3-g; 4-m; 5-f; 6-b; 7-c; 8-d; 9-k; 10-j; 11-e; 12-i; 13-l; 14-n; 15-h.

Problems and Exercises

1. a. The Herfindahl index is calculated by adding the squared value of the market shares of all the firms in the industry. The 4-firm concentration ratio is calculated by adding the market shares of the four firms with the largest market shares.

   PC Market: Before the merger, the Herfindahl index is greater than $14^2 + 11^2 + 9^2 + 8^2 + 3^2 = 196 + 121 + 81 + 64 + 9 = 471$. The exact Herfindahl index cannot be calculated since we do not know the market shares of all the firms in the market. The 4-firm concentration ratio before the merger is $14 + 11 + 9 + 8 = 42$. The Herfindahl index after the merger is at least $17^2 + 11^2 + 9^2 + 8^2 = 289 + 121 + 81 + 64 = 555$. The

4-firm concentration ratio after the merger is $17 + 11 + 9 + 8 = 45$.

Windows-based PC market: Before the merger, the Herfindahl index is at least $18^2 + 14^2 + 12^2 + 9^2 + 5^2 = 324 + 196 + 121 + 81 + 25 = 747$. The 4-firm concentration ratio before the merger is $18 + 14 + 12 + 9 = 53$. The Herfindahl index after the merger is at least $23^2 + 14^2 + 12^2 + 9^2 = 529 + 196 + 144 + 81 = 950$. The 4-firm concentration ratio after the merger is $23 + 14 + 12 + 9 = 58$. (760)

   b. I would use the broader PC-based computer industry definition because the Herfindahl indexes and concentration ratios are lower in this market indicating more competition. (760)

   c. The merger would be expected to decrease competition because within the PC market the Herfindahl index rises from 471 to 555 and the 4-firm concentration ratio rises from 42 to 45. This indicates the merger would result in a less competitive market. The larger merged company will have more ability to set prices above marginal costs, resulting in a loss to society. Welfare loss with a monopoly is shown on page 625 in the chapter on monopoly. (760)

   d. This merger might be expected to increase competition if Compaq and AT&T cannot compete separately against the other three firms in the market. A combined Compaq and AT&T might also be more competitive in a global market. Most likely, however, this merger will lower the level of domestic competition. (760, 763)

2. a. I would not recommend setting prices at point A where $MC = MR$ because at that point marginal revenue is less than average total costs. The monopolist would eventually go out of business. This is shown in the graph to the right. (622)

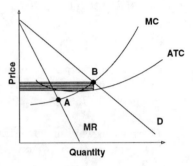

   b. The minimum price I would recommend would be where the marginal cost curve intersects the demand curve at point B in the figure to the right. This eliminates all welfare loss to society associated with a monopoly and is the competitive price and quantity. (622)

   c. The monopolist still enjoys economic profit which is shaded in the graph to the right. (622)

Multiple Choice Questions

1. b.   See pages 748-749.

2. b.   Answer b is correct and answer a is incorrect because the early cases were decided on the performance, or abuse, standard, not on whether the companies were monopolies. Answer c is incorrect because the Act applies to unfair business practices as well as to monopolistic structure. Answer d is incorrect because "disbanded" would mean the companies ceased totally to exist, whereas these two companies were changed by reorganization. See pages 748-749.

3. a.   In the ALCOA case, the Court applied the monopolistic structure standard. See page 750.

4. c.   As discussed on pages 753-754, the government dropped the IBM case.

5. b.   See pages 753-754.

6. a.   See pages 757-758 .

7. a.   See page 760.

8. b.   See page 760.

9. c.   See page 760.

10. d.   When two firms in different industries combine, it has nothing to do with monopoly. See pages 761-762.

11. a.   See page 765.

12. c   See page 764.

Chapter 34: Who Gets What? The Distribution of Income

Chapter at a glance

1. A Lorenz curve is a geometric representation of the share distribution of income among families in a given country at a given time. (770)

   Shows the relative equality of the distribution of income. The farther below the diagonal line, the more <u>unequal</u> the distribution of income.

2. From 1929 to 1970, income inequality in the United States decreased. From 1970 to 1995, it increased. (771)

   These changes occurred mainly because of changes in the progressivity of taxes and government social programs.

3. Poverty is defined by the U.S. government as being equal to or less than three times an average family's minimum food expenditures as calculated by the U.S. Department of Agriculture. (772)

   Is approximately $15,569 for a family of four. Poverty figures, like all statistics, should be used with care. Think about some causes of poverty, and its problems for society.

4. Wealth is significantly more unequally distributed in the United States than income. (776)

   Moreover, world distribution of income is highly unequal. The U.S. has less income inequality than most developing nations but more inequality than many developed countries.

5. Three problems in determining whether an equal income distribution is fair are: (1) people don't start from equivalent positions; (2) people's needs are different; and (3) people's efforts differ. (782)

   When most people talk about believing in equality of income, they usually mean an equality in opportunity to earn income.

6. Three side effects of redistribution of income include: (1) the labor/leisure incentive effect; (2) the avoidance and evasion incentive effects; and (3) the incentive effect to look more needy than you are. (783)

✔ *Know these. The different kinds of taxes are introduced in Appendix B.*

   See also,
   Appendix A: "A Numerical Example of the Problems of Redistributing income."

   Appendix B: "Real-World Policies and Programs to Redistribute Income."

433

Short-answer questions

1. What does a Lorenz curve show? (LO1)

2. What happened to income distribution from 1929 to 1970 in the United States? (LO2)

3. What has happened to income distribution since 1970 in the United States? (LO2)

4. What is the official definition of *poverty*? (LO3)

5. How does the Lorenz curve for household wealth compare with the Lorenz curve for family income in the United States? (LO4)

6. You and your friends are having a lunchtime discussion about fairness. A friend offers a statement that since income distribution has become more unequal in the past few decades, income in the United States has become less and less fair. Assume you are a contrarian. How do you respond? (LO5)

7. "Nevertheless," your friend says, "I believe the current distribution is not fair. The government should do something to make the income distribution more equal." You agree to some extent, but warn that there are side effects of redistributing income. State your argument. (LO6)

B1. What are five expenditure programs to redistribute income? (LO7)

Word Scramble

1. _____ _____   2._____   3._____
   z r o n l e   v u r e c   e o p r t v y   t s r o n n m i i i i d c a

Match the Terms and Concepts to Their Definitions

____ 1.   comparable worth laws

____ 2.   discrimination

____ 3.   Lorenz curve

____ 4.   poverty

____ 5.   size distribution of income

____ 6.   socioeconomic distribution of income

____ 7.   wealth

a.   A geometric representation of the share distribution of income among families in a given country at a given time.

b.   As defined by the U.S. government, a level equal to or less than three times an average family's average annual minimum food expenditures as calculated by the U.S. Department of Agriculture.

c.   Differential treatment of individuals because of physical or social characteristics.

d.   Laws in which government groups will determine "fair" wages for specific jobs.

e.   The value of assets an individual owns.

f.   The relative division or allocation of total income among relevant socioeconomic groups.

g.   The relative division or allocation of total income among income groups.

Problems and Exercises

1.   Use the Lorenz curve on the right to answer the following questions.

a.   What percentage of total income do the top 20 percent of individuals in Ecoland receive?

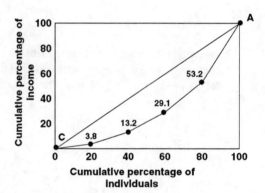

b.   What percentage of total income do the top 40 percent of individuals in Ecoland receive?

c.   Which value, the one in (a) or the one (b), is greater? Why?

d.   What does the straight line represent? Describe points A and C. Why is the Lorenz curve always anchored at those points?

2. Use the following table to answer the questions.

Income quintile	Ecoland	Fantasyland	Textland
Lowest 20%	5%	7%	2%
Second quintile	8	10	6
Third quintile	10	25	9
Fourth quintile	20	25	19
Highest 20%	57	33	64

a. Draw a Lorenz curve for each country.

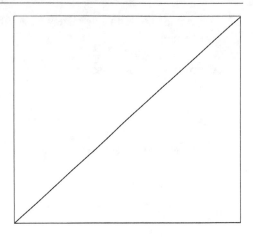

b. Rank the countries from most equal income distribution to least equal income distribution.

B1. You are completing your tax return. You are filing as a single taxpayer. Your income is $87,300. Deductions are $20,000. The rate is 15% for taxable income up to $22,750, 28% of income between $22,750 and $55,100, and 31% of income above $55,100.

a. Calculate your tax liability.

b. Calculate your average tax rate.

c. Calculate your marginal tax rate.

d. Is the tax schedule proportional, regressive, or progressive? Explain your answer.

B2. For each of the following state whether the tax is most likely proportional, regressive, or progressive with income.

    a.   5 cent per gallon tax on gasoline.

    b.   School taxes based on assessed value of a home.

    c.   Poll tax of $100.

    d.   Medical insurance taxes of 1.45% on all income.

Multiple Choice Questions

1.   The Lorenz curve is
    a. a type of supply curve.
    b. a type of demand curve.
    c. a geometric representation of the share distribution of income.
    d. a geometric representation of the socioeconomic distribution of income.

2.   Which of the four curves in the figure on the right has the most income inequality?
    a. A.
    b. B.
    c. C.
    d. D.

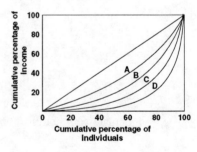

3.   Considering only the direct effects, if the government increases the amount of food stamps and housing assistance it gives out, U.S. poverty, as officially defined,
    a. will be reduced.
    b. will be increased.
    c. will remain unchanged.
    d. cannot be determined from the information.

4.   In the United States in the mid-1990s the poverty income of a family of four is approximately
    a. $3,000.
    b. $10,000.
    c. $15,000.
    d. $20,000.

5. A Lorenz curve for the entire world would show
    a. more income inequality than in the United States.
    b. less income inequality than in the United States.
    c. approximately the same level of income inequality as income in the United States.
    d. no inequality.

6. In a Lorenz curve for the United States, household wealth would
    a. show the same amount of inequality as does family income.
    b. show more inequality than does family income.
    c. show less inequality than does family income.
    d. would show no wealth inequality at all.

7. The gini coefficient is shown by which area in the graph on the right?
    a. A/B
    b. A/(A+B)
    c. B/A
    d. B/(A+B)

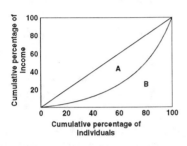

8. On average, women receive somewhere around
    a. 20 percent of the income that men receive to do the same kinds of jobs.
    b. 50 percent of the income that men receive to do the same kinds of jobs.
    c. 75 percent of the income that men receive to do the same kinds of jobs.
    d. 90 percent of the income that men receive to do the same kinds of jobs.

9. The observation that women in two-parent relationships do more work around the house and take more re-
    sponsibility for child rearing than men do is an example of
    a. demand-side discrimination.
    b. supply-side discrimination.
    c. the way things should be.
    d. the way in which men exploit women.

10. The U.S. class system is best represented by
    a. a diamond.
    b. a right-side-up pyramid with upper class on the top.
    c. an upside-down pyramid with upper class on the top.
    d. a square.

A1. Imposing a tax of 40 percent on everyone's income may not be especially effective in redistributing income if
    a. the tax has large incentive effects.
    b. the tax has no incentive effects.
    c. the tax is not progressive
    d. the tax is only proportional.

B1. A progressive tax is one in which the average tax rate
    a. increases with income.
    b. decreases with income.
    c. remains constant with income.
    d. has no loopholes.

B2. The largest government program to redistribute income is
    a. social insurance.
    b. education.
    c. housing.
    d. public aid.

Answers

Short-answer questions

1. A Lorenz curve is a geometric representation of the share distribution of income among families in a given country at a given time. (770)

2. Income became more equally distributed in the United States from 1929 to 1970. (771, 772)

3. Since 1970 income in the United States has become less equally distributed. (771)

4. The official definition of *poverty* is an income equal to or less than three times an average family's minimum food expenditures as calculated by the U.S. Department of Agriculture. (772)

5. The Lorenz curve for household wealth is more bowed than the Lorenz curve for family income. This means that household wealth is less equally distributed than family income. (776-777)

6. Determining whether an equal income distribution is fair is problematic. You tell your friend that first of all people do not start from equivalent positions and income depends upon those initial positions. Second, people's needs differ; some people are happy with less income, while others seem to need a higher income. Lastly, people's efforts differ; some people are willing to work harder than others. Shouldn't that effort be rewarded with higher income? Equality is not synonymous with fairness. (781-783)

7. Although some might agree that a more equal distribution is desirable, there are side effects of redistributing income. They are: (1) A tax to redistribute income may result in a switch from labor to leisure and consequently less production and less total income. (2) An increase in taxes to redistribute income might lead to attempts to avoid or evade taxes, leading to a decrease in measured income. (3) Government programs to redistribute money may cause people to make themselves look poorer than they really are. (783-785)

B1. Five expenditure programs to redistribute income are (1) social security, (2) public assistance, (3) health and medical programs, (4) veterans' programs, and (5) education and housing programs. (791-792)

Word Scramble   1. lorenz curve   2. poverty   3. discrimination

Match the Terms and Concepts to Their Definitions
1-d; 2-c; 3-a; 4-b; 5-g; 6-f; 7-e.

Problems and Exercises

1. a. 46.8%. The top 20 percent of individuals earn 46.8 percent of the income. Calculate this by starting at 80% on the horizontal axis. Draw a vertical line to the Lorenz curve. Look at the value on the vertical axis where this line intersects the Lorenz curve. This is the percent of income that the bottom 80% of individuals earn. To get the amount that the top 20% earn, subtract this number, 53.2, from 100. (771)
    b. 70.9%. Going through the same exercise as in 1(a) but starting at 60%, we find that the bottom 40% earn 29.1% of total income. Subtracting this from 100, we get 70.9%, the percent of total income earned by the top 40%. (771)
    c. (b) is greater than (a). This has to be true, because the vertical axis is the cumulative percentage of income. If the top 20% earn a certain percentage of the total, the top 40% includes that top 20% plus more. (771)
    d. The straight line represents the Lorenz curve if income were equally distributed. Point A says that 100% of individuals earn 100% of the income. This is true by definition. Point C says that 0% of individuals earn 0% of the income. The Lorenz curve is anchored at those points by definition. (771)

2.   a.   First we want to calculate the cumulative percentage of income for each country. We do this below by cumulatively adding together consecutive percentages.

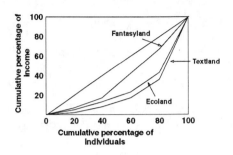

Income quintile	Ecoland	Fantasyland	Textland
Lowest 20%	5%	7%	2%
Second quintile	13	17	8
Third quintile	23	42	17
Fourth quintile	43	67	36
Highest 20%	100	100	100

         We then graph the values and connect the points. This is shown to the right of the table. (775)

   b.   Fantasyland; Ecoland; Textland. The country bowed out to the right the most has the least equal income distribution. It is Textland. The country bowed out the least has the most equal income distribution. It is Fantasyland. Ecoland is in the middle. (775)

B1.   a. $16,252.5. First deduct $20,000 from $87,300 to get taxable income of $67,300. You pay 15% on the first $22,750, 28% on income $22,751 - $55,100, and 31% on the remaining $12,200. Your taxes are .15 x $22,750 + .28 x 32,350 + .31 x $12,200 = $3,412.5 + $9,058 + $3,782 = $16,252.5. (789-790).

   b.   18.6%. Your average tax rate is total taxes divided by total income: $16,252.50/$87,300. (789-790).

   c.   31%. Your marginal tax rate is the rate at which your last dollar earned is taxed. This is 31%. (789-790).

   d.   The tax schedule is progressive. Progressive tax is one in which the average tax rate increases with income. As can be seen by the tax schedule, the marginal tax rate is increasing. Since the marginal tax rate is increasing, and it is above the average tax rate (because of deductions), the average tax rate is increasing too. (789-790)

B2.   a.   5 cent per gallon tax on gasoline is a sales tax and sales taxes tend to be slightly regressive since poor people often spend a higher percentage of their incomes on gasoline than do rich people. That is, the income elasticity of gasoline is less than one. If the income elasticity is 1, the tax would be proportional and if the income elasticity were greater than one, the tax would be progressive. (789-790)

   b.   School taxes based on assessed value of a home are considered to be roughly proportional since the value of a person's home is related to income. That is, the income elasticity of housing is about 1. If the income elasticity were greater than one, the tax would be progressive. (789-790)

   c.   Poll tax of $100 is regressive. The absolute amount remains the same as income rises, but as a percentage of income it declines as income rises. (789-790)

   d.   Medical insurance taxes are proportional since the rate is 1.45% on all income, no matter how high or low. (789-790)

Multiple Choice Questions

1.   c.   See page 770.

2.   d.   The flatter the curve, the more equality. See pages 770-771.

3.   c.   These aspects of income are not taken into account in determining U.S. poverty figures. See pages 772-773.

4.   c.   See page 773.

5.   a.   Since the world income is unequally divided among countries, the world Lorenz curve would have to show more income inequality. (775)

6.   b.   Wealth is considerably less equally distributed than income in the United States. See Exhibit 6, page 777.

7. b. See page 775.

8. c. See page 778.

9. b. This is definitely an example of supply-side discrimination. The answers c or d involve explicit value judgments upon which individuals may differ, and which do not fit with the "it depends" philosophy of this book. See pages 778-779.

10. a. As shown in Exhibit 8, page 781, the U.S. class system is best seen as a diamond. There is a small upper class and a small lower class, and a large middle class.

A1. a. As discussed on pages 788-789, incentive effects can undermine attempts to redistribute income. The c and d answers have little meaning and were placed among the answers only to provide two definitely wrong choices.

B1. a. See page 789.

B2. a. As shown in Exhibit B2, page 791, social insurance is the largest program for redistributing income.

Chapter 35:
Work and the Labor Market

Chapter at a glance

1. Applying rational choice theory to the supply of labor tells us that the higher the wage, the higher the quantity of labor supplied. (795)

    The higher the wage, the more "expensive" it is to "goof-off." So, we work, more; or at least more people decide to work. As wages increase, the quantity of labor supplied increases. We get an upward-sloping supply curve of labor.

    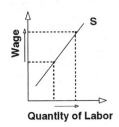
    Quantity of Labor

2. An increase in the marginal tax rate is likely to reduce the quantity of labor supplied because it reduces the net wage of individuals and hence, via individuals' incentive effect, causes them to work less. (797)

    Higher marginal tax rates reduce the incentive to work.

3a. Elasticity of market supply depends on individuals' opportunity cost of working, the type of market being discussed, the elasticity of individuals' supply curves, and individuals entering the labor market. (799)

    An elastic supply of labor means workers are quite responsive to a change in the wage rate. For example, an increase in the wage will result in a relatively large increase in the quantity supplied of labor (number of people looking for work).

3b. Four factors that influence the elasticity of demand for labor are: (800)
    1. The elasticity of demand for the firm's good.
    2. The relative importance of the factor in the production process.
    3. The possibility of, and cost of, substitution in production; and
    4. The degree to which marginal productivity falls with an increase in the factor.

An elastic demand for labor means employers are quite responsive to a change in the wage rate. For example, an increase in the wage will result in a rather dramatic reduction in the number of workers employed.

4. A monopsony is a market in which a single firm is the only buyer. A bilateral monopoly is a market in which a single seller faces a single buyer. (803)

    Monopsony will hire fewer workers and pay a lower wage compared to the competitive outcome.

    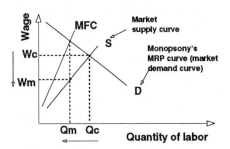

5. Real world labor markets are complicated and must be explained by all three invisible forces; the invisible hand, the invisible handshake, and the invisible foot. (806)

    What we see in the real world is a consequnce of the interaction of these three forces.

6. Three types of discrimination are: (1) discrimination based on individual characteristics that will affect job performance; (2) discrimination based on correctly-perceived statistical characteristics of the group; and (3) discrimination based on individual characteristics that don't affect job performance or are incorrectly perceived. (808)

    One can think of discrimination as treating equals unequally, or treating unequals equally.

    See also, Appendix A: "Derived Demand."

Short-answer questions

1. Use the theory of rational choice and the concept of opportunity cost to explain why firms generally offer time-and-a-half for workers to work on Thanksgiving Day. (LO1)

2. Suppose Congress passes an increase in the marginal income tax rate. What is the likely effect on work effort? (LO2)

3. List two factors that influence the elasticity of labor supply and two factors that influence the elasticity of labor demand. (LO3)

4. Define the terms *monopsonist* and *bilateral monopoly*. (LO4)

5. On average, women earn about 75 cents for every $1 earned by men. Use the three invisible forces to discuss this phenomenon. (LO5)

6. What are three types of discrimination? (LO6)

Word Scramble

1._____ _____ 2._____ _____ 3._____

    a b l o r   t r m k e a   v r i e e d d   a d d e m n   y s m n n o o o p

Match the Terms and Concepts to Their Definitions

___ 1. bilateral monopoly

___ 2. closed shop

___ 3. comparable worth laws

___ 4. derived demand

___ 5. downsizing

___ 6. Dutch disease

___ 7. efficiency wages

___ 8. focal point phenomenon

___ 9. incentive effect

___ 10. labor market

___ 11. marginal factor cost

___ 12. marginal tax rate

___ 13. monopsony

___ 14. union shop

___ 15. outsourcing

a. A market in which only a single firm hires labor.
b. A firm in which all workers must join the union.
c. A market with only a single seller and a single buyer.
d. A firm in which the union controls hiring.
e. Wage that is above the going market wage; paid to keep workers happy and productive.
f. Factor market in which individuals supply labor services for wages to other individuals and to firms that demand labor services.
g. Decision not to work because marginal tax rates are so high while welfare and medical benefits are guaranteed whether one works or not.
h. How much a person will change his or her hours worked in response to a change in the wage rate.
i. A firm shifting production from its own plants to other firms, either in the United States or abroad, where wages are lower.
j. Laws mandating comparable pay for comparable work.
k. Phenomenon where a country focuses on another country as a site for business primarily because it knows the conditions in the country it is considering, while ignoring other countries that may be just as good but about which it has little knowledge.
l. The additional cost to a firm of hiring another worker.
m. A reduction in the workforce of major corporations, especially at the level of middle management.
n. The demand for factors of production by firms; the nature of this derived demand depends upon the demand for the firm's products.
o. The tax you pay on an additional dollar.

Problems and Exercises

1. Use the graph of supply of labor (S$_{L0}$) shown to the right to answer the following questions.

    a. Why is the labor supply upward sloping?

    b. What is the elasticity of supply of labor between A and B? (Use the arc elasticity convention.)

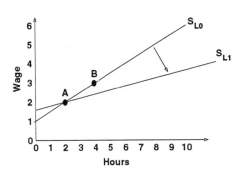

    c. What would happen to the elasticity of labor supply if the curve rotated to S$_{L1}$ as shown?

2. Use the graph to the right to answer the following questions.

    a. Label equilibrium wage and number of workers.

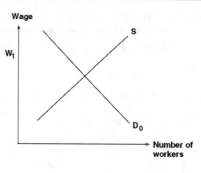

    b. If wages were set by the government at W_1, what happens to
        the supply and demand for labor? How do they differ?

    c. Show how a technological innovation that leads to a higher demand for labor affects equilibrium wage
        and quantity of labor.

3. Answer the following questions using the graph to the right.

    a. Label the equilibrium wage and number of workers if the
        market is competitive.

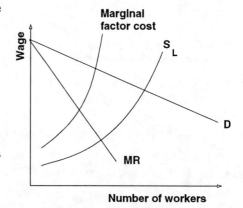

    b. Label the equilibrium wage and number of workers under a
        monopsonist.

    c. If there is a worker's union, what would be the equilibrium wage and level of employment?

A1. Complete the table below for a perfectly competitive firm that produces halogen light bulbs. Each light bulb sells for $1. (Marginal values refers to the marginal change of increasing to that row, i.e., the marginal physical product of going from 23 to 24 workers is 9. The same goes for marginal revenue product.)

	Number of workers	Total product per hour	Marginal physical product per hour	Average product per hour	Marginal revenue product
	20	200		—	
A	21	—	—	—	15
B	22	228	—	—	—
C	23	—	—	10.39	—
D	24	—	9	—	—
E	25	—	—	10.16	—
F	26	259	—	—	—

a. Draw the corresponding labor demand curve, labeling the points on the graph that correspond to the lines of the table.

b. Suppose the price of halogen light bulbs falls to $.50 per bulb. How does your answer to (a) change?

c. If halogen light bulbs sold for $1 per bulb as in (a), how many workers would the firm hire if wages were $5 per hour? If the government set minimum wages at $9 per hour, how many workers would the firm hire?

Multiple Choice Questions

1. Generally, economists believe
    a. the higher the wage, the higher the quantity of labor supplied.
    b. the higher the wage, the further to the right the supply of labor is.
    c. the higher the wage, the further to the left the supply of labor is.
    d. the higher the wage, the lower the quantity of labor supplied.

2. The "Dutch disease" is
    a. a disease involving a lack of incentive to work.
    b. a bacterial disease that reduces work effort.
    c. a viral disease that reduces work effort.
    d. a disease caused by high exports that reduces work effort.

3. The irony of any need-based program is that
    a. it increases the number of needy.
    b. it decreases the number of needy.
    c. it creates other needs.
    d. it destroys needs.

4. The elasticity of supply at Point A in the graph at the right is approxi-
       mately
    a. 0.
    b. .5.
    c. 5.
    d. 10.

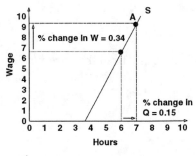

5. The elasticity of supply at Point A in the graph at the right is approxi-
       mately
    a. 0.
    b. .3.
    c. 3.
    d. 10.

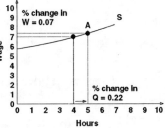

6. The elasticity of labor supply for heads of household (primary workers) is less than that for secondary workers
       because of all the following *except*
    a. institutional factors, such as hours of work, are only slightly flexible.
    b. there are many more new secondary workers who cannot enter the market than there are primary workers.
    c. heads of households have responsibility for seeing that there's food and shelter for the household members.
    d. there are more secondary workers than primary workers.

7. The term "derived demand" refers to
    a. demand by consumers for advertised products.
    b. the demand for luxury goods that is derived from cultural phenomena such as fashion.
    c. the demand for factors of production by firms.
    d. the demand for derivatives.

8. The more elastic the demand for a firm's good,
    a. the more elastic the firm's derived demand for factors.
    b. the less elastic the firm's derived demand for factors.
    c. The elasticity of demand for a firm's good has nothing to do with the firm's derived demand.
    d. The elasticity of demand could cause the elasticity of the derived demand to be either higher or lower.

9. The more important the factor is in the production process
   a. the less elastic the derived demand.
   b. the more elastic the derived demand.
   c. The importance of a factor in the production process has nothing to do with the firm's derived demand.
   d. The importance of a factor in the production process could cause the elasticity of the derived demand to be either higher or lower.

10. Economists distinguish entrepreneurship from labor because
    a. entrepreneurship is more like capital.
    b. entrepreneurship has nothing to do with labor.
    c. entrepreneurship is such an important part of labor that it needs a specific discussion.
    d. entrepreneurs receive only profit.

11. A firm has just changed from being a competitive firm to being a monopolist. Its derived demand for labor
    a. will increase.
    b. will decrease.
    c. might increase or might decrease.
    d. is unaffected because whether the firm is a competitive firm or a monopolist has no effect on the firm's derived demand for labor.

12. A monopsony is
    a. a market with only a single seller and a single buyer of labor.
    b. a market with only a single seller of labor.
    c. a market with only a single buyer of labor.
    d. a market with one seller and two buyers.

13. If firms were controlled by workers rather than by managers, and are expanding,
    a. in that expansion the worker-controlled firms would likely hire more workers.
    b. in that expansion the worker-controlled firms would likely hire fewer workers.
    c. there would be no effect on the number of workers hired.
    d. the number of workers would change, but the effect cannot be determined.

14. The term, efficiency wages, refers to
    a. paying wages equal to marginal revenue product.
    b. paying wages in terms of the product used.
    c. using a bonus system for wages as opposed to a fixed numerical wage.
    d. paying wages above marginal revenue product.

15. A union shop is a shop in which
    a. the union controls hiring.
    b. unions are allowed.
    c. all workers must join the union.
    d. all aspects are controlled by the union.

A1. The marginal revenue product for a competitive firm is defined as
    a. $MPP \times P$.
    b. $MPP \times C$.
    c. $MRP \times C$.
    d. $P \times C$.

A2. The graph on the right shows the marginal revenue product of workers. If the wage is $10, approximately how many workers should it hire?

a. 4.

b. 8.

c. 12.

d. 16.

A3. The marginal product of input A is 20. The marginal product of input B is 40. The price of input A is 2. The price of input B is 3. Which of the following would be the best recommendation you could give based on this information? The firm should

a. hire more A and less B.

b. hire more B and less A.

c. hire more of both A and B.

d. not change its hiring of A and B.

A4. The marginal product of input A is 20. The marginal product of input B is 40. The price of input A is 2. The price of input B is 4. Which of the following would be the best recommendation you could give based on this information? The firm should

a. hire more A and less B.

b. hire more B and less A.

c. fire some of both A and B, but fire more A.

d. not change its hiring of A and B.

Answers

Short-answer questions

1. Work involves opportunity cost. By working one more hour, you have one less hour to devote to nonmarket activities. The theory of rational choice in the case of work means that you will supply work as long as the opportunity cost of working is less than the wage received. Since the opportunity cost of working on a holiday is greater than on other days, firms must offer workers higher wages to work on Thanksgiving Day. This demonstrates that the supply curve for labor is upward sloping: the higher the wage, more labor is supplied. (795)

2. An increase in the marginal tax rate is likely to reduce the quantity of labor supplied because it reduces the net wage of individuals and hence lowers the opportunity cost of not working. (797)

3. Factors that affect the elasticity of labor supply include (1) the individuals' opportunity costs of working, (2) the type of labor market, (3) the elasticity of the individuals' labor supplies, and (4) the individuals entering the market. Factors that influence the elasticity of labor demand are (1) the elasticity of demand for the firm's good, (b) the relative importance of labor to production, (c) the possibility of, and costs of, substitution in production, and (4) the degree to which marginal productivity falls with an increase in labor. (799-800)

4. A *monopsonist* is a firm in a market where it is the only buyer of labor. A *bilateral monopoly* is a market in which a single seller faces a single buyer. (803)

5. Real-world labor markets are complicated and must be explained by all three invisible forces. For example, the fact that women earn about 75 cents for every $1 earned by men must be explained by the invisible hand, the invisible foot, and the invisible handshake. Here are some of the many ways in which these forces can explain this phenomenon: It is argued that employers discriminate against women, paying them less for the same job because they have a distaste for hiring women. This is an example of the invisible handshake. This would result in lower wages. Women's lower pay may also result from social forces that discourage mothers from working outside the home so that women will supply labor intermittently, lowering their wage. This is an example of the invisible handshake and the invisible hand. Comparable worth laws, antidiscrimination laws, and affirmative action laws have been passed in an effort to counteract this pay inequality. These are examples of the invisible foot. (795, 805-809)

6. Three types of discrimination are (1) discrimination based on individual characteristics that affect job performance, (2) discrimination based on correctly-perceived statistical characteristics of the group; and (3) discrimination on individual characteristics that do not affect job performance or are incorrectly perceived. (808)

Word Scramble   1. labor market   2. derived demand   3. monopsony

Match the Terms and Concepts to Their Definitions

1-c; 2-d; 3-j; 4-n; 5-m; 6-g; 7-e; 8-k; 9-h; 10-f; 11-l; 12-o; 13-a; 14-b; 15-i.

Problems and Exercises

1. a. The labor supply curve is upward sloping because the opportunity cost of not working increases as wage get higher. (795)
    b. The elasticity of labor supply is percent change in quantity supplied divided by the percent change in wage. Between points A and B it is $[(4-2)/3]/[(3-2)/2.5] = 5/3$. (798)
    c. The elasticity of labor supply becomes greater with a flatter curve such as S_{L1}. (798)

2. a. Equilibrium wage and number of workers with demand, D_0, and supply, S, is shown on the right as W_E and Q_E. At this point labor demand equals labor supply. At a wage above W_E, there will be pressure for wages to fall as the quantity of labor supplied exceeds the quantity of labor demanded. At a wage below W_E, there will be pressure for wages to rise as the quantity of labor demanded exceeds the quantity of labor supplied. (803)

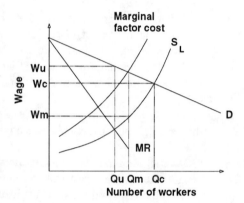

b. If wages were set by the government at W_1, the quantity of labor supplied would rise to S_1 and the quantity of labor demanded would fall to D_1. Quantity supplied would exceed quantity demanded. This is shown in the graph to the right. (803)

c. A technological innovation that leads to a higher demand for labor will lead to a higher equilibrium wage and higher quantity of labor employed as the demand curve shifts to the right from D_0 to D_1. Equilibrium wage is now W_1 and equilibrium labor is S_1. (803)

3. a. If the market is competitive, the wage and employment level will be where the demand and supply curves for labor intersect. This is at W_c and Q_c respectively on the graph to the right. (804)

b. The monopsonist will hire workers where the marginal factor cost of labor intersects the demand for labor. A monopsonist would hire Q_m workers, less than the competitive level, and pay a wage W_m, lower than the competitive wage. (804)

c. Unions would push for higher wages than a firm in a competitive market or a monopsonist would be willing to pay. Wage would be at somewhere between W_u and W_m and would depend upon the negotiating skills and other noneconomic forces. The number of workers hired would then be somewhere between Q_u and Q_m depending upon the negotiated wage. (804)

A1. Below is the completed table for a perfectly competitive firm who produces halogen light bulbs. (Marginal values refers to the marginal change of increasing to that row, i.e., the marginal physical product of going from 23 to 24 workers is 9. The same goes for marginal revenue product.)

	Number of workers	Total product per hour	Marginal physical product per hour	Average product per hour	Marginal revenue product
	20	200		10	
A	21	215	15	10.24	$15
B	22	228	13	10.36	13
C	23	239	11	10.39	11
D	24	247	9	10.29	9
E	25	254	7	10.16	7
F	26	259	5	9.96	5

We use the following relationships to fill in the table: Marginal physical product equals the change in the total product. Average product is the total product divided by the number of workers. Marginal revenue product equals marginal physical product times price of the product. (814-816)

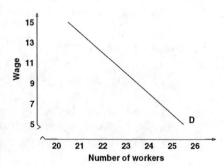

a. The corresponding labor demand curve is shown on the right. Labor demand is a derived demand. A firm is willing to pay the marginal revenue product of the additional worker to hire that additional worker. The wage at each level of workers is equal to the marginal revenue product. (815)

b. Suppose the demand for halogen light bulbs fell and their price fell to $.50 per bulb. The marginal revenue product would be halved and the demand curve for labor would shift in as shown in the figure on the right. The marginal revenue product is shown in the table below. (Marginal values refers to the marginal change of increasing to that row, i.e., the marginal physical product of going from 23 to 24 workers is 9. The same goes for marginal revenue product.) (815)

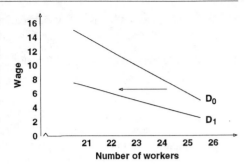

Marginal physical Number of workers	Total product per hour	($0.5) product per hour	Average product per hour	Marginal revenue product
20	200		10	
A 21	215	15	10.24	7.5
B 22	228	13	10.36	6.5
C 23	239	11	10.39	5.5
D 24	247	9	10.29	4.5
E 25	254	7	10.16	3.5
F 26	259	5	9.96	2.5

c. At $1 per bulb and wages of $5 per hour, the firm would hire between 25 and 26; At $1 per bulb and minimum wage of $9 per hour the firm would hire between 23 and 24. A firm in a competitive industry will hire up to the point where the wage equals *MPP* times *P*, or the fifth column of the table in (a). *MPP* times *P* is $5 between 25 and 26 workers. When wages are $5, it will hire between 25 and 26 workers. If the minimum wage were $9, the firm would hire workers to where *MPP* times *P* equals, $9, or between 23 and 24 workers. (814-816)

Multiple Choice Questions

1. a.   The supply curve of labor is considered upward sloping. When there is a movement along the supply curve caused by an increase in the wage, the movement is called an increase in the quantity supplied, not an increase in supply. See page 795.

2. a.   As discussed on page 797 of the text, a is the correct answer. The others we simply made up.

3. a.   As discussed on pages 797-798, a need-based program reduces people's incentives to prevent themselves from becoming needy, and thus a need-based program increases the number of needy.

4. b.   The percent change in quantity is approximately .14; the percent change in wage is approximately .3, so the elasticity is approximately .14/.3 or approximately .5. See pages 798-799, especially Exhibit 2.

5. c.   The percent change in quantity is approximately .2; the percent change in wage is approximately .07, so the elasticity is approximately .2/.07 or approximately 3. See pages 798-799, especially Exhibit 2.

6. d.   The number of primary workers compared to the number of secondary workers has nothing to do with elasticity. See pages 798-799.

7. c.   As discussed on page 800, the derived demand is the demand for factors that is derived from consumer demand.

8. a.   When a rise in price will cause significant loss of revenue (which it does when its demand is elastic), the firm takes that into account in its decision of what to pay workers. See page 800.

9. a.   See page 800.

10. c.   Entrepreneurship is a type of creative labor that is very important and needs a separate discussion. Answer d is not correct because entrepreneurs can receive more than merely profits. See page 801.

11. b.   As is discussed on pages 803 and 804, the monopolist uses marginal revenue, which is lower than the price that the competitive firm uses, and therefore the monopolist's derived demand for labor is lower.

12. c.   As discussed on page 803, a monopsony is a market in which only a single firm hires labor.

13. b.   When there are worker-controlled firms, they will want to have a higher marginal revenue product for existing workers. Thus, they will hire fewer workers. See pages 802-804.

14. d.   The correct answer is d. As discussed on page 806, firms might pay workers more than their marginal revenue product if the firms want to keep their workers' emotional state positive and thus make workers more productive.

15. c.   As discussed on pages 809-810, in a union shop, individuals are required to join the union, but the firm does the hiring.

A1. a.   See page 814.

A2. b.   The firm should hire workers until the wage equals the marginal revenue product. See pages 814-815.

A3. b.   The marginal revenue per dollar is higher for input B so it should hire more of B if it is going to hire more. The other answers do not meet the cost minimization condition. See page 818.

A4. d.   The marginal revenue per dollar is equal for inputs A and B so it should not change the proportional amounts used. The other answers do not meet the cost minimization condition. See page 818.

Chapter 36:
Nonwage and Asset Income: Rents, Profits, and Interest

Chapter at a glance

1a. Rent is the income from a factor of production that is in fixed supply. (821)

A fixed supply means the supply curve is perfectly inelastic (vertical).

1b. As long as land is perfectly inelastic in supply, landowners will pay the entire burden of a tax on land, as in the graph below. (822)

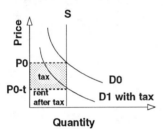

2. Rent seeking is the restricting of supply in order to increase its price. It is an attempt to change the institutional structure and hence the underlying property rights. (823)

Rent seeking is an attempt to make more money by trying to create ownership rights or institutional structures that favor the rent-seeker.

3. Normal profits are the amount that an entrepreneur can get by supplying entrepreneurship to the market. Economic profits are the entrepreneur's return above and beyond normal profits. (824)

Normal profits equal the opportunity cost of the entrepreneur (an amount of profits just sufficient to keep that entrepreneur in that line of business.)

4. An entrepreneur seeks market niches because within those niches lie economic profits. (825)

To make economic profits may also require rent seeking behavior.

5a. Interest is the income paid to savers—individuals who produce now but do not consume now. (826)

The interest rate is the reward to savers for forgone current consumption, but is the cost of borrowing to businesses (and other borrowers).

5b. Interest plays an essential role in the present value formula. (826)

Present value (PV) is determining the current worth of money received in the future. The greater the interest rate or time frame, the smaller the PV.

6a. PV = X/i states the annuity rule: Present value of any annuity is the annual income it yields divided by the interest rate. (X is a specific flow of income.) (827)

For example:
$40 received annually for 30 years when i = 8% = .08 is worth $40/.08 = $500 today.

6b. The rule of 72 states that 72 divided by the interest rate is the number of years in which a certain amount of money will double in value. (828)

$100 at 6% will double in 12 years (72/6 = 12)

7. Marginal productivity theory states that factors of production are paid their marginal revenue product. (829)

Also depends on ownership rights—who owns what.

Short-answer questions

1. What is *rent*? (LO1)

2. Say the government places a tax on the user of land. What will the tax do to the quantity of land supplied? What will the tax do to the price of the land? And who will end up bearing the burden of that tax? (LO1)

3. Recently, Qualitex, a maker of ironing board covers, successfully petitioned the Supreme Court to patent the color of its covers. The firm spent millions in lawyer fees to pursue the patent. This is an example of what type of economic behavior? (LO2)

4. How is rent-seeking related to property rights? (LO2)

5. What is the difference between normal profits and economic profits? (LO3)

6. Why are market niches important to entrepreneurs? (LO4)

7. What is *interest*? (LO5)

8. Suppose the interest rate is 6%, what is the present value of $100 to be received in 10 years? What happens to the present value of that $100 if the interest rate falls? Why? (Use Exhibit 4 on page 827 to find the answer.) (LO5)

9. Use the rule of 72 to calculate how long it will take for $100 to double if the interest rate is 4%. What happens to the number of years it takes for that $100 to double if the interest rate rises? Why? (LO6)

10. What does marginal productivity theory imply about income distribution? (LO7)

Word Scramble

1. _____ _____   2._____   3._____
     t s r p n e e   v u l e a   e e i n r s t t   t r e n

Match the Terms and Concepts to Their Definitions

_____ 1. annuity rule

_____ 2. contractual legal system

_____ 3. economic profits

_____ 4. interest

_____ 5. marginal productivity theory

_____ 6. market niche

_____ 7. normal profits

_____ 8. present value

_____ 9. profit

_____ 10. property rights

_____ 11. quasi rent

_____ 12. rent

_____ 13. rent seeking

_____ 14. the rule of 72

_____ 15. zoning laws

a. 72 divided by the interest rate is the number of years in which a certain amount of money will double in value.
b. A return on entrepreneurial activity and risk taking.
c. A return on entrepreneurship above and beyond normal profits.
d. An area in which competition is not working.
e. Any payment to a resource above the amount that the resource would receive in its next-best use (also called producer surplus).
f. Factors of production are paid their marginal revenue product.
g. Laws that set limits on the use of one's property.
h. Method of translating a flow of future income or savings into its current worth.
i. Payments to entrepreneurs as the return on their risk taking.
j. Present value of any annuity is the annual income it yields divided by the interest rate.
k. The income from a factor of production that is in fixed supply.
l. The income paid to savers—individuals who produce now but do not consume now.
m. The restricting of supply in order to increase its price.
n. The set of laws that govern economic behavior.
o. The rights to use specific property as one sees fit.

Problems and Exercises

1. Recently the Supreme Court decided that the shade "Sun Glow" (Brass No. 6587) used by Qualitex to dye its pressing-machine pads could be patented. Show with supply and demand for Brass No. 6587 how Qualitex will earn rents from its patent.

2. Demonstrate graphically how the price of a good which is in fixed supply is determined.

   a. Show the effect of a tax on the price and equilibrium quantity for that good.

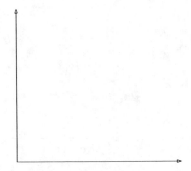

b.   In the short-run, apartments are in fixed supply. The local municipality is considering increasing property taxes on apartments. How would the tax affect the landlords? How would it affect the renters?

3.   A representative firm in a competitive market is earning economic profits.

a.   Draw the *MC, ATC,* and *MR* curves for this firm.

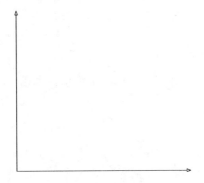

b.   Explain what happens in the long run to economic profits. Demonstrate this situation for the representative firm. Does the firm enjoy normal profits?

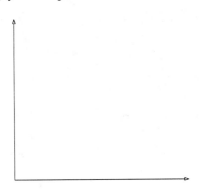

c.   Is it possible that the market never reaches long-run equilibrium? How?

4.   Calculate the present value of receiving $10 each year.

a.   To be received for 7 years. Interest rates are 6%.

    b.   To be received for 15 years. Interest rates are 6%.

    c.   To be received for 15 years. Interest rates are 3%.

    d.   Of a, b, or c, which would you prefer to receive?

    e.   What is the present value of $10 to be received in perpetuity given interest rates in (b) and (c)?

5.   Determine the present value of the following.

    a. $100 to be received in 5 years. Interest rate is 6%.

    b. $100 to be received in 10 years. Interest rate is 4%.

    c.   Assuming the interest rates in (a) and (b), how long will it take to double a $100 investment?

Multiple Choice Questions

1.   If one imposes a tax on a factor with perfectly inelastic supply,
    a. the quantity supplied will decrease.
    b. the supply will decrease.
    c. the quantity supplied will increase.
    d. none of the above.

2. In the graph on the right at point A on the supply curve, a quasi-rent going to an individual A
    a. would be Q*A.
    b. would be AB.
    c. would be Q*B.
    d. cannot be determined from the graph.

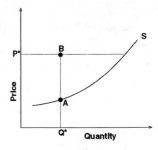

3. When suppliers rent-seek they
    a. use the present value formula to determine what the values of flows of money are.
    b. use the present value formula to determine the values of annuities.
    c. attempt to restrict supply in order to increase the price they get.
    d. attempt to tax land.

4. Rent-seeking causes waste. Therefore
    a. rent-seeking should be prohibited.
    b. rent-seeking should be taxed.
    c. the government should take a laissez-faire position on rent-seeking.
    d. it depends.

5. If a market is in disequilibrium, economic profits must be
    a. positive.
    b. negative.
    c. zero.
    d. none of the above.

6. You are to receive $100 per year forever. The interest rate in the economy is 10 percent. The present value of that $100 forever is
    a. $100.
    b. $1,000.
    c. $10,000.
    d. Infinite, because it goes on forever.

7. If the interest rate is 8 percent, how many years will it take for a fixed amount of money to double?
    a. 1 year.
    b. 9 years.
    c. 14 years.
    d. 72 years.

8. Human capital is
    a. smart machines.
    b. robots.
    c. a type of labor.
    d. both (a) and (b).

9. Marginal productivity theory is
    a. a complete theory of distribution.
    b. a theory of distribution given property rights.
    c. a theory of present value.
    d. a theory of interest.

Answers

Short-answer questions

1. *Rent* is income from a factor of production that is in fixed supply. (821)

2. The quantity of land supplied will not change. The price of the land will not change and landowners will bear the entire burden of a tax on land because the supply of land is perfectly inelastic. (821-822)

3. This is an example of *rent seeking*, an attempt to create ownership rights in order to restrict supply and increase price of the good to be owned. (823)

4. Rent-seeking is an attempt to change underlying property rights. (823)

5. Normal profits are the amount that an entrepreneur can get by supplying entrepreneurship to the market. Economic profits are the entrepreneur's profits above and beyond normal profits. (824)

6. Market niches are where entrepreneurs can capture economic profit. (825)

7. *Interest* is income paid to savers — individuals who produce now but do not consume now. (826)

8. The present value of $100 to be received in 10 years when the interest rate is 6% is $56. The present value of that $100 rises when the interest rate falls because as the interest rate falls, you need more today to reach $100 in ten years with the lower interest rate. (826-828)

9. Using the rule of 72 to calculate when $100 will double if the interest rate is 4%, we divide 72 by 4 to get 18 years. If the interest rate rises, it will take fewer years for $100 to double because you are earning a higher return each year on that $100 with a higher interest rate. (828)

10. Marginal productivity theory states that factors of production are paid their marginal revenue product. So, income is distributed based upon marginal revenue product. (828-829)

Word Scramble   1. present value   2. interest   3. rent

Match the Terms and Concepts to Their Definitions
1-j; 2-n; 3-c; 4-l; 5-f; 6-d; 7-i; 8-h; 9-b; 10-o; 11-e; 12-k; 13-m; 14-a; 15-g.

Problems and Exercises

1. Rent is income from a factor of production that is in fixed supply. Since Qualitex has a patent on Brass No. 6587, it can restrict supply from Q_C to Q_F as shown in the graph to the right. The resulting price, P_F, is above P_B, the opportunity cost of supplying the color. The difference between the cost, P_B, and the price, P_F, is rent earned by Qualitex. (821-822)

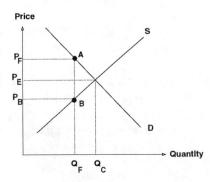

2. A factor with a fixed (inelastic) supply is shown by a vertical supply curve. An inelastic supply together with a downward-sloping demand curve is shown on the right. Price is determined by the intersection of the two curves and is $P*$ in the graph. Quantity will always be the quantity at which the factor is fixed, $Q*$. This is also shown in Exhibit 1 on page 821. (821)

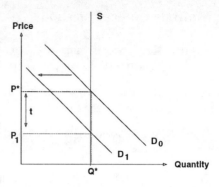

a. The effect of a tax on the price and equilibrium quantity for a factor in fixed supply is shown on the graph to the right. A tax of t will shift the demand curve down from D_0 to D_1, leaving the after-tax price that the consumer pays constant but lowering the after-tax price that the supplier receives by t. Quantity will remain constant. (821-822)

b. The landlords would bear the entire burden of the tax as shown by the graph for 2(a). Landlords receive an after-tax price of $P_1 = P* - t$. The renters would pay the same after-tax rent of $P*$. (821-822)

3. a. The *MC, ATC,* and *MR* curves for a representative firm earning economic profits in a competitive market are shown below on the left where price $= P_0$. Price must be above *ATC* for the firm to be earning economic profits. (824)

    b. In the long run more firms enter the market and bid the price down from P_0 to P_1. All economic profit is competed away as shown in the graph below on the right. The firm still enjoys normal profit. (824-825)

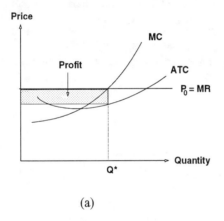

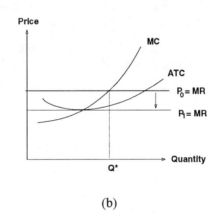

(a)   (b)

c. Firms who are operating in market niches can continue to earn economic profit as long as price is kept above average total costs. This can happen, for example, if the firm has an innovation that is patented. In these cases the "profit" is generally called rent. (825)

4. Use the annuity table found in Exhibit 4(b) in your text on page 827. The annuity table gives the value of $1 per year. Find the number of years and interest rate and multiply this number by $10 to find the value of the $10. (827)

    a. $55.80. Find row for 7 years, column for 6%. Multiply this by 10. (827)
    b. $97.10. Find row for 15 years, column for 6%. Multiply this by 10. (827)
    c. $119.40 Find row for 15 years, column for 3%. Multiply this by 10. (827)
    d. Assuming I am rational, which I am, I would select the one with the highest present value, which is c. (827)
    e. (b) $166.67; (c) $333.33. Use the annuity rule (Present value = annual payment divided by the interest rate.) For (b) this is $10/.06. For (c) this is $10/.03. (826-827)

5. Use the present value table found in Exhibit 4(a) in your text on page 827. The present value table gives the value now of $1 to be received in a certain number of years in the future. Find the number of years and interest rate and multiply this number by the amount to be received. (827)

    a. $75. Find row for 5 years, column for 6%. Multiply this by 100. (827)
    b. $68. Find row for 10 years, column for 4%. Multiply this by 100. (827)
    c. (a) 12 years; (b) 18 years. Using the rule of 72 (the number of years it takes for a certain amount to double in value is equal to 72 divided by the rate of interest), divide 72 by six for (a) and divide 72 by 4 for (b). (826-828)

Multiple Choice Questions

1. d. The answer is "none of the above," as discussed on pages 821-822 of the text. If the supply is perfectly inelastic, all the tax will be paid by the supplier; output will not change. See Exhibit 1, page 821.

2. b. The quasi-rent is measured by the distance between the supply curve and the equilibrium price. See Exhibit 2, page 823.

3. c. As discussed on page 823 of the text, the answer is to restrict supply in order to increase the price they receive.

4. d. As with just about any policy question in this text, the author believes that what policy should be undertaken depends upon the specifics. Since this question gives no specifics, d is the correct answer. See pages 823-824.

5. d. Economic profits are a return above and beyond normal profits. In disequilibrium, economic profits may be either negative or positive, leaving d as the only correct answer. See pages 824-825.

6. b. The annuity rule from page 827 of the text states that the present value is equal to the annuity divided by the interest rate. Therefore we know that this flow is valued at $1,000. (827)

7. b. Using the rule of 72, we divide 72 by 8 and determine that the answer is 9 years. See page 828.

8. c. As discussed on page 829 of the text, human capital is a type of labor. Individuals use the concept "human capital" to emphasize that there are profit and rent components to wages.

9. b. The text emphasizes that to have a complete theory one must explain why property rights are what they are. Marginal productivity theory plays a role in a complete theory of distribution, but it is not a complete theory. See page 829.

Chapter 37:
International Trade Restrictions

Chapter at a glance

1. The primary partners of the United States are Canada, Western Europe, Latin America, Japan, and Southeast Asia. (834)

   See Exhibits 1, 2, and 3 on pages 835-836.

2. The principle of comparative advantage states that as long as the relative opportunity costs of producing goods differ among countries, there are potential gains from trade. (834)

   ✔ *When countries specialize in the production of those goods for which each has a <u>comparative advantage</u> and then trades, all economies involved benefit.*

3. Three determinants of the gains of trade are: (838)
   1. The more competition, the less the trader gets.
   2. Smaller countries get a larger proportion of the gain than larger countries.
   3. Countries producing goods with economies of scale get a larger gain from trade.

   Also: countries which specialize and trade along the lines of comparative advantage are able to consume more than if they did not undertake trade (they are able to escape the confines of their own production possibility curves).

4. Reasons for restricting trade include: (839):
   1. Unequal internal distribution of the gains from trade.
   2. Haggling by companies over the gains from trade.
   3. Haggling by countries over trade restrictions.
   4. Specialized production; learning by doing and economies of scale.
   5. Macroeconomic aspects of trade.
   6. National security.
   7. International politics.
   8. Increased revenues brought in by tariffs.

   ✔ *Understand these motives for trade barriers and be able to explain why they may be fallacious.*

5. Economists generally oppose trade restrictions because: (843)
   1. from a global perspective, free trade increases total output;
   2. trade restrictions lead to retaliation; and
   3. international trade provides competition for domestic companies.

   Economists argue that the benefits of free trade outweigh the costs—especially over time.

6. Three policies used to restrict trade are: (844)
   1. tariffs (taxes on internationally traded goods),
   2. quotas (quantity limits placed on imports), and
   3. regulatory trade restrictions (government-imposed procedural rules that limit imports).

   Countries can also restrict trade through
   a) *voluntary restraint agreements*
   b) *embargoes*
   c) *nationalistic appeals.*

   See also, Appendix A: "The Geometry of Absolute Advantage and Comparative Advantage."

Short-answer questions

1. Who are the primary trading partners of the United States? (LO1)

2. What is the principle of comparative advantage? (LO2)

3. What are three determinants of the gains of trade? (LO3)

4. In a talk to first-year Congresspeople, you reveal that you believe in free trade. Hands fly up from people just waiting to tell you why they want to restrict trade. What are some of their reasons? (LO4)

5. After listening to their remarks, you gather your thoughts and offer them reasons why you generally oppose trade restrictions. What do you say? (LO5)

6. The first-year Congresspeople disregard what you said and ask you what are the ways they can restrict trade. Although you are a proponent of free trade, you oblige. (LO6)

Word Scramble

1._____   2._____   _____   _____   3._____   _____
    a q t u o   d r w l o   d r e t a   a n o t i g o z i r a n   a c e g i r s t t   r n n i i g g b a a

Match the Terms and Concepts to Their Definitions

___ 1. economies of scale

___ 2. embargo

___ 3. World Trade Organization

___ 4. free trade association

___ 5. General agreement on Tariffs and Trade (GATT)

___ 6. infant industry argument

___ 7. learning by doing

___ 8. most-favored nation

___ 9. principle of comparative advantage

___ 10. quota

___ 11. regulatory trade restrictions

___ 12. strategic bargaining

___ 13. tariff

___ 14. trade adjustment assistance programs

a. A tax governments place on internationally traded goods—generally imports.

b. All-out restriction on import or export of a good.

c. As long as the relative opportunity costs of producing goods differ among countries, there are potential gains from trade, even if one country has an absolute advantage in everything.

d. Costs per unit output go down as output increases.

e. Country that will pay as low a tariff on its exports as will any other country.

f. Demanding a larger share of the gains of trade than you can reasonably expect.

g. Government-imposed procedural rules that limit imports.

h. Group of countries that allow free trade among its members and put up common barriers against all other countries' goods.

i. Periodic international conference held in the past to reduce trade barriers.

j. Programs designed to compensate losers for reductions in trade restrictions.

k. Quantity limit placed on imports.

l. An organization whose functions are generally the same as were those of GATT—to promote free and fair trade among countries.

m. With initial protection, an industry will be able to become competitive.

n. You become better at a task the more you perform it.

Problems and Exercises

1. a. State whether there is a basis for trade in the following:
   Case 1: In Country A the opportunity cost of producing one widget is two wadgets; In Country B the opportunity cost of producing two widgets is four wadgets.

   Case 2: In Country C the opportunity cost of producing one widget is two wadgets; In Country D the opportunity cost of producing two widgets is one wadget.

   Case 3: In Country E the opportunity cost of producing one widget is two wadgets; In Country F the opportunity cost of producing one widget is four wadgets.

b. On what general principle did base your reasoning?

c. Assume that is Case 3 there are constant marginal returns and constant returns to scale. Country E is currently producing 10 widgets and 4 wadgets. Country F is currently producing 20 widgets and 20 wadgets. Can you make an offer involving trade that will make both countries better off?

d. How would your answer differ if each country experience economies of scale?

2. Suppose the U.S. is considering trade restriction against EU-produced hams. Given the demand and supply curves drawn on the right, show a tariff and quota that would result in the same quantity of imported hams.

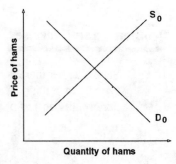

a. Which would result in higher government revenue?

b. Which would the EU prefer?

c. Which would American ham producers prefer?

d. Which would American consumers prefer?

A1. Suppose country A and country B are potential trading partners. Each country produces two goods: fish and wine. If country A devotes all its resources to producing fish it can produce 1000 fish, and if it devotes all it resources to producing wine, it can produce 2000 bottles of wine. If country B devotes all its resources to producing fish it can produce 3000 fish, and if it devotes all its resources to producing wine it can produce 3000 bottles of wine.   For simplicity, assume the production possibility curves of these countries are straight lines.

    a. Draw the production possibility curve for country A on the axes to the right. In country A, what is the opportunity cost of one bottle of wine in terms of fish?

    b. Draw the production possibility curve for country B on the axes for (a). In country B, what is the opportunity cost of one bottle of wine in terms of fish?

    c. Does country A have an absolute advantage in producing either wine or fish? Does country B have an absolute advantage in producing either wine or fish?

    d. Does country A have a comparative advantage in producing either wine or fish? Does country B have a comparative advantage in producing either wine or fish?

    e. Suppose country A specialized in that good for which it has a comparative advantage and country B specialized in that good for which it has a comparative advantage. Each country would then trade the good it produced for the good the other country produced. What would be a fair exchange of goods?

A2. Suppose two countries A and B have the following production possibility tables:

% resources devoted to machines	Country A		Country B	
	Machines produced	Food produced	Machines produced	Food produced
A 100	200	0	40	0
B 80	160	8	32	40
C 60	120	16	28	80
D 40	80	24	24	120
E 20	40	32	16	160
F 0	0	40	0	200

a. Draw the production possibility curves for country A and country B to the right of the table.

b. Which country has the absolute advantage in the production of food?

c. Which country has the comparative advantage in the production of food?

d. Suppose each country specializes in the production of one good. Explain how country A can end up with 50 food units and 150 machines and country B can end up with 150 food units and 50 machines. Both points are outside the production possibility curve for each country without trade.

Multiple Choice Questions

1. As a percentage of GDP, the U.S. imports are approximately
    a. 1 percent.
    b. 10 percent.
    c. 18 percent.
    d. 28 percent.

2. The graph on the right demonstrates Saudi Arabia's and the United States's production possibility curves for widgets and wadgets. Given these production possibility curves, you would suggest that
    a. Saudi Arabia specialize in widgets and the United States in wadgets.
    b. no trade should take place.
    c. Saudi Arabia specialize in wadgets and the United States in widgets.
    d. Both countries should produce an equal amount of each.

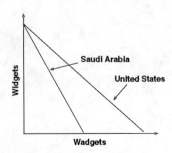

3. A widget has an opportunity cost of 4 wadgets in Saudi Arabia and 2 wadgets in the United States. Given these opportunity costs, you would suggest that
   a. Saudi Arabia specialize in widgets and the United States in wadgets.
   b. no trade should take place.
   c. Saudi Arabia specialize in wadgets and the United States in widgets.
   d. Both countries produce an equal amount of each.

4. Country A's cost of widgets is $4.00 and cost of wadgets is $8.00. Country B's cost of widgets is 8 francs and cost of wadgets is 16 francs. Which of the following would you suggest?
   a. Country A should specialize in widgets and Country B in wadgets.
   b. no trade should take place.
   c. Country A should specialize in wadgets and Country B in widgets.
   d. Both countries should produce an equal amount of each.

5. In considering the distribution of the gains from trade
   a. smaller countries usually get a large proportion of the gains.
   b. larger countries usually get a larger proportion of the gains.
   c. the gains are generally equally split equally between small and large countries.
   d. no statement can be made about the general nature of the split.

6. In regard to the gains from trade, the countries producing goods with economies of scale
   a. usually get larger gains from trade.
   b. usually get smaller gains from trade.
   c. usually get no gains from trade.
   d. It is impossible to make any general statement about gains from trade and economies of scale.

7. Reasons for restricting trade include all the following *except*
   a. the existence of learning by doing and economies of scale.
   b. national security reasons.
   c. the increased revenue brought in from tariffs.
   d. the fact that trade decreases competitive pressures at home.

8. Economists generally oppose trade restrictions for all the following reasons *except*
   a. from a global perspective, free trade increases total output.
   b. the infant industry argument.
   c. trade restrictions lead to retaliation.
   d. trade forces domestic producers to be more efficient.

9. A tariff is
   a. a tax government places on internationally-traded goods.
   b. a quantity limit placed on imports.
   c. an all-out restriction on imports.
   d. a government-imposed procedural rule that limits imports.

10. An embargo is
   a. a tax government places on internationally-traded goods.
   b. a quantity limit placed on imports.
   c. an all-out restriction on imports.
   d. a government-imposed procedural rule that limits imports.

A1. The graph on the right demonstrates Country A's and Country B's production possibility curves for widgets and wadgets. Given these production possibility curves, you would suggest that
   a. Country A should specialize in widgets and Country B in wadgets.
   b. no trade should take place.
   c. Country A should specialize in wadgets and Country B in widgets.
   d. Both countries should produce an equal amount of each.

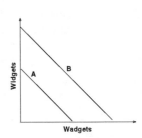

Answers

Short-answer questions

1. The primary trading partners of the United States, those to whom we export or from whom we import most, are Canada, Western Europe, Latin America, Japan, and Southeast Asia. (834)

2. The principle of comparative advantage is that as long as the relative opportunity costs of production differ among countries, there are potential gains from trade, even if one country has an absolute advantage in everything. (834)

3. Three determinants of the gains of trade are (1) the more competition, the less the trader gets and the more will go to the countries who are trading; (2) smaller countries get a larger proportion of the gain than larger countries; and (3) countries producing goods with economies of scale get a larger gain from trade. (838)

4. Their answers might include: (1) although foreign competition might make society better off, some people may lose their jobs because of foreign competition (unequal internal distribution of the gains from trade); (2) some foreign companies are taking tough bargaining positions, and restricting trade is our only weapon against that (haggling by companies over trade restrictions); (3) some foreign countries are threatening us with trade restrictions (haggling by countries over the gains from trade); (4) trade restrictions will protect nascent U.S. industries until they learn to be competitive (learning by doing and economies of scale); (5) imports hurt U.S. domestic income in the short run, and the economy needs to grow in the short run (trade can reduce domestic output in the short run); (6) some restrictions are needed to protect our national security; (7) we do not want to trade with countries who violate our human rights standards or whose ideology conflicts with our democratic ideals (international politics may dominate trade considerations); and (8) tariffs bring in revenue for the U.S. government. (839)

5. I would say that I generally oppose trade restrictions because (1) from a global perspective, free trade increases total output, (2) trade restrictions lead to retaliation, and (3) international trade provides competition for domestic companies. (843)

6. Three policies countries use to restrict trade are (1) tariffs, (2) quotas, and (3) regulatory trade restrictions. (844)

Word Scramble   1. quota   2. World Trade Organization   3. strategic bargaining

Match the Terms and Concepts to Their Definitions
1-d; 2-b; 3-l; 4-h; 5-i; 6-m; 7-n; 8-e; 9-c; 10-k; 11-g; 12-f; 13-a; 14-j.

Problems and Exercises

1. a. There is a basis for trade in Cases 2 and 3. (834)
    b. The general principle is that there are gains from trade to be made when each country has a comparative advantage in one or the other good. (834)
    c. I would have country E specialize in widgets and country F specialize in wadgets. Since country E is currently producing 10 widgets and 4 wadgets I would have it produce 12 widgets and no wadgets, promising that I will give it 5 wadgets for the extra two widgets it produced. I would have Country F produce 28 wadgets and 18 widgets, promising that I will give it 2 widgets in return for 7 of its wadgets. After I made this trade both countries are one wadget better off. I am two wadgets better off. (These two wadgets is the return to me for organizing the trade. (834, 836-837)
    d. If there were economies of scale, there would be an even stronger argument for trade. (834)

2. A tariff would shift the supply curve to the left by the amount of the tariff. A quota with the same result would be at Q_1. Equilibrium quantity would fall from Q_0 to Q_1. Equilibrium price would rise from P_0 to P_1. This is shown on the right. (844-845)

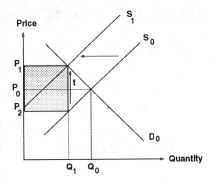

a. The government receives no revenue from the quota, but receives the shaded region as revenue from the tariff as shown on the graph on the right. (844-845)

b. Germany would prefer the quota since it will receive a higher price, P_1, for the same quantity of goods, Q_1 as it would with a tariff. With a tariff it would receive P_2, for Q_1. (844-845)

c. American ham producers prefer the quota because any increase in domestic demand would be met by domestic supply. (845)

d. American consumers do not prefer either since the resulting price and quantity is the same with both. If, however, the tariff revenue were to lead to lower taxes or higher government services, they might prefer the tariff over the quota. They also might prefer the tariff to the quota because any increase in domestic demand will be partially met with imports, keeping domestic producers more efficient than under a quota system. (843, 844-845)

A1. a. The production possibility curve for country A is the curve labeled A in the graph to the right. In country A the opportunity cost of one bottle of wine is 1/2 fish. Each fish forgone frees up resources sufficient to make two bottles of wine. (851-854)

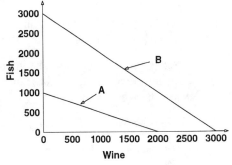

b. The production possibility curve for country B is the curve labeled B in the graph to the right. In country B the opportunity cost of one bottle of wine is one fish. Each fish forgone frees up resources sufficient to make one bottle of wine. (851-854)

c. Country A does not have an absolute advantage in the production of either because if it devoted all of its resources to fish or wine it would still produce less than if country B devoted all of its resources to one or the other. Country B has an absolute advantage in producing both wine and fish. (851-853)

d. Country A has a comparative advantage in wine since it has to give up only 1/2 a fish for each bottle of wine while country B has to give up 1 fish for each bottle of wine. Country B must necessarily have a comparative advantage in fish. (851-854)

e. A fair exchange for B would be giving up one fish for one bottle of wine or better since that is its opportunity cost of producing one fish. A fair exchange for A would be giving up two bottles of wine for 1 fish or better since its opportunity cost of producing two bottles of wine is one fish. Any exchange between these two such as 2 fish for 3 bottles of wine, would be a fair exchange. (851-854)

A2. a. The production possibility curves for country A and country B are drawn on the right. (851-854)

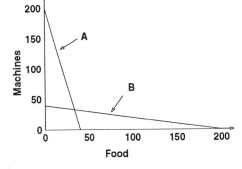

b. Country B has the absolute advantage in the production of food because it can produce more food if it devotes all its resources to the production of food than can country A. (851-854)

c. Country B has the comparative advantage in the production of food since it has to give up only 1/5 machine to produce one unit of food while country A has to give up 5 machines to produce one unit of food. (851-854)

d. Country A would be willing to supply 5 machines for 1 unit of food. Country A would be willing to supply 5 units of foods for one machine. Let's suppose they trade 1 for 1. Country A would produce 200 machines, selling 50 to country B for 50 units of foods. Country B would produce 200 food units, and sell 50 to country A for 50 machines. This way they each reach their desired level of consumption. (851-854)

Multiple Choice Questions

1. b. See page 835.

2. a. The opportunity cost for Saudi Arabia of wadgets in terms of widgets is higher than the opportunity cost for the United States. So Saudi Arabia should specialize in widgets and the United States in wadgets. See pages 834, 836-837.

3. c. The opportunity cost for the United States of wadgets in terms of widgets is higher than the opportunity cost for Saudi Arabia. So the United States should specialize in widgets and Saudi Arabia in wadgets. See pages 834-839.

4. b. The opportunity cost of widgets and wadgets is equal in both countries so neither country has a comparative advantage in either good and there is no basis for trade. See pages 834-839.

5. a. Smaller countries usually find that their production possibilities are changed more, and hence they benefit more. See pages 837-839.

6. a. When there are economies of scale, trade reduces the country's cost of production, giving it more of the advantages of trade. See pages 838-839.

7. d. As discussed on page 839, all are correct except for "trade decreases competitive pressures at home." Trade actually increases competitiveness.

8. b. See pages 842, 843-844. The infant industry argument is an argument in favor of trade restrictions, not against. Economists' response to the infant industry argument is that history shows that few infant industries have ever grown up.

9. a. See page 844.

10. c. See page 846.

A1. b. Since the curves have the same slope, no country has a comparative advantage in either good and there is no basis for trade. See pages 851-855.

Chapter 38:
Growth and the Microeconomics of Developing Countries

Chapter at a glance

1. Seventy-five percent of the world's population lives in developing countries, with average per capita income of under $500 per year. (856)

   Be careful in judging a society by its income alone. Some developing countries may have cultures preferable to ours. Ideally, growth would occur without destroying the culture.

2. The "dual economy" refers to the tendency of developing countries to have two somewhat unrelated economies—one an internationally-based economy, the other a traditional, often nonmarket, economy. (859)

   There is a large discrepancy between the rich and the poor as a consequence. The challenge is to increase the standard of living of the traditional sector.

3. Six microeconomic problems facing developing countries are: (861)
   1. Political instability.
   2. Corruption.
   3. Lack of appropriate institutions.
   4. Lack of investment.
   5. Inappropriate education.
   6. Overpopulation.

   ✔ *Know why these are problems!*
   ✔ *The opposite constitutes the ingredients for growth. Remember them!*

4. When rights to conduct business are controlled and allocated by the government, economic development can be hindered. (862)

   Bribery, graft, and corruption are a way of life in most developing countries. This increases the costs of investment and therefore less economic activity is undertaken and growth is hindered.

5. With per capita incomes of as low as $300 per year, poor people in developing countries don't have a lot left over to put into savings. (864)

   Savings (funds) are need for investment. Without investment there's no growth.

6. Four debates about strategies for growth are: (868)
   1. Balanced vs. unbalanced growth.
   2. Agriculture vs. industry.
   3. Infrastructure vs. directly productive investment.
   4. Export-led growth vs. import substitution.

   ✔ *Think about and list the ingredients for growth (e.g. must have political stability, integrity of public officieals, appropriate institutions, investment in capital accumulation, appropriate education, and policies to compensate for overpopulation.)*

7. Economic development is a complicated problem because it is entwined with cultural and social issues. (869)

   There's no easy solution. Only by having a complete sense of a country, its history, culture, and norms can one decide whether it's the right time and place for this or that policy. That is the art of economics!

Short-answer questions

1. What percentage of the population of the world lives in developing countries? (LO1)

2. What is the average per capita income in developing nations? (LO1)

3. What is the dual economy? (LO2)

4. What is the relevance of the dual economy for developing countries? (LO2)

5. Economists can't tell developing countries, "Here's what you have to do to grow." But they can identify six problems facing developing countries. What are they? (LO3)

6. How can the fact that in some developing countries corruption has become institutionalized make the market function in inappropriate ways? (LO4)

7. Why is it is difficult for developing countries to generate investment? (LO5)

8. Economists do not agree about the formula for growth, but have offered various strategies. What are four debates about strategies for growth? (LO6)

9. Jeffrey Sachs is an economist who has advised Russia for some years now on how to grow economically. Can his knowledge about how to make Russia grow economically be used to solve the problems of growth in African countries? Why or why not? (LO7)

Word Scramble

1. _____ _____ 2._____ _____ 3._____ _____

     l u d a   y o o n m e c   n r b a i   n i a d r   r o n i g f e   i d a

Match the Terms and Concepts to Their Definitions

____ 1. Asian Tigers

____ 2. balanced growth plan

____ 3. brain drain

____ 4. credentialism

____ 5. dual economy

____ 6. the Dueling Duals

____ 7. economic takeoff

____ 8. foreign aid

____ 9. infrastructure investment

____ 10. purchasing power parity

____ 11. unbalanced growth plan

a. A stage in the development process when that process becomes self-sustaining.

b. Debate whether a country should focus development on agriculture or on industry.

c. Funds that developed countries lend or give to developing countries.

d. Group of Asian countries that have achieved economic growth well above the level of other developing countries.

e. Investment in the underlying structure of the economy, such as transportation or power facilities.

f. Plan that spreads money around in trying to spur development in all sectors simultaneously.

g. Plan that focuses on one sector of the economy in the hope that that will generate development in other sectors.

h. Situation where individuals who hold the highest educational degrees get the best jobs simply because they have the credentials.

i. Tendency of developing countries to have two somewhat unrelated economies—one an internationally-based economy, the other a traditional, often nonmarket, economy.

j. The outflow of the best and brightest students from developing countries to developed countries.

k. Method of comparing income by looking at the domestic purchasing power of money in different countries.

Problems and Exercises

1. a. List six obstacles to economic growth.

   b. Briefly explain why each of them is a problem.

c.   Explain one possible way in which a country might overcome three of these obstacles

Multiple Choice Questions

1.   Which of the following would be the closest to correct?
     a. GDP per capita in developing countries is approximately $50 per year and in developed countries is approximately $20,000 per year.
     b. GDP per capita in developing countries is approximately $300 per year and in developed countries is approximately $28,000 per year.
     c. GDP per capita in developing countries is approximately $50 per year and in developed countries is approximately $10,000 per year.
     d. GDP per capita in developing countries is approximately $4,000 per year and in developed countries is approximately $20,000 per year.

2.   Two methods of comparing countries are the purchasing power parity method and the exchange rate method. Of these
     a. the exchange rate method generally gives a higher relative measure to the income in developing countries.
     b. the purchasing power parity method generally gives a higher relative measure to the income in developing countries.
     c. the purchasing power parity and exchange rate methods generally give approximately equal measures of the income in developing countries.
     d. sometimes one gives a higher relative measure to income in developing countries, and sometimes the other gives a higher relative measure.

3.   In the recent past, from the 1970s to the 1990s, the highest growth rate of any groupings of countries belongs to
     a. the Latin American Cougars.
     b. the African Elephants.
     c. the Asian Tigers.
     d. the Central American Leopards.

4.   Foreign aid is
     a. the primary source of income of the poorest developing countries.
     b. one of the top three sources of income of the poorest developing countries.
     c. one of the top three sources of income of developing countries who have ties to the United States.
     d. a minor source of income for developing countries.

5.   One of the likely reasons for a country reaching economic takeoff would be:
     a. economies of scale in production.
     b. diseconomies of scale in production.
     c. diminishing marginal returns in production.
     d. credentialism.

6.   Economics was given its nickname, the dismal science, because
     a. the law of diminishing marginal productivity predicted famine.
     b. the law of diseconomies of scale predicted famine.
     c. learning supply and demand economic models is dismal.
     d. it predicted that economic takeoff would seldom be reached.

7.   If populations grows geometrically, the amount of land is fixed, and there are diminishing marginal returns,
     then
     a. famine is in the future.
     b. income per person will decrease but there will not necessarily be famine.
     c. famine is not in the future if there is technological development.
     d. famine may or may not be in the future.

8.   Which of the following would be most conducive to an unbalanced growth plan?
     a. Diseconomies of scale in production.
     b. Diminishing marginal returns in production.
     c. Economies of scale in production.
     d. None of the above.

9.   Which of the following best represents the textbook author's view of development?
     a. Optimal strategies for growth are country-specific.
     b. A country's development strategy should include as much education as possible.
     c. Countries should focus on infrastructure investment.
     d. Countries should follow a policy of laissez-faire.

Answers

Short-answer questions

1. 75 percent of the population of the world lives in developing countries. (856)

2. The average per capita income in developing nations is under $500 per year. (856)

3. The dual economy is the bifurcation of an economy into two somewhat unrelated economies — one which is internationally based and the other which is a traditional, often nonmarket, economy. (859)

4. Dual economies often exist in developing countries where some groups of individuals have life-styles and incomes similar to those in developed countries and everyone else who participates in the traditional economy has low incomes. (859)

5. Six problems facing developing countries are (1) governments in developing countries are often unstable, (2) governments in developing countries are often corrupt, (3) developing countries often lack appropriate institutions to promote growth, (4) developing countries often lack the domestic savings to fund investment for growth, (5) developing countries tend to have too much of the wrong education, and (6) developing countries are often overpopulated so that raising per capita income is difficult. (861)

6. When there is no well-developed public morality that condemns corruption, market forces can be distorted. Graft and corruption can become institutionalized and create barriers to growth. Knowing that bribes must be paid to import, to develop a business, or to do business in general in developing countries keeps people from undertaking activity that can lead to growth. (862-863)

7. It is difficult for developing countries to generate investment because income is so low there is insufficient savings to fund investment. (864-866)

8. Four debates about strategies for growth are (1) balanced vs. unbalanced growth — should the policy develop all sectors equally or concentrate on only one?; (2) agriculture vs. industry — do you invest in industry to create a base for exports or do you invest in agriculture where most developing countries already have a secure history of production?; (3) infrastructure vs. directly productive investment — should you invest in infrastructure that is indirectly productive or in things that are directly productive such as fertilizer?; and (4) export-led growth vs. import substitution — do you invest in developing industries to compete in the world market or in goods targeted at the domestic market? (868-869)

9. It is possible that some of the lessons Jeffrey Sachs has learned about growth in Russia can be applied to African countries, but economic development is a complex problem that is complicated by cultural and social issues that differ by country. Issues are often country-specific, which means that one must be very careful about transferring lessons from one country to another. (869)

Word Scramble   1. dual economy   2. brain drain   3. foreign aid

Match the Terms and Concepts to Their Definitions
1-d; 2-f; 3-j; 4-h; 5-i; 6-b; 7-a; 8-c; 9-e; 10-k; 11-g.

Problems and Exercises

1. a. Six obstacles to growth are political instability, corruption, lack of appropriate institutions, lack of investment, inappropriate education, and overpopulation. (861)
    b. (1) Without political stability, firms cannot make long-run plans. (2) Corruption makes it impossible for rational economic decisions to be made, and diverts resources to inefficient ends. (3) Without appropriate

institutions, the needed institutional coordination does not take place. (4) Without investment, the technology and machines do not exist to produce. (5) Inappropriate education directs individuals away from development. (6) Overpopulation brings about diminishing marginal returns and reduces output per worker. (861-868)

   c. Overcoming each of these is difficult, and nothing is guaranteed. Some of the possibilities to ponder are: (1) For political stability, one needs dedicated leaders. To foster that, future leaders might be sent to get significant eduction in ethics. (2) For inappropriate eduction, small locally based schools might be established concentrating on basic skills rather than esoteric topics. (3) For over population, a one-child policy such as that attempted by China might be tried. There are many other possibilities, none of which is necessarily the right policy. (861-869)

Multiple Choice Questions

1. b. As shown in the table on page 858 of the text, b is the closest.

2. b. As discussed on pages 858-859, the purchasing power parity method of comparing income cut income differences among countries in half.

3. c. See pages 859-860 and Exhibit 2, page 860.

4. d. As discussed on page 864, total foreign aid comes to less than $14 per person for developing countries. While this does not preclude b or c, it makes it very difficult for them to be true, and, in fact, they are not true.

5. a. This answer is not directly presented in the text in the discussion of economic takeoff on page 864-866. However, since economies of scale require firms to grow to become economically viable, it is the only answer that fits. Even without knowing that, the fact that b and c discourage development taking place in one area, and a knowledge that credentialism limits production, means that one could have deduced that a is the answer.

6. a. As discussed on page 867, Thomas Carlyle gave economics this nickname because the Malthusian doctrine said that population grows geometrically and the means of subsistence grow arithmetically due to diminishing marginal returns, and that therefore famine was in the future. Answer c may be true, but it was not the reason economics got its nickname. Answer d is incorrect because the concept of economic takeoff did not exist in Carlyle's and Malthus's time (the 19th century).

7. d. As discussed on pages 867-868, the Malthusian doctrine predicted famine based on the elements of this question. That doctrine did not, however, take into account technological development. Technological growth can offset the tendencies for famine. But technological growth does not necessarily have to offset those tendencies; thus c is wrong, and d is the only correct answer.

8. c. Unbalanced growth plans are discussed on pages 868-869, and none of these categories of production is mentioned. However, as was the case with the answer to question 3, it can be deduced that c is the best answer. Economies of scale lead one to focus on certain sectors to achieve those economies; thus they lead one toward an unbalanced growth plan.

9. a. As discussed on page 868, the author believes the problems of economic development are entwined with cultural and social issues and hence are country-specific. The other answers do not necessarily fail to reflect the author's viewpoint, but he presented arguments on both sides when discussing them. Thus, a is the best answer.

Chapter 39:
Socialist Economies in Transition

Chapter at a glance

1. The theory of modern socialist economies originated in the early 1800s when a group of writers reacted to the excesses of unregulated capitalism. (872)

   Unbridled capitalism of the past and its abuses gave rise of socialism. Welfare capitalism of today has blunted some of the sharp edges associated with "pure" capitalism.

2. In a centrally planned economy, central planners decide the general direction the economy will take. They make the *what, how,* and *for whom* decisions. (873)

   Central planners in a socialist economy don't have to take consumers' desires into account. They follow whatever set of principles they think best.

3. Most Soviet-style socialist countries suffered from consistent shortages of goods because the planners chose too-low prices relative to demand. (877)

   Planners set prices at levels they believe are "fair" or reflect the "social worth" of the product–in short, at whatever level they want. But economic forces are still present.

4. Five problems that tend to undermine central planning are: (878)
   1. Nonmarket pricing and perverse incentives.
   2. Inability to adjust prices quickly.
   3. Lack of accurate information about demand.
   4. Ambiguous production directives.
   5. Inability to adjust plans quickly to changing situations.

   ✔ *Know why these are problems.*
   They are the same kinds of problems facing many large U.S. firms.

5. The problems faced by transitional economies include the lack of political will to decide on an institutional structure, determining initial property rights, and developing a legal and physical infrastructure within which the economy can function. (883)

   Markets aren't going to solve many of the political and social problems that most transitional economies face. Markets require solutions to political problems before they can operate.

6. Four cautionary lessons for transitional economies are: (1) the Nirvana caution, (2) the QWERTY caution, (3) the tombstone caution, and (4) the transplant caution. (885)

   There are always the 3 invisible forces present–economic, political and social. The challenge for the transitional countries is to develop economic institutions that reflect each country's unique political and social sensibilities as well.

Short-answer questions

1. What are the historical roots of socialism? (LO1)

2. How does a centrally planned economy work? (LO2)

3. Why do most Soviet-style socialist economies suffer consistent shortages of most goods? (LO3)

4. What are five major problems of a centrally planned economy? (LO4)

5. What are some transition problems former Soviet-style socialist countries are experiencing? (LO5)

6. Your friend, a know-it-all in economics, is preparing for an interview with an international organization to advise transitional countries. He has been studying Western institutions so that he can show the interviewers that he is ready to teach the officials of the transitional economies about Western institutions. He is planning to tell them, "If they just adapt them in their own countries, all their problems will be solved." You say, "Wait a minute. Be careful about what you say." What cautions would you tell your friend about following his policy advice? (LO6)

Word Scramble

1. _____ _____
   a a l n n p r s t t   u t o n i c a

2._____
   n a c e g i l n n o p r t u n

3._____ _____
   e e p r r s v e   v t n n i i e e c

Match the Terms and Concepts to Their Definitions

_____ 1. centrally planned economy

_____ 2. counterplanning

_____ 3. market-determined prices

_____ 4. material balance

_____ 5. Nirvana caution

_____ 6. perverse incentive

_____ 7. QWERTY caution

_____ 8. Soviet-style socialist economies

_____ 9. tombstone caution

_____ 10. transplant caution

a. Economy in which government decides the general directions the economy will take.

b. Incentive to use goods in a manner that does not reflect that use's cost to society.

c. Prices are determined by supply and demand, with suppliers free to adjust their prices to make the quantity demanded equal the quantity supplied.

d. Process by which central planners adjust incoming and outgoing quantities of materials until supply equals demand (at least on paper).

e. Process that lets individuals low in the hierarchy influence the planning decisions of those higher in the hierarchy.

f. Remembering that when an institution is borrowed by one economy from another, the institution can be rejected if it doesn't fit the cultural or social aspects of the economy to which it is transplanted.

g. Remembering that some economies have developed for reasons that were not necessarily the most efficient or most desirable.

h. Remembering that markets may not be the cause of high efficiency but instead may be merely covering over disputes about the distribution of property rights.

i. Taking care not to assume that a country that looks extremely fortunate does not have any problems of its own.

j. Centrally planned economies in which the state owns most of the means of production.

Problems and Exercises

1. Central planners can set prices at whatever level they want. That, however, does not free them from the invisible hand. Setting prices at other than equilibrium has consequences that they must deal with.

    a. Say they set the price above the equilibrium price. What will be the consequences? Demonstrate your answer graphically.

    b. Say they set the price below the equilibrium price. What will be the consequences? Demonstrate your answer graphically.

c.   Does economic theory tell us that setting prices at other than equilibrium prices is wrong? Why?

d.   If the central planners persist in setting price below equilibrium price what are the likely consequences?

Multiple Choice Questions

1.   In the early 1990s the primary economic question most formerly socialist countries were focusing on was:
     a. how to create a more equal distribution of income.
     b. whether to start a transition toward a market economy.
     c. how fast the transition toward a market economy should be.
     d. how to make their centralized planning more efficient.

2.   Which of the following is true?
     a. A market economy involves no planning while a centrally planned economy involves planning.
     b. A market economy involves planning while a centrally planned economy involves no planning.
     c. Centrally planned economies and market economies both involve planning.
     d. Neither centrally planned economies nor market economies involve planning.

3.   Shortages of consumer goods in the former socialist countries resulted from all the following *except*
     a. central planners' decision to focus on investment goods.
     b. the high prices central planners placed on many luxuries.
     c. the low prices central planners placed on many luxuries.
     d. the low prices central planners placed on necessities.

4.   In a centrally planned economy, the price of a good is set at $2 and there is a shortage of the good as shown in the graph to the right. What would you predict would happen?
     a. The price would rise to $3.
     b. The price would rise above $3.
     c. The price would fall below $2.
     d. There is no reason to predict the price would change.

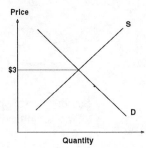

5.   In a market economy, the price is $2 and there is a shortage of a good. What would you predict would happen?
     a. The price would rise to $3.
     b. The price would rise above $3.
     c. The price would fall below $2.
     d. There is no reason to predict the price would change.

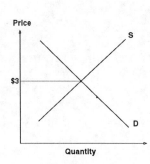

6. Most Western economists do not like central planning. Their reasons include all the following *except*
   a. they believe that central planning creates bureaucratic nightmares.
   b. they believe that central planning tends to undermine democratic political institutions.
   c. they believe that central planning does not achieve the goals it was meant to.
   d. they oppose the equality that central planning brings about.

7. Problems that economists identified that undermine central planning include all the following *except*
   a. inability of prices to adjust quickly.
   b. inefficiency of non-market prices.
   c. inability to adjust plans to changing situations.
   d. lack of information about supply.

8. The former Soviet Union had the heaviest railroad locomotives in the world. Based on the text discussion of centrally planned economies, this was likely due to
   a. the socialist planners' concern for safety.
   b. the low cost of steel in the Soviet economy.
   c. production quotas being specified in weight.
   d. heavier locomotives being more profitable for the firms producing them.

9. The centrally planned economies lagged market economies in technological development because
   a. their people weren't as educated as those in market economies.
   b. their people weren't as innovative as those in market economies.
   c. central planning incentives did not reward development of new technologies.
   d. planners opposed technological developments.

10. The formerly socialist economist were
    a. more environmentally conscious than Western market economies.
    b. about as environmentally conscious as Western market economies
    c. less environmentally conscious than Western market economies.
    d. more environmentally conscious in regard to water, but less environmentally conscious in regard to air, than Western market economies.

11. The problems faced by transitional economies include all the following *except*
    a. the need to determine initial property rights.
    b. the need to develop an institutional infrastructure within which markets can work.
    c. how to improve their educational systems so that they come close to those in the West.
    d. establishing an accepted political foundation to provide stability.

12. The four cautions given in the text for transitional economies about implementing markets include all the following *except*
    a. the QWERTY caution.
    b. the TANSTAAFL caution.
    c. the tombstone caution.
    d. the transplant caution.

Answers

Short-answer questions

1. The theory of modern socialist economies originated when a group of writers in the 1800s reacted to the excesses of unregulated capitalism such as the 10-hour work day, child labor, poor working conditions, highly unequal distribution of income, unemployment, and starvation. (872-873)

2. In a centrally planned economy, central planners make the *what*, *how*, and *for whom* decisions. (873)

3. Soviet-style socialist economies suffered consistent shortages of most goods because they chose too-low prices relative to demand. (876-877)

4. Five major problems of a centrally planned economy are (1) nonmarket pricing that does not reflect costs and perverse incentives that result in less-than-optimal use of goods; (2) inability to adjust prices quickly; (3) lack of accurate information about demand, resulting in shortages and surpluses; (4) ambiguous directives leading to inefficient production practices; and (5) inability to adjust plans quickly to changing situations. (878)

5. Some transition problems the former Soviet-style socialist countries are experiencing include (1) the lack of political will to decide on an institutional structure, (2) determining initial property rights necessary for a market economy to function, and (3) developing a legal and physical infrastructure within which the economy can function. (883)

6. I would tell him that economics does not say that transitional economies should adopt Western institutions. I tell him four cautionary lessons for transitional economies in their decision to adopt Western institutions. They are (1) the Nirvana caution — Western economies have their own problems; (2) the QWERTY caution — Western institutions may not exist because they are efficient; but, rather may exist to serve one group's self interest; (3) the tombstone caution — the settling of disputes may be more important than establishing a market and may even be necessary to a working market economy; and (4) the transplant caution — Western institutions may be inappropriate to the cultural or social aspects of a transitional economy. (885)

Word Scramble   1. transplant caution   2. counterplanning   3. perverse incentive

Match the Terms and Concepts to Their Definitions
1-a; 2-e; 3-c; 4-d; 5-i; 6-b; 7-g; 8-j; 9-h; 10-f.

Problems and Exercises

1.

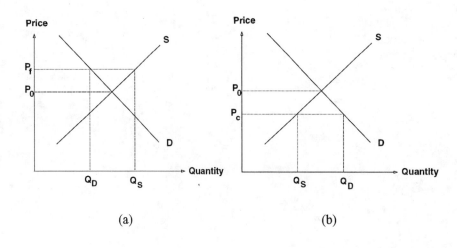

(a)   (b)

a. If they set the price above the equilibrium price the quantity supplied will exceed the quantity demanded, and there will be surpluses as in graph (a) above. (876-877)

b. If they set the price below the equilibrium price the quantity demanded will exceed the quantity supplied, and there will be shortages as in graph (b) above. (876-877)

c. No, economic theory does not say that setting prices at other than equilibrium is wrong. It simply says that doing so will have consequences. One's value judgment about those consequences determines one's judgment about those consequences. (877)

d. There will be continual shortages and the consequences will depend upon how the government deals with those shortages. A black or grey market will likely develop and the actual price many people will pay will be much greater than the stated price, or even the market equilibrium price. The quality of goods will decrease as individuals will be happy to get the good, whatever the quality. Those people who are rationed the good at the low price will be made better off. The others will be made worse off. (876-877)

Multiple Choice Questions

1. c. As discussed on page 873, most transitional countries had made the decision to move toward a market economy. While they may have been concerned with the other questions, the primary one was how fast a transition to make.

2. c. As discussed in the text on pages 873-874, all economies require planning. The difference between them involves who does the planning and what their motives in that planning are.

3. b. Although the prices central planners placed on luxuries were high relative to the prices in Western countries, those high prices could not have been a cause of shortages. High prices eliminate shortages; given people's opportunity cost, the high prices were too low, which makes b the only acceptable answer. See page 877.

4. d. In a centrally planned economy there is no reason to expect the price to change, since market forces are held in check by the planners. Because they generally accept shortages, there is no reason to assume that they wouldn't keep the price at $2. See page 877.

5. a. In a market economy, shortages create strong incentives for firms to raise their prices. So as long as price were below equilibrium price of $3.00 we would expect it to rise to $3.00. See pages 876-877 and Chapter 2.

6. d. Economists may or may not oppose equality, but that is not a reason most economists oppose central planning. First, in reality, central planning did not bring about equality; and, second, good economists would separate their normative views from their consideration of economic systems. True, the belief in democratic political institutions involves normative judgments, but they are the judgments of our society, not of economists alone. See pages 878-881.

7. d. Central planners had plenty of information about supply. Their problems concerned demand and adjusting to changing situations. See pages 878-881.

8. c. Answer c is the obvious choice. There is no discussion in the text about the socialist planners' concern for safety, and prices and profits were not part of the Soviet planning system, all of which eliminates the other answers. See page 879.

9. c. The problem was one of incentives, not education or people's creativity. It was extraordinarily difficult to design plans that involved new technologies because new technologies involved doing things in new, unplanned, ways. See pages 879-880.

10. c. As discussed in the text on page 882, one of the great ironies of the socialist economies is how little attention they paid to environmental issues in their attempt to grow economically.

11. c. The formerly socialist educational systems were excellent, and despite severe shortages of resources, they still do as good a job as Western systems, at least with regard to education through secondary school. Even if you didn't know this, the others are all problems faced by transitional economies so answer c, which represents a problem transitional economies do not face, can be arrived at through elimination. See pages 882-884.

12. b. As discussed on page 885 of the text, TANSTAAFL does not refer to one of the cautions, but refers to the central idea of economics that transitional economies should keep in mind. See pages 884-886.

Pretest V
Chapters 28 - 39

Take this test in test conditions, giving yourself a limited amount of time to complete the questions. Ideally, check with your professor to see how much time he or she allows for an average multiple choice question and multiply this by 40. This is the time limit you should set for yourself for this pretest. If you do not know how much time your teacher would allow, we suggest 1 minute per question, or about 40 minutes.

1. A firm is making no profit. If there is X-inefficiency, what can we conclude?
   a. The firm is operating economically efficiently.
   b. The firm is operating technically efficiently.
   c. The firm is operating less efficiently than technically possible.
   d. We can say nothing about the efficiency of the firm.

2. When there is little competitive pressure, large organizations have a tendency to
   a. make decisions that benefit the consumer.
   b. make decisions that benefit the managers.
   c. make decisions that benefit the owners.
   b. none of the above.

3. In the graph on the right, if suppliers restrict output to OL, what area represents the welfare loss to society?
   a. A + B.
   b. B + C.
   c. C + D.
   d. A + D.

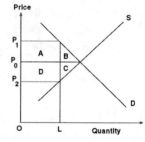

4. If average total costs are decreasing throughout the relevant range of production, the industry will be
   a. a natural monopoly.
   b. a prime target for rent-seeking.
   c. a lazy monopolist.
   d. an example of monitoring problems.

5. Agriculture is a highly productive industry. This enormous productivity has
   a. caused agriculture to increase in relative importance as a percent of output.
   b. caused agriculture to decrease in relative importance as a percent of output.
   c. caused farmers to be rich and prosperous.
   d. increased the share of the labor force working in agriculture.

6. In the graph to the right, what area represents the final income going to farmers after the supply shifts out from S_0 to S_1?
   a. A + B.
   b. B + C.
   c. A + C.
   d. A + B +C.

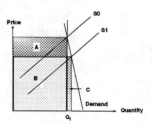

7. The general rule of political economy in a democracy states
   a. small groups that are significantly affected by a government policy will lobby more effectively than will large groups who are equally affected by that policy.
   b. large groups that are significantly affected by a government policy will lobby more effectively than small groups who are equally affected by that policy.
   c. large groups will always win in majority rule situations
   d. Congress will always be inefficient.

8. In the graph at the right, the government gives enough economic incentives to suppliers to decrease output sufficiently so that the price rises to $5. The area best representing the amount of those incentives is
   a. A.
   b. A + B.
   c. A - B.
   d. A + B + C.

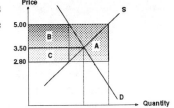

9. You are the adviser to the president who wants to subsidize the price of wheat so that consumers pay a price of $1.50 per bushel. The current price of wheat is $2 and 100 bushels are being demanded. The president asks you what the program will likely cost. You respond
   a. $0.
   b. something, but less than $50.
   c. $50.
   d. more than $50.

10. A Pareto-optimal policy is
    a. a policy that hurts no one.
    b. a policy that benefits all.
    c. a policy that benefits some people and hurts no one.
    d. a policy that benefits more than it hurts.

11. An economist might advise a developing country to turn down the offer of a free dialysis machine because
    a. the marginal cost of using it exceeds the costs of other, more beneficial, life-saving technology.
    b. the average cost of using it exceeds the costs of other, more beneficial, life-saving technology.
    c. there is no such thing as a free machine.
    d. other developing countries may need it more.

12. Suppose that filtering your water at home reduces your chances from dying of giardia (a disease caused by an intestinal parasite) by 1/450. The filter costs you $400 to install. You have chosen to install the filter. Which dollar value best reflects the value you implicitly place on your life?
    a. $180
    b. $1,800.
    c. $18,000.
    d. $180,000.

13. Laissez-faire is
    a. the philosophy that government should intervene in the economy as little as possible.
    b. the philosophy that government should intervene in the economy as much as possible.
    c. the philosophy that government should not exist.
    d. the philosophy that externalities should be internalized.

14. An externality is
    a. the effect of decisions not taken into account by decision makers.
    b. another name for exports.
    c. events that happen that are external to the economy.
    d. the external effect of a government policy.

15. In the graph on the right, if the government were attempting to set an effluent fee, the amount of that effluent fee should be

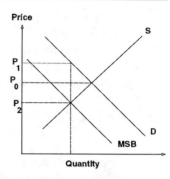

   a. P_1.
   b. P_2.
   c. $P_1 - P_0$.
   d. $P_1 - P_2$.

16. Mr. B is using 20 gallons of gas a day and Mr. A is using 10 gallons of gas a day. The marginal cost of reducing gas consumption by 3 gallons a day is $4 for Mr. A and $3 for Mr. B. The government issues a regulation requiring equal reduction so that each has to reduce consumption by 3 gallons a day. Economists would conclude

   a. the reductions are inefficient because they are equal.
   b. the reductions are efficient because they are equal.
   c. the reductions are inefficient because they are based on regulation.
   d. the reductions are inefficient because they do not equalize the marginal costs of reduction.

17. In reference to the A and B groups whose demands are shown in the graph on the right, the group most likely to support a marketable permit program to reduce demand as opposed to regulatory solutions is

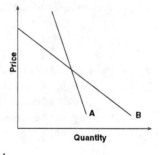

   a. A.
   b. B.
   c. Neither A nor B is more likely to support a marketable permit solution.
   d. Both A and B are equally likely to support a marketable permit solution.

18. In reference to the graph on the right, if there is a severe shortage of landfills, which of the following might be true?

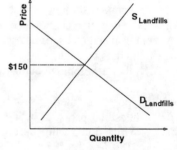

   a. The price being paid for landfills is currently at 50.
   b. The price being paid for landfills is currently at 200.
   c. The price being paid for landfills is currently at 400.
   d. None of the above.

19. An important law in the U.S. regulation of markets is

   a. the Standard Oil Antitrust Act of 1890.
   b. the Sherman Antitrust Act of 1890.
   c. the ALCOA Antitrust Act of 1890.
   d. The Lincoln Antitrust Act of 1890.

20. The resolution of the AT&T antitrust case of the 1980s was

   a. AT&T agreed to split up into three operating divisions.
   b. AT&T agreed to split up and allow the Baby Bells to be independent.
   c. AT&T was combined with MCI and Sprint.
   d. MCI and Sprint were broken off from AT&T and developed as competitors to AT&T.

21. When one of two merging companies supplies one or more of the inputs to the other merging company, the merger is called

   a. a horizontal merger.
   b. a vertical merger.
   c. a conglomerate merger.
   d. a takeover merger.

22. Which of the four curves in the figure on the right has the most income inequality?
    a. A.
    b. B.
    c. C.
    d. D.

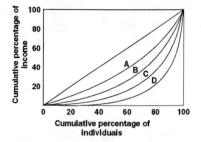

23. A Lorenz curve for the entire world would show
    a. more income inequality than in the United States.
    b. less income inequality than in the United States.
    c. approximately the same level of income inequality as income in the United States.
    d. no inequality.

24. The observation that women in two-parent relationships do more work around the house and take more responsibility for child rearing than men do is an example of
    a. demand-side discrimination.
    b. supply-side discrimination.
    c. the way things should be.
    d. the way in which men exploit women.

25. The irony of any need-based program is that
    a. it increases the number of needy.
    b. it decreases the number of needy.
    c. it creates other needs.
    d. it destroys needs.

26. The term "derived demand" refers to
    a. demand by consumers for advertised products.
    b. the demand for luxury goods that is derived from cultural phenomena such as fashion.
    c. the demand for factors of production by firms.
    d. the demand for derivatives.

27. A firm has just changed from being a competitive firm to being a monopolist. Its derived demand for labor
    a. will increase.
    b. will decrease.
    c. might increase or might decrease.
    d. is unaffected because whether the firm is a competitive firm or a monopolist has no effect on the firm's derived demand for labor.

28. If firms were controlled by workers rather than by managers, and are expanding,
    a. in that expansion the worker-controlled firms would likely hire more workers.
    b. in that expansion the worker-controlled firms would likely hire fewer workers.
    c. there would be no effect on the number of workers hired.
    d. the number of workers would change, but the effect cannot be determined.

29. If one imposes a tax on a factor with perfectly inelastic supply,
    a. the quantity supplied will decrease.
    b. the supply will decrease.
    c. the quantity supplied will increase.
    d. none of the above.

30. Rent-seeking causes waste. Therefore
    a. rent-seeking should be prohibited.
    b. rent-seeking should be taxed.
    c. the government should take a laissez-faire position on rent-seeking.
    d. it depends.

31. You are to receive $100 per year forever. The interest rate in the economy is 10 percent. The present value of that $100 forever is
    a. $100.
    b. $1,000.
    c. $10,000.
    d. Infinite, because it goes on forever.

32. The graph on the right demonstrates Saudi Arabia's and the United States's production possibility curves for widgets and wadgets. Given these production possibility curves, you would suggest that
    a. Saudi Arabia specialize in widgets and the United States in wadgets.
    b. no trade should take place.
    c. Saudi Arabia specialize in wadgets and the United States in widgets.
    d. Both countries should produce an equal amount of each.

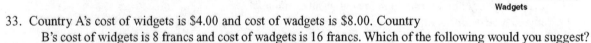

33. Country A's cost of widgets is $4.00 and cost of wadgets is $8.00. Country B's cost of widgets is 8 francs and cost of wadgets is 16 francs. Which of the following would you suggest?
    a. Country A should specialize in widgets and Country B in wadgets.
    b. no trade should take place.
    c. Country A should specialize in wadgets and Country B in widgets.
    d. Both countries should produce an equal amount of each.

34. Economists generally oppose trade restrictions for all the following reasons *except*
    a. from a global perspective, free trade increases total output.
    b. the infant industry argument.
    c. trade restrictions lead to retaliation.
    d. international politics

35. An embargo is
    a. a tax government places on internationally-traded goods.
    b. a quantity limit placed on imports.
    c. an all-out restriction on imports.
    d. a government-imposed procedural rule that limits imports.

36. One of the likely reasons for a country reaching economic takeoff would be:
    a. economies of scale in production.
    b. diseconomies of scale in production.
    c. diminishing marginal returns in production.
    d. credentialism.

37. Which of the following would be most conducive to an unbalanced growth plan?
    a. Diseconomies of scale in production.
    b. Diminishing marginal returns in production.
    c. Economies of scale in production.
    d. None of the above.

38. Which of the following is true?
    a. A market economy involves no planning while a centrally planned economy involves planning.
    b. A market economy involves planning while a centrally planned economy involves no planning.
    c. Centrally planned economies and market economies both involve planning.
    d. Neither centrally planned economies nor market economies involve planning.

39. In a centrally planned economy, the price is $2 and there is a shortage of the good as shown in the graph to the right. What would you predict would happen?

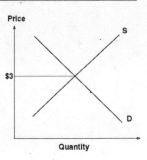

a. The price would rise to $3.

b. The price would rise above $3.

c. The price would fall below $2.

d. There is no reason to predict the price would change.

40. The centrally planned economies lagged market economies in technological development because

a. their people weren't as educated as those in market economies.

b. their people weren't as innovative as those in market economies.

c. central planning incentives did not reward development of new technologies.

d. planners opposed technological developments.

Answers

1. c (28:2)	11. a (30:5)	21. b (33:8)	31. b (36:6)
2. b (28:4)	12. d (30:7)	22. d (34:2)	32. a (37:2)
3. b (28:8)	13. a (31:1)	23. a (34:5)	33. b (37:4)
4. a (28:10)	14. a (31:3)	24. b (34:9)	34. b (37:8)
5. b (29:2)	15. d (31:7)	25. a (35:3)	35. c (37:10)
6. b (29:5)	16. d (32:5)	26. c (35:7)	36. a (38:5)
7. a (29:7)	17. a (32:8)	27. b (35:11)	37. c (38:8)
8. a (29:9)	18. a (32:12)	28. b (35:13)	38. c (39:2)
9. d (29:13)	19. b (33:1)	29. d (36:1)	39. d (39:4)
10. c (30:2)	20. b (33:5)	30. d (36:4)	40. c (39:9)

Key: The figures in parentheses refer to multiple choice question and chapter numbers. For example (1:4) is multiple choice question 1 from chapter 4.